Hong Kong Connections

Hong Kong Connections
Transnational Imagination in Action Cinema

Edited by Meaghan Morris, Siu Leung Li and Stephen Chan Ching-kiu

Duke University Press
Durham and London, 2005

Hong Kong University Press
Hong Kong, 2005

This book is among a series of titles co-published by Duke University Press and Hong Kong University Press, a collaboration designed to make possible new circuits of circulation for scholarship. This title is available in Asia, Australia, and New Zealand from Hong Kong University Press; in the Americas and Europe from Duke University Press; and from either publisher in the rest of the world.

Library of Congress Cataloging-in-Publication Data
Hong Kong connections: transnational imagination in action cinema/edited by Meaghan Morris, Siu Leung Li, and Stephen Chan Ching-kiu
p. cm.
Includes bibliographical references and index.
ISBN 1-932643-19-2 (cloth : alk. paper)
ISBN 1-932643-01-X (pbk. : alk. paper)
1. Adventure films—History and criticism. 2. Adventure films—China—Hong Kong—
   History and criticism.
I. Morris, Meaghan.
II. Li, Siu Leung.
III. Chan, Stephen Ching-kiu.
PN1995.9.A3H66 2005
791.43′655′095125—dc22
2005023603

Duke University Press
Box 90660
Durham, North Carolina
27708-0660
www.dukepress.edu

Hong Kong University Press
14/F Hing Wai Centre
7 Tin Wan Praya Road
Aberdeen, Hong Kong
www.hkupress.org

Printed and bound by United League Graphic & Printing Co. Ltd., Hong Kong, China

Contents

Acknowledgments

Any collective volume incurs many debts in the course of its preparation, perhaps especially when an international conference inspires and informs the text. The essays published here were developed from papers given at the *Hong Kong Connections: Transnational Imagination in Action Cinema* conference organised by the Department of Cultural Studies and the Kwan Fong Cultural Research and Development Programme at Lingnan University, Hong Kong, January 6–9, 2003. Not all of the conference presenters were free to write for this book, but all of them helped to shape it by generously sharing their learning, their ideas and their enthusiasm over three days of intense discussion. The editors gratefully acknowledge the major contribution made to *Hong Kong Connections* by Chris Berry, Esther M. K. Cheung, Law Kar, Leung Ping-kwan, Lin Wenchi and Lo Kwai-cheung. Our thanks also to John Nguyet Erni, Mette Hjort, Pang Laikwan, Lo Wai-luk, Wong Ain-ling, Jacob Wong and Emilie Yeh Yueh-yu for their active participation. The conference organisation was assured by Heidi Ng Hei-in and her team of student helpers; special thanks are due to Vitinie Ho Wing-wa, Rachel Lo Fung-yee and Alex Leung Kwok-kin (for taking such good care of Titus). The staff from Lingnan University's ITSC gave us the opportunity to see more wonderful clips and visual materials in better conditions than most academics generally dream of enjoying.

Like the wider research project of which it formed a part, the *Hong Kong Connections* conference was supported by a two-year Competitive Earmarked Research Grant to the three editors from the Research Grants Council of Hong Kong (CB01A2: LU300301H: "Transnational Imagination in Action Cinema: Hong Kong and the Making of a Global Popular Culture"). This funding gave the editors the benefit of an outstanding

Research Assistant, Shelley Chan Shek, whose work informs not only our contributions to this volume but our overall perspective on the transnational dimension of Hong Kong cinema and its history. The support provided by the grant also enabled us to discuss this project with colleagues elsewhere, and the editors are grateful in particular to Jenny Lau Kwok-wah, our panel respondent at the 2003 Society for Cinema and Media Studies Annual Meeting; to Lin Wenchi, for hosting us at the Film Studies Center of National Central University, Jong-li, Taiwan; and to Iain McCalman and the staff of the Humanities Research Centre at Australian National University in Canberra, where Stephen Chan Ching-kiu enjoyed the luxury of a Visiting Fellowship in July 2004.

The enthusiasm and drive of Mina Cerny Kumar led us to bring this project to Hong Kong University Press, where the experience of working with Phoebe Chan and Colin Day has been a much appreciated reminder of what a pleasure it can be to work with a serious academic publisher; this book has benefited greatly from their editorial expertise, and from the fine copy-editing of Jamie Cox. Closer to home in the Department of Cultural Studies, Dr Chan Shun-hing and Dr Lau Kin-chi unstintingly provided both learned and inspired assistance with translation problems of sometimes unforeseen complexity and often immediate urgency. We thank Verbal Chan Man-ching for her help in finalising the manuscript, and Selina Lo Tak-man for her good humour in handling our endless printing requests. Finally, our special thanks must go to our Departmental secretary, Josephine Tsui Wai-shuen, whose contribution both to the conference and to this volume was not limited to any one of its aspects but was (as it always is) both pervasive and decisive for the project as a whole.

Contributors

Nicole BRENEZ teaches Cinema Studies at the University of Paris-1. A graduate of the Ecole Normale Supérieure, she has published several books including *Shadows de John Cassavetes* (Nathan, 1995) and *De la Figure en général et du Corps en particulier. L'invention figurative au cinéma* (De Boeck Université, 1998). She has a book forthcoming on Abel Ferrara (Illinois University Press). She has organised many film events and retrospectives, notably "Jeune, dure et pure, une histoire du cinéma d'avant-garde en France" ["Young and Dangerous: A history of avant-garde cinema in France"] for the French Cinémathèque in 2000. She is curator of the Cinémathèque Française's avant-garde film sessions.

Stephen CHAN Ching-kiu is Professor of Cultural Studies and Director of the Master of Cultural Studies Programme at Lingnan University, where he began the BA (Hons) Cultural Studies programme in 1999. Previously, he directed the Hong Kong Cultural Studies Programme at The Chinese University of Hong Kong. He edited the bilingual *Hong Kong Cultural Studies Bulletin* (1994–1998) and the book series *Hong Kong Cultural Studies* (Oxford University Press China), editing for the latter *Identity and Public Culture, Practice of Affect: Hong Kong Popular Song Lyrics*, and *Cultural Imaginary and Ideology*. Co-author of *Hong Kong Un-Imagined: History, Culture and the Future* (Taipei: Rye Field, 1997), Chan's interests range from cultural representation and urban sensibility to transnational flows and critical education through popular genres. Recent essays include "Figures of Hope and the Filmic Imaginary of Jianghu in Contemporary Hong Kong Cinema" (*Cultural Studies*, 2001), "Building Cultural Studies for Postcolonial Hong Kong" (*Cultural Studies: Interdisciplinarity and*

Translation, Rodopi, 2002), and "Burst into Action: The Changing Spectacle of Glamour Heroines in Contemporary Hong Kong Cinema" (*Cultural Studies Review*, 2004).

DAI Jinhua has taught in the Department of Literature of the Beijing Film Institute for ten years. Now Professor of the Institute of Comparative Literature and Comparative Culture and Director of the Cultural Studies Workshop of Peking University, she is also Visiting Professor to the Department of East Asia, Ohio State University, USA. She has published widely on film history, mass culture and feminist literature. Her books in Chinese include *Surfacing from History: A Study of Contemporary Women's Literature* (1989), *A Handbook of Film Theory and Criticism* (1995), *Breaking Out of the City of Mirrors: Women, Film, Literature* (1995), *Invisible Writing: Cultural Studies in China in the 1990s* (1999), *If in the Mirror: Interviews with Dai Jinhua* (1999), *The Views in the Mist: Chinese Film Culture 1978–1998* (1999), and *Writing Cultural Heroes: Cultural Studies at the Turn of the Century* (2000). Her most recent work, *Cinema and Desire: Feminist Marxism and Cultural Politics in the Work of Dai Jinhua* (ed. Jing Wang and Tani Barlow, Verso, 2002) is a translated collection of her important articles.

David DESSER is Professor of Cinema Studies at the University of Illinois, Urbana-Champaign. A Visiting Scholar in the Department of Cinema/ Television at Hong Kong Baptist University for 2002–03, he recently co-edited *The Cinema of Hong Kong: History, Arts, Identity* (with Poshek Fu, Cambridge, 2000) and he is the author and editor of numerous books on Japanese cinema including *Eros Plus Massacre: An Introduction to the Japanese New Wave* (Indiana University Press, 1988) and *Ozu's "Tokyo Story"* (Cambridge, 1997). He recently provided a full commentary track for *Tokyo Story* in the Criterion Collection DVD series.

Laleen JAYAMANNE is a Senior Lecturer in cinema studies at the University of Sydney. She has recently published *Toward Cinema and its Double: Cross-Cultural Mimesis* (Indiana University Press, 2001) and has also written on Jackie Chan. She has edited *Kiss Me Deadly: Feminism and Cinema for the Moment* (Power Publications, 1995) and co-edited *The Filmmaker and the Prostitute: Dennis O'Rourke's The Good Woman of Bangkok* (Power Publications, 1997). She is currently working on a book on an avant-garde Indian filmmaker entitled *Cinematographic Avatars: the Cinema of Kumar Shahani* for Indiana University Press.

KIM Soyoung is Associate Professor of Cinema Studies at Korean National University of Arts. She has also taught at UC Berkeley and UC Irvine as a Visiting Professor. Her publications in Korean include *Hollywood/ Frankfurt (1993)*, *Cine-Feminism* (1996), *Cinema: Blue Flower in the Land of Technology* (1997), *Spectres of Modernity* (2000) and *Blockbusters in Korean Mode; America or Atlantis* (2001). Her articles in English have appeared in *The UTS Review*, *Traces*, *Inter-Asia Cultural Studies* and *Postcolonial Studies*, and articles in Japanese appear in *Gendai Shiso, Shiso, Impacts* and *Eureka*. She has also made films: *Koryu; Southern Women/ South Korea* (2000) and *Images of Women in Korean Cinema* (2002) and *A Runner's High* (2003) which were widely screened at international film festivals.

Siu Leung LI is currently Associate Professor of Cultural Studies at Lingnan University. He previously taught in the Humanities Division at the Hong Kong University of Science & Technology. His academic publications include *Cross-Dressing in Chinese Opera* (Hong Kong University Press, 2003), and "Kung Fu: Negotiating Nationalism and Modernity" (*Cultural Studies, 2001*). He also co-authored *Fouxiang Xianggang: lishi, wenhua, weilai"* [Hong Kong un-imagined: history, culture, future] (Taipei: Rye Field, 1997). Also trained in European classical music and flute performance, Li is a flute player and collects late-nineteenth century French flutes.

Adrian MARTIN is the author of *Phantasms* (Penguin, 1994), *Once Upon a Time in America* (British Film Institute, 1998) and *The Mad Max Movies* (Currency, 2003), and co-editor of *Movie Mutations* (BFI, 2003) and *Raúl Ruiz: Images of Passage* (Rouge Press/International Film Festival Rotterdam, 2004). He has books forthcoming on Terrence Malick (BFI), Brian De Palma (Illinois University Press) and John Cassavetes (IB Taurus). Since 1995 he has been film critic for *The Age* newspaper (Melbourne, Australia). He is currently a Doctoral candidate in the Faculty of Art and Design, Monash University, Melbourne, and co-editor of a new Internet film journal, *Rouge*.

Meaghan MORRIS is Chair Professor of Cultural Studies, Lingnan University. A former film critic, she has written widely on popular historiography, cultural studies, and feminist cultural theory. Her books include *'Race' Panic and the Memory of Migration*, co-edited with Brett de Bary (Hong Kong University Press, 2001); *Too Soon, Too Late: History* *in Popular Culture* (Indiana University Press, 1998); *Australian Cultural Studies: A Reader*, co-edited with John Frow (Allen & Unwin, 1993); and *The Pirate's Fiancée: Feminism, Reading, Postmodernism* (Verso, 1988). She is currently completing a study of action cinema as popular historiography and her related articles include "White Panic, or Mad Max and the Sublime", in Kuan-Hsing Chen, ed., *Trajectories: Inter-Asia Cultural Studies* (Routledge, 1998), and "Learning from Bruce Lee: Pedagogy and Political Correctness in Martial Arts Cinema", in Matthew Tinckcom and Amy Villarejo, eds, *Keyframes: Popular Film and Cultural Studies* (Routledge, 2001).

S. V. SRINIVAS is a Fellow at the Centre for the Study of Culture and Society, Bangalore. When he is not studying the circulation of Hong Kong cinema in India, he works on Telugu cinema. Srinivas has published in *Economic and Political Weekly* and *Deep Focus* and his recent essays include "Is there a Public in the Cinema Hall?" *Framework* 42 (online edition, Oct. 2000); "Film Culture, Politics and Industry", *Seminar* 525 (2003); and "Hong Kong Action Film in the Indian B Circuit." *Inter Asia Cultural Studies* 4:1 (2003).

Stephen TEO is the author of *Hong Kong Cinema: The Extra Dimensions* (BFI: London, 1997; expanded edition forthcoming), and *Wong Kar-wai: Auteur of Time* (BFI, forthcoming). He was awarded his doctorate by RMIT University, Melbourne for a dissertation on the *wuxia* genre, which he plans to publish as a book. He has taught a course on Asian cinemas at RMIT, and has published widely on Hong Kong cinema. His articles include 'Tsui Hark: National Style and Polemic" in Esther Yau (ed.), *At Full Speed: Hong Kong Cinema in a Borderless World* (University of Minnesota, 2001), and "The *Wenyi* Genre: Melodrama with Chinese Characteristics" in Steven Schneider, et al (ed.), *Traditions in World Cinema* (University of Edinburgh, forthcoming).

Valentina VITALI teaches comparative film theory at the University of Ulster (Northern Ireland), where she obtained a PhD for her thesis *The Aesthetics of Cultural Modernisation: Hindi Cinema 1947–1957*. Her work has appeared in *Framework: the Journal of Cinema and Media* (42 and 43.2), *Southern Review: Communication, Politics & Culture* (35.2), *Women: A Cultural Review* (15.2), *Journal of Asian Studies* (63.2), *Kinema* (Fall 2004) and *Inter-Asia Cultural Studies* (6.2). She has contributed to *The Indian Cinema Book* (edited by Kaushik Bhaumik and Laila Jordan, BFI, forthcoming), and is co-editor, with Paul Willemen, of *Theorising National Cinema* (BFI, forthcoming).

Paul WILLEMEN was a member of the *Screen* editorial board in the 1970s, edited *Framework* in the 1980s, worked at the British Film Institute and is now Professor at the University of Ulster. He is the author of *Looks and Frictions* (Indiana University Press and BFI, 1994), co-author of the *Encyclopaedia of Indian Cinema* (with Ashish Rajadhyasksha, Oxford University Press 1998) and has recently published the essay "Detouring Through Korean Cinema" (*Inter-Asia Cultural Studies,* 2002).

Rob WILSON is a Professor and Graduate Chair of Literature at the University of California at Santa Cruz. His scholarly works include *Reimagining the American Pacific* (Duke University Press, 2000), *Waking in Seoul* (Mineumsa Press, 1988) and *American Sublime* (University of Wisconsin Press, 1991) and the co-edited collections *Global/Local* (Duke University Press, 1996) and *Asia/Pacific as Space of Cultural Production* (Duke University Press, 1995). He is presently at work on a study of conversion and counter-conversion in the Pacific called *Henry, Torn from the Stomach* and a collection of cultural criticism called *Worldings: Doing Cultural Studies in the Era of Globalization* (New Pacific Press).

WONG Kin-yuen is Head of English Studies at Shu Yan College, Hong Kong where he teaches technoscience culture and intercultural studies as well. He was Department Head of Modern Languages and Intercultural Studies, and Director of Cyberculture Centre for Research and Development, Research Institute for the Humanities at the Chinese University of Hong Kong. His recent publications include the forthcoming *Cultural Cyborgs* (in Chinese).

Kinnia YAU Shuk-ting is Assistant Professor in the Department of Japanese Studies at the Chinese University of Hong Kong. In 2002 she completed a doctoral thesis in the Department of Culture and Representation, Tokyo University, on "The Interrelation between Japanese and Hong Kong Film Industries", a comprehensive study of the history of exchange between the Japanese and Hong Kong cinemas from the 1930s to the 1990s, which argues that this collaboration between two Asian filmmaking centres has proved to be one of the most significant elements for the globalization of Hong Kong cinema, as well as for the consolidation of the present Asian film network. Yau's thesis includes personal interviews with twenty related filmmakers from both Hong Kong and Japan.

YUNG Sai-shing is currently Associate Professor in the Department of Chinese Studies, National University of Singapore. His research interests include traditional Chinese drama, Chinese ritual theatres, Cantonese opera, and the social history of Chinese opera in Singapore. He published his first book, entitled *An Anthropology of Chinese Drama: Ritual, Theater, and Community,* in 1997 (Taipei: Rye Field). He is now completing the manuscript of his second book, which studies the cultural history of the gramophone record industry of Cantonese opera and music during the first half of the twentieth century.

Introduction:
Hong Kong Connections

Meaghan Morris

This book explores the proposition that Hong Kong cinema since the 1960s has played a significant role in shaping what is now one of the world's most widely distributed popular cultural genres: action cinema. Hong Kong action has not only seized the imaginations of filmmakers working in many countries, cultural traditions and styles (a very long film could be compiled of scenes from world cinema remaking such Hong Kong signature moments as Bruce Lee's shoulder-rolling, neck-cracking stretch from *The Way of the Dragon*, John Woo's flying doves and bullet ballets, or Ringo Lam's "three-way, guns-drawn standoff" from *City on Fire*[1]), but Hong Kong films have also proved popular over the decades with audiences worldwide. Building fan bases that persist across generations and continue to grow unevenly through phases of relative inactivity in the Hong Kong industry and neglect from mainstream film institutions elsewhere, Hong Kong films are watched, copied, collected, discussed, pirated, re-made, parodied and appropriated in many different viewing situations all over the world. How do we account for this transnational appeal, and how can we understand it historically?

Problems of context and perspective assail any serious effort to answer these questions directly. Their complexity is rendered overwhelming by the sheer diversity of materials, situations and angles available for study and the multiplicity of ways to establish connections between them. A popular "cultural" genre is one in which people take up aesthetic materials from the media and elaborate them in other aspects of their lives, whether in dreams and fantasies, in ethical formulations of values and ideals, or in social and sometimes political activities. Thus action culture today encompasses not only the real or simulated militarism of the corporate

weekend warrior — by no means only a Western phenomenon, as I
found when I fell over a camouflaged dummy soldier on my way to the
Ladies Room in the "war-game themed" tourist hotel in Shenzhen that
was hosting my university's retreat — and the macho soap of extreme
sports and AXN cable TV ("movies for guys who like movies"), but the
cyber-active fantasy lives of a multitude of sedentary workers, male and
female scholars included. Hong Kong-inflected action culture also shades
into tenderly self-shaping autobiographical zones ("my old poster of Bruce
Lee" is a motif of the contemporary *bildungsroman* that would repay
comparative study),[2] and fosters DIY modes of spiritualism as well as of
physical and ethical culture. It also sponsors "self-defence" and "self-
esteem" movements communally embraced from social or psychic
positions of disadvantage and vulnerability.

Meanwhile, for the cinemas and film cultures newly flourishing in
recent years across the Asian-Pacific region, Hong Kong cinema is now a
benchmark of achievement, a site of inspiration and cross-cultural
borrowing, a model for emulation and a target of rivalry: the title of a recent
critical guide to "the latest Korean New Wave" is *Korean Cinema: The New
Hong Kong.*[3] A Google sampling in June 2004 of the 25,900 English-
language web pages then dealing with the sensational Thai martial arts
film *Ong-bak* suggested that almost all fans and critics compared the impact
of its *muay thai* sequences performed by Phanom Yeerum (a.k.a Tony
Jaa) with the early achievements of Jackie Chan and Jet Li ("I felt what it
must have been like to watch the Hong Kong film industry when it first
exploded onto the international scene all those decades ago") before
declaring the supersession of the Hong Kong model ("there are enough
elaborate stunts and power moves in *Ong-bak* to put every Hong Kong
action movie I've seen in the last 10 years to shame").[4] One review presents
the film as an effort by the director Pracha Pinkaew and his "kung fu
obsessed" young star to "reclaim *muaythai* as a valid martial art in its own
right" in response to those "chop socky flaunting video imports from Hong
Kong" which "besiege" the Bangkok market stalls, pervading Thai action
sequences with "kung fu stylings" at the expense of "the domestic combat
discipline".[5]

At the narrative level, *Ong-bak* is not a rivalry story about Hong Kong
and Thailand, or kung fu and *muay thai*, focussing rather on the primal
ethical struggle between traditional rural virtues and cosmopolitan urban
corruption which organised Bruce Lee's *The Big Boss* (a.k.a *Fists of Fury*,
1969; directed by Lo Wei) as well as the film Lee directed himself, *The
Way of the Dragon* (a.k.a *Return of the Dragon*, 1971). However, the
nationalist scenario used to promote *Ong-bak* can itself be traced through

Hong Kong cinema, where Chinese fighters have been testing their strength in Thailand at least since *The Big Boss* and Zhang Che's *Duel of Fists* (1970), and followed through to such Thai-themed Western remakes of the latter as David Worth's influential *Kickboxer* (1988), with Jean-Claude van Damme. More diffusely, the same scenario shapes such Hong Kong-US joint exploitation ventures in Thailand as the late Cold War production by Seasonal Films of Corey Yuen Kwai's *No Retreat No Surrender 2 — Raging Thunder* (1987), starring Loren Avedon, Cynthia Rothrock and Patra Wanthivanand, and featuring co-presence of the evil Soviet army and a band of Shaolin monks. The vicissitudes of this wildly inventive, commercially hybrid geo-political imaginary of combat (and the force of *Ong-bak*'s riposte to its impact in Thai cinema) suggest a historical depth to the transnational invocation and contextually complex uptake of the Hong Kong action "model" that students of inter-cultural dialogue and cross-cultural media circulation, as well as of film industries, national film cultures, and their relays in domestic, regional, and global popular cultural formations, might want to investigate more closely.

However, a marked imbalance or asymmetry in the disciplinary organisation of cinema studies makes this kind of discussion difficult. On the one hand, most English-language accounts of "action cinema" overwhelmingly focus on Hollywood, limiting Hong Kong's influence at best to the 1970s kung fu craze focused on Bruce Lee, plus a few famous figures (Jackie Chan, Jet Li, Chow Yun-fat, John Woo, Tsui Hark, Yuen Wo-ping) making forays in the US today, and the CGI-enabled download ("I know kung fu!") of Yuen's choreography into the *Matrix* trilogy and its spin-offs.[6] Unsurprisingly, this norm-setting focus on Hollywood has shaped critical interest in action as a *genre*. On the other hand, the many action films made in Hong Kong, Japan, India, Thailand, Korea, Indonesia or the Philippines tend to be studied, if at all, by specialists in *national* or, sometimes, regional ("Asian") cinema.[7] Hong Kong cinema in particular is now the object in English of a distinct, rapidly expanding field of scholarship modelled on "national cinema" studies — a problematic framing, to which I will return.

However understandable it may be in terms of the political realities of global film distribution and the resistant affect at stake for people affirming other cinemas and film cultures against Hollywood's industrial dominance, this division of critical labour installs in cinema studies the schema whereby a universalizing West produces "theory" (of film genre, in this instance) for a "Rest" that is rich in eccentric cultural particulars — a division further institutionalised in Western popular culture by fan celebrations of the "weird", the "wacky" and the "zany" in East Asian media production.[8] In the process, this division impoverishes both film theory and film history by missing some vital connections. Action cinema has long had a complex economy in which not only do Hollywood and other North American or Western producers trade (however unequally) filmmakers, styles and stories with the Hong Kong industry, but Hong Kong cinema famously draws on a long history of interaction with other cinemas in Asia as well as in the West — and over some of the former it has exerted its own export-oriented forms of domination (a "marginal imperialism", in Ding-Tzann Lii's apt phrase[9]). At the same time, dubbed into multiple languages, Hong Kong films circulate not only as "Hong Kong cinema", or "Chinese cinema", but as a vital part of the *local* film culture in particular places. Given the dispersal of large ethnic Chinese communities across South-east Asia, it is not surprising if this absorption should occur in Indonesia or Vietnam.[10] A more remarkable imaginative adoption takes place with the "Deadly Kung Fu Fights in India" series of VCDs from Diskovery Video in Mumbai, dubbed in Hindi or English, sometimes subtitled in both, and presenting old Hong Kong films in packages adding Indian figures and inventive new titles to the cover image design.[11]

Cultural circulation of this complexity deserves concerted study. *Hong Kong Connections* brings Hong Kong and action cinema specialists together to explore Hong Kong as a virtual as well as actual cultural location through which filmmakers and audiences in Japan, Korea, India, Australia, France, the UK and the US as well as Taiwan, Singapore and the Chinese mainland have interacted to create a transnational genre. Based on an international symposium held at Lingnan University, Hong Kong, in January 2003, this volume also aims to deepen understanding of action cinema's popular force, and thereby to reflect on the critical problems involved in the transnational *study* of globally popular forms. These problems are not easily avoidable, not least because much of the social and historical work on which film scholars depend for a detailed sense of context maintains the national boundaries and geo-political discontinuities that have shaped the modern disciplines. As Esther Yau notes in her Introduction to *At Full Speed: Hong Kong Cinema in a Borderless World*, too often we simply do not know enough to be able to discuss cinema historically *in* a transnational register — as distinct from talking with cultural compatriots "about" transnational cinema.[12] As a starting point, then, this book assumes that we need to develop collectively an account of action cinema's "Hong Kong connections" that is capable of articulating the differences as well as the links that globally constitute popularity.

IMAGINING FILM STUDIES TRANSNATIONALLY: ACTION CINEMA

The differences most intensively marked at present in debate about action cinema are internal to Western English-speaking societies. If Hollywood blockbusters are often reduced by critics everywhere to their special effects and violence, action cinema has been explored more seriously in recent years as "military entertainment", as a showcase for technological research and development, and above all for the issues of gender, race, sexuality and class raised for Western critics by its emphasis on "hard bodies", "tough girls" and "heroes in hard times".[13] Accordingly, most work in English on Hollywood action reflects the wider moral and political priorities of (broadly speaking) contemporary "multicultural" American and British criticism. Useful as it is, this literature mainly conceives of "global Hollywood" as a distribution outlet for *American* stories of social and political conflict.[14]

Implicitly taking a national cinema approach to a global film phenomenon, such readings attempt little of the dialogue that was common thirty years ago with film critics writing in French or Italian, and rarely consider the uptake of Hollywood films in other parts of the world and by the non-Western language communities to which English essays on cinema are, like the films, exported. Yet as Lo Kwai-cheung points out in relation to the fun had in *Rush Hour* with jokes about Chinese and African-Americans, the "gazing stance" of audiences elsewhere cannot necessarily be construed (for example) "along racial and ethnic lines" in the ways that matter to most Americans: "it is almost unimaginable for Hong Kong local audience to laugh … not for the reason [of being] offended by the racist slurs, but for the fact that they do not have a strong enough idea of racial stereotypes in American culture to understand the gags".[15]

However, polemical calls for an expanded study of reception are easy to make, the research materially difficult, and more "thick" description of the practices of a more diverse range of interpretive communities will not alone suffice (highly desirable though this would be) to reorient film studies in a direction more compatible with the formulation of a transnational critical agenda.[16] As Toby Miller, Nitin Govil, John McMurria and Richard Maxwell point out in their industrial study of *Global Hollywood*, "the cultural audience is not so much a specifiable group *within* the social order as the principal site *of* that order. Audiences participate in the most global (but local) communal (yet individual) and time-consuming practice of making meaning in world history".[17] So unless we also find ways to account from multiple perspectives for the *connections* between otherwise disparate and often mutually indifferent film communities that transnational popularity entails, a shift of emphasis towards audience ethnographies may only achieve an increased weighting of the "'other' cultures" side of the division in cinema studies while allowing the division itself to function normally — preserving what S.V. Srinivas calls "the shortcomings of analytic frames that operate under the assumption that Hollywood is the norm and every other cinema requires a separate theory".[18]

Studying the material interactions between specific film industries and their modes of distribution and exhibition is an indispensable condition for the kind of study we have in mind, as the chapters here by David Desser, Kim Soyoung, Stephen Teo, Valentina Vitali, Paul Willemen and Kinnia Yau Shuk-ting attest. At the same time, alongside the profit-oriented "macro-level synergies that hold today's media culture together" there are also, as Thomas Elsaesser reminds us, those "more internal, micro-links" involving the "pleasure-oriented" connections that film critics usually work with; it is these, in the end, that assure the growing political as well as economic power of media conglomerates as they manufacture "dreams that 'work'".[19] Elsaesser's own speculations on the powers of the Hollywood blockbuster stress its "themes that dramatize time and temporality, that connect the past with the future", the imaginative hold it establishes from childhood in the rhythm of individual lives, and the ways in which marketing and release patterns allow the blockbuster to "rival" nature by "dividing the year and ringing the changes of the seasons": "across mythical stories of disaster and renewal, trauma and survival", he concludes, "it thus reconciles us to our mortality".[20]

While some cross-cultural testing of this last claim would be interesting, a socially grounded as well as textually sensitive approach to understanding the pleasures afforded audiences by a cinema of "temporalities and lifelines" (in Elsaesser's phrase) is another way to initiate a comparative discussion of the political-economic force of action movies across different contexts; perhaps also it is a way to extend discussion to the ambitions and impacts of other film industries that may dream of but do not rival the Hollywood industry's scale and global reach. Hong Kong producers of the stature of Shaw Brothers and Raymond Chow have aspired, since the 1960s in the former case and the 1970s in the latter, to achieve a mode of globalisation based on "the Hong Kong ecumene" (in Steve Fore's illuminating phrase).[21] However, the action-based temporalities and intimate, as well as public, lifelines explored here in the chapters by Stephen Chan Ching-kiu (on Hong Kong Cantonese films of the 1980s and 1990s) and by S. V. Srinivas (on the Telugu "mass-film" genre developed in the state of Andhra

Pradesh in India over much the same period) are organised at significantly local levels of language community and affective mobilisation.

It is precisely this analytical emphasis on locality and context that gives the essays in this volume their methodological force for studying transnationally popular cinema. Action cinemas generally mobilise or reanimate aspects of an old form of story-telling (whether myth, epic, legend, folktale, saga, annals or chronicle) whereby a hero, or a band of heroes, faces an unknown land or confronts intruders at home. Classically in the social *practice* of such modes of narration, the recitation of the hero's exploits affirms and defines community for those who make his story their own; fan networks do much the same today, as they establish partial, temporary or sporadic modes of "community" — modes that may take shape and thrive in time rather than (or as well as) being actualised or anchored in space. Action cinema also inherits the European historical novel's interest in the nature of "world-historical" heroism in modern social conditions, working fictionally across the terrain once occupied in the Western historical tradition by imperial and national histories of "great men and great events", absorbed with conflict and war.[22] Correspondingly, action may become a significant cultural genre in a range of otherwise diverse societies where the very idea of modernity is tied up with historical experiences of violence as colonisation and as rapid capitalist development — issues explored here in a Hong Kong context by Siu Leung Li; in Korean film history by Kim Soyoung; around the Pacific by Rob Wilson; and in Laleen Jayamanne's Australian-Sri Lankan approach to the "belatedness" of Charlie Chaplin and Jackie Chan.

Whether particular films play a critical, conservative or frivolous role in shaping popular images of worldly issues, the point is that they circulate fictions about them and in doing so give them a fragile but pervasive currency in real places and for definite social groups. Action films are blatantly concerned with *difficulties* of community, with social and geo-political conflict, with nation-building (consider Zhang Yimou's *Hero* as well as James Cameron's "Gulf War comedy" *True Lies*) and, on the grand scale, with civilizational clashes and the "ends" of the world as we know it. Having absorbed elements of both science fiction and the "period" adventure, action films can also deal in the culture shocks of time travel to other societies, or, with ethnographic force, to your own in another phase of its development. Like the deep-frozen Ming Dynasty imperial guards reanimated in pre-handover Hong Kong by Clarence Fok Yiu-leung's *Iceman Cometh* (*Time Warriors*) in 1989, the year of the Tiananmen Square massacre, then converted in Hollywood by Marco Brambilla's *Demolition Man* (1993) into a white cop/black gangster dyad cryogenically imprisoned then released by a politically correct dictatorship in the future of Los Angeles, this "other phase" of time may be historically pressing but chronologically remote, or it may be just "a few years from now" (*Mad Max*) or "the day after tomorrow". Whatever their fictive historical setting, as they tell stories of local, national or global heroes saving their world, be it large or small, from annihilation, action films stage and resolve the conflicts and uncertainties of *our* time.

Along with comparative industry studies, and textually attentive analyses of the force and significance of media temporalities, a third way of understanding action as a global cultural formation explores the uses and practices of the technologies that enable popularity. Yvonne Tasker early drew attention to the social diversity of the audiences renting action films from video stores in Britain in the early 1990s, and to the role that video was playing in forming new consumption networks.[23] Some years later Lee Server observed that video was creating transnational audiences for Asian popular cinemas unable to secure theatrical release of their films in the US — a point recently elaborated by David Bordwell when he allows in *Planet Hong Kong: Popular Cinema and the Art of Entertainment* that video, zines and Webculture have established "another way" besides theatrical release "in which a popular cinema can go global".[24]

As they cross territorial borders in cheap, accessible forms (video tape is still typical across much of the world, while the VCD rules in Asia with the exception of Japan), action scenarios are transformed imaginatively by the local needs and experiences of the people who not only watch, enjoy, discuss and share but also sometimes remake them, whether they do so in their capacity as artists, like the research-oriented French avant-garde filmmakers discussed by Nicole Brenez and the action directors essaying the "force and bliss" of Hong Kong style in Adrian Martin's experimental history; as "new cinephiles", whose internet-enhanced labours of love are explored in Desser's essay; or as the ordinary post-human spectators predicated and welcomed by Wong Kin-yuen.

IMAGINING HONG KONG CINEMA

A transnational critical discussion cannot be one that marginalises the aesthetic and historical issues or the interpretive frameworks of interest to Hong Kong-based and Chinese scholars, and yet this all too easily occurs in Western effusions about global "popular" culture. In a discussion of the uptake of kung fu and other martial arts imaginaries in computer games today, Leon Hunt rightly cautions against easily blurring "East/West binaries" in accounting for the interface between martial arts games and films, pointing out that this interface seems rather to take the form of "a three-way dialogue" between "Hollywood ('blockbuster'-spectacle, CGI, *The Matrix*), Japan (*anime*, manga), and Hong Kong (action aesthetics, kung fu films and stars)".[25] Little is gained conceptually by effacing in simple models of "inter-mixing" those pragmatically grounded associations between locales and distinctive cultural traditions which we recognise and use every day, especially since the blurring Hunt refers to is most likely to be effected successfully from a parochially "Western" perspective that is capable of imagining "the East" or "Asia" as one half of a binary in the first place.

Nevertheless, the question arises of what we *do* when we affirm an equivalence between "Hollywood", "Japan" and "Hong Kong". These proper names are commonly used in English to identify internationally well-known film industries. They also designate, respectively, an area of a much larger city in the United States, Los Angeles; an entire nation-state; and a former British colonial territory, which is larger than the urban areas of Hong Kong Island and the Kowloon peninsula that dominate its image as a "city", and which has been since 1997 a Special Administrative Region (the HKSAR) of the People's Republic of China. Within these asymmetries of everyday talk about film there is no doubt a good story to be told about the cognitive eccentricities of Anglo-centric cultural mapping. However, the difficulties of settling the status of the "Hong Kong" in "Hong Kong cinema" famously exceed this routine critique, all the more so in that Hong Kong's films, and its action genres in particular, have such a vivid and solid identity for both fan and scholarly literature.

Compared with what was available in English ten years ago, there is no shortage of scholarship now on the *specificity* of Hong Kong cinema. Studies such as Stephen Teo's history, *Hong Kong Cinema: The Extra Dimension,* and the bi-lingual volumes published in recent years by the Hong Kong Film Archive provide rich resources for studying Hong Kong's action films in the context of a wider cultural and industrial history firmly anchored in the territory of Hong Kong, but implicated in linguistically and politically complex commercial and cultural relations with other Chinese film industries, as well as in a regional economy of "border-crossing" and trade.[26] To these historically-inflected studies, Lisa Odham Stokes and Michael Hoover add a powerful argument in their book *City on Fire* that Hong Kong cinema has to be understood through the territory's distinctive political economy; for Stokes and Hoover, the Hong Kong industry has a "dark underbelly" of the hyper-exploitation of labour (dramatised in *Ah Kam*, Ann Hui's 1996 film about an action movie stunt woman), piracy and criminal connections typical of early capitalism, while supporting "the screen glamour and fanzine hoopla" of the late capitalist commodity culture at which Hong Kong also excels.[27] On the aesthetic side, Bordwell's *Planet Hong Kong* develops a strong account of Hong Kong cinema's "art of entertainment" by vividly relating everyday filmmaking practices in Hong Kong to the formal properties of film texts.

The specificity of Hong Kong cinema is not in doubt. However, one of the most debated issues in Hong Kong film scholarship is how to *frame* that specificity within a discipline that tries to organise film worlds beyond Hollywood with the category "national cinema". There are good reasons for the insistence of the national model in cinema studies, but it poses problems for active filmmaking areas or states that are not "nations" in any meaningful sense of the term.[28] Thus Poshek Fu and David Desser suggest that in these terms "Hong Kong presents a theoretical conundrum … a cinema without a nation, a local cinema with transnational appeal" — and one which became the third most active cinema in the world and is still "per capita the most active in the world by far".[29] In recent years this problem has been complicated further by the awkwardly hybrid national framework with an expiry date ("one country, two systems" until 2046) installed for the HKSAR as the condition of its reintegration with China.

The issue of *negotiating* "the national" increasingly preoccupies Hong Kong filmmakers, both thematically (in crime genres alone, consider Andrew Lau's *Young and Dangerous* cycle of the 1996–98 period, the great *Infernal Affairs* "undercover" trilogy of 2003–04 directed by Lau with Alan Mak,[30] or Derek Yee's poignant *One Nite in Mongkok* and Johnnie To's more playful *Breaking News*, both from 2004) and economically, as the opportunities and difficulties of co-producing, making and releasing films on the Mainland begin to affect the shaping of Hong Kong stories — with implications on both sides of the border, as Dai Jinhua's essay here suggests. Not a national cinema, certainly, and yet no longer exactly a cinema *without* a nation, a "one country, two systems" cinema is also no longer unequivocally local — if indeed Hong Kong cinema overall ever was "local" *as a cinema*, given the aggressive export drive of its major studios and producers, the formative tension between Cantonese and Mandarin-language filmmaking in its past, and its increasingly multi-glossic orientation today. Yet Hong Kong cinema still does not fit easily into anthologies bravely attempting a transnational approach to "Chinese cinemas", not least because the diversity and scale of Hong Kong's industry exceeds their grasp.[31]

In the most comprehensive discussion to date of the literature arising from this "conundrum" of situation and naming, Esther M. K. Cheung and Chu Yiu-wai introduce their *Between Home and World: A Reader in Hong Kong Cinema* by reminding us that if this cinema has basically achieved a national status even as it "evades definition because of its complex and paradoxical history", the primary task remains one of "addressing the difficulties involved and arriving at some ways of *understanding* this complex cultural entity — not simply to grant it a name in the final analysis"[32]. Among the efforts they review are such models of Hong Kong's cinema as "popular cinema", "urban cinema", and "transnational cinema", to which we can add "postmodern cinema", "ethnic cinema", and the Chinese mainland term, "Tsui Hark films", explored in this volume by Dai.[33] "Crisis cinema" is the model which Cheung and Chu prefer, for its capacity to take account of the "various kinds of mutations that Hong Kong is caught up with", and to emphasise "the multiplicity of cinematic expressions" to which this variety continues to give rise across a spectrum from action to queer cinema.

Perhaps the most problematic of the non-national models applied to Hong Kong films is the notion of a "subcultural cinema" as used by David Bordwell. The problem is not that particular uptakes of Hong Kong cinema cannot usefully be called subcultural (or, in a related phrase, as "cult"); of course they can, especially in urban milieux around the developed world. The problem follows rather from the rigorous logic of Bordwell's insistence on the primacy of a theatrical model of *cinema*: a "truly global cinema", he argues, is one which significantly occupies screen space in developed and developing countries alike. On those terms there is indeed only one such cinema and it is, as he says, American: indisputably, "the Hollywood of the East is Hollywood" and Hong Kong cinema is, by comparison, a "cottage industry".[34] However, when Bordwell turns to accounting for that other, non-theatrical way for a popular cinema to "go global", the unavailability of the national paradigm allows subculture to slip in as a handy way of mediating the local and the global: "a local cinema has achieved international reach by becoming a subcultural cinema".[35]

Here, the term "subcultural cinema" is doing the same work that "national cinema" does when crudely used as a label to signify, as Cheung and Chu put it, cinematic "varieties of 'otherness', namely how they are different from Hollywood films".[36] It also takes for granted what comparative research would need to establish, namely that the cultural mode of Hong Kong's cinema's video-borne "reach" into many different countries, *and* to diverse communities therein, can uniformly be described as subcultural. A light-hearted World Film analogy with the marketing category "World Music" further makes it clear that "sub"-culture for Bordwell is not a set of social practices and identification rituals shaped in response to a dominant "culture", but just a bunch of non-American cultural *stuff*: "Japanese *anime*, Indian melodramas, Italian horror, Mexican masked-wrestler films, Indonesian fantasies, and other off-center [sic] media materials from various countries".[37] Hong Kong cinema is at the leading edge of this exotic wave of stuff, its "salsa or reggae".

By this logic anything not produced in the US is "subcultural" when it travels, while American media materials are "global" wherever they go. To be fair, Bordwell is no doubt simply describing the assumptions of his own cultural habitus, as the term "off-center" suggests: *anime* cannot sensibly be called off-centre in Japan, nor is melodrama "off" in India. However, if we have good reason to accept the unique worldly status of Hollywood, it does not follow that a corresponding "centrality" should be accorded in cinema studies to the middle American consumer. Whether Japanese media products are off-centre everywhere in India, Italy or Mexico is a question to be asked; and whether they are positioned *in the same way* across India as they are in Hong Kong (where they are not really "off-centre" at all) or in Korea (where cultural imports from Japan were banned between 1978 and 1999) is another question again. One of the aims of this volume is to bring such questions to bear on the circulation of Hong Kong action cinema: any cultural "ecumene" (including that of Hollywood) has a deeply folded and differentiated texture which critical scholarship needs to explore.

HONG KONG CONNECTIONS

Our project is not to organise from one location a comparative study of the uptake of Hong Kong action in various places, useful though that might be. Rather, with Hong Kong action cinema as its convergence-point, this book initiates a multilateral discussion between scholars who centre themselves in various national or other geopolitical frames (migrancy included) and also in relation to different disciplines and intellectual cultures; the contributors draw on political economy, history, opera, and music and literary as well as cinema studies, and their questions arise in work environments that range from universities in Hong Kong and elsewhere to the French Cinémathèque, an independent research centre in India and a major newspaper in Australia. This volume is not based in the North American academy, and only a quarter of the book's contributors and one of the book's three editors are native speakers of English.

However, it is not an eclectic international assembly: the reader will find here both a strong "regional" emphasis on East Asian and Asian-Pacific perspectives, social experiences and critical debates, and a conscious effort to bring these "centrally" into dialogue with the preoccupations of scholars from other parts of the world.

In an important sense, however, this is not a book *about* Hong Kong action cinema and the reader will encounter detailed discussion of issues in Korean, Telugu, Hindi, French, Australian and mainland Chinese film history. Our objective in initiating this project was to create a contact zone of transnational discussion that could be rendered coherent by a shared sense of connection *to* Hong Kong cinema, but in which the problem of articulating connections might itself become the primary theme. In this process of articulation, the links that materialised between participants and papers were often more striking than the differences, as various "ways of understanding" Hong Kong action cinema emerged. The touchstone texts to which many scholars referred, for example, turned out to be not the canonised films of John Woo or Tsui Hark, but the action comedies or "rubbish films" of Stephen Chiau and the critically "abjected" recent work of Jackie Chan (in particular, *Tuxedo*) as well as the problematic instance of Ang Lee's *Crouching Tiger, Hidden Dragon*. More subtly, collaborative themes and motifs came together across the boundaries of individual essays. For example, Wilson's notion of martial arts as a "training to live with digital technology" is taken up in Li's reflections on the cultural meaning of technological anachronism and kung fu in Cantonese films, connects with Martin's model of the martial-arts trained body as "already technology-in-action", and finds itself theorised in Wong's magisterial essay on embodiment and *wuda pian* in the era of new technologies. Another path to Wong's themes can be traced from Yung Sai-shing's pedagogy of the operatic "moving body" through to the "impaired" action star bodies discussed by Kim, the "secrets of movement" pursued by Brenez, the transnationally mobile acts of "miscegenation" explored by Jayamanne, the fantastically capitalised film bodies analysed in different contexts by Vitali and Willemen, and to Wilson's spectral "bio-poetics" of trans-Pacific globalisation.

Nevertheless, any collective volume promotes an argument imposed by the editors. Our thesis here is twofold: first, that action cinema works as a generic zone in which cross-cultural logics of contact and connection (audio-visual and socio-cultural as well as bodily and technological) are acted and tested out; and, second, that a Hong Kong-*based* but not exclusively Hong Kong-focused account of these logics can contribute to cinema studies a cosmopolitan model of how to understand global cinema from local contexts that are neither "centred" by Hollywood nor exclude or disavow its influence. We also assume that the contexts of film production as well as reception must be studied not only from different perspectives but in historical depth; it is from within this "depth" — that is, of time, memory and experience — as well as in the encounters and the connections that form and unfold in space, that any popular cultural products are invested with meaning by concrete communities and possibilities for innovation and change arise.

We begin, therefore, with a section on "History, Imagination and Hong Kong Popular Culture", in which scholars from Singapore, Japan (Yau's location at her time of writing), Hong Kong and the Chinese mainland examine the distinctive modalities of historical imagination at work in Hong Kong action cinema. Hong Kong's "art of entertainment" is famously interactive, borrowing from a range of Chinese arts, genres and cultural traditions as well as from many foreign cinemas, and in that sense its action films have long been addressing densely local, indeed, deeply parochial concerns in cosmopolitan cultural forms, some of which travel widely and translate well.[38] Two of the Hong Kong action cinema's most significant links historically have been with Chinese opera on the one hand, and Japanese cinema and media culture on the other; however, the nature of these links is rarely explained in detail for readers of English. Yung's essay here on "inter-generic influence" between action cinema and diverse forms of Chinese opera not only explores the translation of a performance culture from opera aesthetics to cinema, but shows how the pressure of cinema's rising popularity across South-East Asia in the 1930s led Teochew opera troupes to introduce "special effects" — such as wires and "flying swords" — that would migrate back to cinema for a long journey around the world that has taken them to Hollywood only in relatively recent times.

Kinnia Yau's essay also begins with opera, as she points out that the importance of "action" in Japanese and Hong Kong cinema alike derives from the cultural legacy of their respective traditional theatres (*kabuki* in the case of Japan). Her study of the interactions between the two cinemas from the mid-1950s to the mid-1970s not only deepens our understanding of what Hong Kong filmmakers borrowed from Japan in this key period, and of the wider regional industrial initiatives that made this borrowing desirable, but also works the other way round to consider the reception in Japan of Hong Kong cinema, in particular the flagrantly anti-Japanese kung fu films of the early 1970s. Li and Chan take up the issue of how to "read" in films the politically complex affect and the memories that a popular cinema can mobilise for its "local" audience, as they link action texts historically with wider issues of Chinese modernity (Li) and with the everyday life of Cantonese popular culture in Hong Kong (Chan). These essays introduce to the volume key concerns of Chinese contemporary cultural studies, concerns which are relayed and resituated by Dai in the complicated cultural politics of the Chinese mainland in the late 1980s and early 1990s. Drawing deeply on Chinese film and cultural history, Dai's essay opens up the theoretical question of the "popularity" of Hong Kong action cinema (and the diversity of its cultural uptakes) in a layered analysis of the differences between specific *moments* of popularity in Hong Kong cinema's circulation in China.

The second section, "Action Cinema as Contact Zone", takes its title from Kim's historical analysis of the significance in South Korea of the encounter between two genres, Hong Kong "action", and Korean *Hwalkuk* ("living theatre", originally a popular, male-oriented action entertainment during the colonial era); she reflects in particular on co-productions, on the resonance of action landscapes for local audiences, and on the capacity of the figure of an injured or impaired action star to invoke a "marred" modernity that still retains a sense of promise. Srinivas takes up the themes of contact between genres and the mobilising power of the star-protagonist as he considers Hong Kong kung fu cinema's connections with and yet, in another sense, its lack of significance for, the profoundly political Telugu "mass film", as the latter is reworked by the Telugu martial arts film that he discusses in detail, *Bhadrachalam*. Examining more oblique but no less material modes of contact — the echo, the relay and the resonance — Vitali studies the political economy of the Hindi film industry during the 1970s and 1980s, as its relation to American "globalisation" was mediated both by the Indian state and by the industry's resistance to state control, in order to see how and why "martial art" came to play the role that it did in Hindi action at the time, and what "values", economic and symbolic, invest its choreography of Hong Kong-resonant but indigenous "acrobatic mastery".

Jayamanne draws on her memories of the popularity of Charlie Chaplin as a "Third World" hero in her native Ceylon in order to discuss the technologically as well as culturally miscegenating body of Jackie Chan's recent work featuring an African (*Who Am I?*) or African-American connection (*Rumble in the Bronx, Rush Hour*); in these films which have been despised by critics, in Hong Kong as in the US, Jayamanne sees the creation of new "kinship" networks and generic modes of intimacy. Giving intimacy a different inflection, Brenez closely reads "three modest, unknown and unique French experimental films" — *Samouraï* by Johanna Vaude, *Révélation/Chunguang Zhaxie* by Xavier Baert, and *Lighting* by a collective under the direction of Othello Vilgard — to show how they materially and conceptually use Hong Kong action cinema in their search for solutions to the problem of representing movement. In the section's final essay, Martin argues that experimental cinema is a special branch of action cinema; suggesting that "Hong Kong cinema begins with *Mad Max*", his own practice of intimate reading explores the scene rather than the film "text", and his study of "the edge of the cut" in action montage follows the Hong Kong style from the work of George Miller through to cinematic moments of intensity in Johnnie To's *Running Out of Time*, Martin Scorsese's *Cape Fear*, Wong Kar-wai's *Ashes of Time*, Tsui Hark's *The Blade*, and James Wong's *The One*.

The essays in the first section explore Hong Kong cinema's distinctive historical formation and its ways of imagining and representing historical experience for local and Chinese communities, while the second section moves outward and away from Hong Kong territory to other zones of popular cinema and historical imagination. The third part of the book, "Translation and Embodiment: Technologies of Globalisation", addresses the "how?" of Hong Kong action cinema's transnational reach in a globalising economy of new media in which film is only one element. Key preoccupations for all the essays in this section are, on the one hand, the modes of translation — between circuits of production and technologies of distribution as well as genres, traditions and languages — that enable new formations of "popularity" to emerge across historic cultural boundaries, and, on the other hand, the impact in "action" *bodies* of the forces of historical change and technological experiment.

Returning us to the transnationalism of Chinese popular cinema, Teo assesses the "globalising postmodernism" of *Crouching Tiger, Hidden Dragon* (Ang Lee 2000) as a prototype of what he calls "late" transnational production; discussing the techniques adopted for presenting the film to Western audiences (including the use of live synch-sound), Teo suggests that the popular *wuxia* genre has now gone well beyond its "core centre" in the Hong Kong film industry and its markets in the Chinese diaspora to become, at the very least, a pan-Asian genre with an uncertain future. Desser takes a more optimistic view in his detailed account of the *practices* of "new cinephilia" enabled by as well as based in new media such as VCD and the World Wide Web; taking issue with Susan Sontag's vision of a "decay of cinema", Desser examines the expansion of film appreciation that is occurring as not only Hong Kong, Japanese and Korean but Hindi films as well enter a global mainstream, and as this development reaches American suburban communities and begins to impact on Hollywood cinema.

Willemen is sceptical both about the analytical value of the term "action cinema", and about the scale and timing of Hong Kong's influence on Hollywood, which for him is not significant before the mid- to late-1990s. Examining the history of "action" as a marketing as well as a production category, he traces its changing uses in the trade magazine *Variety* and goes on to link the rise of the video market, and the related mainstreaming by Hollywood of the features of a hitherto marginal "exploitation cinema", to changes in the nature of labour power under finance capitalism — and in the body images that fantasmatically register and deal with those changes. Wilson explores literary as well as filmic inscriptions of lived experiences of that capital as it flows through and fragments global cities around the Pacific Rim; finding the "hauntings" of cultural memory at work in passages of action, Wilson follows "spectres" and "global souls" as they wander between San Francisco, Seoul and Hong Kong. Wong then concludes the volume by drawing on classical "Chinese Kung fu discourse", on the temporal philosophies of Henri Bergson and Gilles Deleuze, and on recent theories of digital culture to explore the implications of new technologies for cinema. Dissenting from those who (like some fans of *Ong-bak*) regard the use of digital effects in such films as *Matrix*, *The One* and Tsui Hark's *Legend of Zu* as the end of Hong Kong action's creativity, Wong sees in these films "a real attempt at presenting the 'outside' for thought"; for Wong's philosophy of the virtual, such experimentation holds great promise both for thinking "beyond writing", and for renewing not only the *wuda pian* tradition but perhaps, too, the life force in "global souls".

Ultimately the question addressed by this book is how we ourselves might most productively *imagine* the "transnational" flows and movements in culture that are so often invoked in critical rhetoric today. To ask this question is not to reject the tasks and responsibilities of criticism, forsaking scholarship for fantasies and dreams. On the contrary: acts of imagining enable as well as shape our research projects and our analytical priorities, and studying the history of action cinema is a useful way to think in concrete terms about pressingly transnational cultural developments. Theories of globalisation abound these days, many of them purely rhetorical constructs assembled from bibliographies of the "must read" texts *du jour* for the Euro-American academy. Detailed empirical studies, in textual and performance aesthetics as well as in political economy and history, are needed now to advance our understanding of how globalising forces are actually working, or not working, in culture; urgently needed, too, is a greatly expanded geographical frame of scholarly reading and discussion. However we define it, action cinema is a useful *case* for study both because its transnationalism is not new, and because the diverse generic practices connected by the term "action" explicitly dramatise the conflict-ridden conditions of their own production, circulation, and popular status. With this volume, we suggest that Hong Kong's action cinema and its uptakes and relays elsewhere provide an exemplary model for such a case study. We hope, too, that this book is a positive example of what a collaborative rather than a unilateral approach to "transnationally imagining" film scholarship both entails and is able to do.

Part 1

History, Imagination and Hong Kong Popular Culture

1

Moving Body:
The Interactions Between Chinese Opera and Action Cinema

Yung Sai-shing

> *[Cantonese opera:] Inheriting the traditions of Kunshan and Luantan operas; Absorbing the essences of northern and southern theatrical styles; Paying respect to and learning from Peking opera as its elder brother; treating the motion picture as its loyal friend who never hesitates to remonstrate.*
>
> Mak Siu-ha, *A Brief History of Cantonese Opera*[1]

INTRODUCTION

Shortly after the publication of *A Brief History of Cantonese Opera,* quoted above, its author Mak Siu-ha (Mai Xiaoxia 1904–1941) was killed during the bombing of Hong Kong Island by the Japanese Artillery in December 1941.[2] Recognized today as the first scholarly study on the history of Cantonese opera, the article has been used extensively in the classrooms of academies and universities of China and overseas. Mak was a talented Hong Kong artist of the 1930s. He was at the same time a playwright of Cantonese opera, a songwriter for Cantonese movies, an amateur Cantonese opera actor, a skilful martial art practitioner, a painter-cum-designer, a public relations officer of Cantonese opera troupes, and a director of Cantonese movies who had graduated from the Chinese Academy for Actors.[3]

As an insider, Mak Siu-ha witnessed the unprecedented changes experienced by Cantonese opera during the 1920s and 1930s. I have no intention of providing a thorough study about this central issue in the research of the history of Cantonese opera in this short essay. It suffices to point out that in the citation above, Mak clearly indicates that innovative elements emerged on the Cantonese opera stage in the 1930s, and were the result of interactions between Cantonese opera, Peking opera and motion pictures. These interactions took place mainly in the decade when the talkies had been newly introduced to the urban centers of China and Southeast Asia, including Shanghai, Hong Kong, and Singapore.

This phenomenon of inter-generic influence should be no stranger to the students of the histories of Chinese cinema and opera; the connections between Chinese regional operas and Chinese cinema have been close since the beginning of the Chinese film industry. The present paper, however, concentrates on the interrelationships between Chinese theatrical arts and action cinema. Although the time frame stretches from the 1930s to the present, and Chinese operas from different provincial origins will be touched on, this paper attempts to investigate two issues. First, in what ways has action cinema been influenced by Chinese theatrical art? And, in reverse, how have motion pictures, and action cinema in particular, affected the presentation and aesthetics of Chinese opera? In answering the first question, I shall use the careers of Yuen Wo-ping and Jackie Chan as cases studies; unavoidably then, the present study will center mainly on Hong Kong film productions. At the same time, I shall discuss passages from the Teochew opera, Kunshan opera and Peking opera, in order to compare these with the fight scenes and choreographic designs created by these two major figures in Hong Kong action cinema.

THE ARRIVAL OF THE "NORTHERN STYLE": THE EMERGENCE OF LOCAL MARTIAL ARTISTS

The story has to go back to Mak Siu-ha. In the quotation above, Mak highlights the changes taking place in Cantonese opera in the 1930s. One of these major changes was a process of synthesis with the northern theatrical arts. Here, "synthesis" in fact means learning and borrowing from Peking opera, especially the vigorous, forceful, and eloquent acrobatic/martial forms of the latter, which appeared to be more appealing to the theatergoers of Cantonese opera. A new term, *beipai* — literally, the "northern school" or the "northern style" — thus emerged to label these bustling martial forms newly borrowed from northern China, whereas the term *nanpai* was used to designate the native combat style indigenous to the Cantonese opera of southern China. Starting from the 1930s, the "northern school" has been gradually replacing the "southern school". Today, the latter has almost completely vanished from the Cantonese opera stage.[4]

One of the key figures who brought this fashionable northern martial style to Hong Kong was Yuen Siu-tin (Simon Yuen, 1912–1980), the father of the famous Hong Kong director and choreographer Yuen Wo-ping. Yuen Siu-tin was originally a Peking opera actor in Shanghai. He joined a troupe when he was as young as six years old, and trained to be an opera actor of the "male martial role".[5] In the 1930s, Yuen was recruited by the eminent Cantonese opera actor Sit Kok-sin (Xue Juexian, 1904–1956), to be one of the four actors performing the "northern style" martial art in his *Juexiansheng* Theatre Troupe.

From a poster of the *Juexiansheng* Theatre Troupe in 1937, probably designed by Mak Siu-ha, we find that there existed two categories of martial art performers in the troupe. Consisting of seven members, the first type is categorized as *dawu yiyuan*, literally the "martial artists". They are the original martial artists performing the native "southern style". To their left, one finds the names of another four actors. Highlighted in a larger font, they are labeled and especially promoted as the "actors of martial male roles in northern style, recruited by high pay". The first name on the list is Yuen Siu-tin, the others being Yuan Caixi, Zhang Deming, and Xiao Yuelou. These four newcomers were performing in a play freshly written by Mak Siu-ha, revised and directed by Sit Kok-sin.[6]

Before we move further into the discussion of Yuen Siu-tin, it is worth noting two points. The first concerns the intimate relationships between Cantonese opera and Cantonese movies. Sit Kok-sin started his career in film production as early as 1925, when he set up his own film company in Shanghai. It seems to have been a one-man-business in which Sit acted simultaneously as the company manager, scriptwriter, movie director and actor. His first production, *The Playboy (Langdie)*, was a silent film produced in 1926. However, the Cantonese film that caused a sensation for Sit Kok-sin was the *White Golden Dragon (Bai Jinlong)*. Produced in Shanghai by the Tianyi Company of the Shaw brothers in 1933, this film was the movie version of the Cantonese opera of the same title. The story was an adaptation from the Hollywood movie *The Grand Duchess and the Waiter* (Malcolm St. Clair 1926). Its production reflected the interactions between Hollywood films, Cantonese opera, and the Cantonese film industry in the 1920s and 1930s. We will come back to this issue later.

Second, the 1930s saw a fashion in Cantonese opera circles of learning from Peking opera. For instance, Chen Feinong who was famous for his impersonation of female roles, acquired the arts of ribbon dance and martial art from the Peking opera actress Shisan Dan.[7] Another distinguished actor, Xin Ma Shizeng (1916–1997), learned Peking opera from Lin Shuse.[8] Sit Kok-sin was also a dedicated student of Peking opera.

He was fascinated particularly by the performing style of Zhou Xinfang (1895–1975), the founder of the vocal style of the Qi School. Furthermore, Sit had also staged Peking opera publicly on different occasions.[9]

Among the four Peking opera actors recruited from Shanghai by Sit Kok-sin, Yuen Siu-tin is the most significant in the later development of Hong Kong action cinema. Yuen was no stranger to Hong Kong movie audiences during the 1950s and 1960s. Characterized by his Cantonese spoken with a strong northern accent, Yuen Siu-tin acted frequently in fighting scenes in the low-budget martial art and swordsman films directed by such Hong Kong directors as Wu Pang (Hu Peng, 1909–2000) and Ling Wan (Ling Yun, 1925–), including the Wong Fei-hung series directed by the former from the early 1950s.[10] In the 1950s and 1960s Yuen was one of the most influential martial art directors in the Hong Kong film industry, and led a group of martial art directors working for various studios. In those same decades, he also trained young martial artists, some of whom would later become famous action movie actors, choreographers and directors: Yuen Wo-ping and Tong Kai being two outstanding examples.

Yuen Wo-ping, today an internationally renowned action choreographer and action movie director, received rigorous and intensive training in Peking opera from his father. Recollecting his training life in the 1950s, Yuen Wo-ping says:

> The life of learning at that time was tough. My father basically taught what he knew (about martial arts) to his sons and daughters. Perhaps it is as the Chinese say: A son inherits his father's profession. We practiced basic skills every morning, and then went to have Dim Sum at the restaurant. In the afternoon, we would learn the skills of playing weapons, like blade, spear, sword, and halberd. We also practiced Chinese boxing and somersaulting. At that time people were generally poor. Besides coaching his sons and daughters, my father also had a large group of students. They all slept and ate in our house, all relying on my father. It was something like a hostel.[11]

In fact it was a traditional practice for a Peking opera teacher to feed and house his disciples, in a way similar to a boarding school. At the age of about seven or eight, Yuen Wo-ping began to stage Peking opera publicly in Hong Kong at banquets. Through his father, he was also exposed to production work at movie studios, paving the way for his later career in filmmaking.[12]

Tong Kai was one of the chief disciples of Yuen Siu-tin. Trained by master Yuen, Tong began his career as a "Dragon-Tiger Master" for Hong

Kong swordsman and kung fu movies. Following the career path of his master, Tong Kai started a career as an action choreographer in the 1960s. His first film (co-choreographed with Lau Kar-leung) was *South Dragon, North Phoenix*, directed by Wu Pang in 1963. From the late 1960s Tong worked closely with Lau Kar-leung to choreograph action movies for Shaw Brothers, including the classics *One-Armed Swordsman* (1967) and many others. Tong Kai recalls the life of training under Yuen Siu-tin in his teens:

> Master Yuen Siu-tin had three genuine disciples under his wing. One was Fatty Ying, another was Yuen Sing-chau, and I was the third … . We learned somersaults — it wasn't proper kung fu then, but the kind of somersaults and skill of pulling horses performed in the Cantonese opera "The Investiture of the Minister for the Six Kingdoms". These actions were done by Dragon-Tiger Masters. At that time, those people responsible for somersaults and pulling horses on the opera stage were called Dragon-Tiger Masters.[13]

"The Investiture of the Minister for the Six Kingdoms" is a traditional ritual play in the repertoire of Cantonese opera. Its performance involves extensive displays of somersaults and acrobatics, which are performed by the "Dragon-Tiger Masters". The interview above reveals the connection between Chinese opera and action cinema: the skill and concept of the action choreography of the martial artists comes from their training and knowledge in Chinese opera.

The famous director Lau Kar-leung, who was the working partner of Tong Kai for years in action choreography, once explained the nature of "Dragon-Tiger Master" in Cantonese opera and Cantonese action movies:

> "The Dragon-Tiger Master" was a Cantonese opera term for martial artist, originally known as the "Five Army Tigers". The name didn't sound nice in marquees so they changed it to the "Dragon-Tiger Master". I know that the first generation of Dragon-Tiger Master were Yuen Siu-tin, Chow Siu-loi, Kei Yuk-kwun, Cheung Yuk-sing, and others … . The second generation masters were Tong Kai, Lau Kar-leung, Tsui Chung-hok, Han Yingjie, Kwan Ching-leung, Siu Kei-lun … . The third generation includes many people; the famous ones are Jackie Chan, Yuen Wo-ping, Yuen Cheung-yan, Sammo Hung … The fourth generation artists are the people now — like Ching Siu-tung.[14]

Two points deserve special attention here. First, when naming the "first generation" Hong Kong martial artists, Lau Kar-leung placed Yuen Siu-tin first on the list. This shows the reputation and importance of Yuen Siu-tin in his circle. In fact, Yuen served as the "leader" ("snake head") of the martial art directors in those decades. [15] Second, a majority of the artists listed by Lau had received proper training in Peking opera. Kwan Ching-leung is a disciple of the master Yu Zhanyuan, who trained the famous "Seven Little Fortunes". Han Yingjie was the action choreographer in King Hu's martial art films. Two of the most well known are *Come Drink with Me* (1966) and *A Touch of Zen* (1971). King Hu recalls his relationship with Han Yingjie and the "Seven Little Fortunes":

> I used Han Yingjie as martial arts director beginning with *Come Drink with Me*. His assistant was Sammo Hung. The children who appeared in *Come Drink with Me* included Jackie Chan, Ng Ming-choi and Ching Siu-tung. I was the board member of a few Peking opera schools and of course I didn't demand a salary — and they wouldn't have given me one because they were so poor.[16]

After 1949, due to the changed political situation in mainland China, Peking opera actors from Shanghai moved and settled in Hong Kong. They brought with them their skills and knowledge, and started to establish their private academies. According to King Hu, there were four major academies of Peking opera in Hong Kong in the 1950s and 1960s.[17]

These private academies of Chinese opera in Hong Kong after World War Two served as the key cultural institutions through which the traditional Chinese operatic art was transmitted and preserved. Here, "transmission" has both the senses of disseminating the art from northern China to the British Crown Colony in the south, and handing down the skills of performance from the pre-war generation to the local Hong Kong actors. These institutions, either formally operating in the form of an academy, or conducting private tuition, cultivated a new generation of Hong Kong martial artists. Through severe and demanding training, these operatic academies played a decisive role in nurturing new blood for the Hong Kong action cinema. I have summarized the relationships between major Hong Kong martial artists, their masters, and the related Peking opera schools in Hong Kong in the following table:[18]

The "Masters"	The Disciples / Martial Artists	Academies of Peking Opera in Hong Kong
Yuen Siu-tin	Yuen Wo-ping (and the Yuen Brothers); Tong Kai	
Yu Zhanyuan	Kwan Ching-leung (Guan Zhengliang), Jackie Chan, Sammo Hung, Yuen Biao, Yuen Wah	Chinese Drama Academy
Fen Juhua	Lam Ching-ying (Lin Zhengying), Tung Wai (Dong Wei)	Spring and Autumn Drama School
Tang Di	Ching Siu-tung (Cheng Xiaodong), Mars (Chiang Wing-fat)	Eastern Drama Academy
Ma Chengzhi	Tsui Chung-shun	Chung Wah Drama Academy

FROM OPERA STAGE TO SILVER SCREEN: THE ACTION CONTINUED

The previous section discussed the historical linkage between Chinese operatic art and action cinema, contextualizing their interactions in the histories of Cantonese and Peking operas in Hong Kong. Here, I will analyze the connections between Chinese opera and action cinema from an aesthetic point of view.

The family of Chinese opera is constituted by more than 360 regional genres, originating from and performed in different provinces and localities. For example, while the dominant operatic genre in Hong Kong is Cantonese opera, Teochew, Hoklou and other regional forms also exist.[19] In Singapore, the four most popular genres are Teochew, Hokkien, Cantonese, and Hainan operas. These theatrical forms are differentiated from each other mainly by their musical variations and dialect differences. On the other hand, they also share common aesthetic principles and performance skills.

The contents of the Chinese theatrical art are best represented by and summarized in the two terms *sigong* and *wufa*, literally the "Four Arts" and the "Five Skills". The "Four Arts" denotes the arts of *chang* (singing), *nian* (reciting), *zuo* (choreographic movements), and *da* (martial and acrobatic arts). The meaning of the "Five Skills", however, is not as clear-cut as the "Four Arts"; there is sometimes disagreement on what is meant by the name of one of the skills. The five Chinese characters of the *wufa* denote: "hand" (*shou*), "eye" (*yan*), "torso" (*shen*), "method" (*fa*), and "step" (*bu*). Since the other items without exception refer to parts of the human body, the fourth, *fa*, seems not to belong in the same category. Thus, another version of the *wufa* postulates that the written character for the term *fa*, rather than being the character to denote "method", should be the character that means "hair" which specifies the skill of spinning "hair". The confusion is a result of the same pronunciation of the two different characters.

Obviously, the components of the *sigong* and *wufa* have a lot to do with the actions of a performing body. They are the rules that govern the movements of the various parts of the body in motion, synchronized and coordinated in a harmonious manner. The "Five Skills" are the codes and methods of body movements on stage. As for the "Four Arts", it can be further subdivided into two groups. Whilst *chang* and *nian* (singing and reciting) are the expressive arts presented orally, *zuo* and *da* are the stylized and choreographic actions, appealing to the visual sense of the audience.

In other words, a major part of the visual pleasure of the theatergoers derives from the body movements and choreographic actions of the actors. On the actors' side, they have gone through extensive, rigorous training in order to present accurate and beautified actions, following the guidelines specified by the "Four Arts" and "Five Skills". Thus from the very beginning Chinese opera is an actor-oriented theater. The theatergoers' focus is concentrated on the actors' performing skills, constituted by their singing, reciting, body movement, and choreographic and acrobatic actions. Closely related to this aesthetic feature is the nature of an "abstract theater". It is quite well known that traditional Chinese opera uses a minimal set. On a traditional Chinese opera stage, one finds limited stage properties and the simplest scenery. The most typical sets are composed of one table and two chairs, with a plain curtain as the backdrop; changes of setting are made known to the audience through the performance of the actors. As the proverb postulates: "Scenes exist on the actor's *body*" (*jing jiuzai yanyuan shenshang*); the scenic settings of the play are created, defined and revealed by the body movement and performance of the actors. This implies that the stage of Chinese opera assumes no specific meaning until an actor has entered. Once he or she has entered and is in movement, the actor(s) invest their surroundings with meaning through singing and acting.

These two aesthetic features — "actor-oriented" and "abstract" — are interconnected. They work hand in hand in order to ensure that the audience will give primary attention to the "Four Arts" and "Five Skills" displayed by the actors, without being distracted by over-elaborated scenery and lavish props. Under such aesthetic principles, the physical virtuosity and acting skills of the actors are foregrounded, whereas the importance of the theatrical spectacle has been minimized accordingly. The aesthetic focus of the audience concentrates on the performing artistry exhibited by an individual actor. To an initiated audience, an actor's skill and competence (including choreographic actions and martial/acrobatic arts) are the focal objects to be viewed and appreciated. The theme, characterization, and plot development of the play might not be their main concerns.

I would argue that such a principle of highlighting the action/body of the actors has "moved" from the traditional opera stage to the contemporary action cinema. To a certain extent, the visual concentration on the body in motion in Hong Kong action cinema is a continuation and extension of Chinese theatrical aesthetics. When distinguishing Hong Kong action cinema from its Hollywood counterparts, David Bordwell argues: "From the 1960s swordplay films and 1970s kungfu movies to the cop movies and revived *wuxia pian* of the 1980s and 1990s, this filmmaking tradition has put the graceful body at the center of its mise-en-scène".[20] As I have pointed out, "putting the graceful body at the center" has always been the dominant aesthetic principle of Chinese opera. What Bordwell describes as the aesthetics of Hong Kong action cinema is also applicable to, if not derived from and rooted in, the Chinese operatic art. The only difference is that the "opera stage" has been replaced by the "mise-en-scène", which serves as the new/modern frame in which the actors exhibit their bodies and actions. Hence, the "tradition" as mentioned by Bordwell should be further linked to that of the Chinese theater. Bordwell further elaborates his argument: "my key point is not that Hong Kong films employ death-defying stunts; that is not news. What is important is that the stunts are staged, shot, and cut for readability".[21] Interestingly, Bordwell uses the word "staged". In Hong Kong action cinema, the actions are stylized, the body movements are aestheticized, and the performances are maximized. The cinematic techniques are there to help foreground the actions of an actor. They are employed in order to encourage the audience to concentrate on the actions displayed in the mise-en-scène. Like its counterpart on the Chinese opera stage, the body of an actor has become the spectacle.

In his movies, Jackie Chan tumbles, somersaults, leaps, and spins in an effortless way. It is a common understanding that such skills developed from his training in Peking opera. I would like to point out that some of these actions/performances owe a direct debt to the "Four Arts" and "Five Skills". For example, the "step" he uses in performing the "drunken fist" in *Drunken Master*, is derived from the "drunken step" (*zuibu*) in the "Five

Skills". Displaying a specific skill of body movement, it is usually used on the Chinese opera stage to represent the walking manner of a drunken person.[22]

What the action choreography in action cinema owes to the heritage of Chinese opera is also reflected in the use of props. As mentioned above, Chinese opera is an abstract theatre. The basic set in the Chinese theater is composed of two chairs and a table. These simple objects are used to signify a wide range of settings and things, from a courtroom to a bedroom, from a small bed to the Great Wall. At the same time, these basic props on the opera stage become the most convenient objects for the opera actors to show off their acrobatic and stunning actions. Hence, Chinese opera actors have developed special skills in acting with these basic props. The sets of actions/skills centered on a chair or a table are sometimes labeled as *yizigong* and *zhuozigong*, the "chair skill" and the "table skill". A play that shows fabulous *yizigong* is *Blocking the Horse* (*Dangma*), a well-known piece from the contemporary Kunshan opera.

Such traditional skills have been adjusted and then adopted in the action cinema. It is not difficult to identify fight scenes in Jackie Chan's movies involving chairs and tables, with the actors circling around these objects. For example, in *Drunken Master*, after the naughty Wong Fei-hung (Huang Feihong) (played by Jackie Chan) has successfully cheated his master Beggar So (played by Yuen Siu-tin), he meets the villain Yan Tiexin in a deserted temple. As expected, a fight starts. In this scene, Jackie Chan demonstrates his "chair skill": being pulled backward and forward on the chair, lying horizontally and falling from the back top, and rolling around with the chair on the ground. Similar actions making use of chairs and tables can also be found in his other movies, for instance, *Project A, Project A II,* and *Miracles*, where they are staged in various settings, including a bar, a Chinese teahouse, a police station, and a private club.

Another simple prop used by opera actors to perform acrobatics is the ladder. One example is the *Haunted Storeroom* (Chaifanghui), a classic of Teochew opera. The story concerns a kind-hearted merchant (played by the male comic role) who is forced to stay overnight in the storeroom of an inn. At night, a female ghost appears and asks him to do her a favor. Terrified by the ghost, the actor climbs up to the top of the ladder, performing a series of funny but stunning actions: leaning the body backward 90 degrees, slipping down, climbing up again, standing on one leg, and rolling down. In action cinema, both Jackie Chan and Yuen Wo-ping like to use ladders in fight scenes. In *Project A II*, Jackie Chan tries to help Maggie Cheung jump down from the roof of a warehouse. He performs a set of breathtaking actions: jumping on the top of the ladder, swinging the ladder to the opposite building, sliding down from the top, and rolling down before touching the ground.

Needless to say, the most remarkable and elaborated ladder fighting scene is the final duel between Jet Li and Yam Sai-kwun in *Once Upon a Time in China*. The idea of such a ladder fight was initiated by the director of the movie, Tsui Hark, while Yuen Wo-ping, a guest action choreographer, helped choreograph this special scene.[23]

NEW COMPETITION, NEW AESTHETICS, NEW SPECTACLE

Earlier I discussed a poster designed by Mak Siu-ha in 1937 for the Cantonese opera troupe *Juexiansheng*. On the front of the poster, there are two lines of characters on each side of a photograph of Sit Kok-sin. Printed in a fairly large font, they represent the selling points promoted specially by the troupe. They read: "Newly introduced three-dimensional scenery; recently acquired costumes in embroidery style". These promotional words review the changes introduced to Cantonese opera in the 1930s in response to the new challenges Cantonese opera troupes were facing.

As mentioned above, Chinese operatic art prioritizes the personal skills and artistry of an actor. Elaborate sets are not preferred or required for encouraging the audience to focus on the "Four Arts" of the actors. In this form of actor-oriented theatre, the actions and acting of the actors are privileged at the expense of theatrical spectacles — because the body and its action have become the spectacle. Such aesthetic principles and staging methods began to face new challenges at the turn of the last century, when Chinese encountered new modes of modern entertainment imported from the West. The competition was more intense in the urban centers during the 1930s. Among the main sources of this new competition were the silent movies, and later, the talkies.

How did the Cantonese opera respond to these challenges? An answer shared by the troupes was: self-enrichment through absorbing the strong points of the competitors. This explains why Mak Siu-ha says: "learning from Peking opera as its elder brother; treating the motion picture as its loyal friend who never hesitates to remonstrate." The question that immediately follows is: what did they learn?

In the mid 1930s, Sit Kok-sin began his project of staging the "Four Classical Beauties of China". In 1938, his *Juexiansheng* Theatre Troupe staged *Diao Chan* (*The Beauty Diao Chan*) at the Hong Kong Lee Theatre. In an advertisement from the newspaper *Huaqiao Daily*, which promoted this new piece, we find the following passage:

Dedicated to presenting Chinese operatic art in pure form, our troupe originally did not favor fanciful sets. We have always upheld this principle, and our audience has always admired and supported it. However, in view of the recent need to revive Cantonese opera and promote the national art, our troupe has commissioned highly paid experts to produce spectacular scenery for this play. We have newly acquired more than ten sets of "seven-layer scene", hundreds of pieces of costume in the style of the Han dynasty, countless vessels and artifacts in ancient style. Their fabrication has been based on meticulous studies. All this is to ensure that *Diao Chan* will be a grand and spectacular piece, able to compare and compete with the movies. Now that the play has been staged, we are pleased to see that our play has captured all the good qualities of movies, but that the reverse does not apply.[24]

The advertisement also lists the 12 sets of "seven-layer scene" in details. Supported by electric power and lighting, these three-dimensional backdrops could be removed and shifted instantly. When first introduced in the urban theaters, the audience was greatly fascinated and astonished by these innovative spectacles on the stage.[25]

The writer of the above passage (very probably Mak Siu-ha) stressed that initially the troupe had been staging Cantonese opera in a conventional ("pure") way, until they realized the severity of the competition from the movies. Aiming to attract a bigger audience, the troupe invested substantially in acquiring extravagant props, spectacular scenery, and flamboyant costumes. The *Juexiansheng* Theatre Troupe was not the only troupe that adopted such new visual spectacles. Another oft-quoted example is the famous actress Li Xuefang who performed in a robe decorated with light bulbs. During the performance, the light bulbs would be switched on, dramatically illuminating the whole robe.

I am not arguing that the opera actors of the 1930s totally repudiated the traditions of the "Four Arts" and "Five Skills". What I am trying to point out is that the opera troupes had chosen to modify the traditional aesthetics in order to fight this difficult battle with their new competitor: the talkies. When introducing new stage spectacles, the attention of the audience was now directed to the dazzling scenery, fanciful sets, astonishing stage mechanics, and even bizarre stage effects. Responding to the new challenges, Cantonese opera moved from "abstract" to "real", from "displaying body action" to "showing stage spectacle".

In fact, such changes on the traditional opera stage were not confined to the Cantonese opera. In the same decade, the Teochew opera troupes in Singapore and Thailand also introduced new visual effects onto their stages. Probably influenced by the swordsman films produced in Shanghai, particularly the *Burning of the Red Lotus Temple* (*Huoshao Hongliansi*), the Teochew troupes developed the visual effect of "flying swords". In such scenes, the swordsmen would release flying weapons (like missiles!) from their bodies to attack their enemies. The flying weapons sent by the two rival parties would hit and fight each other in the air, controlled by a white beam sent from the swordsmen's palms.

This emphasis on stage spectacle continued after World War Two. In 1957 the six major Teochew opera troupes of Singapore-Malaysia jointly performed a play to celebrate the second anniversary of their trade union. The title of this Teochew opera play is now globally well known: *Crouching Tiger, Hidden Dragon*. According to the founder of the Union, Yang Liujiang, who is now in his early 90s, the staging of the play turned a new page in the history of Singapore-Malaysia Teochew opera. It was the first time the six troupes collaborated in staging one piece. The most renowned playwright Lin Rulie (1906–1981) was invited to write the script. In order to present eye-catching spectacles, they commissioned a specialist from Thailand to design scenery for this performance. From a photograph, we can see the emphasis on theatrical spectacle in the 1950s. The scenery of the "roof-top" is foregrounded, placed at the centre of the stage. Having successfully stolen the precious sword, the female character Yu Jiaolong (played by Zhang Ziyi in the modern film version) strolls and jumps freely on the roof. Interestingly, the swordsman chasing after her in the photograph of the production is not dressed in traditional Chinese opera costume. Rather, he looks like a cowboy in a Hollywood Western.

CONCLUSION

In this paper, I have studied the interactions between traditional Chinese opera and action cinema, both from a historical and an aesthetic perspective. I have argued that both Chinese theatrical art and Hong Kong action cinema share a common aesthetic appeal: foregrounding the body in motion of an actor. On a more technical level, the acrobatics and martial arts exhibited on the opera stage have been continued and extended to the silver screen. Although the martial techniques used in action cinema may come from several sources, Chinese theatrical art serves as one of their most influential origins. In my paper, these connections are further historicized in the context of the history of Cantonese opera in the 1930s, the role of Chinese opera academies in Hong Kong after 1949, and the Hong Kong film industry in the 1950s and 1960s. These inter-generic connections have been studied against the backdrop of the cultural history of Hong Kong.

In addition to these interactions among operatic and cinematic genres, I have highlighted the geographic/cultural connections between Shanghai, Hong Kong, and Singapore. This paper began with a discussion of the significance of Yuen Siu-tin, who brought the "northern style" martial form from Shanghai to Hong Kong. After 1949, more Peking opera actors/actresses from Shanghai arrived in Hong Kong, and they were significant in cultivating a new generation of Hong Kong martial artists, including Yuen Wo-ping, Jackie Chan, Ching Siu-tong and many others. In studying the emergence of the new emphasis on spectacle, I have also analyzed the impact of Shanghai's action movies on local operas during the 1930s. Special effects, such as the "flying sword" and "flying swordsman", began to appear on Chinese opera stages. Such cinematic techniques, originating from Shanghai, were retained in Hong Kong action cinema after 1949. The production of *Zu: Warriors from the Magic Mountain* (1983) by Tsui Hark is a re-make of the genre in a modern package.

2

Interactions Between Japanese and Hong Kong Action Cinemas

Kinnia Yau Shuk-ting

This essay is a study of the interrelations between action movies made in Japan and Hong Kong, primarily from the mid-1950s to the mid-1970s. First, however, a note on terminology: I use the term "action movies" here to refer in general terms to both Japanese *judo* film and *samurai* film (also known as *jidaigeki* or *chanbara*) as well as to Hong Kong's "new-style" swordplay film (also known as new-style *wuxia pian*) and to kung fu film. In Japanese and Hong Kong film history alike, "action" has always been considered one of the most important film genres; some version of it has existed ever since the Japanese and the Chinese began making their own motion pictures in the early twentieth century. The close conceptual tie between "action" and "movie" in these two national cinemas clearly derives from the cultural legacy of their respective traditional theatres, particularly *kabuki* in Japan and Peking opera in China — in both of which "action" is an indispensable traditional element. *Kabuki* is a highly stylized dramatic form tracing back to the feudal Tokugawa period (1598–1867), and David A. Cook has pointed out that the earliest Japanese fiction films were versions of famous *kabuki* plays.[1] As Japanese cinema grew into a large-scale domestic industry in the first two decades of the twentieth century, the stylized conventions of *kabuki* became the mainstream conventions of Japanese narrative film. Meanwhile, the first Chinese-directed motion picture, *Dingjunshan* (1906, Yin Jingfeng), is actually a documentary of a Peking opera troupe.

POSTWAR INITIATIVES: HONG KONG

From the 1950s onwards, Japanese filmmakers were eager to work with Hong Kong companies for the purpose of expanding their Southeast Asian markets. In return, Hong Kong filmmakers were also willing to borrow and learn from their Japanese counterparts for the purpose of improving their technical skills. It is important to recognize at the outset the substantial role played by the Southeast Asian Motion Pictures Producers Association and the Southeast Asian Film Festival in promoting Japan-Hong Kong co-operation in this period. Co-founded by Masaichi Nagata and Run Run Shaw in 1953, the Southeast Asian Motion Pictures Producers Association was the organizing body behind the first Southeast Asian Film Festival, held in 1954. When the third festival was held in Hong Kong in 1956, the founders took the opportunity to restructure the organizing body; it was expanded and renamed the "Asian Motion Picture Producers Association". Henceforth this body would hold the annual Asian Film Festival, and Festival participants were member countries or regions of the Association, including Hong Kong, Japan, Singapore, Malaysia, the Philippines, Korea, Thailand, Taiwan and South Vietnam.

Film company executives from all these countries would meet during the festival, talk shop and make production and distribution deals. Given the growing awareness of Japanese cinema around the world after Daiei's *Rashomon* (Akira Kurosawa 1950) won the Golden Lion Award at the Venice International Film Festival in 1951, film distributors were more confident in exporting Japanese movies to Hong Kong, Taiwan and Southeast Asia. However, since the mainstream Japanese audience at the time had no interest in movies from other Asian countries, only three Hong Kong productions — namely, *Sorrows of the Forbidden City* (Zhu Shilin 1948), *Lady Balsam's Conquest* (Zhang Shankun and Yi Wen 1955) and *The Kingdom and the Beauty* (Li Hanxiang 1959) — secured a release in Japan before the early 1970s.[2] Consequently, interaction between the Japanese and Hong Kong action cinemas mainly occurred on a one-way basis before the release of Bruce Lee's *Enter the Dragon* (Robert Clouse 1973): Japanese films influenced Hong Kong movies but not vice versa. When *Enter the Dragon*, co-produced by Warner Brothers and Concord (a company co-founded by Raymond Chow and Bruce Lee), was released in Japanese B-picture theatres on 22 December 1973 it immediately became a blockbuster hit to rival *The Exorcist* (William Friedkin 1973).

Yet the early development of action cinema in China was not at all encouraging. Although *The Burning of the Red Lotus Monastery* series

(1928–1931) of film adaptations by Zhang Shichuan from Pingjiang Buxiao Sheng's novel *Legend of the Strange Hero* did spark off a *wuxia pian* craze in the late 1920s, it soon came under the fire of political criticism: it seems that the fantastic depiction of martial arts was deemed harmful to the elevation of the Chinese people's spirit.[3] This attitude probably had its roots as far back as the Sung and Ming Dynasties (the fourteenth to the seventeenth centuries), when the country as a whole valued art and culture over military pursuits.

Before 1949, Chinese "action movies" were mostly understood to be black and white Cantonese, Hong Kong-made *wuxia pian* — films generally poor in quality because of their financial and technical insufficiencies. The first "Wong Fei-hung" picture, *The Story of Wong Fei-hung*, directed by Wu Pang, was made in 1949 and its realistic fighting style marked a watershed in the history of Cantonese action movies. The most representative Hong Kong action film genre during the 1950s, the "Wong Fei-hung" series strongly conveys a Confucian code; the master of the southern school of kung fu, Wong Fei-hung (played by Kwan Tak-hing), was regarded as an exemplary Confucian martial artist. However, the "Wong Fei-hung" series bore no relation to Japanese *judo* film or *chanbara*, and the "Wong Fei-hung" filmmakers showed no interest in seeking technical help from Japan. Japan-Hong Kong collaboration at this time was basically confined to that between the Japanese and Mandarin cinemas.

The president of Shaw Brothers, Run Run Shaw, had in fact sought to strengthen Hong Kong's Mandarin action movies as early as the late 1950s, when his studio made a series of *wuxia pian* including *The Adventure of the 13th Sister* (Li Hanxiang 1959), *The Swallow* (Yue Feng 1961) and *Revenge of a Swordswoman* (Yue Feng 1963). However, despite having cinematography provided by two Japanese cameramen, Tadashi Nishimoto and Isamu Kakita, these films had no significant relation with Japanese action cinema.[4] Shaw Brothers' first attempt at upgrading Hong Kong action cinema was not particularly successful; apparently the time was not yet right for this genre to flourish. Shaw Brothers was specializing at the time in Chinese historical costume epics such as *The Kingdom and the Beauty, Magnificent Concubine* (also known as *Yang Guifei*, Li Hanxiang 1962) and *The Empress Wu Zetian* (Li Hanxiang 1963) and most Hong Kong people preferred the "feminine" genres, such as the *huangmei* opera film[5] and the sentimental romance (i.e., *wenyipian*, "literary arts" film) to the "masculine" swordplay and action genres.

THE POSTWAR JAPANESE ACTION CINEMA

In contrast, a golden age of *chanbara* emerged in Japan between the mid-1950s and the mid-1960s. *Chanbara* had been suppressed during the American Occupation (1945–1952), after the Civil Information and Education Section (or CI&E) proclaimed that Japan should not make films to glorify feudalism, imperialism or militarism.[6] This edict necessarily eliminated the whole genre of *chanbara* and encouraged the production of *Meiji-mono* (stories with settings in the Meiji period) and films of contemporary life. Under these circumstances, notable *chanbara* stars such as Tsumasaburo Banto, Chieizo Kataoka, Utaemon Ichikawa and Kanjuro Arashi had to change their screen personae from swordsmen to gunfighters. The situation of the veteran *chanbara* director Hiroshi Inagaki was worse — without exception, all of his proposals were banned.

Production of *chanbara* resumed immediately after the end of the American Occupation. The first *chanbara* to be shown in postwar Japan was Kurosawa's *The Men Who Tread on the Tiger's Tail*, originally made in 1945 but released in 1952. This initiated an extraordinary interest in *chanbara* and supply followed demand; big budget *chanbara* productions began to appear in quantity. Inagaki's *Samurai* series (also known as the *Miyamoto Musashi* series, 1954–1956, Toho version) and Kurosawa's *Seven Samurai* (1954) were credited with elevating *chanbara* to new artistic heights; coincidentally, both films cast the great postwar Japanese action star Toshiro Mifune in the leading role. *Seven Samurai* has been praised by most Japanese film critics as the most brilliant motion picture ever made in Japan: its production cost set a new record — a total of 2.1 billion yen, seven times more than the average Japanese picture at that time. The golden age was also marked by international awards at festival after festival. *Samurai* won the Academy Award for the Best Foreign Film, while *Seven Samurai* won the Silver Lion at the Venice International Film Festival, and the Academy Award for the Best Foreign Film. Following the boom of the 1950s, Japanese filmmakers continued to make high quality *chanbara*: Kurosawa directed *The Bodyguard* (also known as *Yojimbo*, 1961) and *Sanjuro* (also known as *Tsubaki Sanjuro*, 1962); Tomo Uchida began the *Miyamoto Musashi* series (1961–1965, Toei version)[7] in 1961; and in 1962 Kenji Misumi began to shoot the "Zatoichi" series, depicting the blind swordsman played by Shintaro Katsu. All of these featured vigorous fight scenes not commonly seen in the films of the 1950s.

The early 1960s were a turning point in the development of action cinema in the West as well as in Japan, with Hollywood's "James Bond" series and Italian "spaghetti Westerns" creating a new wave of interest worldwide. Starring the new action hero Sean Connery, the first picture about the British secret service agent James Bond, *Dr No* (Terence Young 1962), was released in the midst of the Cold War between the US and the Soviet Union. The mix of sex, violence and campy humour that characterized the Bond films exerted a tremendous impact on Asian action cinemas, and from the mid-60s onwards modern action films were mass-produced in Hong Kong: *The Golden Buddha* (Lo Wei 1966) and *The Black Falcon* (Takumi Furukawa 1967) are only two examples. All of the films mentioned above featured a James Bond-type hero confronting criminal organizations while surrounded by hostile spies, bevies of beautiful women from around the world, and newfangled gadgets. In this context a Nikkatsu-Shaw Brothers co-production *Asia-Pol* (Akinori Matsuo) was made in 1966, starring Jimmy Wang Yu and Ruriko Asaoka as special agents pursuing gold smugglers in Hong Kong, Bangkok and Yokohama; a Japanese version was shot at the same time, featuring Hideaki Nitani in the male lead.

During the same period Sergio Leone made his first "spaghetti Westerns", *A Fistful of Dollars* (1964), and *The Good, the Bad and the Ugly* (1966), mixing the Hollywood Western with elements from Kurosawa's *The Bodyguard*.[8] The new genre created a global sensation and made a TV cowboy, Clint Eastwood, into an international star.

THE EMERGENCE OF HONG KONG'S NEW-STYLE *WUXIA PIAN*

It is worth noting that at least six of the eighty-eight Hong Kong theaters were showing Japanese movies in the mid-60s, namely the London, May Fair, Rialto, Cathay, Winner and Pearl theaters.[9] *Chanbara* such as Kurosawa's *Seven Samurai, The Bodyguard, Sanjuro,* and the series of "*Tange Sazen*", "*Nemuri Kyoshiro*", "Zatoichi" and "Kogarashi Monjiro" were immensely popular with the Hong Kong audience, and with the arrival of the new action film genres from Japan and the West, Cantonese *wuxia pian* and the "Wong Fei-hung" series no longer satisfied local moviegoers. To a large extent it was these external influences that led to the rise of the "new-style" Hong Kong *wuxia pian*.

New-style *wuxia pian* emerged in the midst of specific social-economic developments in Hong Kong in the 1960s. The first of these was a demographic shift: the generation born after World War Two was reaching adolescence and young adulthood, while the 1961 census revealed that out of a population of over 3 million, more than 1.2 million were below 15 years of age. Cheuk Pak-tong has pointed out that this age group eventually replaced the older generation to constitute a big movie-going audience in the pre-television age (the golden age of television in Hong Kong took shape only gradually during the 1970s).[10] Secondly, Hong Kong began to embark on the road to an industrial future, leading to her future status as one of the "Asian dragons." The result was an increase in the number of young people entering the workforce and becoming more economically independent. Movies became an important entertainment for such workers in their spare time; unlike the older generation, this newly educated group wanted the cinema to express more local feelings and ambitions. In these circumstances it was not surprising that Cantonese opera film and *huangmei* opera film faded out. Even the long-lived "Wong Fei-hung" series of films began to decline, as the new generation generally considered them out-dated.

In the transitional period between the late 1950s and the early 1960s, there was also a new development in Hong Kong literary culture. As Sek Kei has noted, the new-style martial arts novels published in this period were extremely popular and inspired a new surge of interest in the fantastic mode of the martial arts world.[11] The works of the two foremost new-style martial arts novelists, Liang Yusheng and Jin Yong, exerted a tremendous influence on the new-style *wuxia pian* produced in Hong Kong and Taiwan; Liang Yusheng's *The Jade Bow* and Jin Yong's *The Story of the Book and the Sword* and *Legend of the Brave Archer* sparked a continuous line of screen adaptations, and there is little doubt that the popularity of new-style martial arts novels was one of the main factors contributing to the birth of the new-style *wuxia pian*. Sek Kei also points out that the latter's rise in popularity coincided with the outbreak of the Cultural Revolution (1966–1976) in mainland China. Hong Kong was affected by serious social unrest in the early stages of the Cultural Revolution; in 1966 riots were sparked by a protest over a rise in Star Ferry fares, and a labor dispute at a plastic flower-manufacturing factory spilled over into street riots in 1967. Shaw Brothers was attacked by leftist groups, reportedly making Run Run Shaw give up his scheduled hosting of the 14th Asian Film Festival. The depiction of violence and bloodshed in Hong Kong's new-style *wuxia pian* was widely considered a reflection of the social disorder occurring at the time.

Between the mid-1960s and the early 1970s, Hong Kong's Mandarin cinema was basically dominated by Shaw Brothers. The Cathay Organisation had gradually lost its competitive edge after the premature death of president Lu Yuntao in 1964 and, in the face of the expansion of Shaw Brothers, independent film production companies like Xinhua and

Lingguang had all but retreated to Taiwan. The production output of Great Wall, a studio supported by the People's Republic of China, was affected by the Cultural Revolution and had begun to fall. Now the dominant force in Hong Kong's Mandarin film industry, Shaw Brothers was ready to start its own revolution by upgrading both the quality and the quantity of its productions, and by increasing the variety of its film genres with such ventures as the new-style *wuxia pian*, spy thrillers, modern musicals, psychological murder thrillers and youth romances. Among these experiments the new-style *wuxia pian* was considered the most successful, both commercially and critically. Run Run Shaw reportedly bought a collection of Japanese *chanbara* for his directors, including King Hu and Zhang Che (Chang Cheh), to study. Another Shaws director, Xu Zenghong, was even dispatched to Japan to learn the production techniques of *chanbara*. This trio became well known for pioneering the genre and two of Shaw Brothers' earliest new-style *wuxia pian*, *Come Drink with Me* (King Hu 1966) and *One-Armed Swordsman* (Zhang Che 1967), displayed heavy stylistic influences from Japanese *chanbara*.

Cantonese cinema, however, was a step ahead of Shaw Brothers in introducing elements of Japanese *chanbara* into its *wuxia pian*. From the mid-1960s onwards, Cantonese filmmakers had felt the urgent need for change to keep abreast of the new movie-going generation; they began to adopt special effects, use younger actors, and take as their models both Japanese *chanbara* and Hollywood's fantasy pictures.[12] The "*Mangxia chuanxinjian*" [The blind swordsman's heart-piercing sword] series (Lee Fa 1965), *The White Dragon* (Wong Fung 1968), *The Little Warrior* (Lee Tit 1969) and *Three Encounters* (Yeung Keun 1969) were all Cantonese *wuxia pian* inspired by Japanese *chanbara*. Judging from the title of *Mangxia chuanxinjian*, we can assume that the film was a mixture of *The Story of Zatoichi* (Kenji Misumi 1962) and *Sanjuro*, of which the respective Chinese titles in Hong Kong were *Mangxia tingshengjian* [The blind swordsman's hearing sword] and *Chuanxinjian* [Heart-piercing sword]. In *The White Dragon, The Little Warrior* and *Three Encounters*, the well-known teen star Bobo Fung appears in the costume of a boy *samurai*, and fights in Japanese style. It may seem interesting that she played a boy, a young hero who was able to rescue not only the elderly and women, but also adult males. In fact, the casting of Bobo Fung could probably be considered a compromise between the traditional martial worlds of Japan and China. On one hand, a *samurai* was supposed to be a male in Japanese culture; on the other hand, the fantasy of "strong and beautiful teenage girls" had a long history in the Chinese literary tradition.

The Chinese title of *Three Encounters* is *Sanjiaoliao*, literally meaning "ending a combat with three strikes", also suggests inspiration from Japanese *chanbara*. The fight scenes in old-fashioned Cantonese *wuxia pian* were usually of a relatively long duration. Swordsmen were shown fighting with flying daggers or palm powers enhanced by animation drawn directly on the film. However, *chanbara* made by Akira Kurosawa or Kenji Misumi used a totally different fighting style and technique: the heroes mostly stood still in silence for some moments before drawing their swords. Once their blades were unsheathed, the editing was cut so fast that the audience might even miss what was really going on. Although the fights in *chanbara* always ended in an instant, they built up a breath-taking rhythm of alternating stillness and motion. One of the most extraordinary fight scenes in *chanbara*, for instance, was the duel between Toshiro Mifune and Tatsuya Nakadai in *Sanjuro*. The atmosphere of this sequence was expertly engineered, mounting to the spectacular climax when the two heroes confront each other in profile.

Cantonese new-style *wuxia pian* films were able to capture the attention of the local Hong Kong audience as well as Southeast Asian filmgoers, and in order to compete for these markets Shaw Brothers determined to revolutionize its own *wuxia pian*. Shaw Brothers' new-style *wuxia pian* effort was initiated in 1965 by Xu Zenghong's *Temple of the Red Lotus* and *The Twin Swords* and the genre came to maturity with the release of King Hu's *Come Drink with Me* and Zhang Che's *One-Armed Swordsman* in 1966 and 1967 respectively. Following the example of the Cantonese new-style *wuxia pian*, Shaw Brothers also emphasized youthfulness by casting younger stars like Cheng Pei-pei, Yue Hua, Jimmy Wang Yu, David Chiang and Di Long. However, the stories of the Shaw Brothers' *wuxia pian* were more rebellious than those of the Cantonese films, and their fight scenes were enriched with realistic and, in a sense, more violent touches and more bloodshed, as well as more effective editing.

Along with their Japanese and Hollywood flavors, the themes and fighting style of Shaw Brothers' new-style *wuxia pian* were at the same time characterized by a strong sense of Chinese tradition. This might explain why Run Run Shaw never asked any of the Japanese directors who had come to join the studio in the 1960s to contribute significantly to this genre. By the early 1970s Shaw Brothers had employed six Japanese directors — Umetsugu Inoue, Takumi Furukawa, Koh Nakahira, Koji Shima, Mitsuo Murayama and Akinori Matsuo — to direct films of different genres, including spy action, modern musical, suspense and romantic comedy, etc. However, although the new-style *wuxia pian* took as its model the Japanese *chanbara*, the Japanese contribution to new-style *wuxia pian* at Shaws was strictly limited to cinematography (Tadashi Nishimoto and Yukio Miyaki) and choreography. Moreover, apart from using Kentaro Yuasa,[13] Shaw Brothers also invited the Chinese action choreographers Han Yingjie,[14] Lau Kar-leung and Tong Kai[15] to supervise fight scenes for the sake of preserving traditional Chinese fighting techniques.

King Hu claimed that he had never seen the "Zatoichi" series before directing the new-style *wuxia pian* for Shaw Brothers.[16] Looking at his early works, however, it is difficult not to perceive some touches of *Zatoichi*. To a degree even *Dragon Gate Inn* (1967), a popular hit that Hu made in Taiwan, had a certain Japanese flavor. Certainly the "Zatoichi" series enjoyed considerable popularity in Hong Kong and throughout Southeast Asia in the 1960s, sparking numerous Chinese imitations; *Paid with Blood* (Xin Qi 1970) and *The Deaf and Mute Heroine* (Wu Ma 1971) are two typical examples. *Paid with Blood* was basically an adaptation of *Zatoichi*, with Zhang Qingqing playing a blind swordswoman. The deaf and dumb swordswoman played by Helen Ma in *The Deaf and Mute Heroine* can also be seen as inspired by the physically handicapped but powerful swordsman of the "Zatoichi" series. Meanwhile, the Zatoichi character also appeared in a number of Asian productions made outside Japan, one of which was *One-Armed Swordsman vs. Zatoichi* (Kimiyoshi Yasuda, Xu Zenghong 1971), a film co-produced by Katsu Production and Golden Harvest. The story was about a duel between the Japanese hero Zatoichi and the one-armed Chinese swordsman played by Jimmy Wang Yu. Interestingly, the picture had two different endings; Zatoichi won in the Japanese version, but lost in the Hong Kong version.

The character of the one-armed swordsman, Fang Gang, originated from Zhang Che's *One-Armed Swordsman*, already mentioned as one of the earliest Hong Kong new-style *wuxia pian* reflecting Japanese influences. The film opened with a pre-credits action sequence in which the hero's father was killed. The use of a "prologue", a sequence preceding the title or accompanying the credits, was a common editing technique in Japanese *chanbara*, especially in the 1960s. In the case of *One-Armed Swordsman* the opening sequence provided a justification for the hero to learn martial arts in order to avenge his father's death. In contrast with his counterpart King Hu, Zhang openly confessed to being inspired by Japanese *chanbara*. He even claimed that the location shooting in Japan of his *Golden Swallow* (1968) was insignificant compared to what he could learn from the production techniques of Japanese *chanbara*.[17] Afterwards, Zhang invited the cameraman Yukio Miyaki to come to Shaw Brothers.

Up until the late 1970s, Miyaki was the cinematographer for such Zhang Che movies as *The Singing Thief* (1969), *Return of the One-Armed Swordsman* (1969) and *The Flying Daggers* (1969),[18] in which he upgraded the hand-held camera technique used in Hong Kong action cinema.[19]

THE KUNG FU FILM CRAZE IN JAPAN

In the 1970s, kung fu film took over the role of the new-style *wuxia pian* and became the most significant Hong Kong film genre. Although it reached a peak with the appearance of Bruce Lee's first martial arts feature *The Big Boss* (Lo Wei 1971), the kung fu film genre had already appeared in the 1930s,[20] and was consolidated by the "Wong Fei-hung" series from the late 1940s. However, it seems that the kung fu films of the 1970s were strikingly different from the earlier films, and one of the main differences was the inclusion of foreign elements.

In 1970, Zhang Che made *Vengeance!*, a film which shifted the fighting style from the "saber and sword" [*diaojian*] to the "fist and leg" [*chuanjiao*], and in doing so paved the way for the emergence of several other kung fu films that subsequently established the genre, such as *The Chinese Boxer* (Jimmy Wang Yu 1970), *The Big Boss*, *The Bloody Fists* (Ng See-yuen 1972), *Crush* (Tu Guangqi 1972), *King Boxer* (Zheng Changhe 1972) and *Fist of Fury* (Lo Wei 1972). Zhang himself has claimed that his choice of an early Republican Chinese setting in such films as *Vengeance!* and *The Duel* was inspired by Japanese movies set in Meiji Japan because he found many similarities between the Meiji period and early Republican China.[21] Most of the plots of the early 1970s kung fu films were, in fact, based on duels between Chinese and foreign (usually Japanese) martial artists. Unlike Wong Fei-hung, young Chinese heroes like Jimmy Wang Yu, David Chiang and Bruce Lee fought in a mixed style of *judo*, *karate*, Korean *taekwondo*, Thai boxing and Western boxing.[22] Influenced by Japanese *chanbara* or *judo* films like *Sugata Sanshiro* (Akira Kurosawa 1943), Hong Kong kung fu movies displayed a great deal of blood and violence, but invariably demonstrated anti-Japanese sentiments at the same time.

In *Fist of Fury*, Bruce Lee played the hero Chen Zhen whose mission was to search for the murderer of his mentor Huo Yuenjia. Despite the anti-Japanese sentiment and the negative depiction of Japanese people throughout the film, *Fist of Fury* was a big hit when it was released in Japan. Japanese were portrayed in a very funny way in *Fist of Fury*, wrongly wearing *hakama* and even sporting blonde wigs. However, most Japanese spectators claimed that they did not feel any sense of resentment because they did not recognize themselves in these grossly unreal and "stupid" characters. Moreover, apart from the dynamic fighting style portrayed in the film, the spirit of the Chinese warrior was admired as a "lost treasure" by some of the Japanese audience — a spirit once found in their own *bushido* (or *samurai*) movies.[23] Nevertheless, Raymond Chow, the president of Golden Harvest, reportedly worried that the anti-Japanese sentiment in *Fist of Fury* would irritate the Japanese audience[24] and this may explain why certain changes were made in the Japanese version. One of these was the famous scene where several Japanese are teasing Chen Zhen in front of a signboard outside a park reading "No Dogs and Chinese Allowed". One of the Japanese says to Chen, "If you walk like a dog of our Japanese Empire, I'll take you in [the park]", but the Japanese subtitle was simplified to: "If you walk like a dog, I'll take you in". The scene of a Japanese stripper dancing at a feast was also cut out in order to protect the image of Japan from denigration.

Despite the close link between Japan and Hong Kong in filmmaking practice over the years, most Japanese people showed no interest in Hong Kong movies until the arrival of the kung fu genre. Before the Japanese release of *Enter the Dragon* Raymond Chow approached Shintaro Katsu, without success, to secure the distribution of Bruce Lee's earlier films such as *The Big Boss* and *Fist of Fury*. Katsu's refusal revealed the low esteem in which Hong Kong movies were generally held by Japanese filmmakers in the early 1970s and it was only with the release of *Enter the Dragon* in 1973 that Hong Kong movies began to enjoy some popularity in Japan. Lee's martial arts features were released overseas in the order of America first, then Europe, and then Southeast Asia; in other words, Japan was actually the last major foreign market in which his films were released.[25] The film critic Koyo Udagawa called 1973 "The Year Zero" for Hong Kong movies in Japan,[26] and *Enter the Dragon* undoubtedly changed Japanese attitudes towards Hong Kong movies; afterwards, big companies like Toho Towa and Toei fought each other for the rights to distribute Bruce Lee's pictures. Eventually, Toho Towa won *The Big Boss*, *Fist of Fury* and *The Game of Death*, while Toei won *The Way of the Dragon*. In 1974, about thirty Hong Kong martial arts films were released in Japan. However instead of using the term "kung fu" people at the time spoke of the "boom in *karate* movies". Japanese television stations even began to broadcast Hong Kong movies in prime time.

Japan also began making adaptations of Hong Kong kung fu films. *Onna hissatsuken* (Kazuhiko Yamaguchi 1974), starring Etsuko Shihomi and Shinichi Chiba,[27] was in fact a Toei version of *Enter the Dragon*, in which Shihomi played a Chinese kung fu fighter who infiltrated a Triad group in order to save her brother. This picture was followed by *Onna hissatsuken kiki ippatsu* (Kazuhiko Yamaguchi 1974), featuring Yasuaki Kuruta,[28] an action star familiar to the Hong Kong audience; and then came *Kaettekita onna hissatsuken* (Kazuhiko Yamaguchi 1975) and *Onna hissatsu godanken* (Shigehiro Osawa 1976). Imitating Bruce Lee's action hero image, Shinichi Chiba took the nickname Sani Chiba [Sonny Chiba], and played the leading role in two 1970s kung fu series, namely "*Satsujinken*"[29] and "*Jigokuken*".[30] This was an unprecedented moment in that Japanese action cinema was for the first time being inspired by Hong Kong.

CONCLUSION

The Japanese film industry reached its zenith with a total annual box-office attendance figure of 1.12 billion in 1958; that is, every single Japanese citizen went to the cinema an average of 11.2 times a year. However, that number had drastically dropped to 550 million in 1967.[31] It is worth noting that the downfall of the Japanese film industry and the golden era of Shaw Brothers were occurring simultaneously. Although Shaw Brothers' new-style *wuxia pian* eventually displaced Japanese *chanbara* as the leading force in Asian cinemas, the influence of the latter could still be seen in some Hong Kong swordplay films made in the 1970s and the 1980s, such as Tsui Hark's *The Butterfly Murders* (1979) and Ching Siu-tung's *Duel to the Death* (1983), both of which brought the martial arts film genre into the realm of high technology and modern special effects. Ann Hui has also commented that her *Romance of Book and Sword* (1987) was partly inspired by *Seven Samurai* and *Yagyu ichizoku no inbo* (Kinji Fukasaku 1978).

However, most Hong Kong filmmakers were never satisfied by carbon-copying Japanese *chanbara*. The main reason being that they were mindful of preserving Chinese traditions, such as the motif of pursuing revenge for a parent's death, as well as adapting Chinese fantasies of "palm power" and "weightlessness technique". Slow motion technique was another characteristic of Hong Kong *wuxia pian*. Interestingly, slow-motion was seldom seen in the Japanese *chanbara* or gangster film (also known as *banzai eiga*) and according to Zhang Che his own use of slow-motion was largely inspired by *Bonnie and Clyde* (Arthur Penn 1967) and *The Wild Bunch* (Sam Peckinpah 1969).[32] It was by incorporating both Eastern and Western elements, old and new, that Hong Kong Chinese *wuxia pian* evolved a unique style and developed it to a remarkable degree of refinement. For example, in Hong Kong's new-style *wuxia pian* we rarely see heroes portrayed in the carefree manner of Toshiro Mifune or Clint Eastwood; the Chinese heroes are always tangled up in troubles with relationships and revenge. Japanese swordsmen seldom fought over the death of their *sifu* (martial arts teachers) or their parents. It was not until another martial arts novelist, Gu Long, became popular in the early 1970s that Chinese martial arts heroes, such as Lu Xiaofeng and Chu Liuxiang, were transformed into characters in the symbolic mould of the handsome, smart and carefree James Bond.[33]

A slowdown in Japanese interest in kung fu films appeared after the release of Bruce Lee's third and self-directed martial arts feature, *The Way of the Dragon* (1972). In 1975, only seven kung fu films were released in Japan; three came out in 1976, two in 1977, and two more in 1978. The main reason for this declining interest was that the Japanese audience soon grew tired of the repetitive storylines and corny kung fu action sequences.[34] Up until 1978, Lee's pictures aside, only three kung fu films succeeded in making substantial box-office in Japan: *One-Armed Boxer* (Jimmy Wang Yu 1972), *Call Me Dragon* (Ng See-yuen 1973) and *The Man from Hong Kong* (1975, Brian Trenchard-Smith).[35] The release of Lee's last picture, *Game of Death* (1978, Robert Clouse, Sammo Hung) in 1978 ended the first kung fu film craze in Japan. However another action star, Jackie Chan, soon emerged and reached a new climax of popularity with his *Drunk Monkey in the Tiger's Eyes* (Yuen Wo-ping 1978) and *Snake in the Eagle's Shadow* (Yuen Wo-ping 1978). Avoiding Lee's realistic style of kung fu, Chan consistently explored the slapstick potential in kung fu film and deliberately tried to dismantle the conventional heroic image. His trademark became a blend of kung fu acrobatics and Michael Hui's comic touch — a combination which served as a new "weapon" to secure Japanese interest.

Up to the 1980s, all the Chinese-language films that were well received in Japan belonged to the kung fu and action-comedy genres. Films by certain popular stars such as Jackie Chan, Sammo Hung, Yuen Biao, and Jet Li were guaranteed decent sales. Peter Lam and Lau Fong have pointed out that in the 1980s Chinese-language films became more aggressive in opening up the Japanese market.[36] In 1983, three Chinese-language films were included among the top 20 box office hits in Japan: *Security Unlimited* (Michael Hui 1981), *Dragon Lord* (Jackie Chan 1982) and *Shaolin Temple* (Zhang Xinyan 1982). From a box-office perspective, Japan, being populous and geographically expansive, was undoubtedly an overseas market with enormous potential. If this potential could be fully tapped, sales in Japan alone would equal the total of Taiwan and Southeast Asia combined.[37] As a result of the increasing importance of the Japanese market, the anti-Japanese sentiments in Hong Kong martial arts films began to be minimized. For example, Jackie Chan played an anti-Japanese hero in his early films like *Not Scared to Die* (Xiang Zi 1973) and *The New Fist of Fury* (Lo Wei 1976), but after he became a superstar in Japan, anti-Japanese feeling was no longer emphasized in his pictures. Indeed, in a relatively recent remake of Bruce Lee's *Fist of Fury* — *Fist of Legend* (Gordon Chan 1994), the Chinese warrior Chen Zhen (now played by Jet Li) even marries a Japanese woman — played by the young idol, Shinobu Nakayama.

3

The Myth Continues:
Cinematic Kung Fu in Modernity

Siu Leung Li

"Back then I thought the era of using the sword would soon be passé. That's why I sold my sword": thus speaks the poverty-stricken, low-rank samurai Seibei, living in the last years of the Tokugawa period, to his opponent and to us, the film's spectators — explaining why he has surprisingly drawn out a bamboo sword in the critical final duel of the recent award-winning film *Twilight Samurai/Tasogare Seibei* (2002).

Seibei is ordered by his lord to take out a disobedient fellow samurai who is reputed to be the clan's best swordsman. Although relying only on his shorter sword, still a real one made of metal, Seibei turns out to be the last master swordsman and reluctantly kills his opponent in the duel that takes place inside a house. At the close of the film, the scene has changed to the post-Meiji reform period in early modern Japan. Having donned a most elegant kimono, Seibei's grown-up daughter, the narrator who frames the story, is paying her respects to her father at his tomb. She tells us with an air of lightheartedness and respect that after the duel the honest, humble and dutiful Seibei was rewarded by his lord and had a couple of relatively better off years with his family. He was then killed by gunfire in the power struggle between Emperor Meiji and the samurai clans which opposed the reforms leading to westernization. The revelation that Seibei was killed by gunfire is very likely nothing more than an aside, yet the irony of the uselessness of martial arts in the shadow of modern firepower immediately brings to mind the death of the kung fu master Yen Zhengdong in Tsui Hark's *Once Upon a Time in China/Huang Feihong* (1991).

Directed by the renowned veteran filmmaker Yoji Yamada (famed for the urban comedy film series "Tora san") and winning almost every major and minor film award of the year in Japan, *Twilight Samurai* is not an action adventure, nor is its primary concern with martial arts. The link between this film and the question of cinematic kung fu in modernity is complex and goes beyond the limit of film genre. In this rather compressed human drama of an ordinary member of a specific class of people who, as the film title suggests, were coming to the end of their days, the hero Seibei was played, interestingly enough, by Hiroyuki Sanada who first rose to fame in the 1980s as an action actor and a protégé of international action superstar Shinichi Chiba (generally known as Sonny Chiba in the West). Unlike many swordplay and kung fu films from Hong Kong, there is no mythicization of Japanese martial arts in *Twilight Samurai*, which features only two significant yet "unglamorous" duel scenes. Nevertheless, the film echoes, though only obliquely, the concerns of those kung fu films that address the complex issues of the negotiation between an Asian national culture and European modernity in the era of European imperialism in East Asia. Wong Fei-hung (*Once Upon a Time in China*), Chen Zhen (*Fist of Fury/Jingwumen* [a.k.a. *China Connection*] [1971] and *Fist of Legend/ Jingwu yingxiong* [1994]) and Seibei are the burning yet fading martial art figures embodying a "pre-Euromodernity" national culture in contestation and negotiation with the West.

What are "martial arts" and the national tradition that they represent to do in the high era of European modernity? For better or worse, like it or not, modernity is here. Resistance is futile; yet resistance there has been and still is — in kung fu cinema and in the larger Chinese context. Chinese nationalism and modernity are more often in a troubled relationship than not. But in *Twilight Samurai*, the transition from the society of a samurai-dominated feudal system to a modern nation seems to be a "seamless" progress, maybe with an intense sadness but with not much trace of anxiety — the anxiety concerning catching up with modernity or failing to do so, the anxiety (not infrequently manifested in Hong Kong Chinese kung fu films) over losing one's national esteem and cultural identity in the face of European modernity. In the last scene of *Twilight Samurai*, the peaceful countryside and the Meiji-style rickshaw seem also to imply that the national has accommodated the modern. The loss of Seibei the samurai, the father, the tradition is remembered without anguish, hatred and anxiety, quite unlike the nationalistic discourse that often recurs in the kung fu imagination in Hong Kong (Chinese) cinema.

In the Chinese context a nationalistic discourse, whether in the form of hailing how China has stood on its feet ("see, we have gained membership in the WTO, we won 32 gold medals at the 2004 Athens Olympics, we are to host the 2008 Olympics, we now have the magnetic levitation train,"), or criticizing how China has remained pre-modern in various aspects, is two sides of the same coin — a coin of anxiety. This anxiety must derive from complex factors. One can attribute at least one of these to the possibility that China, compared to its neighbors such as Japan, may have experienced bigger obstacles and problems in "the quest for modernity".[1] The cinematic re-imaginations of kung fu in the past three decades can reveal to us significant things about China's problems on the road to modernity.

Bruce Lee once said, "To me, ultimately martial art means honestly expressing yourself".[2] I would say, "To me, ultimately kung fu means honestly expressing our anxiety of becoming and unbecoming modern". I should note that here "kung fu" means the cultural imagination of kung fu, not real-life martial arts. As a personal obsession, I am always perplexed by how the Japanese (popular) cultural imagination continuously eternalizes their World War Two war machines, iconized by the battleship *Yamato* (the largest of its kind in military history) and the Zero fighter plane (the most advanced fighter in the early years of World War Two) as proud symbols of power in modern times.[3] I wonder if in Japanese popular culture karate and judo, or, in Korea, taekwondo, were ever mythicized in the way that we have mythicized kung fu in the face of the challenge of Western modernity.[4] For one thing, historically China in the early part of the twentieth century never produced any notable military weapons, meaning that we were really (or perhaps still are in a way, regardless of the PRC being a nuclear power) behind the others in the quest for modernization and modernity.

THE FANTASTIC AND THE SCIENTIFIC IN THE SWORDPLAY WORLD

I would like to suggest that the nationalistic mythicization of kung fu or more broadly, *wugong* ("martial skills" — a more inclusive term meaning both hand-to-hand combat kung fu and the fighting skills of using weapons) in our cinematic imagination at once betrays a tremendous anxiety over the hitherto not-so-successful negotiation with Western modernity. This anxiety seems to have been so burdensome that it did not need to wait until the rise of the kung fu genre in the 1970s to surface. In one peculiar moment in a 1964 Cantonese fantasy swordplay film, a fracture of meaning opens up in terms of the *wugong* imagination negotiating Western modernity. I refer to the scene in *Buddha's Palm 2/ Rulai shenzhang 2* (1964), where the hero Long Jianfei, a palm-power user with the skills of the formidable "Buddha's Palm", is trapped in an underground matrix filled with all kinds of hidden killing devices and booby traps. At first the hero fails to break open a metal gate with his palm power and he mutters to himself: "Why? Mmmm, I think this must be a *steel* gate! That's why it can't be cracked open" (emphasis added).[5]

Such an anachronistic placement of steel in an obviously very distant past may in reality be the result of some sloppiness in filmmaking, but textually it coincidentally juxtaposes the mythic power of *wugong* with modern technology and seems to expose the limitations of *wugong* and its inferiority to modern technology. A few moments later, the hero encounters another steel door and this time he tells everybody that he will try breaking it using the third strike of the Buddha's Palm — there are altogether nine strikes in this set of skills and now we, the spectators, realize that he must have employed the first or second strike in the previous encounter with the steel door. A bit of a surprise, this time he breaks through the door! This may very well suggest that if one's *wugong* is strong enough, one can overcome modern technology. But as the common saying goes, "do not cheer too soon"; at the very moment of Long's breaking open the gate, two robots appear to block his way. What could be more imaginative than the inclusion of two metal box-headed and rectangular-bodied 1950s sci-fi styled robots into a fantasy swordplay world set in a once-upon-a-time China — the archetypal backdrop that *Crouching Tiger, Hidden Dragon/Wohu zanglong* (2000) builds upon? Nevertheless, Long fights the robots with his unique weapon, a sleek, shiny dragon-headed metal bar the length of a common sword. We have no clue why he does not strike with his Buddha's Palm skills and he is injured by the robots before he finally runs away with the help of his two female companions. This oscillation between being subdued by, and overcoming, modern technology, and the rather naïve and clumsy handling of the physical escape of the hero demands further questioning, and I shall come back to this briefly when I discuss Stephen Chow's *From Beijing with Love/ Guochan linglingqi* (1995).

The intrusion of the Western sci-fi imagination of modern high technology (robots) out of nowhere into the fantasy swordplay world of this film makes this scene truly "outlandish" in both the senses of "bizarre" and "of foreign origin". The crossing of borders between worlds — the martial arts and the sci-fi, traditional China and the modern West — constitutes a rupture in the traditional imagination of *wugong* that assumes a monolithic Chinese identity. Could the steel and the robots emerge out of a hidden cultural anxiety at large derived from the confrontation between the native and traditional on the one hand, and the foreign and technological on the other? In addition the Buddha's Palm coincidentally implies a linear progressive notion; the film emphasizes that the first principle for the user of the Buddha's Palm is that he only advances and never goes backward. This linear progression and self-improvement in the progression of movement is not at all in contradiction with the spirit of modernity.

Returning from the swordplay world to mainly hand-to-hand combat kung fu action, I shall now discuss three non-orthodox "kung fu" films by Stephen Chow in order to critically examine the imagination of kung fu negotiating modern technology, before concluding with a discussion of Jackie Chan's recent Hollywood film *Tuxedo* (2002).

KUNG FU SOCCER

Stephen Chow, arguably the reigning king of comedy in Hong Kong cinema and an avowed admirer of Bruce Lee, made this declaration of intention in *Shaolin Soccer/Shaolin zuqiu* (2001) through the character that he plays:

> My real identity is a postgraduate student, studying ways to effectively develop and promote Shaolin martial arts … . I have always been finding ways to re-package kung fu so that you ordinary people can get a better understanding of it.

Chow's character is a Shaolin Temple kung fu disciple who, along with his former Shaolin classmates, has turned into one of *les misérables* in contemporary modern Shanghai. They are poor low-lifes collecting garbage or washing dishes for a living in an ever-intensifying capitalist-oriented market economy that obviously has no use for "kung fu" whatsoever. In the film, no one is even interested in taking kung fu lessons as a pastime. This really is pathetic when we contrast it with the reality that many performance-major music graduates earn their bread by teaching private students. The film goes on to tell the story of how these former Shaolin pupils, after many hardships and humiliations that are of course presented farcically, successfully adapt kung fu to play soccer and become rich and famous — and ultimately, internationally famous when Stephen Chow teams up with his girlfriend (played by Zhao Wei), a practitioner of *tai chi chuan*, and become stars in the bowling world. In the last shot of the film they appear on the cover of *Time* magazine. In reality, Chow himself did make it to the cover of the special "Asian Heroes 2003" issue of Time Asia (28 April 2003, Vol. 161, No. 16).

I would like to read Chow's words quoted above on two levels: first, as a self-referential remark on the film itself; second, on a wider cultural horizon, as a reference to the metamorphosing cinematic imagination of kung fu — originally a traditional and native practice — in negotiation with the modern condition.

The film itself can be read as one of the attempts in commercial cinema to further commodify kung fu beyond the conventional "kung fu genres", crossing kung fu over to other genres to produce an often hybrid form in order to make money. The "original" kung fu genre — as exemplified by what is widely accepted as the *first* really "kung fu film", *The Chinese Boxer/ Longhudou* (1970) directed by and starring Jimmy Wang Yu, or the more recent *Once Upon a Time in China* saga (1991–97) by Tsui Hark — imagined kung fu as an essential part of traditional Chinese culture and a means to empower and revive China in the face of alien invasions in "modern times", often located during the late Qing–early Republican period. But of course kung fu films set in contemporary times also appeared at almost the same time; Bruce Lee's *The Way of the Dragon/ Menglong guojiang* (1972) (re-titled *Return of the Dragon* in the US) being a well-known example. In any case, the "late Qing–early Republican" kung fu films were dominant up to the early 1980s.[6]

The comic kung fu genre, fully established by *Snake in the Eagle's Shadow/Shexing diaoshou* and *Drunken Master/Zuiquan* both of 1978, is also mostly set in this historical period. The "re-packaging" of kung fu became large-scale after 1983 when the market required a genre change. That year saw Jackie Chan making action films with a contemporary setting while featuring action with easily recognizable traces of kung fu. Police-gangster kung fu action films were prevalent from the mid-1980s and throughout the 1990s. Meanwhile, Tsui Hark revived the late Qing-early Republican kung fu genre in *Once Upon A Time in China* in 1991 and, interestingly, also struck a last gesture (up to the present moment) in 1997 with his final installment of the series, signifying the symbolic demise of this genre. Kung fu has in many countries disseminated into, permeated and hybridized many other genres from vampire horror (Wesley Snipes's *Blade*) through cookery (Stephen Chow's *The God of Cookery/Shishen*; Tsui Hark's *The Chinese Feast/Jinyu mantang*), screwball comedy (the Korean film *Volcano High*), to cyberpunk and cyber fantasy (the *Matrix* trilogy, *Mortal Combat*). After *The God of Cookery* (which from midway onward virtually turns into a kung fu film in the guise of a cookery story),

Stephen Chow cleverly timed his next project to coincide with the interest in soccer's 2002 World Cup and made *Shaolin Soccer* in 2001.

In an earlier paper on kung fu films, I argued through an analysis of several significant "nationalistic" late Qing–early Republican kung fu films that they operate in a self-negating mode that denies kung fu's effectiveness in modern life.[7] This filmic representation of kung fu often envisions a contest between tradition and modernity with a self-denial of modernity caught in a liminal temporal space imagined somewhere in modern history. These films re-imagine the myth of kung fu as all powerful and yet at once self-reflexively point to the uselessness of kung fu in the modern era of Western firearms. The hidden question that is to be dealt with is: how do we re-place kung fu in our times? My larger concern is, as I said before, to look into how we have negotiated (Chinese) tradition and (Western) modernity in this popular cultural cinematic re-imagination of kung fu. Put in yet another way: how do modern Chinese people live their lives in negotiation with modernization and modernity, with popular cultural imagination a dominant fact of reality?

Shaolin Soccer is a recent practical example of this negotiation with a tint of self-reflexivity in the form of a non-kung fu genre. Chow's intention is probably mostly pragmatic: with the decline of Hong Kong movies since the mid-1990s, how can we cash in with kung fu again in a new genre or form when existing genres no longer have markets? Chow's making of *Shaolin Soccer* is paralleled by his Shaolin characters' struggle for survival in the movie. We must not forget that Chow experienced great difficulty in getting financial support for the film. No one was interested or dared to invest in such a film, especially at this time of the "death" of the Hong Kong film industry. In the end he secured investment from Universe, a company with its origins in video marketing now also investing in making films in order to supply software for its video trade. But the two parties started a big feud as soon as the film began to break box-office records here and there. A long lawsuit ensued amid news that Chow might be making a US version of the film. The project had not yet taken any concrete shape when *Shaolin Soccer* was released in the US in late 2003.

While Chow was reconceptualizing "kung fu cinema" in light of the new media (for example, filmic CG after *Matrix*'s "bullet-time" editing and the rise of the DVD/VCD mode of "film" consumption) and the new market (Hong Kong cinema's way out is to cross its geopolitical and cultural boundary with mainland China to the north, and head overseas in all other directions), the Shaolin pupils in the film were placed in a condition of re-thinking the place, space and use of kung fu in the modern world. This contradiction between kung fu and modernity is nowhere more self-conscious in the film than in the scene where Stephen Chow tries to persuade one of his former classmates who is now a very broke stock broker to join him to form a soccer team turning kung fu *into* soccer. Chow is taunted at point blank by his friend in a highly self-reflexive undertone: "Jet planes are all over the sky; computers are everywhere in the streets. What kind of world are we living in now? You, wake up please!"

Right, it is high time that we woke up from the dreams of the mythic worlds created by the traditional kung fu imagination since the 1970s; there is no escape from the techno-reality of jets and computers. *The Matrix* (1999) demonstrated one of Hollywood's approaches to capitalizing Chinese kung fu — a mode that integrates jets and computers *with* kung fu. It must, therefore, be noted that kung fu action is only one of the ingredients of that film's huge worldwide success. As a matter of fact, the box office of *The Matrix* in Hong Kong was lower than that of *Star Wars: The Phantom Menace, The Mummy,* and *The Sixth Sense,* all released in the city in the same year, 1999.[8] One may conclude that Yuen Wo-ping action choreography was nothing new in the eyes of Hong Kong movie-goers, not to mention the nakedly amateurish strikes and kicks of Keanu Reeves and his like; this explains why, even with the latest advances in CG, Jet Li the master martial-artist-turned-actor is still very much sought-after in Hollywood, including for cyber sci-fi projects like *The One* (2002). The "novelty" of the action in *The Matrix* lies more in the innovative "bullet-time" editing than in kung fu per se. Packaged with the best that Hong Kong cinema could offer to catch up with post-*Matrix* computer special effects, *Shaolin Soccer* also resolved the contradiction between a virtually outdated kung fu and the reality of jets and computers — a problem also solved, as the Shaolin soccer group finally succeeds, by reinforcing the transformativity and timeless power of kung fu. Furthermore, this successful re-placement of kung fu signifies the triumph of pre-modern technological culture over modern technology (or what Wong Kin-yuen calls "technology per se"),[9] since the Shaolin team's arch opponent, the Evil soccer team, relies on the latest high-tech drugs to boost their body power, whereas the Shaolin players are natural products of physical kung fu training. This immediately reminds us of the binary structure used in *Rocky IV* (1985): Sylvester Stallone versus Dolph Lundgren.

The irony in *Shaolin Soccer* is that the super-, if not mythical, power of pre-modern Shaolin kung fu is remarketed via digital technology to bring out the message that the traditional is not merely still useful in this high-tech media age but also ultimately superior to the modern. It is precisely digital technology that has enabled this instance of the successful re-placement of a cinematic kung fu that is at once represented in the film as human, natural and in opposition to the posthuman high-tech devices and products. Perhaps part of the relevance of kung fu in relation to our techno age is aptly revealed by a spontaneous remark of Rob Wilson's: "Martial arts have become a training to live with digital technology".[10]

THE 007 FROM THE IMPERIAL CITY

In 1995 and 1996 Chow made a pair of very successful movies following the same basic formula of parodying the James Bond films. One had a modern setting (*From Beijing with Love*) and the other the outer form of a swordplay film (*Forbidden City Cop/Danei mitan linglingfa*). In *Forbidden City Cop*, the realization that there is something called "Western science and modern technology" confronting traditional kung fu, and that the products and practice of this technoscience seem to be overwhelming, underlies and underlines the text. Although it takes the guise of a swordplay film, there is much more hand-to-hand combat kung fu in this film than fighting with weapons. It is the story of an imperial guard, played by Chow, whose duty is to protect the emperor and who is assumed to be supreme in *wugong*. However, he has no *wugong* at all and is only interested in designing and experimenting with "useless" gadgets of various kinds, based on what the audience will immediately recognize as "scientific knowledge". Chow's experimental gadgets in the film connect the character with the Leonardo da Vinci who sketched the conceptual technological designs of the flying machine and submarine. Likewise, some of Chow's gadgets can potentially be used as weapons — among a variety of things that he invents, there is a "mouth-gun".

The story goes that a group of villains is plotting to assassinate the emperor; they easily kill all the imperial guards who demonstrate dazzlingly impressive kung fu at the beginning of the film, while Chow can only manage a clumsy, child's play somersault. At the critical moment however, it is Chow who annihilates all the villains except one, using his self-invented mouth-piece shotgun. The emperor is safe for the time being. Momentarily, the film displays an attempt at rationalizing combat power in terms of scientific thinking at the expense of the power of kung fu. The film has its reflective moments of dismantling the myth of kung fu. However, in the last formulaic duel scene in which Chow the kung fu-less imperial guard confronts the arch villain and master of kung fu, Chow resorts to the ultimate mysterious *wugong* — a swordplay strike recorded on a sacred scroll of a swordplay manual that he involuntarily acquires through an accidental lightning-strike during the final duel — and thereby annihilates the last villain who is interestingly named, in literal translation, the "King of Face-Off" (*wuxiangwang*). The film rethinks and destabilizes the myth of kung fu in terms of science and technology but returns to the shelter of this cultural myth of self-power that it tries to un-imagine.

This structure of the conservative turn is also seen in *From Beijing with Love*, released a year before. This time the special agent from mainland China — a caricature of 007 — is a vulgar pork seller who uses a Chinese chopper. Nevertheless this character, played by Chow, also calls himself a "swordsman" (*daoke*). His opponent is a high-tech bullet-proof armored man with an invincible golden gun (*The Man with the Golden Gun* plus *Robocop*). This villain has shot "002" dead at the beginning of the film. At the end it is the "swordsman's" *wugong* that literally butchers the villain. The final duel is an imitation of the classic style of the samurai genre best exemplified by Akira Kurosawa's *Yojimbo*. The villain in his armor is literally gashed from the head to the abdomen by a single strike from Chow's butcher's chopper. Once again, the ending implies that when one's kung fu is spectacular enough one can overcome advanced technology, just as the hero Long Jiangfei in *Buddha's Palm* did to escape from the cellar.

Yet the reflection on kung fu in *From Beijing with Love* is not as straightforward as this example implies; in fact, it is full of contradictions and twists. Earlier on in the film, Chow is set up by some corrupt communist cadres in the Mainland police/military force and is tied up before a firing squad. Next to him is another convict sentenced to death. Chow, a kung fu master, immediately gets his legs (which are incidentally not tied) into position to make a big leap. At the same moment, Chow is startled to see that the condemned convict next to him is striking the same posture and muttering to himself with a sneer: "Thirty years of rigorous training and today, at long last, this can be put to great use! Do you think you can kill me, the Iron-Leg Water-Surfer, so easily?" Here is another hidden kung fu master who excels in a kind of kung fu called "iron-leg water-surfing" (*tietui shuishangpiao*), a term adapted from the linguistic style of the swordplay/martial arts novel (*wuxia xiaoshuo*). On the screen we see him strike the ground with his foot, cracking it with a deep fissure. Stirring up mud and dust, in a split-second he is flying in the air. But in another split-second he is blasted into pieces by a bazooka operated by a military officer in a most disciplined and efficient manner, signifying the triumph of modern military technology and efficiency over mythic kung fu and the human body.

Yet this mockery of kung fu as a myth in *From Beijing with Love* is, as the analysis of the final duel reveals, negated by a return to the ultimate embrace of the myth of kung fu as the force to overcome evil and correct the wrongs of reality. The same structural turn in *Forbidden City Cop* is of greater significance and perhaps brings more frustration, too, because in this film there is a much larger investment in and emphasis on the representation of science to confront kung fu. There is an underlying tension and anxiety deriving from a radical failure to negotiate the opposition between a native tradition that carries a tint of the mystic and a foreign culture that appeals to European post-enlightenment rational thinking and technology. Perhaps it is only when the kung fu imaginary is capable of forgetting and leaving behind the nostalgic return to its myth that this popular cultural imagination can break through to be at full ease with modernity.

JACKIE WEARS A TUXEDO

We have a reversal of the story that I am narrating at the moment when Jackie Chan dons an American tuxedo in Hollywood. *Tuxedo* (2002) shares one major element with the two Stephen Chow films just discussed: they all subvert the myth of kung fu in one way or another framed by the discourse of modern technology; meanwhile they also parody the Bond film to different degrees. James Tong, the name of Jackie Chan's character in *Tuxedo*, who repeatedly imitates James Bond by introducing himself with "My name's Tong, James Tong," has absolutely no kung fu skills at all. He is a taxi driver in New York and he tells us at the beginning of the film that "Not everybody Chinese is Bruce Lee". Well, James Tong shares the same family name with Bruce Lee's character in *The Way of the Dragon*, "Tong" (Tong Lung) — Tong meaning "Chinese" or "China". At the same time James Tong shares James Bond's given name. In name, he has the best of both worlds.

    Tuxedo is quite a dismantling of the myth of kung fu in several ways. In the film, combat and other powers do not come from the human body, but from the suit, which is a product of modern technology. Jennifer Love Hewitt plays a scientist, the female hero in the film, and she describes the tuxedo as "the most incredible piece of technology on this planet". Although it is also said that "it is 90% the tuxedo, 10% you" — thus mostly material and a little human — the film did not convince me that there was even a 10% human contribution to the action performed when wearing the tuxedo. Moreover, even if the 10% were really there, it would already be denigrating enough to the status of the human body in the relationship between human and object.

The tuxedo-type hero is not new, however. There is a vein of comic book heroes/heroines, both American and Japanese, who gain or enhance combat power through a special costume. The notable thing here is that the tuxedo is not an extension of the body, as we often see in many sci-fi heroes and heroines who by their own bodies are already fighting machines, while the clothing or gadget extension merely enhances their power and they fight through the armor extension. Here, the tuxedo itself is an assimilation of the kung fu body. The tuxedo/object moves the body/subject, not the other way round.[11] It is the tuxedo fighting through the human body.

The screen image of Jackie Chan in *Tuxedo* is a far cry from what he has done so far as "Jackie Chan" — making films (*Drunken Master, Project A* and so on) in which the body, and often the kung fu-trained body, is the source of power. Without the tuxedo, Chan's character in this film really is an ordinary man, literally. The aura of the kung fu body is very much absent, especially in relation to what Stephen Teo has written about Bruce Lee's body:

> In *The Way of the Dragon*, before his gladiatorial bout with Chuck Norris in the Roman Coliseum, Lee prepares himself, stretches his muscles, reaches down to his feet, creaks all his joints. Here is a specimen of superb training, a fighter *all too humanly plausible — not the imagined warrior of an action movie director*. Lee's appeal lies here. A Chinese audience who sees him knows that *Lee has done all Chinese proud*; they know that his skill is *achievable*, a result of fitness and training and not a given. Lee is a common man hero.[12]

While Bruce Lee's aura is built upon his authentic body-powerful and authentic martial arts, Jackie Chan's aura is built upon his authentic stunts. Whereas in 1998 Jackie Chan jibed at the CG effects of Hong Kong's first cyber age comic book-based fantasy action film *Stormriders* as "kindergarten",[13] he has now made a film himself that is heavily dependent on digital technology. This is not to say that Chan did not perform most of his stunts in *Tuxedo*; it is the "kindergarten" level of the stunts compared with his previous numerous daredevil stunts that disappointed many fans and translated his image from the realm of the authentic/real to that of the digital/virtual. Even in *The Matrix*, kung fu skills have to be acquired through training, although this happens almost instantaneously through the computer implant and virtual reality. In *Tuxedo*, no training is needed at all. In the logic of my argument, ironically, this may not be a bad thing and may even be desirable. For *Tuxedo* comes close to a total destruction of the mythic kung fu body and an affirmation of technology. Let us not forget that this is an American movie. We shall see how the kung fu myth continues or discontinues in subsequent Hong Kong, Korean, Indian or other cinemas.

4

The Fighting Condition in Hong Kong Cinema: Local Icons and Cultural Antidotes for the Global Popular

Stephen Chan Ching-kiu

THE CONDITION OF FIGHTING

In Hong Kong action cinema, the inevitable condition of fighting usually, though not always, ends up in one of the fighters winning the show, another losing it, such being a popular convention in matters of martial art. Culturally, the spectacle of any good fight is a matter for public appreciation, discourse, and indeed consumption, though the outcomes of any particular game could sometimes be whimsical, intangible or simply inconsequential. For politically Hong Kong is indeed rather intangible; the city has grown into perhaps one of the most sensitive ideological battlefields in the world, with its own unique cultural formation shaping a modern city life with a unique kind of colonial modernity.[1] To grow from that groundwork of history, and indeed to build on the basis of the cosmopolitan framework involved, some local politicians would insist that we need prosperity and stability to keep intact the power bloc as defined and delimited by the status quo of the late colonial rule up to 1997, the year of the big historical spectacle when the people saw themselves, as it were, eventually winning the game of (de-)colonization. Have the winners somehow now lost their grip on the object of their show? And how will they appreciate that ambivalent passage from colonial to postcolonial subjection, an inevitable passage of power as of sensibilities, supposedly allowing the Hong Kong people to start setting the rules of the game in the Hong Kong Special Administrative Region after the transfer of sovereignty in 1997?

Historically, it is ironic that the amazing "success" of Hong Kong has been built on winning the peculiar game of an established colonial institution that effectively, until two decades ago, shielded the territory from the political trauma, dislocation and "cultural revolution" the Chinese people had to experience north of its border. But this mediatory "border", almost a magical shock neutralizer, has been changing its social form and function at an incredibly rapid rate since China moved to re-enter the global market following the end of the Great Cultural Revolution in the late 1970s. Hence, in between the postcolony (island) and the nation (mainland) the realities of border-crossing and cultural interface have undergone significant transformation, particularly in the past decade.

To be sure, cross-border imaginations and their ensuing cultural translations are routinely accelerated and continuously dramatized by the great tolerance among some of us — the pragmatic Hong Kong people — who could hardly wait for the ex-colony, now Chinese Special Administrative Region (SAR), to turn into a more integral ("effective") part of the motherland and, thus, to be subject to a more severe ("authentic") form of Chinese sovereignty. Cultural translations, as well as the circulation, transformation and re-negotiation of identity-traces involved, have become part of a fluid and non-systematic process of social signification in the postcolonial formation of culture in Hong Kong. Given the anxiety, bewilderment, frustration, cynicism and despair traceable everywhere in the public spectacle being offered to us (whether local movie-goers or not) during the latest course in our peculiar decolonization process, the problematics of the local appear to have been tied up with the trajectory of meaning-reproduction informing our collective plight in the long, melodramatic fight for a future haunted increasingly by the year 2047. Fifty years after 1997 do seem unimaginatively short, living amid the "inevitable" (also called "status quo" during the 1990s) experienced as a historical condition in which people are kept waiting for drastic sociopolitical changes of some kind, if not cultural actions of magnitude upon that very "status quo".

Having been so deeply and effectively implanted in the popular imaginary, this collective emotional complex smacks of typical Hong Kong pragmatism, moving toward, across and beyond the timeline of 1997. Only now its aggressiveness, its proto-typical economic value and competitive function in war-games of all sorts, appear to be both individually and socially problematic for the local people who have survived the historical changes and crises of the 1990s. To the public of this so-called Asian world city today, postcolonial pragmatism has now confirmed that it is not so much sovereignty, nationality or even citizenship that matters, but real assets in terms of money, security and perhaps the capacity to dream on location (in that order and logic). The everyday play of the socio-ideological contradictions involved in contemporary spectacles and trauma is not unfamiliar to the Hong Kong people, as far as popular imagination through local cultural productions and circulations is concerned. As the trying scenario of re-instituting postcolonial locality becomes ever so difficult to anchor, moves to turn to globality as a relatively more facile source of relevance, a welcome digression from legitimacy, and a mode of sensibility for the local inhabitants become more prominent in Hong Kong's attempt to re-read, re-invent and re-play its "success" narratives after 1997.

Amid all our attempts to negotiate some sort of renewed sense of identity for the local community after colonial rule, how, then, do the troubling strategy and the tactics of pragmatism relate to the global spectacle of action cinema? During the last few decades, our "success" narratives provided an increasingly stable social condition for the ordinary people to receive a way of life, perception and thinking we refer to as the Hong Kong popular imagination. In what ways would this mode of imagination play a role in precipitating such forms of cultural relevance, legitimacy and sensibility? For the action cinema we are concerned with, there are many ways of staging and enjoying a fighting scene. The question to consider is: what do we fight with or indulge in *when we submit ourselves voluntarily to the condition of action* in general, and *fighting* in particular, *through action cinema*? I want to address this issue in the context of local Hong Kong cultural imagination as framed by the condition of play and the negotiation of the sociocultural factors suggested here. With a perspective on the specific transnational dimension of our culture, my discussion will deal with a few representative action figures of identity taken as instances of the local/(trans)national in shifting relationships. The guiding principles informing the game of winning and losing will be examined, as well as the cultural condition under which pleasure materializes through "the fighting showcases" at issue.

FIGHTING ON SCREEN

Let me start with the view I borrow from Marilyn Mintz's seminal work *The Martial Arts Films* (1978), that films are a cultural antidote. To highlight this idea I shall focus on selected key moments of fighting in the shaping of local icons, sensibilities and subjectivities through contemporary Hong Kong cinema since the 1980s, focusing on the 1990s. Writing in the late 1970s, Mintz summarizes the condition of the martial arts as cultural action in the following way:

As a microcosm of the whole social structure, the martial arts film is a parallel or metaphor in action for what is occurring on the larger plane. Beginning with the individual, then the immediate family, the clan, the town, the collective, the province, the country — each reacts to the other, influencing action and thought. Loyalty to one group need not be exclusive, but there are degrees of primary interests or priorities that are constantly determining and swaying individual behavior.[2]

To study the formation of local icons with reference to the cinematic acts of code-making I begin with their "positional values", which vary according to the generic conventions, cultural bias and social evils as bound up in the context of action-making. "Codes and traditions", Mintz points out, "were all created to serve an end, to give *everyone* a sense of perspective of a greater purpose". Complete with their own systems of codes, modes of behaviour, and techniques of fighting, the martial arts films "go to the very core of human behavior, values, and survival plots".[3] For the audience of the traditional *wuxia pian* (martial arts/ swordplay films), what is important is to see some favorite *wuxia* heroes *in action* functioning effectively on screen, and to enjoy the way these iconic figures fight with style, and hopefully win through the exercise of "violence", which is often (though by no means necessarily) tied in with the "action" framed. But clearly, this is not sufficient. Today, violent action *per se* would be a necessary but not sufficient condition for pleasurable consumption in the genre, though in the early history of cinema it was hardly necessary for people on screen to "fight" realistically at all. For the Hong Kong action genre, code-making involves the re-positioning of the values of martial arts and the re-definition of heroes, as much for the fans of local icons as for addicts of the global popular genre. It may also work via the transferal of the contemporary consciousness into a period context. All factors considered, this means that the global popular can be viewed as the multi-faceted reality where cultural flows operate and exert influence on our daily action. "In the martial arts films, there are men [sic] dying like flies, or men [sic] fighting for something they believe in".[4]

In an account of the historical trajectory of the *wuxia pian*, the Chinese critic Chen Mo suggests that from the technical point of view there are two types of cinematic limit for screen violence, namely, (i) the degree of "cruelty" (*canren*) or level of "tyranny" (*canbao*) (re-)produced; and (ii) the extent to which fighting scenes are presented in the entire film. The former refers to the intensity of the action concerned, while the latter has to do with the proportion (measured by time/frame) in which "action" is represented. In other words, the extent of violence/action delimits the scope of plot events whose meaning and relevance in a film is commonly geared toward something cruel or tyrannical.[5] If iconic figures can fight for ideals on the screen, the one key I would want to emphasize here is people's right to have dreams, to escape through the cinema into that which they trust they would enjoy.

While Mintz points out that it is the ordinary people's right to have dreams (and hence, to "escape") through the cinematic fantasy of fighting, in the Chinese context there has always been the strong reminder that *wuxia* is the national dream of the people. The dominant logic seems to have always suggested that through *wuxia* the Chinese people could dream for an ideal nationhood. For instance, it has been argued that since the national dream of *wuxia* has been a product of an agricultural civilization: "it entails the last dream the people had of their country before the advance of modern civilization in China".[6] Hence, as a form of cultural imagination, the fighting spirit has to be decoded properly in order to understand the condition of *wuxia* in the imaginary register, in other words — more so through the allegorical function of the "great heroic dream" than social fantasies about justice or salvation.

Indeed, there must be good reasons for *fighting* to happen *on screen*. For most of the Hong Kong audiences, the security of home has always been articulated as the baseline for entry into modern, world-conscious urbanity with a distinctive local touch bordering on national ambivalence and transnational hybridity. At the same time, securing a long-term place in global capitalism has lately also been much favoured in public discourse as a strategy to protect home from the possible threat of the nation-state, and to map home's position in relation to the changing global order. In the following, I shall draw from a number of distinctive fighting scenes in the local cinema in order to explore this issue. Above all, I would very much want to ask: can the action that captures the popular imagination allow one to have a sweet dream and rest peacefully and joyfully for a few hours afterwards? And if so, what can we learn from such an experience? That is a basic question for me, in my role as a student of the "glocal" cinema, which I am still trying to understand here.

LOCAL ACTION

Since the postwar period in Hong Kong, local action heroes have been fighting with forces of the national and transnational, which interact at crucial moments in the shaping of the global popular as the new cultural dominant. The generic status of the "local icons" evolves with the fury and weaponry in their actioners. From here we may examine the ways in which some of these Hong Kong action scenes serve as cultural antidotes for the social condition the local heroes have always fantasized about; for what came before the contemporary forms of such fantasies; and for what seems so transient in the estranged postcolonial state of affairs.

Here I have in mind first of all a whole range of classic icons, including those epitomized by local heroes dating back to Jackie Chan's common-guy-next-door figures in the early Yuen Wo-ping films, all the Wang-Yu-style martyrs in Zhang Che (Chang Che), Bruce Lee's melodramatic anti-imperialist China-man rebels, as well as Kwan Tak-hing's local version of the Confucian *kung fu* master found in the classic Wong Fei-hung series. According to Mintz, martial arts films "depict a certain range for rebellion and pose possible alternative behaviors that appeal to the suppressed and the suppressors as a true expression of *fantasy* and forerunner of *change*".[7] If indeed new roles following the fantastic trajectory of such iconic heroism have to be re-articulated in Hong Kong cinema today, my concern is which key changes to identify for capturing the significance of the range of local actions that help position the ordinary spectators in the course of their subjection to the city's unique course of (post)colonial formation.

It is often said that in *wuxia* films self-narration dominates the representational form, thus framing the cultural composition of the heroic icons and the sociohistorical value of the individual. To represent the changing shape of identity, therefore, one has to dwell on the fantastic form of self-in-struggle, allowing it to traverse personal and collective levels as if striving for a kind of tragic reconciliation of irreducible dramatic tensions. So in the world of *jianghu* re-captured in Tsui Hark's *Dragon Inn* (Film Workshop 1992; prod. Tsui Hark, dir. Raymond Lee/Ching Siu-tung, Tony), both modern values (independence, freedom) and traditional values (such as loyalty and piety) are put under persistent narrative focus and analysis. Such critical concerns have always pre-occupied Tsui Hark to some extent, as we know.[8]

To put this in a comparative perspective, we may note that attempts have sometimes been made by critics from the Chinese mainland to anchor the significance of Hong Kong *wuxia* cinema in the nationhood of its cultural tradition, referring to some "progressive spirit in self-improvement" as a concrete manifestation of the essence of Confucian cultural values they trace in the local cinema. Hence, for instance, a certain version of "eternal life" rooted in the "spirit" of the imagined totality "Hong Kong people" is identified as part of the proto-national context within which the local *wuxia* cinema would supposedly operate. As a result, traces of Daoism in *Dragon Inn*, such as the adoption of Zhuang Zi in "Butchering the Bull" are taken as crucial contributions of traditional Chinese culture to the modern cinematic spectacle of *wuxia*.[9] Many would agree that the pragmatic individualist turn is indeed tied to a certain form of pro-active nationalist spirit and imagination, which seems to be as prominent in Bruce Lee, Yuen Wo-ping and Tsui Hark, as in many local series ranging from the "Wong Fei-hung" of the 1950s, to anything you might expect to see in a Wong Kar-wai, Wong Jin or Stephen Chiau film during the 1990s. Let us look at this with a few examples.

Miracle Fighters (1982) by Yuen Wo-ping (*Drunken Fist*, 1978) is fascinating in its imaginative rendition of a certain pragmatic Chinese localism, in which the traditional Guangdong (sometimes Cantonese) culture we inherit from the past dominates the plot, action and the whole common appeal of the *kung fu* comedy. Regardless of the film's setting in the Qing Dynasty of the seventeenth century, what Yuen's *kung fu* imagination offered to the local audience of the 1980s was the Hong Kong variant of our Guangdong heritage in popular culture, now appearing in its *residual* form (to use Raymond Williams' term). Unlike the nostalgic films of the 1990s, however, here the representation of past local customs and common tricks of daily life could not have been seen as lost collective experience by the contemporary audience. Rather more likely, they were translated via readily accessible social settings in the film into spectacular practices of everyday life and everyday "action". Physical action is rendered immensely pleasurable here as an integral part of ordinary life gradually being forgotten socially, cherished now on the local screen against the micro-context of some negotiable pre-urban daily activities for the contemporary audience of late capitalist Hong Kong. Captured in a highly original and fabulously exaggerated work of action imagination, the hilarious fighting scenes we find in *Miracle Fighters* are conceivable, indeed re-presentable only under cultural conditions that were largely free from any pervasive sociopolitical tensions or unrest. This would be the Hong Kong of the early 1980s, de-familiarized, making its way through three decades of relative stability and prosperity as a subordinate British territory, with the majority of its people subjecting themselves rather naturally as Chinese colonized in the back-garden of their giant motherland.

Whereas Tsui Hark has always been much pre-occupied with issues of national or ethnic identity for the Chinese people, with a touch of common wisdom and simplicity, Yuen's action fantasia re-enacts the system of iconic action codes, the modes of cinematic fighting, and the surprising articulation of a contemporary Hong Kong consciousness. In *Miracle*

Fighters, these are all dealt with in such locally signifying terms and conditions that little reference is needed to the transnational or even the national imagination per se. For instance, a commonplace (now completely out-dated) Cantonese practice of street-side facial care for women popular in the local community during the 1950s and 1960s is translated in cinematic terms into the pre-text and context for playful fighting between the two individuals concerned — the traditional female cosmetician and the woman having the beauty treatment, typically seated on a backyard chair. In the most amazing ways imaginable, through Yuen Wo-ping's masterful rendition of the fight, the cosmetic act takes shape in a sequence of fascinating bodily *kung fu* moves played out with threads, needles and face-powder, between the two male impersonators respectively performing the roles of the standing cosmetician and the woman-on-the-chair. Under the circumstances, short of embracing the *local* as a lived moment of the specific *colonial* way of life (resulting in the bracketing of any dominant nationalist-imaginative effects), Yuen addresses his audience as subjects positioned within the living space of an earlier mode of communal imagination, complete with old-fashioned fantasies about the extraordinary power of the minor bodily acts, which are nevertheless based on and expressed in a cinematic language of exceptionally skilful and liberating fighting tactics.

The special effects make the action imaginary the convincing gateway to fantasy experience. Well-known now for the action choreography he did for *Hero* (Zhang Yimou 2002), Tony Ching Siu-tung created some of the best local icons for action cinema during the 1990s with such highly acclaimed popular works as *Swordsman II* (1992) and *The East is Red* (1993). The local audience will always remember scene after scene of memorable moments of action spectacle that Ching generated through the icon of The Invincible East rendered by the glorious performance of Brigitte Lin in these films. Iconographic conventions and special effects are likewise brilliantly integrated in *The Heroic Trio* and its sequel *The Executioners* (Johnnie To 1993), in which the three heroines (Anita Mui, Michelle Yeoh, and Maggie Cheung) keep making bodily flights between buildings and across streets.

In *Miracle Fighters*, the typical Hong Kong imaginary takes the form of a mixture of residual and dominant traces of the local culture. The traditional articulation of the *kung fu* movements to a nationhood-based *wuxia* spirit has been translated onto the screen in such a way that fighting assumes the function of play through physical fitness and the common-sense intellect for the ordinary people. Such a hilarious form of local action becomes possible on screen perhaps because the broader condition of social life had remained relatively calm in the early 1980s. Prior to the official disclosure of the 1997 political handover issue, crisis had yet to be registered; hence the playful and creative attitude that befits this particular social milieu. Fighting is a delicate, happy and harmless non-violent game, when stability seems to be the least of problems for the community and the status quo is accepted as the given frame for any quest for action. With *The Heroic Trio*, all the fighting scenes are presented in stylistic bodily moves across the well-composed frame. Working with director Johnnie To, Ching punctuates the action movements of his three leading women warriors throughout the film with dynamic moments of kinetic energy. The simple narrative of crisis, framed like a contemporary pop legend, is anchored nicely in the nostalgic adventurous chase featuring the trio (on horseback or motorcycle) racing along an empty highway along the shore one after another.

For the martial arts movies, as Mintz points out, the generic chase is indeed "a highly evocative element" which "stimulate[s] anticipation as two entities speed through time — one eventually to be thwarted; the other, egoistically rewarded".[10] This particular action sequence in *The Heroic Trio* provides the clues for us to reach at the relevance and sensibility of all the fighting spectacles found in the rest of the film, with a noticeably local, non-conforming landscape set as backdrop to the thematic chase, which is played out to the familiar tone and jolly beat of Anita Mui's reassuring Cantopop soundtrack. Female bonding, one of the key motifs of the film, becomes tied instantly to the local significance of pride, indulgence and cynical playfulness that together contribute to shaping the popular in its rather disjunctive mode of ordinary sensibility for the local movie-goers of the early 1990s.

LOCAL SENSIBILITY AND REGIME OF THE POPULAR

With its origin in *wushu*, or the martial arts, action has always provided the local cinema with an approach to "heroism" that serves to capture the national imagination of a people. In the words of the critic Lau Tai-muk, *wuxia* films "bring the audience back to a simple old world ... whereby problems that cannot be solved in reality can be solved [in cinema]".[11] In Hong Kong, the generic innovation pioneered by Tsui Hark's Film Workshop has produced a series of very refined and successful modern *wuxia* works, through which a disturbing form of national imaginary spoke loudly in a euphoric sensibility in the midst of the territory's rather gloomy decolonization process. In this connection, Ching's intense action sequences serve to supply an additional, double-edged perspective with signs of hyperactivity and despair cohabiting in the spectacular guise of screen violence. Call these the symptoms of cynical (post)colonial politics, and you would be fully disillusioned, for what you get more often than not in case of a problem is the return to the popular for a pragmatic resolution. Consuming action, the ordinary people would be content to work their way through fantasies of the spectacular amid the uneasy sociopolitical climate they had to live with during the last decade in Hong Kong's transition to its postcolonial status.

Fighting transforms the local action icons into legendary heroes whose world exists only for the cinema they cling onto. The martial arts are about "aggression, action, collision, and intensified use of energy".[12] As a dominant form in popular cinema, masculinity (*yanggang*) was popularized by Zhang Che (1912–2002) and John Woo in the 1970s and 1980s respectively, when the particular visual and kinetic form of martial arts pictures did provide one perspective for the audience to feel for the times. As the action-movie master Zhang Che once admitted, "the 60s and 70s were the most energetic periods of Hong Kong — the period when young people exerted themselves ... The masses were striving ahead in a rebellious mood and the colonial administration was receiving a shock to the system".[13] The critic Law Kar observes that in Zhang's movies, the heroes are all death-defying male fanatics always ready to resist authority and the establishment. The so-called "violent" and "bloody" nature of his films is therefore symptomatic of Hong Kong people's lack of a socially imaginative perspective in seeing cinema as a way of coping with the politics of culture at the time.[14] Zhang made the now classic *One-Armed Swordsman* in 1967, when riots broke out in Kowloon. During the riots, *The Assassin* was filmed. All subsequent local icons of the *kung fu* or action genres have since been male dominant.[15] As a result, all subsequent masculine bondings in the local genre are firmly built on the Confucian system of values, making all forms of local politics an aspect of familial norms set down in the hierarchy of social relationships based on the traditional values of piety and loyalty.

And so it seems that no politics is effective outside of the scenario of one male fighter struggling against another. In this context, the regime of the popular is the limit condition in which the male fighter can win without even having to engage much in actual deeds of bodily or swordplay combat. This is the case with all the heroes in Wong Kar-wai's *Ashes of Time* (1994). If To and Ching have transposed the issue of locality, or the location of culture as experience by shifting the focus onto the female heroines in *The Heroic Trio*, Wong gets rid of the need for dealing with morality altogether by situating the regime of action, as it were, in the inertia of the ultimate desert. He deals with all variants of border-crossing casually and brings home routinely to the audience a version of decadent pragmatism under the fighting condition of the limitless *jianghu*, where no killing is meaningful, and no desire effective. We see a lot of rapid movements, and then again, nothing much stirs, except for chunk after chunk of monologue and voice-over narration. People fight in all the stories we hear from the all-star cast Wong put together for his audience, working against the grain and shocking them with an anti-generic work of *wuxia* film.[16] The conditions of belief and trust have indeed been put to serious test in the counter-generic world of the alternative *wuxia pian*, where people fight for very little and believe in even less. This work has surely transgressed the two cinematic limits mentioned earlier, namely, the degree of cruelty and tyranny, as the proportion of fighting scenes in all the sequences shows. One could argue that the film's shortcoming in terms of the extent of action represented is compensated by the intensity in the emotional complexity embodied; or perhaps it is displaced by the extent to which some fans are given to adoring the local icons in some of their most glamorous and touching performances on screen.

It is with the post-*wuxia* imagination that we are asked to experience anew both the depth and hollowness of the contemporary cultural crisis. While *The Heroic Trio* shifts the local cinema to a hybrid action mode, Hong Kong style, *Ashes of Time* moves beyond all generic boundaries of *wuxia* to attain an anti-*wuxia*, even a post-*wuxia* mode of sensibility representative of the postcolonial mood in local transition. Capturing the condition of action under different modes of cinematic expression of what fighting may mean, both films arguably re-invented the genre in the course of their respective attempts to come to grips with the form and implications of decolonization in Hong Kong, if only in *Ashes of Time*'s specific cultural act as mediated in the *wuxia* mode of performance. Fighting can be cruel; it may even generate a sense of the terror of imagination, or, if you want, a tyranny of the senses. Amid cruelty of action, the fighting spirit of the individuals is put to the test. Aside from all the inter-textual richness and generic fascination embodied in scene after scene of unconventional narration, the films make the condition of fighting so spectacularly enjoyable and amorally uplifting that any resonance with the contemporary situation of Hong Kong may be heard only as an aside. The national and the local are not necessarily opposite forces in the circuit of identity formation. In many ways, "the strategy of local resistance misidentifies and thus masks the enemy",[17] as the theorists of "global empire" would have it. The common field of tensions today is the specific regime of global relations under which the dream of a way out is no longer dependent on the power of national imagination but, as both *The Heroic Trio* and *Ashes of Time* show, is founded on the dislocated popular experience and sensibility, and indeed on stylistic action spectacles in the process of mediation. Thus conceived, the popular tactics of local cinematic action must be re-considered, and not be taken simply as a transition from the national to the transnational mode of identity formation.

Citing Bruce Lee, Mintz sees that in the classical situation, fighting is the art of "fighting without fighting".[18] She suggests that through the martial arts genre filmmakers have generally developed "a type of expressionistic, impressionistic style", where the use of images and landscapes is extremely significant, evoking a "total effect" somewhat like visual poetry.[19] But how would the local scenarios of cultural action or translation involve the re-negotiating and re-mapping of boundaries? It seems to me that the current discourses on (post)colonialism are to a large extent incapable of offering grounded insights to the specific condition of Hong Kong's local cultural crisis. Hong Kong works at the margin (some say at the mercy) of the red capitalist dragon that is surely to become her political sovereign, national figure, and cultural authority in the decades ahead. In this context, "self" and "other" are constantly played against each other in the politics of recognition and mis-recognition. The people of Hong Kong may still be able to uphold its integrity as a relatively autonomous community, as promised, at least until 2046. To invoke the socio-historical context for such identity formation, we might want to ask how Hongkongers have been projected, received, and tolerated as a people as they witness their community being transformed into a postcolony under the historical "One Country Two Systems" construct.

Now, what one might call "Hong Kong subjectivity" is discernible in various cultural-political forms of imagined identity the people have become familiar with since the mid 1990s. The local subjects concerned simply want to distinguish their dislocated "selfhood" historically from those whose subject-positions they do not want to, and still cannot, tolerate *now*, while reconstructing their relative autonomy as Chinese subjects in the meantime. As a result, different manifestations of "otherness" have been registered through the effective alienation of the community in transit ever since the signing of the Sino-British Joint Declaration in 1984. The ensuing power transition has given rise to a drastic shift in, or indeed a consolidation of, *sensibility*. Such changes have been evident in the public space of culture, in which various kinds of social practices are to be understood in light of the sort of repressed and repressive jubilation, as it were, brought about by impacts of the Return, following the trauma caused by the Tiananmen massacre of 1989 less than a decade before.

MEDIATION: ANTIDOTES FOR GLOBAL IMAGINARY

To understand the gap or tension between global appeals and local drives is to see it as part of a differential scheme of cultural-political flows, in which local moments of cultural action yield to the dominating forces of translation exerted by both the national and the transnational formation. On the other hand, the global moment actively draws on the dynamics of the local-national interflow in its residual, dominant, or emergent modes. As Hardt and Negri point out, "it is false, in any case, to claim that we can (re-)establish local identities that are in some sense *outside* and protected against the global flows of capital and Empire".[20] Thus, the regime of the popular can be viewed as the formation of a multi-faceted reality where cultural flows operate and exert influence on our daily actions. It is clear that throughout the development of action cinema in Hong Kong, various "glocal" moments of glory have become focal points for the film industry to foster the mobility of cultural flows: Bruce Lee, King Hu, Jackie Chan, Ang Lee, Wong Kar-wai, Yuen Wo-ping. What might be some of the specific local mappings that could be seen as resistant to global negotiations? Approaching 1997 it seemed that a new space would be necessary for invoking the local in a new post-colonial discourse. This new geopolitical condition for the practice of a postcolonial cultural space for the local in relation to the mutable calls of the national in the new global configuration of power came about with a social imaginary that was also being gradually re-inscribed into the transnational mode of cultural production and representation.

Stephen Chiau's *The God of Cookery* (1996) offers an example of how the action code is re-generated in the context of cuisine both as a game (play and contest) and a represented space for kung fu exercise in the ordinary scheme of cultural activity (cooking in this case). If we analyze the local icons in the context of specific cinematic acts of code-making, we are obliged to position Chiau's heroic figures, not as kung fu masters, but as the re-imagined fighters of daily life. The actors of kung fu are now either fully engaged in a contemporary consumerist spectator's culture such as the glocal soccer game, or casually proficient in a range of everyday practices such as the street-side performance of steam-bun making, and the boarding of a double-decker bus in a busy urban shopping area via weightless leap. In its different manifestations, the generic set-up for fighting is brilliantly re-adjusted to create maximal comic effect; in the process, the relevant terms of the fight are thoroughly re-contextualized, leading to an unforgettable re-definition of the function of the martial arts.

Thus we witness the classical spirit of fighting operating in such a way that ordinary spectatorship is drawn to share and identify with the dis-located action imaginary, in times of increasingly widespread sociopolitical crisis. For the subject of the martial action, all signs of fury and weaponry are not eliminated, but re-coded, re-presented in the open and forward-looking action narratives of the original local heroes. Though physical, Chiau's moves are never bloody or violent. The hilarious *Shaolin Soccer* (2001) offers the best case yet for Chiau's action farce; his tactics are sometimes called *mo-lei-tou* (*wulitou* 無厘頭), or nonsensical play, though they really represent the tactical attitude of "no nonsense". Digital special effects are used to pre-figure the ordinary hero (a cook, a soccer player) in the role of super-hero. These create a sense of absurdity and urgency, culminating in that shaping of sensibility which is symptomatic of the sense of disorientation found in late- and post-colonial Hong Kong society.

With the fantastic form of self-in-struggle, tensions in Chiau's comic rendition of action are fully resolved, and the audience's latent energy for local sensibility is heightened. It suddenly became clear for many of us that *wuxia* is not only useful for the common individual on a personal level (you'd eat better, and walk down the main street with a sense of pride like a well-respected consumer), but useful also on the national level (Shaolin can modernize; its skills are endlessly useful for urban life-situations such as parallel parking). Recognizing that the power of culture "is anchored in a capability to induce meaning, which makes interpretation the clue to critique", Johan Fornäs has pointed out the need for "developing an understanding of mediation between texts, subjects and contexts" as a key function in cultural studies.[21] With Chiau's films, the function of *wushu* is now made exceedingly pragmatic, and the question of *wuxia* spirit translated into the terms of instrumental value, with an eye always on making a big score under the conditions of everyday competition. Fantasy and change have emerged in a form capable of liberating ordinary spectators' imaginations and their positions in relation to the dominant discourses. Instead of nostalgia, *The God of Cookery* dwells on practices of everyday life, so that the ordinary folks living through times of great uncertainty throughout the 1990s will now be able to re-imagine the uses of power and pleasure they found in the bodily tactics revealed by Yuen Wo-ping's *Miracle Fighters* of an earlier period.

Many would agree that Ang Lee has been highly successful in his skilful translation of traditional Chinese culture for the world market of the twenty-first century. *Crouching Tiger, Hidden Dragon* (Ang Lee 2000) globalizes the circulation of conventional signs of *wuxia*, rendering them "international Chinese elements" that appeal to Western eyes. Making

Chinese aesthetics, culture, calligraphy and choreography accessible to the global market is the main strategy adopted by Lee. There are practically no untranslatable local data of any sort in the film; the director has made sure that the spectacular action flights are rendered both aesthetically and culturally approachable. The whole point is to popularize "Chinese culture" for "the world", thus re-developing the *wuxia pian* as a new transnational genre.[22] By contrast, most works made in the local cinema during the 1980s and 1990s (by Yuen Wo-ping, Tsui Hark, Ching Siu-tung, Wong Kar-wai, Stephen Chiau, Jeff Lau, and Corey Yuen) contain substantial local elements difficult to translate readily to a non-local viewer without deep and thorough cultural de-coding and re-coding. Law Kar has said that it is difficult "to pin down on the 'ethnicity' of Hong Kong cinema whether in artistic or cultural terms", even though Hong Kong cinema has been the most successful in reaching for the "world market".[23] Nonetheless, we realize that the majority of Tsui, Ching and Yuen's works would defy ready global imagination because their local sensibility is deeply rooted in popular history and imagination, drawing from a whole range of contemporary sociolinguistic accents and the sociocultural repertoire of daily life experience. The same may also be said of the action movies of Chiau, Lau, Wong, and many others.[24]

In the end, we all might agree that "[t]he martial arts affect all areas of life, either directly for the fighter, or indirectly for those who must respect the resolution of the conflict".[25] Referring to the significant moments in which conflicts have been resolved for the people through fights, an *Oriental Daily* editorial commentary signed by "The Oriental Tea House" entitled "Long Live the Chinese" stated for the local Chinese readers in 1996: "We need to think hard about why such a scene can appear only in the kung fu movie, while in real life, whenever we have a chance to fight a war, the opposite scenario would often be seen".[26] Citing the glorious history of national super-star Bruce Lee breaking "The Sick Man of East Asia" board into pieces with his famous kicks in the film *Fist of Fury* (1972), the author laments that in reality the Chinese still could not stand up and argue their case against the Japanese in the dispute over the controversial Diaoyu Islands. The ambivalent reproduction of the national-local here is an important factor to consider amid historical and political differences over the strengths and weaknesses of the postcolonial nation-state. Dreams of nationhood may indeed take various forms: there are dreams distracted and dis-articulated (Tsui Hark), dreams utterly and permanently lost (Wong Kar-wai), dreams that are either displaced and re-located (Johnnie To, Ching Siu-tung), remembered and reconstructed (Jeff Lau, Corey Yuen), or destroyed and re-invented

(Stephen Chiau) through dominant and emergent forms of localness. Action, life, movie: these may well be the enduring terms of Hong Kong's new eclectic dance.[27]

The local, the national, and the transnational may each constitute focal points for shaping the complex form of identity traces. Among the three modes of identity imaginary, the residual form of localism has existed as a part of the inherited regional cultures of various southern origins, including most importantly the Guangdong heritage.[28] This mix of local identity traces was distinctive of the formation of what might be called the Hong Kong Chineseness of the 1950s and 60s, and has since the 1970s been progressively displaced by an emergent mode which has come to constitute the core of what is now commonly known as Hong Kong popular culture. Briefly, the 1970s is now generally recognized as a period of rapid economic growth and gradual social reforms, when the colony could boast a rather rosy image of itself as one of the most prosperous cosmopolitan cities in Asia in the immediate aftermath of the local social riots in 1967. Throughout the 1980s and 1990s Hong Kong people developed through their daily life practices a local and contemporary set of identity imaginaries quite distinct from that of Chinese cities on the Mainland. Ironically, younger generations could readily recognize the colony as a home situated between a range of local, national and transnational positions.

These hybrid articulations have since resulted in the consolidation of cultural sensibilities unique in the history of Chinese modernity. Not only was the subject formation here deeply concerned with the form and substance of a new identity discourse and cultural sensibility, it has become increasingly dependent on the transfiguration of a remarkable array of social imaginaries which was to become typical of Hong Kong's location as a "post-colony" since the mid-1990s. Such a general tendency in the displacement of one mode of local identification by another may also obtain in the development of the local action genres, resulting in the predominance of localness at the expense of national imagination. By the 1980s, as Law Kar would admit: "Compared with films made in the Chinese mainland and Taiwan, Hong Kong cinema lacks national distinctiveness (*minzu tese,* or ethnic characteristics). Having been subjected to prolonged rule by Britain, local culture grew under historical conditions that were full of constraints and repressions. But this is also how the local cinema has always been left alone to feed on what it's worth, to make do constantly with a space for survival, by absorbing whatever comes along from film cultures Chinese and foreign alike".[29]

What the local imagination can attain is surely something we have yet to fully examine. During the last decade of colonial history in Hong Kong, the particular form of local eclectic consciousness has been re-articulated to the territory's moments of crisis, in which the colonial-international mode of operation worked hand in hand with the new logic of post-imperialist global order. What was the local, then, in the 1990s? It is not easy at all to unpack the cultural imaginary that has been setting limits to the condition of possibility of our everyday life. The process is today largely intertwined with the complex network of marketing needs and constraints in which much of Hong Kong's massive cultural productions operate. Such crucial factors as production apparatus, management technology, and human resource planning often play key roles in determining the particular shape and impact of a cultural text or event at issue. I am not asserting that there is some total domination of everyday life realities in Hong Kong. Rather, I would say that the form and tactics of every specific cultural act may be more fruitfully understood in relation to both its social condition of existence and its "political unconscious" working as the subtle flow of its narrative subtext.[30]

Such a critical choice may have to be articulated with the eventual possibility of Hong Kong's re-entry to Chinese modernity, or Hong Kong's re-mapping of senses and sensibility for understanding the cultural-political realities of that modernity.[31] During the last few decades, most local Chinese-Hong Kong people did not necessarily identify themselves as part of an integral community, be it the once-colonized territory, or the newly de-colonized SAR.[32] It is with the integrity of the senses that we have been concerned through this treatment of the fighting condition in examples of action cinema in late- and post-colonial Hong Kong. While developments in the kung fu mode of comedy have been unique for Hong Kong cinema, the hybridization of action cinema more widely in the 1970s and 1980s seems to have laid the foundation for the local imaginary to be articulated yet again with an acutely sensitive and ambivalent national unconscious. The contemporary Hong Kong sensibility has taken shape and taken root within such a context, drawing on but re-shaping a new dominant trajectory of the uniquely eclectic local, whose identity traces are increasingly being re-translated according to various tactics of the global imaginary in the current stage of transnational capitalism. The critical strategy, for us, has been to try and trace the trajectory of its passage by rethinking the condition of fighting as a part of our most recent chapter in action cinema history.

5

Order/Anti-Order: Representation of Identity in Hong Kong Action Movies

Dai Jinhua

In the late 1980s and early 1990s, as the reality was fast approaching that China would resume sovereignty over Hong Kong in 1997 and the power structure in Hong Kong society was beginning to experience gradual changes, a profound anguish and a sense of political powerlessness permeated Hong Kong society. At the level of cultural expression, these feelings of anguish and powerlessness became an oppressing sense of uncertain identity. While Hong Kong's colonial rule of nearly 150 years was coming to an end, the end of the cold war was giving new vigor to globalization. The nation-state was suddenly more ambiguous in meaning, weaker in the imagination, and more brittle in its geographical boundaries. Hong Kong's cultural sense of self and other was thrown into an immense tension of violent joinings and separatings, against the background of the facts that China was in rapid change but maintained a powerful central government, that the British colonial democracy was fading, that the decolonization process was in full swing in Hong Kong, and that the cold war "national" boundary between Hong Kong and the Mainland marks (in reverse) the global division between North and South, i.e., between global wealth and poverty.

Such a strong and oppressive sense of lost identity, the fear of abandonment and desire for belonging, find expression in the Hong Kong film industry at its height and particularly in action movies, often called "Tsui Hark Films" by Mainland film critics.[1]

First appearing were *Dragon Inn* (Li Wai-man 1992), *Swordsman II* (Ching Siu-tung 1992), *Burning Paradise* (Ringo Lam 1994), the series *Once upon a Time in China*, and other movies based on Jin Yong's novels. Next came the huge commercial success in Hong Kong of the series *A*

Chinese Ghost Story and the movie *Green Snake* (Tsui Hark 1993). Also extremely popular were Stephen Chiau's movies, with their distinctive Hong Kong local flavor, often called "*mo-lei-tou* (*wulitou*) Films" ("無厘頭" 電影, films of absurdity or "rubbish films"). Superior to the "Tsui Hark Films" or new martial arts movies, John Woo's "Hero series", also called "Fashion Gunfight Movies" (時裝槍戰片), brought unprecedented fame and glory to the Hong Kong film industry. At the same time, with Jackie Chan as the paramount hero and trademark, the "Police Story" series ("警察故事" 系列) and the *Young and Dangerous* (蠱惑仔) series popular in the 1990s elevated Hong Kong style cop-and-robber movies and gangster movies to the international arena and then brought global recognition.

HISTORICAL BACKGROUND

In the history of Chinese film, *Dragon Inn*, *A Chinese Ghost Story*, and Stephen Chiau's movies in traditional settings all belong to a special subgenre in Chinese films — "*guzhuang baishi pian*" (classical-costumed tales of anecdotal history, 古裝稗史片). In such films, the story is one of ancient times as understood by popular tradition. But the emergence of the *guzhuang baishi pian* was not something special to Hong Kong movies of the 1980s and 1990s. Rather, it is a recurring cinematic phenomenon in the history of Chinese film, popular in stifling times of social upheaval, times of anxiety and uncertainty. I call this phenomenon of recurrence the "transmigration" of *guzhuang baishi pian*. If we say that the *guzhuang baishi pian* are an effective way for popular culture to reorganize the pre-modern Chinese social life experience into modern culture, we can then say that the first wave of the *guzhuang baishi pian,* the supernatural martial arts movies popular just after the revolutionary setbacks in 1927, offered people at that time a way to escape from and replace the difficult reality during a time rife with social and identity crises.

We can look at the issue from the perspective of another branch of Chinese popular culture: the new martial arts fiction that arose in the late Qing and early Republican Era. By re-articulating the common binary themes of "Order/Anti-order", "Law/Outlaw", and "Orthodox/Unorthodox" in pre-modern Chinese narrative, the new martial arts fiction opened up a new discourse on the value of the individual and on the existence of imaginary space. Undoubtedly, this was one of the social and cultural functions of the earliest *guzhuang baishi pian,* supernatural martial arts movies. The new martial arts fiction voiced the intellectual's dream of being a roaming chivalrous swordsman, representing the modern transformation of the Chinese literary tradition and a tangled link between the literati and the mass culture. On the other hand, the new martial arts movies (*guzhuang baishi pian*) have developed closely along the lines of interest of urbanites and mass culture.

The main characteristics of the Hong Kong martial arts movies of the 1980s and 1990s are the re-adaptation and mockery of the historical anecdotes portrayed in Chinese fiction. There is an intertextual relationship among the different genres such as prose fiction, television drama, and cinema. Hong Kong martial arts movies also look back to supernatural *guzhuang baishi pian* in earlier Chinese film history. The earlier *guzhuang baishi pian* took their themes from pre-modern Chinese drama, folklore, vernacular short stories or *huaben* (話本), storytelling or *pingshu* (評書), storytelling to the accompaniment of stringed instruments or *tanci* (彈詞), essays on miscellaneous subjects or *bijiwen* (筆記文), and the novels and martial arts fiction (new and old styled) of the Ming and Qing periods. In the 1930s when Shanghai fell to the Japanese occupation and became an "isolated island", the first transmigration of the *guzhuang baishi pian* took place. This subgenre was then already a re-remaking of the classical themes. The *guzhuang baishi pian* have formed a very popular subgenre of films especially for overseas Chinese, originating with the Tianyi / Nanyang / Shaoshi Film Studio which operated in occupied Shanghai and then in Southeast Asia and Hong Kong. In view of the political and cultural separation between mainland China and Hong Kong in terms of film developments after 1949, one would not be surprised to see that the *guzhuang baishi pian* have become a prominent and even characteristic element of Hong Kong film.

However, we must point out that as in the last two decades of the twentieth century the *guzhuang baishi pian* phenomenon in Hong Kong became a series of variations on specific older films, carrying a strong post-modern nostalgia. Outside of art films such as *Time Flies* (Yim Ho 1984), *Center Stage* (Stanley Kwan 1992), and *In the Mood for Love* (Wong Kar-wai 2000), the nostalgia evinced is not a sentimental yearning for bygone days, but rather a negotiation of many layers of significance involving belonging/abandonment, order/resistance, and identification/rejection. The film *Burning Paradise* seems to return to the original splendor of the early supernatural *guzhuang baishi pian* by tracing a "Century of China". *Dragon Inn* was a remake of the famous movie *Dragon Gate Inn* (1967) directed by King Hu, with a substantially new script. The new "Wong Fei-hung" series, *Once Upon A Time in China*, perfected the Hong Kong film convention of a unified plot following the experiences of one main character throughout. While paying tribute to the politically "orthodox", the "mainstream", and the "(new) order", these films also focus directly on the recognition of Hong Kong identity and its dilemma. The absurdist *mo-lei-tou* (*wulitou*) films, mainly featuring Stephen Chiau, are a revealing part of this wave of quasi-nostalgic remakes. The so-called "Stephen Chiau Films", such as *King of Beggars* (Gordon Chan 1992) and *The Chinese Odyssey Part One and Two* (Jeff Lau 1995), are full of local Hong Kong elements, profaning and mocking the Mandarin of the original films with long and delirious Cantonese speeches, thus creating a text of deconstruction and cynicism in an atmosphere of carnival.

GLOBAL/LOCAL MARKET

If we look at the history of *guzhuang baishi pian* transmigration from the perspective of the film industry, in addition to the social and cultural perspectives, we can observe that this transmigration serves as the connecting point between the global market for Hollywood films which was established after the First World War, and the local Asian film market. In the late 1920s, Tianyi Film Studio began the trend of *guzhuang baishi pian*, and was successful in markets outside China: Southeast Asia, the South Pacific, and overseas Chinese communities worldwide. Targeting Hollywood as the chief competitor, the early supernatural *guzhuang baishi pian* became a successful vehicle for oblique social messages, avoiding direct confrontations while evoking real problems and dilemmas. The *guzhuang baishi pian*, with their fresh "Oriental"/Chinese features, later grew into a genre specially dedicated to these outside markets. Similarly, the golden age in Hong Kong films is marked by its challenge to the Hollywood film industry on a global scale by taking over huge profits from the Southeast Asian film market.

Regarding Hong Kong films of the last twenty years of the twentieth century, one relevant factor is that in the mid-1980s, the Chinese government began to allow outside film studios to enter the Mainland to shoot scenes and to "co-produce" films with Mainland film agencies, thus opening up the Mainland film market. This development has meant some reorientation of the mass culture products of Hong Kong and Taiwan film and television studios in search of markets.

What has most attracted filmmakers and television program producers from Hong Kong and Taiwan are the vast natural resources and cheap labor resources. The Chinese government's decision to lift the ban on film and television crews from outside China made it possible to film on-site scenes in *guzhuang baishi pian* — the Gobi Desert, the ancient silk road paths, the temples, and the imperial palaces — in a relatively economical way. At the same time, these film crews benefited greatly from two things: the fact that the Mainland film industry had been at a low ebb since the mid-1980s, and the large number of well trained martial arts professionals, which provided outside film crews with another cheap and rich human resource. Even though the so-called "co-production" of the films was a way for the Beijing censors to control content, it also provided opportunities for Hong Kong studios (other than the Hong Kong *Yindu Jigou*, a Mainland front organization stationed in Hong Kong) to enter the Chinese film market on a large scale. So for the first time the Hong Kong film industry, which had already taken over the Southeast Asian film market, began to consider the potentially huge box-office profits in the Mainland. If we say that the approach of 1997 prompted the fusion between the historical sense and the present-day consciousness shown in Hong Kong films, then the attraction of the Mainland box-office profits also demanded that in order to lure Mainland viewers, the Hong Kong film industry had to retain its qualities of "pure entertainment" and ideological non-commitment. Also, the co-production of a film meant certain compromises with the Mainland film review board, which meant that the Hong Kong films with an eye for the Mainland market would have to conform to orthodoxy. Such elements involved in filmmaking reinforced in a way the tension between order and resistance, between identification and rejection in the Hong Kong films, particularly the "Tsui Hark Films".

The Mainland government holds the view that allowing outside film companies to enter China to make films is a way to save the slowly collapsing Chinese film industry. At the same time, as a component of Beijing's international cultural and diplomatic strategy, allowing outside film companies to make films in China is a measure of China's "openness" or (to use another image) China's entering the world market. Whatever the motives behind the new policy, it provided official and legally permitted channels for the mature and unique mass culture of Hong Kong films to enter the Mainland cultural mix. Before this policy change in the mid-1980s, Hong Kong films and Hong Kong popular culture could only be accessed on the Mainland through the many illegally installed television antennas in the Pearl River Delta pointing toward Hong Kong, through the many producers and distributors of pirated videotapes, and through the circulation of numerous "aberrant" magazines and newspapers. Even though in the 1980s Hong Kong popular culture was already flooding the Chinese landscape, Mainland official culture still regarded Hong Kong culture as alien and peripheral, as "a piece of background music remote and pleasant to the ear".[2] This "background music remote and pleasant to the ear" served as an excellent close-up demonstration model in structuring the Mainland popular culture industry and stealthily helped transform Mainland social ideology. As the 1980s ended and the 1990s began, Hong Kong movies, though not huge in quantity, almost completely took over the Mainland film market, winning an unprecedented victory at the box office through the legal channels of film co-production. This victory signifies Hong Kong popular culture's official entrance on the Mainland sociocultural stage. Albeit displaced into the position of a latecomer, Hong Kong took its place as one of the most prominent features of the fantastic mosaic of the Mainland cultural scene in the 1990s.

HISTORICAL MASQUERADE: ORDER AND THE RESISTANT "INDIVIDUAL"

In the late 1980s and early 1990s, the setting for most Hong Kong martial arts movies was the late Ming Dynasty or the late Qing Dynasty, when each dynasty was struggling against collapse. The difference is politically significant. To favor the late Ming is characteristic of the new martial arts fiction, particularly the stories by Jin Yong. To favor the late Qing period, on the other hand, is rather troubling, because the "barbarian" non-Han rulers of the Qing empire are seen as less legitimate than the Han Ming rulers. This choice among thrones in the context of the current conventional understandings of the past amounts to a choice among conceptions of the modern Chinese nation-state. In the practical logic of mass culture, this scheme is an effective approach to narrative, perfectly understood both by the filmmaker and the audience. (The first joint-venture film between Hong Kong and the Mainland, *Shaolin Temple* (Zhang Xinyan 1982) was set in the historical background of the high Tang, which like the Ming was a glorious and Han-dominated era.)

The late Ming was a time of an empire falling apart and besieged by internal and external catastrophes; such a setting is full of significance for a film audience. The enemies in the film stories set in this time are often eunuchs who have deceived the Son of Heaven, or heretical evil elements who have usurped the emperor's power, or non-Han forces aspiring to conquer China. The protagonists rise to fight against the evil or the invasion, to protect the imperial power and restore order. But such films often omit what is known to all the viewers — the imminent fall of the Empire. Further complicating matters, the Emperor remains off-stage in most such films, and the evil forces are nominally his agents. Hence even as the protagonists defend the true Imperium, they can be seen as resisting the magistrates in power. On the other hand, the late Qing as a historical setting for a film narrative, with its ambiguous imperial orthodoxy (the minority Manchu nationality ruling the majority Han nationality), grounds a more complicated dialectic between order and resistance among various parties, such as revolutionaries whose goal is to drive out the barbarian Manchu and restore Han China, foreigners seen as agents of aggressive imperialist invasion, and sworn brothers who live by the ethical code of the martial arts.

If we put the Hong Kong *guzhuang baishi pian* side by side with two similar sets of films made on the Mainland from the early 1990s to the present day, the ideological significance of such rendering becomes even clearer. One of the latter is the film series "Assassin", for instance, *Song of the Emperor* (Zhou Xiaowen 1995), *The Assassin* (Chen Kaige 1998), and *Hero* (Zhang Yimou 2003). The other is a group of television programs about the Qing dynasty (*Prime Minister Liu Luoguo, Yongzheng Empire, Kangxi Empire, Kangxi in Disguise, Iron-Mouth Ji Xiaolan,* and others). In "Assassin", although the main narrative is the attempted assassination of the first Chinese emperor, the focus is on the Qin Emperor as a positive symbol, rather than on the assassin. The 1980s film script for the film *Song of the Emperor* was titled *Blood Built,* referring to the building of the Great Wall in which millions of people died. But when it was finally filmed and released in the mid-1990s, it was renamed *Song of the Emperor.* Similarly, the entire plot in Zhang Yimou's film *Hero* is about giving up the opportunities to assassinate the Qin Emperor. The various television series moved their historical setting back from the late Qing to the High Qing period.

One of the social and cultural functions of the new martial arts fiction is to provide narrative and imaginative space for individuals in the social transition from the pre-modern to the modern. In American Western movies, the protagonist kills the bad guys, helps the weak, and departs alone, gloriously and by preference. Such an ending celebrates living outside the social order. By contrast, in the Hong Kong action movies, particularly in the *guzhuang baishi pian,* when the hero departs alone on a horse, the sad implication is one of self-exile and a sense that there can be no home to return to. In other words, in Hong Kong movies it is his own individuality, rather than the nation or community, that burdens the protagonist. Such conflicts between order and resistance, society and the individual, are fully expressed in John Woo's hero films, with their outstanding portrayal of the sworn brotherhood of traditional Chinese culture. But this narrative model is lopsided and dissolved in Wong Kar-wai's post-modern space and Stephen Chiau's absurdist carnivals.

WOMEN WARRIORS DEPARTING

In view of the history of Chinese films, one of the prominent characteristics of the Hong Kong action movies of the late 1980s and early 1990s is that the image of the woman warrior, which always occupied an important position in the *guzhuang baishi pian*, has been pushed to the backstage. What has replaced it is an increasingly re-enforced male world. The male gender has become the only gender for the resolution of social identity and individual crises.

In fact, throughout the history of Chinese films, the woman warrior is a very distinctive figure. Whenever there is a woman warrior in a film, she is never a secondary character, but almost always the dominant focus. And in contrast with the gender assignments in Hollywood or other major commercial films in the West, although the female image (a woman warrior) is an object of the male audience's gaze, she is very rarely an object of desire for the male protagonist. She not only comes to the assistance of other female characters in trouble in the film, but also helps to save the male protagonists. The plot schema "beauty saves hero" makes the image of a woman warrior socially subversive and transgressive. The image of the woman warrior in films bears the influence of the woman warrior in traditional Chinese drama and the influence of the novel *A Chinese Romance*, which wildly exaggerates the stories of women warriors. Still, in most of the films in which a woman warrior is the main character, she can be the action hero, savior, and a person of power, but she cannot gain social acceptance in her world. Like the cowboy of the American Western, she can establish a certain emotional involvement with the male protagonist, but she will eventually act as a go-between for the match between the male protagonist and another woman whom she has helped, and then she will depart with a sword in her hand. We can read such an ending as a surpassing and abandoning of the social order and the gender order codes; but if we put the ending within the contextual structure of the film, such an ending looks more like an exile, or at least a suspension. In the martial arts movies, the fact that the male protagonist meets a martial arts master and becomes his disciple is an important step for him on the path of growth. When he finishes his training and leaves the mountain, he becomes a completely self-governing subject and a hero. Whereas in the woman warrior films, the moment when the woman has finished her martial arts training and becomes a master is the moment when she has given up her gender identity and earthly life. In other words, the completed woman warrior has become an all-powerful and otherworldly saving force, alien to ordinary social existence, serving as an Other for the imaginary world of the audience.

In other films in which the woman warrior is not only the action hero but also the subject of desire, she can eventually become the mate of the man she loves (although after this happens she loses interest for the audience). In order to achieve such an ending, the entire film has to be built on double or more than double structures of masochism. For it to be fully legitimate that the male protagonist is both the object of her desire and the beneficiary of her help, he often has to be placed in a paralyzed and helpless state, both real and metaphorical. If the audience identifies with the male protagonist, they too will have to go through a masochistic experience. Alternatively, in order to gain her love, a woman warrior must go through torture, misunderstanding, and other tests much more severe than a male protagonist would have to face. In order for the audience to identify with the woman warrior's actions, they must also have a masochistic appreciation of her experience.

In a sense, woman warrior films constitute a subgenre of Chinese martial arts films. They reflect fast changing and turbulent times, the pressure of a reality in which there are no ways out and no solutions. These films become a vehicle of transference for those who feel politically powerless and helpless. There are two modes: 1) the woman warrior is a savior from the outside, thus providing an imaginary solution to real life problems, or 2) the pressures of real life are transferred to a masochistic choice and pleasure.

Perhaps this interpretation can explain the disappearance of the image of woman warrior in the Hong Kong action movies of the late 1980s and early 1990s. It is my view that during this time Hong Kong movies, particularly the action movies, try to address issues of identity and power between Hong Kong and China, at least at the level of the political unconscious. The hero in the action movies and the martial arts movies tends to represent Hong Kong and the self. In the conventional power scheme, the female is a weak figure on the margin, so for the protagonist representing Hong Kong to be female would cut too close to the quick. On the other hand, Hong Kong's painful experience and sense of political powerlessness came from forces external to Hong Kong society: the British government's abandonment, and the Mainland's heavy-handedness and overwhelming force. Such outside powers produced multiple rifts in the Self/Other power relationships, and in the Chinese identity that had been taken for granted although not highlighted in the past. Therefore, the imaginary savior from real predicaments could not be an external, alien image in the form of a woman warrior. Rather, salvation had to come from within the male hero himself, as he gathered potential strength from despair to wage a life-and-death fight against a decidedly superior force.

In fact, in the Hong Kong martial arts movies, one narrative element necessary in the martial arts plot — the suffering of the main protagonist[3] — has faded or disappeared as well.[4] The reason is no doubt similar to the reason for the disappearance of the woman warrior, but other influences are at play here. For one thing, Hong Kong's post-modern writing is full of jest and mockery, a mode that does not easily bear the melancholy and "solemnity" that is required in the narration of a suffering protagonist. Also, Tsui Hark's films glorify the aesthetics of violence, and their market requires a rapid succession of action scenes. Substantial description of suffering by the protagonist would slow the narrative and has to be eliminated.

THE "INDIVIDUAL" AND GENDER RHETORIC

If we place the action movies of the 1980s and early 1990s in the context of local Hong Kong mass culture, we find that these movies both continue and break with the traditional gender descriptions in Hong Kong martial arts fiction. The quintessential works of Hong Kong martial arts fiction are those by Jin Yong. Departing from previous martial arts writing, Jin Yong used a main theme in modern Western fiction: the story of a man growing up, searching for his father, and killing his father. A basic characteristic common to Jin Yong's works is the original fatherlessness of the protagonist and his search for his father. The protagonist usually takes as his father or master an evil man, and later comes to recognize that his father or master is evil. Jin Yong's romance stories also often show clear traces of a son's Oedipal love for his mother. Recent gender theory involving global anticolonialism and decolonization shows that in colonial and post-colonial cultures the "Father" and paternal power are seen as symbols of the colonizing metropolis, whereas "Mother" often represents the native land, the ancient country before colonization, or the future nation-state to be established after gaining independence.

Jin Yong's novels written in the 1950s and 1970s reveal the political unconscious of the Hong Kong colonial and anti-colonial experiences. His novels have been a continuous source of material for other products of mass culture. However, an important change in the gender rhetoric of films based directly or indirectly on Jin Yong's work among the *guzhuang baishi pian* of the late 1980s and early 1990s is the disappearance of the plot described above, in which a son finds an evil father and then comes to recognize this evil. In these films, fatherlessness becomes a pre-existing or *a priori* personal/subject identity of the protagonist. If abandoning the growing-up theme affirms the subject or personal identity of the protagonist and suspends the anti-colonial and decolonial implications in the narrative, it becomes more interesting to observe the gender rhetoric about the female or "mother" in these films. In many Hong Kong films, including mainstream movies, action movies, and even art films, a common theme is a son's searching for and then killing his mother. The most characteristic of these films are *Days of Being Wild* (Wong Kar-wai 1990) and *The Day the Sun Turned Cold* (Yim Ho 1995). The former shows a son desperately searching for his birth mother, only to stop short at her door and leave without meeting her. The latter shows a symbolic matricide by a son when he finally testifies in court that his mother murdered her husband.

In the *guzhuang baishi pian* of the late 1980s and early 1990s, another feature of the gender rhetoric is misidentified gender or gender ambiguity. The eunuchs in the late Ming stories became symbols of both order and rebellion, while their identity as neither male nor female is a traditional characteristic of "evil spirits". In the film *A Chinese Ghost Story* (Ching Siu-tung 1987), the tree spirit ("Grandma") has a changeable voice — sometimes male, sometimes female — showing the spirit's position as authority and evil spirit, as both patriarchal and matriarchal power. A tree is inherently a phallic symbol, but the tree spirit's ability to suck and devour represents a castration threat by the matriarchal power. A tree a thousand years old, with its twisted roots and gnarled branches, fully demonstrates the complicated relationships of rejection and identification with the expressions of order and resistance, political community, and individual identity. Another example is the Hong Kong movie *Swordsman II*, which is based on Jin Yong's novel *Swordsman*, with several important changes. In the novel, the main story line is that the hero, a martial arts disciple disowned by his master, fights to regain the trust of this father figure. In the film version, the character called "Dongfangbubai", a minor character in the original story, becomes the main character. In the original story, Dongfangbubai castrated himself to become a eunuch in order to work in the imperial court — recall that a eunuch is an evil spirit in traditional gender rhetoric. In the movie *Swordsman II*, Dongfangbubai is played by the famous female star Brigitte Lin and thus is identified by the movie's viewers as a "male" pretty woman. The "male" pretty woman Dongfangbubai overshadows the "authentic woman" Ren Yingying, the hero's sworn sister, in a comically ambiguous gender position. As played by Brigitte Lin, Dongfangbubai operates both as the male protagonist's opponent and as the object of his questionable desire, turning the entire movie into a playful take-off on Jin Yong's original Oedipal story. Dongfangbubai, as an image of misidentified gender and gender ambiguity, works as an obstacle to the male protagonist's firm grasp on his own identity. The movie, by excising the "search-for-father" storyline and suspending the love story to incompleteness through gender ambiguity, makes it difficult to locate the expression of identity in the individual's position. The expression of identity can only be accompanied by Stephen Chiau's absurdist ecstasy and cynicism, by the aesthetics of violence and the strong brotherhood in "resistance in despair" shown in John Woo's movies, and by the post-modern imaginary space and nostalgia in Wong Kar-wai's movies.

FILLING AND REBUILDING

It can be said that the Hong Kong action movies of the late 1980s and early 1990s are effective expressions of, and imaginary solutions to, the identity crisis in Hong Kong society before and after the 1997 handover of Hong Kong to China. Interestingly, such movies became central to the early 1990s Mainland cultural market. In symbol and subterfuge, Hong Kong action movies gave expression to the idea of rejecting Mainland political power. However, throughout the 1990s, Mainland mass cultural development wholeheartedly welcomed and identified with Hong Kong and Taiwan social and popular culture. Such a phenomenon enabled China to locate itself in the process of rapid globalization. Hong Kong and Taiwan popular culture not only serve as models and forerunners for the Mainland production of popular culture, but also work to fill gaps and construct transitions for the ideological collapse and discursive perplexities in the transformation of the Chinese social system.

If we say that Hong Kong action and martial arts movies were introduced to the Mainland film market as "mere stories" and "mere forms", separated from their original contexts of production and reception in Hong Kong to meet different understandings and imaginings on the Mainland, we can also say that the cultural expression of estrangement and suspension in the Hong Kong movies of the late 1980s and early 1990s became, on the Mainland, the best carrier for post-June-Fourth-1989 cynicism and nihilism about reality and history. The ambiguous and painful sense of "no man's land" for individuals as shown in Hong Kong action movies provided an effective imaginary hide-out for Mainland young people who had experienced the June-Fourth governmental repression and felt they had no place of refuge. Indeed, in the early 1990s mainland

China was in an ideological vacuum, following the political shutdown and the serious wounds and disruptions of the June-Fourth event. Chinese society went from a broad opening in the 1980s to a sudden closing after 1989, complicated by the ambiguous international political situation following the fall of the Soviet Union. After June Fourth the dream of democracy or at least reforms in the Chinese political system was suspended. The articulation of the cruel fact of the widening division of Chinese social classes was forbidden. Chinese society sank deep into a voiceless identity crisis. The vacuum and crisis in the Mainland found absurd though accurate expression in the popular movies of Hong Kong. The multiple layers of identification versus refusal, order versus resistance, in the Hong Kong martial arts films took on new meanings in the Mainland. In the name of "co-producing" films with Hong Kong companies, Mainland filmmakers turned the *guzhuang baishi pian* into an alternative to the officially approved mainstream films. Such was the cultural reality in Mainland society in the early 1990s.

In addition to the showing of Hong Kong action movies in Mainland theaters, the current trend is for the Chinese audience to access these movies through pirated VCDs and DVDs imported from Hong Kong, and also by downloading from the Internet. The *guzhuang baishi pian* shown in Chinese cinemas had at first served to fill an ideological vacuum on the Mainland. But through the 1990s, Hong Kong and Taiwan popular culture gradually came to occupy the mainstream of culture on the Mainland, becoming one of the most active constructive forces in commercial consumer ideology and popular culture. The popularity of Hong Kong films has been a cultural preparation for the individualism fomented by global consumer culture. Whereas at the beginning of the 1990s, the Hong Kong movies popular in the Mainland cinema worked as an imaginary space and cultural release for the real and spiritual post-June-Fourth-1989 pressure, they soon became a reference for the self-identity and self-expression of Mainland young people growing up in the fragmented and ineffective ideological space between the imagination of globalization and local reality.

A certain aura of "late-comingness" surrounds the arrival and popularization of Hong Kong (and Taiwan) popular culture on the Mainland. But the Mainland's coming late to these films is not simply a matter of China's being a latecomer to the process of modernization. For one thing, the time difference is more complex. Movies that appeared simultaneously in Hong Kong are shown successively on the Mainland: first Tsui Hark's films, and then John Woo's films, to be followed by Wong Kar-wai's films and "Stephen Chiau films". Grouped in this way, the films are more intelligible to the Chinese market. This phenomenon can be seen as a local trace in the new ideological construction, or as an interval of imaginary solution to the dilemmas of commercialized individualistic expression.

Perhaps we can view the interactions of mass culture production and consumption in Hong Kong, Taiwan, and mainland China, even the whole of East Asia, as one of the movements in the localization of a global spectacle. In this way, the cultural realities within the Mainland and the rest of the region are the local spectacles of globalization. A different cultural landscape is formed by the movies of Jackie Chan, John Woo, and Ang Lee, and by the rise of South Korean films and Korean popular culture (which is also called the "Korean Wave"). But I shall address this topic on another occasion.

Translated by Zhang Jingyuan

Part 2

Action Cinema as Contact Zone

6

Genre as Contact Zone: Hong Kong Action and Korean *Hwalkuk*

Kim Soyoung

SPECTERS OF COMPARISON

The South Korean cinema has recently won attention on international film circuits in the form of either the art cinema or the blockbuster in the Korean mode. The commercial releases of *Chunhyang* (2000), *Memento Mori* (1999), *Nowhere to Hide* (1999), and *Shiri* (1999) in North America as well as in Asia and Europe mark a new momentum for the Korean cinema. *Chunhyang* is an art house film. As a teen horror film, *Memento Mori* invites cult fans locally, at festivals, and on the art-house circuit. *Nowhere to Hide* and *Shiri*, however, are action movies. For the last few years action movies featuring gangsters have been topping the box office in Korea. This is unprecedented. Hitherto, action cinema or *Hwalkuk* survived at the margins of the film industry, which had largely sustained itself by privileging melodrama, comedy, and female spectators.

The Hong Kong–Korea connection was formed in the late 1960s and has persisted to the present day. The 1970s were a pivotal time when two modes of connection were established: co-production (including funding, use of locations, co-directing, and mixed casts) and generic appropriation. Hong Kong action itself resurfaced in the Korean market toward the end of the 1980s with the release of *A Better Tomorrow* (1986) and *As Tears Go By* (1988) as "Hong Kong Noir". Recent Korean hits like *Shiri* (1999) and *Nowhere to Hide* (1999) were repeatedly compared to Hong Kong action movies when they were released in America. *The Village Voice* describes *Nowhere to Hide* as "an ongoing series of epic foot pursuits that transpire so breathlessly that a slow-mo swashbuckler like Chow Yun-fat would be left wheezing in the rain".[1]

Overall, Korean cinema has been marked by three golden ages: the mid-1920s to the mid-1930s; the mid-1950s to the 1960s; and from the late 1990s to the present. The colonial period (1910–1945) provides a contour of the "national" cinema to come. The following two golden ages are, respectively, marked by modernization and globalization. The experience of Korean modernity, propelled and fractured by Japanese colonialism and Americanism, presents itself as a Medusa's head to those intriguing questions about modernity that have been haunting contemporary minds both in the West and the rest of the world. In fact the impacts of modernity on non-Western nations such as Korea reveal a topology of the uncanny (*unheimlich*). As Freud demonstrates, *heimlich* is a word whose meaning coincides with its opposite, *unheimlich*,[2] and the uncanny aptly gestures at a site of psychic reality known as colonial double consciousness.[3] The colonial double consciousness tends to telescope different temporalities and spatiality into something else.

The anguish-ridden and experimental Korean modernist/surrealist writer of the colonial era, Yi Sang, was possessed by this double consciousness. He often wrote that he was not able to think of Tokyo, New York, and Paris without thinking of Seoul, or Seoul without thinking of Tokyo, New York, and Paris. Yi was undoubtedly an elite modernist writer. He read Baudelaire, greatly admired René Claire and Jean Cocteau, and always wanted to go to Paris. In order to get there, as a colonized subject, he traveled first to Imperial Japan. However he was arrested in Tokyo for being seditious, and was detained there until his death in Tokyo University Hospital in 1937. Around the same time, Na Unkyu, a legendary director whose films such as *Arirang* (1926) attracted numerous moviegoers with anti-colonial sentiments, made *The Wild Rat* (1927), an action movie or *Hwalkuk*. This genre had been introduced as a part of the Japanese Shimpa mode of theater and film by Korean directors like Na Unkyu and other Japanese in Korea. In *The Wild Rat* Na appropriated the action code of *Hwalkuk* to enable a group of young Korean vagrants, known as "The Wild Rat", to fight a rich collaborator who works with the colonialists and aims to marry a local girl, taking her from her poor fiancé. This is a sort of primal scene of Korean action movies — a young boy gazing at a local girl abused by colonial authority. The film mobilizes its critique by appropriating the colonial modern form of representation and enacting a rescue fantasy on the part of a group of male vagrants (not yet gangsters). A crime of justice follows; winning applause from an audience whose status is not in any sense better than that of the wild rat bunch.

This film was immediately recognizable as anti-colonial. *Hwalkuk* was a cheap amusement enjoyed mostly by male subjects during the colonial era, functioning as a site of vernacular colonial modernity in comparison with Yi Sang's Surrealism-tinted modernism. *Hwalkuk* laid the grounds for comparison in/between Imperial Japan and colonized Korea. Four decades later, the grounds of comparison shifted as Korean *Hwalkuk* encountered Hong Kong action movies toward the end of the 1960s. By then the international finance center of Asia, Hong Kong had emerged as a place to long for and emulate. The traumatic colonial past excluded Tokyo as an ideal choice, and US cities were already inside Seoul through places like Itaewon and Yongsan (the US military bases located in the heart of Seoul). For most people, restrictions on travel overseas during the era of military rule excluded the possibility of satisfying this fascination by actually going to Hong Kong. At the same time, the second stage of the state-led economic development plan (1967–1972) emphasized the importance of foreign investment capital in order to facilitate an export-driven industry. There was a need to open up and to look outside without jeopardizing the borderlines drawn by the cold war. In/between the official restrictions on overseas travel and the need to open up to a certain degree, the neighboring city-state of Hong Kong came into the popular consciousness as a new, accessible other.

While South Korea is at the southern end of the Korean peninsula, North Korea borders China, blocking access to the continent from the South Korean perspective. The pervasive cold war mentality paralyzed both the capacity and desire to move beyond the border. In this state of confinement, movies with location shoots in Hong Kong entertained the desire to transcend the walls of the Cold War, and cinema substituted for the endlessly deferred travel beyond the border, especially for male subjects at the margins. Action movies of this kind were shown at theaters in poor neighborhoods, where the poorly paid, the lumpen-proletariat, and high school dropouts were the regular audience. The dominant movie form of the 1970s was melodrama, and in particular the hostess melodrama, films about fallen girls who had migrated from the countryside to Seoul to work in factories but ended up as bar girls. In contrast to this genre, which showed the dark side of Korea's economic development, action cinema often tended to opt for the state ideology to reclaim the marginal male and incorporate him into the industrial labor force.

After the early 1970s, the fever for location shooting gradually faded, and the popular Hong Kong action movie series *One-Armed Swordsman* (first released in 1967) was displaced by the *One-Legged Man* series in South Korea. Both series obviously refer to the *Zatoichi* series (1963 to the present day) featuring Katsu Shintaro as a blind swordsman.[4] Handicapped action heroes in Japan, Hong Kong, and South Korea provide an intriguing and ironic space in which inter-Asian comparisons can be made. The one-legged man in Korean action movies is shadowed by the images of his brother figures from Hong Kong and Japan. Benedict Anderson's inspiring expression "the specter of comparisons" (*el demonio de las comparaciones*) offers a framework to illuminate the double vision and double figures in question.[5] Anderson's term is derived from José Rizal's novel *Noli Me Tangere* in which the young mestizo hero returns to the Colonial Manila of the 1880s from a long sojourn in Europe. He visits the municipal botanical gardens in Manila and sees that the gardens are "shadowed automatically — Rizal says *maquinalmente*— and inescapably by images of their sister gardens in Europe".[6] As if looking through an inverted telescope, he sees them simultaneously close up and from afar. The agent of this incurably doubled vision is called "*el demonino de las comparaciones*", which Anderson translates as "the specter of comparisons".

In what follows I would like to shift this spectral vision from the Philippines and Europe to Hong Kong, Japan, and Korea to look into action movies. Uncanny double consciousness, double vision, or double figures in the representational space are not peculiar to Korean colonial modernity and its cinema, although in that context they do have their own specific configuration (the tracing of which will, at times, require some "doubling back" in my analysis). These doubles are haunting apparitions that plague the space divided by the colonizer and the colonized over some hundred years. Shifting the focus from a doubled vision of Europe and Asia to that of Hong Kong and Korea, this essay aims to shift grounds of comparison in order to contribute to Inter-Asian cultural studies by taking a look at the Hong Kong connection in Korean action movies.

POST-COLONIAL GENRE AS CONTACT ZONE: *HWALKUK* AND ACTION CINEMA

As soon as Korean action movies catch the eye, one enters the uncanny site of a contact zone crowded and haunted by various forces. Korean action movies provide a space contested by Japanese swordplay, Hong Kong action, and Hollywood action. *Hwalkuk* ("living theater", pronounced in Japanese as "*Katsukeki*": see below) is the term used to indicate plays and movies driven by action scenes. The "*hwal*" in *Hwalkuk* is also used in the term *Hwal-dong sajin* ("moving motion pictures") used in early cinema days. In that sense, it betrays the kernel of the early cinematic form that highlights movement and action.[7] The term *Hwalkuk* has been used less since the late 1970s, and "action movie" has become a more familiar term. When *Hwalkuk* is employed to indicate a certain category of films, it now often carries an ironic, comic, or nostalgic tone. For example, the recent cult movie *Die Bad* (2000) promoted itself as *Hwalkuk. Samurai Fiction* (Nakano Hiroyuki 1998) was promoted as a comic *Hwalkuk* emphasizing bloodless samurai action. However, this essay re-employs the term *Hwalkuk* to reveal a genealogy of action movies in South Korea.

Hwalkuk is genealogically related to the Japanese Samurai action cinema introduced during the colonial period (1910–1945). Its literal meaning of "living theater" is dependent on an idea of the body, a lived experience, and commensurability between representation and the real. Korean *Hwalkuk*, an invention of Japanese colonial modernity, is then overlaid with swordplay films, Hollywood action, and Hong Kong action, as I pointed out before. It is, however, the infested and fantastic space of *Hwalkuk* that provides an arguably decolonizing choreography and landscape through the figure of the one-legged fighter acting against the Japanese authorities in 1930s Harbin. Han Yongchol (a.k.a. Charlie Shell), a taekwondo action star, played the one-legged hero in films like *The One Legged Man Returns* (1974) and its sequel (also 1974). Blatantly handicapped action cinema such as Korean *Hwalkuk* must be an amusing nuisance to add to the already intriguing constellation of transnational Hong Kong action cinema. The cluster of films constituting the Korean action cinema is a site where a process of "transculturation" is inevitably inscribed. As Mary Louise Pratt explains, "transculturation" is a phenomenon of the contact zones where subordinated or marginal groups select and invent from materials transmitted to them by a dominant or metropolitan culture.[8] What the term "contact" implies here is also friction and violent bodily encounters. The action movies indeed enable one to imagine the various kinds of contact as the screen transforms into a kind of contact zone.

The "Korean" action movie was born into this contact zone of transculturation crowded with Japanese *hwalkuk* (itself a translation of Western action in the Japanese context), the James Bond series, and Hong Kong action — a composite form of colonial, semi-colonial, and postcolonial contacts. Genre theory based upon the Hollywood model is insufficient to cope with a non-Hollywood action genre like Korean *Hwalkuk*. Genre theory tends to follow two approaches. One is the structuralist project of the 1970s, which assumes "the possibility of a 'system' of genres through a critical gesture that sought to identify the classical Hollywood cinema with a set of discrete, self-evident, and constellated categories".[9] The more recent approach is more attentive to the cultural politics of genres, considering genres in relation to other institutions as well as to other genres. Linda Williams, for example, argues that melodrama is "the fundamental mode of popular American moving pictures" and further claims that "melodrama is a peculiarly democratic and American form that seeks dramatic revelation of moral and emotional truth through dialectic of pathos and action. It is the foundation of the classical Hollywood movies".[10] However, territorial nation-bound claims (for Hollywood, in this case) about the genre and the mode bypass the trajectory of transculturation that genre encounters as it travels outside America. And such claims also fail to account for the incorporation of non-Hollywood generic components, such as the Hong Kong martial arts film, into Hollywood.

Removed from the constraints of genre analysis, *Hwalkuk* action cinema is the product of various cultures and involves contingent, violent, and surprising negotiation on the signification level. For example, a Japanese *Shimpa Hwalkuk* entitled *Pistol Burglar Shimizu Sadayoshi* was translated into Korean and made its theatrical debut as *Six Bullets Gun Burglar* (*Yukhyopogangdo*, 1912). Later, Na Unkyu appropriated the action codes of *Hwalkuk* in *The Wild Rat* (1927) to allow a bunch of young Korean men to avenge themselves against a member of the colonial power. *Hwalkuk* resurfaced in the 1960s as "Continental (*Dairyuk*) *Hwalkuk*". Set in Manchuria, Shanghai, Harbin, and the borderlands between Russia and Manchukuo, Continental *Hwalkuk* mostly depicted the Korean independence army resisting the Japanese colonial authority.[11] The Continental *hwalkuk* series was not highly regarded either by critics or the general audience. During this period, the auteur cinema[12] and melodramas such as *Bitter but Once Again* (*Miwodo dashihanpon*, 1968) were most popular with audiences, critics, and journalists. The audiences for *Hwalkuk* series were mostly non-elite men who frequented shabby neighborhood theaters.

While *Hwalkuk* prevailed mostly on B-circuits in the 1970s, Hong Kong was viewed as a neighboring other, an alternative to Tokyo and the West. When the contemporary cityscape of Hong Kong is evoked in such films as *Golden 70 Hong Kong Mission* (1970), it is represented as a sort of laboratory to learn the workings of capitalism and foresee a desirable future. Hence, "going to Hong Kong" was at one time a colloquial expression in South Korea, meaning "going into a state of extreme gratification". No one really knows the origin of this expression, but it aptly captures what Hong Kong evoked for local people at the time.

Although the censorship governing the Korean movie industry after 1973 was unimaginably harsh, the film industry churned out 189 movies in 1970 alone. However, the actual number of moviegoers dropped. In 1976, ninety films were made but none attracted over a hundred thousand spectators in Seoul, even though the population of South Korea had already exceeded 26 million. There was a general cynical denigration of Korean films, which had not been the case in the 1960s. People joked about how "a womanizer from eight provinces sowed his wild oats in Myongdong [downtown] and Hong Kong"[13] in the films of the period. Movie industry regulations promulgated in 1965 limited newly established foreign film import quotas to film companies that produced local films. Co-productions guaranteed more import quotas, which helped to propel a rush of co-productions (or, at least, claims of co-production, a point to which I will return) between South Korea and Hong Kong in particular. For instance, *Sahak pikwon* (*Snake-Crane Flying Fist*, Kim Jintae and Lo Wei 1978) credits Jackie Chan as a co-star with the Korean actress Kim Chung Ran. *Samunui Sungkag* (*Wandering Monk*, 1979) is a co-production between King Hu (Woo Gam Chuen) in Hong Kong and Han Kapjin in South Korea.[14] There was also a flood of films with "Hong Kong" in the title. Shin Kyong-Kyun directed *A Woman and a Man from Hong Kong* (1970), *Mrs. Chang from Hong Kong* (1970), *Iron Man Park from Hong Kong* (1971) and *Hong Kong Blues* (1971). Another group of films claimed various connections to Hong Kong in the 1970s.[15]

Now, whereas melodrama and comedy have been staples of South Korean cinema, the appearance of action cinema has been sporadic and tied to the use of locations such as Hong Kong, Taiwan, Japan, Manchuria, the Russian-Manchurian border, and Shanghai, most of which were sites of resistance for the Korean independence army during the colonial period. The provisional *Daihan Minkuk* [Korean] government was set up in Shanghai, and the military base for the independence army was in Manchuria.) So it is important to recognize that the shift to Hong Kong toward the end of the 1960s marks a relatively new location in the Korean people's cinematic remapping of Asia.

The Korean action films employing one-legged or other handicapped action characters as protagonists demonstrate how the post-colonial trauma of Japanese rule in Korea found its way into the 1970s action movies that succeeded the Continental *Hwalkuk* of the 1960s. Often set either in contemporary Hong Kong or in the Shanghai of the 1930s, Korean action films of the 1970s were known as *Muhyup* (that is, *wuxia*, the Chinese term for swordplay) *Hwalkuk* and appropriated the generic codes of Hong Kong action cinema to re-stage fights between Japanese colonial agents and the Korean independence army. These films are often hardly distinguishable from gangster films (and vice versa). The Korean action cinema as a de-colonizing text uses not only the generic codes of the Hong Kong action cinema but also the urban space of Hong Kong in contrast with Tokyo and Seoul. This tendency, however, ended with the introduction of the Hollywood inspired new action known as the "*Ttorai*" (Freak) series (1985–1988).

In 1970, two films, *Golden 70 Hong Kong Mission* and *Expo 70 Tokyo Frontline,* were made by the same director, Choi Inhyon. A composite of action (*Hwalkuk*), propaganda, and thriller, the films laid bare the anxieties that prevailed in the early 1970s. *Golden 70 Hong Kong Mission* is categorized as an anti-communist *Hwalkuk* and *Expo 70 Tokyo* is simply categorized as anti-communist propaganda in the Korean Film Archive database. The State-led economic development begun in 1962 moved into a second stage after 1967. To modernize infrastructure, the military regime sought foreign investment capital and internationalization despite maintaining blocks on overseas travel. The rivalry between North and South Korea was used to propel the modernization program. This tension between internationalization and containment is translated into two texts in particular, *Golden 70 Hong Kong Mission* and *The Men from Eight Provinces* (*Paldo Sanai*).

Golden 70 Hong Kong Mission pays obvious tribute to the Bond film *Goldfinger* (1964). The film's protagonist has the code name G07. In *Goldfinger,* 007's mission is to stop a plan to take over the global gold market. In *Golden 70 Hong Kong,* the good-looking Korean agent (G07) acts in alliance with a Korean-American agent (Richard Han) to stop Chinese, North Korean, and Hong Kong gangs who come to Hong Kong to get hold of a counterfeiting plate they plan to use to forge US dollars. In the opening sequence, a man is looking down at the Hong Kong harbor at night. He soon discovers that a man carrying a briefcase is following him. He tries to stab the man who is tailing him, but accidentally kills a Hong Kong woman instead. This kind of misrecognition and misidentification — mixing up South Korean, North Korean, and Chinese and Hong Kong people — creates both a fiasco and a platform in the film. A Hong Kong gangster's moll undergoes cosmetic surgery to look like an agent from China. G07 and the Richard Han character cannot identify each other until the last sequence. The spectators' recognition of differences among North Korean, South Korean, Korean-American, Chinese, and Hong Kong people is purely dependent upon the plot, which is slippery at best.

In spite of the fact that *Golden 70 Hong Kong* is a propaganda film backed by an indirect government subsidy but it barely serves state ideology. This is due to its incoherence and the sloppy citations of the 007 series instanced in the use of sound, props (a James Bond-style briefcase), and a seductive and fatal Bond girl (she turns out to be a North Korean agent) who falls in love with G07. In the end, G07 turns down an offer from the North Korean agent who now possesses the counterfeit plate to flee somewhere other than two Koreas. G07, incompetent as an agent, is determined to tell her that they should instead go back to South Korea. At that moment, the male North Korean agent kills the female North Korean agent. Upon his arrival in Seoul, G07 confidently tells the Korean scientist and his granddaughter who have spent the last seven years in Hong Kong after being kidnapped by Chinese gangs, "You will be surprised! Seoul is an international city now!" In command of the whole film is Richard Han, the Korean-American agent whose gaze upon Hong Kong opens the film. Relying upon the Cold War mentality and the state of emergency imposed upon South Korea at the time, *Golden 70 Hong Kong* affirms the dependence of the South Korean nation-state on the US. Hong Kong is in the end a detour to re-affirm that fact.[16]

In addition to casting Hong Kong as a cosmopolitan background, the other direction of 1970s action cinema is towards the incorporation of marginal male subjectivities into the state apparatus. The Park Chung Hee military regime heavily regulated and directed the movie industry to back up its modernization and decolonization projects from the early 1960s to the late 1970s. In these circumstances, the *Hwalkuk* series provided a way to summon marginalized male subjectivities to perform patriotic decolonizing missions against Japanese rule. As they successfully perform this "historical" mission, they are legitimated. However, decolonization was not always in sync with state-led industrialization. Historical events like the joint agreement between South Korea and Japan in 1965 — primarily to facilitate state loans from Japan — provoked nationwide demonstrations. Modernization and industrialization required capital, but decolonization in the form of popular memory did not sit well with capital from Japan. Popular resentment of this kind has resurfaced in films like 1999's *Phantom: The Submarine*. The disjuncture between industrialization and decolonization left indelible traces in action films, such as the impaired action heroes like Charlie Shell (Han Yongchul).

After the liberation of 1945, South Korea was in a neo- or semi-colonial relationship with the US. When the US Army occupied the heart of Seoul (Yongsan and the Itaewon area) and the northern border leading to the mainland of the Asian continent (China and The Soviet Union) was blocked by North Korea, the evocation of spectacular places like Manchuria and the borderlands, and the display of virile male bodies moving beyond the Korean peninsula should have created an empowering viewing experience for non-elite male spectators of the time. However, in the vast landscape the impaired action hero harks back to the sense of confinement working at the local level. In the Continental *Hwalkuk* of the 1960s, the wandering expatriates, criminals, and gangsters armed with fists and pistols and expelled by the colonial regime are hardly distinguishable from the soldiers of the Korean independence army in Manchuria, who are barely uniformed. Furthermore, diasporic Koreans could not reveal their identities for fear of the Japanese police. Thus, mistaken identities among Koreans often spark fights which in the end facilitate reaffirmation of homosocial bonding or kinship, based on ethnic nationalism in the midst of Manchuria. Characters from the Continental *Hwalkuk* continued to appear in the 1970s when the term *Hwalkuk* was replaced by either *Muhyup* (*wuxia*, or swordplay) *Hwalkuk* or simply rendered as "action movies". The main setting for these action movies shifted from the continent to South Korea, Hong Kong, and other parts of Asia such as Taiwan and Japan.

Meantime, the series entitled *"Paldo Sanai"* (*Men from Eight Provinces*, 1969–1991) was more explicitly focused on local affairs. The series features an outlaw from Chola Namdo Province (a most marginal area), who defeats seven outlaws from seven provinces that excel in various martial skills. Once they are bonded by brotherhood, the leading character persuades them to live according to the law by joining the labor market either as a porter, a vendor, or some other form of manual laborer. When a potential gang fight looms in the second episode, a cop suddenly appears and tells the leading character not to commit a crime. The gentle cop in his stylish trench coat even gives the main character from Chola Namdo Province money for a new start. In the period of state-led and condensed industrialization, it is not difficult to detect the necessity of transforming unorganized but virile male bodies into industrially useful ones. The *Men from Eight Provinces* series also reveals that the parochial regionalism pervasive in the eight provinces is an obstacle to be overcome in the effort to subject the people to the state. Male subjects at the margin are not available as labor power for industrial capital; their agricultural background does not equip them with the skills required for industrial labor. They are a reserve labor force at best and certainly unthreatening. In one film in the series, *The Return of the Men from Eight Provinces* (1969), the leading male character's miserable living conditions are most pointedly expressed when he works as a porter and sets out to deliver a heavy box to a professor who did her PhD in Paris. His subalternity is accentuated by the contrast to the luxurious living conditions enjoyed by the female professor. *Men from Eight Provinces* is meant to resolve the local problems created by regional differences, class differences, and a scarcity of jobs for unskilled labor in the midst of state-led modernization. Their muscular bodies remain in/between the agricultural and the industrial.

Along with *Golden 70 Hong Kong Mission*, the films that involve Hong Kong as a setting are *Hong Kong Blues* (1971), *Madame Chang from Hong Kong* (1970), *A Woman and a Man from Hong Kong* (1970), *A Blind Man with a Cane in Hong Kong* (1970), and *A One-Eyed Man in Hong Kong* (1970). As I noted earlier, the motif of the handicapped action hero as a protagonist was inspired by Zhang Che's *One-Armed Swordsman* (1967) series and, more obliquely, the Japanese *Zatoichi* series (1962–1989) about a blind swordsman played by Katsu Shintaro. The latter's role as a source could only be indirect: the Zatoichi series was not accessible to local audiences due to the banning of Japanese popular cultural products in South Korea. It was Jimmy Wang Yu's role as the one-armed swordsman that found its counterpart in Charlie Shell (Han Yongchul) as the one-legged man in the *One-Legged Man* series (1974).

Shell, professionally trained in taekwondo, assists the independence army in Harbin during the 1930s. In the first picture of the series he cuts off his own left leg in remorse over the accidental killing of his lover's brother in a resistance fight against the Japanese army. But in the second picture of the series, it is the Japanese army that amputates his left leg. Next, he confirms national pride as he defeats a Japanese karate gang and a kung fu master in *The Successor* (1974), set in Hong Kong. The handicapped male hero is quite a new kind of (anti)-heroic figure in Korean film history. Along with the *One-Legged Man* series, there are other action films employing handicapped action heroes and heroines, such as *Sokyangae Ttonagata* (*Leaving in the Sunset*, with Oh Jimyong as a one-armed hero, 1969), *Piyonmaengyoe* (*Flying Swallow Blind Woman*, Kim Jisoo as a blind swordswoman, 1969) and *Palopnun Komgaek* (*An Armless Swordsman*, 1969), and *Uiriae Sanda* (*Live in Justice*, 1970) — a contemporary version of *The One-Legged Man*.

In addition to the generic appropriation behind these action movies, it should also be mentioned that it was quite common to see injured war veterans on the streets in the 1970s due to the Korean War (1950–53) and the Vietnam War (1964–1973). Often these men begged for money by telling stories of these wars in public places. Therefore, handicapped action characters with super powers might have certainly created an ironic resonance with male spectators of the period. Stephen Teo points out that the *One-Armed Swordsman* series is historically related to the Cultural Revolution in China and the riots in Hong Kong against British colonial rule around the same time. In a word, the series expresses the wish to be able to start all over again and be re-strengthened.[17] According to this logic, it is not too difficult to imagine the *One-Legged Man* series and other films with impaired action characters as harking back to the Korean War, the Vietnam War, the partition, and the authoritarian regime. One has to start all over again, but with a fractured body just as with a partitioned nation.[18]

Except for Charlie Shell, Korean action stars are mostly represented as natural born street fighters without professional training. The absence of training scenes in Korean *Hwalkuk* is a notable difference from Hong Kong kung fu movies. The *sifu* (teacher) figure in *wuxia* is replaced by a big brother type, who offers a pseudo-familial tie to other male characters, instead of providing physical training. The learning process is not incorporated in most of the action movies of the 1960s and 1970s. The heroes in these films are full-fledged male heroes from the very beginning. Real heroes are presented as having acquired fighting skills through the steer fights they experience as often as possible. For instance, Kim Doohwan and Sirasoni ("baby tiger") provide models for street fighter-type gangsters or, preferably, fist fighters (*jumok*). The two are legendary gangsters who became resistance fighters against the Japanese authorities. Sirasoni is believed to be an especially powerful kicker. The story has it that while he worked as an errand boy for the resistance army, he had to board moving trains in order to smuggle goods for the army in Manchuria. As opposed to some Hong Kong action films that privilege training at the beginning of the film, male heroes in Korean action films pride themselves on learning from street fights. Often, these characters reaffirm their power by defeating karate, taekwondo and kung fu experts. Even today, TV series continue to worship them.

Returning to the issue of co-production, the Korean film industry hurried into co-productions with Hong Kong-based film companies after the Korean release of *Fists of Fury* and *Enter the Dragon* in the early 1970s. In 1978, Hong Kong director Lo Wei co-directed *Sahak Pikwon* with the Korean director Kim Jintae. Jackie Chan starred in the film. In 1979, King Hu co-produced *Samunui Seung Gaik (The Successor to the School)*. The co-production trend was firstly due to the popularity of Hong Kong movies triggered by Bruce Lee and Jackie Chan. Secondly, however, the government's film regulation and promotion policy also promoted this kind of co-production. It encouraged international festival participation and co-production by allowing the producers of such films to import more foreign films. In *Sahak Pikwon* Jackie Chan is dispatched to the *jianghu* underworld by his *sifu*, a Buddhist monk, to find a killer who stole a precious text from eight masters after developing the new Snake Crane

Flying Fist martial art technique.[19] The Korean actress Kim Chung Ran (Gam Ching Lan in Cantonese), who is trained in taekwondo, joins Jackie Chan in his search. The Korean actor Cho Chun, known as "Twin Lights" because of his shiny bald head, makes a brief appearance as Jackie Chan's opponent. There are scenes which indicate that the outdoor sequences were mostly shot in Korea. The Yi dynasty-style royal tomb site stands in for the mythic space of China. The released video version available in Korea undoubtedly shows Jackie Chan as the leading hero. But the synopsis offered by the Korean Film Archive database tells a different story, in which the Buddhist monk Jikong from Koryo-dynasty Korea is the hero. The synopsis, based upon the information provided by the film production company, informs us that the film is set in the Chinese Yuan dynasty period and that Jikong from Korea triumphs in a martial arts competition held in Yuan China. Thus he becomes the leader of eight schools that collaborate to write a book of Snake and Crane martial art techniques. Upon its completion, however, the book is stolen by a masked man. A young man, Su Yin Fung (Jackie Chan), causes a stir when the lost book is found in his possession. Finally, the Buddhist monk Jikong reappears to sort out the chaos. The reason why there is a marked difference between the released video version and the Korean synopsis is transparent: to secure the import quota and make it appear that the film foregrounded a local hero in the middle of China. But more symptomatically, something else can be read in the film.

Korea's sovereignty in the period before Japanese colonial rule was continually undermined by China. Toadyism is a national stigma, which still troubles the mind of Koreans. Thus China, unlike contemporary Hong Kong, brings forth this collective memory. Co-production with contemporary Hong Kong offers an ironic way to compensate for the historical trauma in relation to China. Location shooting in South Korea transforms a local landscape into a Chinese landscape as if it were mythic.[20] Quite unwittingly, the background of the film — the landscape and the setting — uncovers an involuntary memory that comes from the pre-modern past. In *Sabak Pikwon*, Jackie Chan fights in front of Yi dynasty royal tomb sites. For Korean audiences it is very difficult to miss these settings because they are favorite picnic places.

This is marked as a moment of double consciousness and doubly coded space. Re-presentation of the "real" Korean landscape as mythic China in Hong Kong-Korean co-productions of the 1970s in particular yields a convoluted, fantasmatic, and hybrid space.[21] This is a turn that echoes Anderson's example of the sister gardens in Manila and Europe but with a twist. The double vision operative in the film is an accidental decolonizing process akin to unconscious optics, but nonetheless inhabited by historical specters.

CONCLUSION: SPECTERS AND *HWAL*

Korean action movies are indeed populated by various specters, sister gardens, uncanny double consciousness, and double visions that evoke not only the colonial relation but also an emergent other like Hong Kong. The movies with impaired action stars (such as the *Zatoichi* series, the *One-Armed Swordsman* series, and the *One-Legged Man* series) offer contact zones where alleged East Asian modernity presents itself as marred but as possessing, nonetheless, a hint of a promise for a new start.

The "*hwal*" in *Hwalkuk* means an energetic bodily movement that is closely related to the form of early cinema in the translation "*Hwaldong-sajin*" ("moving motion pictures"). In contrast with power (*kwon-ryok*), *hwal-ryok* signifies vitality. Vitality is the form of energy directed against authority: "It is not non-violence that fights against power, but vitality. Vitality is not the opposing power but the anti-power. It is not centripetal but centrifugal power".[22] The *hwal* (vitality) component in action movies has this potential of the anti-power. One of the propaganda *Hwalkuk* from the 1970s set in Manchuria quite unexpectedly takes up this direction. Three gangsters in *Undo the Chain* (1971), after becoming inadvertently involved with the independence army, refuse their duty to serve the national cause, and set off for places unknown. They refuse to take up national/ethnic identities even though the leader of the independence army implores them to stay, and they disappear into the plains of Manchuria.

The uncontrollable vitality (*hwal*) lurking in action movies that can be traced back to the early form of cinema seems to have potentials that explode the baggage of the historical and the exhausting colonial legacy. Catastrophe? Indeed. But it does not necessarily end in destruction.

7

Hong Kong Action Film and the Career of the Telugu Mass Hero

S. V. Srinivas

Indian cinema's Hong Kong connections can be traced by examining two distinct but related aspects. On the one hand, there is the circulation of Hong Kong action films locally, within industrial and cultural contexts that are distinctly "Indian" in the manner in which an import travels down the chain of distribution/exhibition and becomes available for local audiences/appropriations in the process. In this essay however I focus on the other aspect of Hong Kong action film's circulation, the other connection so to speak, that of how locally produced *films* are impacted by the import. I confine the discussion to the examination of Telugu cinema.[1] Much of this essay is devoted to the understanding of Telugu film, its specific dynamics and history. However, the story I have to tell may not be unrelated to the concerns of those interested in Hong Kong cinema. I suggest that the juxtaposition of Telugu and Hong Kong film underscores the shortcomings of analytic frames that operate under the assumption that Hollywood is the norm and every other cinema requires a separate theory.

What the new frame will be is not entirely clear to me, but it certainly cannot be a version of "exceptionalism" or the "cinema of attractions" argument. Exceptionalism is a familiar problem in the Indian context, where the eminently justifiable demand to take formal and historical specificity into consideration is often conflated with an indefensible claim that a given cinema, say Telugu cinema, is unique and like no other. Similar claims could of course be made of most other non-Hollywood cinemas, especially those that are invested with considerable political or national significance. Exceptionalism also suggests that there is a contradiction between a given instance of the cinema and the filmic (that function of the technology of the cinema and film form, which is a part of a global history) as necessary foci for the study of cinema. David Bordwell's ingenious resolution of this seeming contradiction, in *Planet Hong Kong: Popular Cinema and the Art of Entertainment,* is noteworthy. He declares, "At the limit, all popular film becomes a 'cinema of attractions' ... and the plot simply a pretext for the real *raison d'être,* the parade of spectacles".[2] Having thus situated Hong Kong cinema within the broad category of the popular film, he supplies the contexts of production and reception. However, the context is unnecessary in his own framework where film is "the parade of spectacles". Context therefore presents itself in the book as a gigantic footnote meant for those who are curious to know what this strange object called Hong Kong cinema is all about.

Part of the difficulty in dealing with the circulation of Hong Kong action film in Andhra Pradesh has to do with the excess of what may be viewed as influence. As with other parts of the world, it was the success of Bruce Lee's *Enter the Dragon* (Robert Clouse 1973), released across the state between 1976 and the early 1980s, which inaugurated the era of Hong Kong action films in India. Although the imports have been restricted to kung fu films and action comedies and their economic worth is negligible for the Hong Kong industry, the list of influences is indeed long and varied.[3] In a recent interview the Telugu film star Srihari, who played the lead in the martial arts film discussed at some length below, stated that he decided to become an actor after watching his first Bruce Lee film.[4] From the 1980s, generations of stars have invoked the Hong Kong action film by performing their own stunts and simultaneously claiming to be trained in East Asian martial arts. Individual Hong Kong films were remade locally, namely *Hello Brother* (E. V. V. Satyanarayana 1994), which is based on *Twin Dragons* (Tsui Hark and Ringo Lam 1992). The Telugu female vigilante film of the 1990s draws as much on Western and indigenous "cowgirls" as the female fighting stars of Hong Kong. Yet it is possible to narrate a history of Telugu cinema, as has indeed been done time and time again, as if Hong Kong cinema did not exist. This happens not only because each Indian cinema can be claimed by an exceptionalist argument but also because of the banality of influence: Indian cinemas have always borrowed from every conceivable source and the English film press in India expends considerable energy in "exposing" unacknowledged borrowings. Even if originality, or its contemporary equivalent intellectual property right, is not an issue, tracking influence might degenerate into the "disdainful engagement" with the popular. Of immediate consequence for my argument is the fact that Telugu cinema has remained more or less unaffected at the level of narrative by the numerous borrowings from and remakes of Hong Kong action film.[5] In lieu of a thorough substantiation of my claim, I examine the recent Telugu martial arts film, *Bhadrachalam* (N. Shankar 2001), which is unusual for two reasons. It is among the few full-fledged martial arts films ever made in Telugu but is also a film that remains faithful to the Hong Kong kung fu films from the late 1970s and 1980s in narrative terms. *Bhadrachalam* draws attention to an interesting connection between Telugu and Hong Kong films, one that renders insignificant possible thematic similarities between the two.

Contradicting my claim about *Bhadrachalam* being an example of the rather direct influence of Hong Kong action film on the local industry, the film actually invokes the Jean-Claude Van Damme star vehicle *Kickboxer* (Mark DiSalle and David Worth 1989) much more explicitly than any Hong Kong film itself. There are sequences in *Bhadrachalam* that are quite clearly drawn from *Kickboxer*. Further, those involved in the making of *Bhadrachalam* are reported to have said that the film is based on Van Damme's *Bloodsport* (Newt Arnold 1987) and *Kickboxer*. I do not wish to defend my claim by pointing out that these American films were in turn inspired by the Hong Kong action film.[6] While this is in fact the case, I prefer to ignore this history for the purposes of my argument. Indulging in what would seem to be a sleight of hand at this stage of the analysis, I propose that the direct invocation of *Kickboxer* and the absence of a similar gesture towards any particular Hong Kong film are evidence of the banality of influence. The tracking of influence is misleading because it often draws attention to what is trivial and consequently obfuscates the processes at work in the act of borrowing.

Bhadrachalam's importance lies in the nature of its gesture towards the Hong Kong kung fu film. I will show that the gesture, devoid of any direct quotations, is aimed at working out problems within the generic category, locally known as the mass-film, to which this film belongs. These problems, related to representing the star protagonist, had accumulated since the mid-nineties. Before to I go on to the analysis of the film however, a brief history of the mass-film.

The mass-film is an industry term that refers to star vehicles of a specific kind that emerged in the 1980s.[7] The mass-film is what Paul Willemen calls a "production genre" in that the label "tells us how a film's profit-making potential has been calculated into its very design at the production stage by the way it adheres to or varies from a generic formula".[8] The mass-film involves big budgets and major stars and, as the name indicates, attempts to cater to the widest possible spectrum of the film market. For a variety of historical reasons, the mass-film became identified with a set of themes but more importantly, modes of spectatorial address and a political mandate.

The genre emerged in the early 1980s after the successful entry of the then superstar N. T. Rama Rao ("NTR") into politics.[9] Its appearance in the wake of NTR's crossover resulted in the mass-film's inheritance of his political plank, the assertion of linguistic identity, in interesting ways that I will return to later. The mass-film mobilizes the masses, via the star-protagonist, against the enemies of state and society. The genre is the site of contradictory tendencies. On the one hand films like *Khaidi* (A. Kodandarami Reddy 1983) launched a populist critique, by way of vigilante actions, against figures representing feudal authority. On the other, the mass-film also included anti-urban/ruralist melodramas (for instance *Mangammagari Manavadu*, Kodi Ramakrishna 1984) which in the 1990s resulted in the nostalgic reconstruction of a benevolent feudalism in films like *Pedarayudu* (Raviraja Pinisetty 1995).

In the early 1990s the mass-film increasingly gestured towards the struggles of empowerment of the lower class-caste population, at times representing these struggles with a surprising degree of sympathy, notably in *Mutha Mestri* (A. Kodandarami Reddy 1993). By the mid 1990s however, the mass-film was in a serious state of decline and it was only towards the end of the decade that the genre was revived. *Bhadrachalam*, made in 2001, is one of the more successful attempts at reworking the mass-film's mandate as the most important Telugu genre for working out what M. Madhava Prasad calls the "aesthetic of mobilization".[10]

In the 1980s and 1990s, the mass-film's star-protagonist, quite often a city slum inhabitant with roots in the village, became identified with the local. This identification was not so much because the genre dealt with the politics of linguistic identity in any direct way but because it inherited the mode of representation of the star from an earlier era. This was a mode that made the star-protagonist the bearer of a *history*, which was available to the *spectator*. The interesting relationship between the star and the spectator, who was presumed to know, ensured that the mass-film always presented itself as a highly localized genre (although it was not uncommon for hits of the genre to be dubbed into other south Indian languages or be remade in other languages casting equivalent stars).[11]

I will stay with the issue of the star and *history* for a moment. *Kathanayakudu* (J. Hemambaradhara Rao 1969) names the star-hero (NTR) of the film as the protagonist by using a voice-over narrator in the sequence introducing the character. The pre-credit sequence shows the villains killing an honest schoolteacher and going on to collect money from the public in the dead man's name. Towards the end of the segment, the villains laugh maniacally after they have collected the money. The voice-over narration states that this is the story of every village and city, even as the scene shifts to show a panoramic scene of an unnamed city. "A hero [*kathanayakudu*, literally protagonist] is needed to confront this [evil]", the narrator says, just as there is a freeze frame of NTR walking on a road towards the camera. The film's title appears, labelling the character as the protagonist.

The process of naming ensures that a spectatorial investment is made in the hero at the very moment of introduction based on an implicit trust in the narrative, but it is a trust based on the spectator's awareness of the character's *star* status. This man is going to bring justice and we can trust him to do so *because* he has a history — he is NTR. I suggest that the fact of his being NTR and the spectator's awareness of it is essential for the production of an addressee who is marked by an identity that is named as a *linguistic* one, which is the foundation for Telugu cinema's engagement with the politics of linguistic identity. *Kathanayakudu* foregrounds a process that was already at work in Telugu films of the period by drawing attention to it.

At this point it would be useful to situate the specific story of Telugu cinema in a larger context. The complex interconnection between cinema and politics in Andhra Pradesh (and other southern Indian states) has to be understood in the light of the much more fundamental link between cinema and politics. Ashish Rajadhyaksha argues that:

> a crucial value of a political order is added on to … the baseline of the cinema — the unambiguous, unshakable *fact* that, in one sense, the camera's point of view and hence of the projector, can be nothing more than the view of the actual viewer, and the ensuing *need* to let the viewer recognize this, and then to reassert, acknowledge, this fact at various points in the narrative suturing process. At this level, therefore, when the viewer purchases a ticket, enters the auditorium and "releases" the film saying, "I am here" ("I am present … I help it to be born"), what the cinema is doing is to incarnate one of the most fundamental, if ambiguous at times, rights of democracy.[12]

The imbrication of Telugu cinema with the politics of linguistic identity resulted in the politicization of a narrative strategy (naming the star, offering him for spectatorial investment) which, being a narrative strategy, is available for dissimilar deployment by the Hong Kong industry. As a result of the particular ways in which the Telugu film industry used the strategy, even where there was no explicit reference to the question of linguistic identity NTR star-vehicles could claim to address a linguistic community on the ground that the star himself *embodied* the politics of identity. This embodiment was a consequence of spectatorial foreknowledge and therefore a specifically cinematic way of dealing with the question of identity. Further, the naming of the character as the protagonist-saviour has the effect of producing the history of the star as if it was his *manifest destiny*. Why is character X the saviour? Because (he is a star and) we can trust the star to resolve the crisis. *Therefore* the star is marked by destiny (no other reason is given) to resolve the crisis. This particular notion of manifest destiny facilitates, at the level of the plot, the unfolding of revenge dramas or the accomplishment of superhuman tasks.

The mass-film made infrequent direct references to questions of linguistic identity (it didn't need to because it had NTR's crossover behind it). It nevertheless managed to claim a certain *nativity* or local specificity through the deployment of the star. The mass-film laid emphasis on intertextual references (to the star's biography, earlier roles, names of his earlier films, etc.) as a way of consolidating the existing link between the star's history and the production of the local.[13]

Without going into the details I would like to state that over the past decade or so, in the face of militant Indian nationalism, regional cinemas, particularly the Telugu, Tamil and Kannada cinemas, which have a complex relationship with the politics of linguistic identity/nationalism, have been burdened with the difficult task of finding a new balance between the two kinds of nationalisms. It is no longer viable to posit an antagonistic relationship between linguistic nationalism and Indian nationalism, but at the same time the increasing demands of the latter can only lead to the greater need for the elaboration of the local (linguistic identity, cultural specificity). It is beyond the scope of this paper to go into details of how the industry has attempted to grapple with the situation. But a consequence of the demands of Indian nationalism is the *crisis in the mass-film at the thematic level.*

There is another level at which the mass-film faced a serious crisis and that has to do with the manner in which the star was represented. I will return to this after a brief discussion of the film. It is interesting to note that in *Bhadrachalam* both levels of the crisis in the mass-film are addressed, and the invocation of the kung fu film is crucial to both. The film opens with a renowned master of taekwondo, Parasuram (Vijay Chander), being insulted and assaulted by his student Suraj (Gazar Khan). The master vows that he can produce a hundred martial arts experts. The master has a heart attack due to the scuffle with Suraj. His daughter (Sindhu) goes to their ancestral village to sell land to raise money for the master's treatment. Here she meets Bhadrachalam (Srihari), an honest and hardworking man who helps her overcome the threat from her greedy uncle Pichayya (Narra). She realises that Bhadrachalam is the kind of student her father is looking for and asks Bhadrachalam to come to the city, but he refuses to leave the village. His elder brothers, who feel he has unnecessarily picked a fight with Pichayya, a powerful landowner, throw Bhadrachalam out of his house. Bhadrachalam travels to the city in search of the master's daughter but loses the address when two petty crooks pick his pocket. The petty crooks realize that they can manipulate the simple Bhadrachalam, and without his knowledge they turn him into a slumlord and organize a thriving protection racket. Gangsters (who have lost their protection business due to Bhadrachalam) attack and injure him. The master's daughter discovers him in the hospital and the master spends the money collected for his treatment on Bhadrachalam. Bhadrachalam recovers and begins to train in taekwondo. He goes on to beat the master's bad student Suraj and become India's representatives at the Asia level taekwondo competitions in Bangkok. Suraj is also on the team. An industrialist's daughter (Rupa) takes a fancy to Bhadrachalam and has her father sponsor his trip to Bangkok. In Bangkok she is rebuffed by Bhadrachalam and joins hands with Suraj who is already plotting Bhadrachalam's downfall with the help of the gangster (Vijay). Bhadrachalam is unable to reach the stadium in time for the competition because the gangster and his men attempt to kill him. When he does arrive he finds Suraj getting ready to represent India. He tells Suraj that the nation is greater than either of them and that he should fight to win. Suraj realises that Bhadrachalam is the better martial artist and sends him into the ring. In the finals Bhadrachalam defeats the (racially white) Korean fighter while the entire nation watches on television.

The film is divided into three distinct segments united by the opening fragment (the injury to the master). Segment One introduces Bhadrachalam and serves to recall the history of the mass-film's rural variant. Segment Two takes the story to the city but also extends the recap of the mass-film and brings us to the most significant element of the genre which is its use of the city slum and urban criminal to lay out a framework for working out the politics of representation. Segment Three presents the alternative to the mass-film and proposes a new career for the mass hero. The first two segments simultaneously trace the history of the mass-film and critique the genre as well as the mass-hero. In the last segment the emphasis is on the hero's successful entry into what may be called the global circuit from which he is able to represent the nation. Further, the global itself emerges as a location in which all antagonisms in the space of the village and city are rendered non-existent.

Interestingly, it is to place Bhadrachalam in the global circuit that the film invokes the Hong Kong kung fu film (via *Kickboxer*). The opening fragment in which the master vows to produce a better student than Suraj frames the narrative well within the conventions of the kung fu film, which often involves the training of the hero in order to correct or avenge a historical wrong. This invocation by *Bhadrachalam* certainly addresses the mass-film's thematic shortcomings. The historical wrong is of course the insult to the master but also the mass hero's political career.

The introduction of Bhadrachalam is typical of the mass-film's elaborately crafted introduction of the star-protagonist. Even before we see his face — which is hidden from view — we know that the star has arrived. In fact, the actual introduction of the star occurs in the credit sequences when we are shown multiple images of Srihari attired as a martial artist leaping in slow motion. There is a freeze-frame and the image is labelled Real Star Srihari (Real Star, Srihari's honorific title, appears in English).

Segment One thus begins with the showing of the saviour — the spectator recognizes him as the one the master is looking for, and he proves it soon enough by saving a boatload of people. He, like other mass heroes, is marked by destiny. But the significant difference between this film and earlier mass-films is that this marking is not enough — as it turns out he has to become something, he has to be trained. The emphasis on training, already indicated in the opening fragment through the master's vow to produce a better fighter than Suraj, as the means of entering the global circuit makes a great deal of sense in the context of the new kind of labourer India now exports — the software programmer. Critics have commented upon the growing importance of the non-resident Indian (NRI) and the space of the "global" for imagining the Indian nation. While this film does not address the NRI, it retains the centrality of the global for the production of a nation free of antagonisms. The global itself is presented interestingly in the Asian championship event prominently featuring a *white* Korean (possibly a response to *Kickboxer*'s more-Thai-than-Thai Van Damme). But the white Korean is evidence of the importance the film attaches to the space of the global, which quite obviously is marked by its whiteness. Bhadrachalam has to take on the white man in order to announce his arrival in the global arena.[14]

Bhadrachalam's natural career, it would seem, is to clean up the village or the city — spaces he occupies at different points of time in the film. But that career is rejected. In fact, an indication of the illegitimacy of the mass hero's conventional role is evident from the manner in which Bhadrachalam's short stint as the urban criminal is presented. This phase of his life is an elaborate hoax played by the pair of petty crooks who mislead him into believing that he is actually ridding the city of slumlords. The spectator is fully aware of the trick and the entire segment is presented in a comic light, preventing any spectatorial investment in the hero's temporary job.[15]

I suggest that this rejection is an indication of the increasing inability of the mass-film to address the difficult relationship between the local and the national — the action has to move into another space in order to free the genre of the earlier mandate of the mass-film to represent the obstinacy of the local — which refused to be reduced to the national and drew attention to itself as that something that Indian nationalism had to acknowledge. This is not to suggest that the film does not pay attention to the local. The first two segments of the film in different ways signal the importance of the local. Segment One is not only set in the countryside but also contains a song sequence praising the village (the song starts with the words *Ide Naa Palletooru*, meaning "this is my village"), which is presented as an object of nostalgia — our hero has to move beyond this space. However, an interesting sequence in Segment One underscores the adherence of *Bhadrachalam* to the conventions of the mass-film with reference to spectatorial positioning and the production of the local. The sequence deserves close attention. Pichayya, before a large gathering of villagers, refuses to permit his niece to sell his brother's land. Bhadrachalam tells Pichayya that he is wrong to do so. Pichayya slaps Bhadrachalam for interfering in a family matter. Bhadrachalam slaps him back. Pichayya's sons are infuriated by Bhadrachalam's action and signal their toughs to attack him. A fight ensues. Playing with spectatorial expectation, Bhadrachalam slowly and deliberately salutes the ground (like a trained wrestler), folds up his dhoti and unbuttons his shirt. The sequence in slow motion is about 20 seconds long and is accompanied by the film's signature tune including significantly the chant "Bhadrachalam" on the sound track. He is seen from different directions — members of the crowd are watching him perform the actions. When he salutes the ground, there are three shots in which he is actually saluting the camera (the salutation is done over ten shots), as if Bhadrachalam is seeking the blessings of the spectator before the very first fight of the film breaks out. This sort of gesture/address to the camera-spectator is a routine affair in the mass-film.[16] What is striking is that the positions of the camera when he salutes the ground result in an identification of the crowd, the spectator and the ground with each other.[17] The spectator, the village/soil/earth and the crowd are inseparably bonded by the star-protagonist.

Similarly, the film's long climax depicting the finals of the taekwondo competition in Bangkok deploys a number of techniques used by the mass-film. Thematically, it brings together all the three segments of the film — with the village, the city slum, the taekwondo master and his daughter

situated in different places all watching the fight, along with a flag waving
crowd of spectators, prominently featuring the former villains Suraj and
the gangster, in the stadium itself. It is not merely the fact that people in
various locations are watching the fight that makes the climax interesting.
They are brought together, united, by Bhadrachalam. Half-way through
the fight Bhadrachalam, clearly inferior to the Korean fighter, falls down
and breaks his hand. Suraj, by now a strong supporter of the hero, advises
that the fight be called off. Bhadrachalam insists on going on and has his
hand bandaged. Within seconds he is brought down again. While the
referee begins to count, in various locations people (sometimes looking
directly at the camera that occupies the position of the television set) say
in both English and Telugu, "Get up Bhadrachalam." From Pichayya to
the gangster, all are united in their plea. Sure enough, he gets up eventually
and wins — but not before the boatman in the village prays to the river
and the entire crowd of villagers rushes to the giant statue of Anjaneya
(the god of wrestlers) to pray before it. While this could well be read as
fresh evidence of Hindu nationalism taking over popular cinema, it is useful
to note that by this point "Get up Bhadrachalam" has become something
of a spectatorial injunction. The river and the god are stand-ins for the
crucial relaying function performed by the spectator. For this reason the
two prayers are sandwiched by three recaps of incidents encapsulating
Bhadrachalam's progress and suffering. It is as if the spectator is being
asked to make him get up.

Through a variety of inversions, the mass-film offers itself to be read
as responding to spectatorial demands. The star appears because the
spectator wills him to do so and further, he goes on to actually
acknowledge the presence of the spectator by waving, winking to him/
her.[18] Returning to the film, river and god are only manifestations of the
irrational core of the spectator-star relationship in the mass-film.[19]
Bhadrachalam will not get up unless the spectator wills him to do so, and
within the narrative logic of the film the spectator alone has access to the
physical space and more importantly, the *power* to revive the hero.
Irrational because the spectator cannot make anything happen (of course
we know that) but significant because it demonstrates the centrality of the
spectator in making the film happen (recall Rajadhyaksha's reference to
the famous Metzian formulation, "I am present … I help it to happen").

How is the Hong Kong action film implicated in all this? At the very
outset, *Bhadrachalam*'s gesture towards Hong Kong cinema is found in
its status as a martial arts film. More significantly, the film redefines the
star-protagonist's *political career* in terms of his *performance* (in terms of
the story, the service of the nation through sport — clearly modelled after

cricket nationalism in the Indian sub-continent) rather than in terms of defeating an identifiable (class/national) enemy. The film thus draws attention to, indeed thematizes, the lowest common denominator of the genre — the star-protagonist's ability to perform for the spectator. Not withstanding its very different history, the Hong Kong kung fu film works with a very similar conceptualization of the star/actor-protagonist interplay. I would suggest that the differences between the two genres in the production of stardom draw attention to what they share in common.

I will use the example of *Snake in the Eagle's Shadow* (Yuen Wo-Ping 1978, released as *Vengeance* in India) to re-introduce the question of history and manifest destiny.[20] This film was an early hit in Jackie Chan's career, but notice how it presents him, practically names him as the protagonist. The film's credit sequence has Chan practicing kung fu before the camera against a red background. There can be little doubt that he is performing for the spectator in a direct fashion. In terms of the film's plot, this sequence might belong somewhere in the second half of the film since the film begins at a point of time before the protagonist becomes an expert in kung fu. Expertise in kung fu is his future, his destiny. Like *Kathanayakudu* and *Bhadrachalam*, the credit sequence has the intended effect of naming Jackie Chan as the protagonist of the film. In the Indian version, towards the end of the credit sequence there is a freeze-frame of Chan in an attacking position and a card reading "Jackie Chan in *Vengeance*" appears. Unlike *Kathanayakudu* and the mass-film, the star performing before the camera who is offered to the spectator as being worthy of investment is a relative newcomer. Unlike NTR he has almost no *history* of fulfilling spectatorial expectations.

According to Ng Ho, Hong Kong's kung fu comedies emphasize the image of the protagonist, not because he is a recognizable star but because he is new! In fact Ng Ho suggests that the very structure of the kung fu comedy is determined by the star's lack of history:

> The first third of the narrative is of paramount importance, since it sells the "image" of the protagonist. (This is necessary nowadays because *kung fu* comedies tend to use a lot of new faces, and writer-directors need to expend a great deal of energy on making these newcomers as ingratiating as possible.) The second third depicts the developing conflict between hero and villain. The final third resolves the conflict with a suite of uninterrupted fight scenes.[21]

It may be useful to recall the credit sequence of *The Big Boss* (Lo Wei 1971, *Fists of Fury* in India) which pictures the as yet unknown Bruce Lee demonstrating a flying kick slide across the screen. Clearly, the process of naming the protagonist and, more importantly, seeking spectatorial investment in a relatively unknown star, is older than the kung fu comedy. The point is that spectatorial expectations are not necessarily dependent on known faces. Chan and Lee in the sequences mentioned above appear to the viewer of the mass-film as if they are already major stars insofar as they have become the focus of spectatorial expectations.

However, isn't it possible that rather than being the result of the confusion of a provincial viewer, this is indeed the intended effect? As with an early NTR film I discussed elsewhere, these Hong Kong films call for a high degree of trust in the narrative.[22] In *Snake in the Eagle's Shadow* it is a while before the expectations raised as early as the credit sequence are fulfilled in any satisfactory fashion. Moreover, there is a retroactive logic in operation here — it is as if we are watching the film for the second time for we know what he will be even before the plot begins to unfold. The juxtaposition of the kung fu film and the mass-film therefore foregrounds one of the foundational principles of stardom itself. Recognition of the star is an *effect* achieved by the film and has to be worked into every film, regardless of the stature of the star. In the kung fu film and the mass-film there is a process of naming of the actor as protagonist, as the agent of spectatorial expectation, which is crucial for the effect to be produced.

Now for the training sequences, which I claim are the most important inspiration behind *Bhadrachalam*. The kung fu films of the *Snake in the Eagle's Shadow* vintage have elaborate training sequences where there is a justification of the naming process — we see the protagonist acquiring the stature that was indicated in the credit sequence.[23] The film is therefore about the protagonist becoming what the credit sequence promised. In cinematic terms, the film is about meeting the expectations raised in the credit sequence. The famous training sequences in kung fu film are important for reasons that have nothing do with what the film reduced to its plot would suggest. In the training sequence, the protagonist is seen *working*, quite literally. As a matter of fact, films like *36th Chamber of Shaolin* (Lau Kar-leung 1978) actually make a direct connection between kung fu, the work of the protagonist (in cinematic terms) and actual physical labour (by the hero due to the requirements of the story).

Given this history of the kung fu film, the borrowing from *Kickboxer* could be read as being an instance of banal influence, regardless of the fact that practically the entire training sequence accompanied by the theme song in *Bhadrachalam* is put together from scenes based on *Kickboxer*. However, *Bhadrachalam* invokes the training sequences of kung fu films because the mass-film's star had lost his ability to work: roles no longer matched up to the stature of stars and no crisis at the level of the plot was large enough for the star-protagonist. Stars no longer worked because we had seen it all before and we could not care less whether Bhadrachalam got up or not. As suggested earlier, the training of the hero is crucial for his entry into the global arena, which in turn is important for the resolution of the antagonisms in the village and the city. At the purely performative level, the star had to be seen doing something to retain the high degree of trust in him, which, if found to be misplaced, could result in the film turning out to be a financial disaster. As with the kung fu film, the training sequences are there primarily as proof that the star-protagonist is responding to the spectator's trust in him. Indeed these sequences are among the "highlights" of *Bhadrachalam* in that they are something of a novelty since stars, even fighting stars like Srihari himself, are not normally governed by the kind of authenticity and realism that the training sequence foregrounds.

Finally, what can the Telugu mass-film, a regional genre even in India, tell us about Hong Kong cinema? Specific histories do not make exceptions. Those of us who are looking at non-Hollywood cinemas have for too long lamented the inadequacy of Hollywood-centred theories of the cinema. To modify Rajadhyaksha somewhat, we don't need a theory of Telugu cinema or Hong Kong cinema but a theory of the cinema that can also account for a Telugu cinema and a Hong Kong cinema and, of course, Hollywood cinema.[24] I suggest that an interesting starting point is a juxtaposition of two so-called exceptions.

ACKNOWLEDGMENTS

I would like to thank the participants of the conference for their insights and questions. The research that went into the paper is a part of the project, "Democracy and Spectatorship in India: Telugu Popular Cinema and Hong Kong Action Film" funded by SEPHIS. I am grateful to G. L. N. Reddy, my collaborator in the project, whose work I have used here.

8

Hong Kong–Hollywood–Bombay: On the Function of "Martial Art" in the Hindi Action Cinema

Valentina Vitali

The stunt film, which first appeared in India in the 1910s with US serials, experienced a boom in the mid-1930s with the Hindi films of Homi Wadia. There are indications that the historiographic perception of an autonomous stunt genre at this time derives from the US distributors' and South Asian exhibitors' explicit use of the action ingredient as a marketing strategy. If, from this perspective, the Indian stunt film may be interpreted as an effect of the US film industry's export operation in the Subcontinent, contemporary reviews, stills, plot synopses and the movement of stunt actors reveal a connection between Hindi stunt and mythological films which was not at work in the US serials. This seemingly uniquely Hindi mix parallels an overlap between stunt films, mythologicals and pseudo-historical films that is at work in 1960s Italian "peplums". More to the point here, it also echoes the mix of action, history and myth at work in Hong Kong martial art films — even if there is no direct connection between 1930s "India" and 1960s Italy or Hong Kong.

In the 1970s, a modern action cinema emerged in India — just when it did in the US, but also in Turkey, the Philippines and other countries — that borrowed from Italian westerns and Hong Kong martial art movies, but which was at the same time unmistakably Indian. In order to account for such parallels and discrepancies, that is, in order to begin to grasp the complex relays by which generic categories circulate, it is necessary to think of film genres as structural possibilities rooted in the processes by which films are made and circulate. The symptoms of such processes manifest themselves differently, depending on the specific historical conditions that lend them substance. By way of a re-examination of the historical conditions and economic dynamics out of which a modern action cinema appeared in India in the 1970s, this paper proposes a framework within which questions may begin to be raised as to why its mode of action (its display of human physical energy) should resonate with, among others, that of Hong Kong martial art films.[1] The broader question that is raised, but not directly addressed in this paper, is: how does the array of narrative strategies at work in a film relate to the non-cinematic, strictly material processes by which the film comes to be?

HISTORIOGRAPHY AND FILM GENRE: WHEN WAS "ACTION" IN INDIAN CINEMA?

Film historians have tended to paint the history of the Hindi cinema in two broad brush-strokes: one from the 1930s, when the Indian film industry acquired its current shape, to the consolidation of the "feudal family romance", a form of melodrama also known as "the social", in the mid-1950s; and the other, from the fragmentation of "the social" into more distinctive generic bundles in the early 1970s to date. In this linear historiographic narrative, the emergence of the action film as a mainstream genre has, as a rule, been "discussed" as a *fait accompli*. The problem is not, as some film historians have put it, that the relation between one genre and another has never been addressed satisfactorily, or that the generic categories available to historians of Indian cinemas derive from European and North American cinemas, but that the nature and existence of a film genre is too often assumed from the start. Books on specific bundles of films tend to "define" genres by way of empirical lists of ingredients and similarities. Since generic differences are, essentially, structural differences, the notion of genre can be more productively formulated on the basis of two considerations: the first is that films fall under "base" and "superstructure" alike; the second, that to posit such simultaneity is not to assume a strictly synchronic relation between the two.

The Hindi feudal family romance can be thought of as a body of films dealing, in form and content, with the instauration or the refusal of a set of secular reforms centred on a notion of the individual and presented in what was, in the 1950s, the one official language of the Indian nation, Hindi. Unlike other kinds of films, Hindi feudal family romances were, and to a large extent continue to be, distributed across the national territory. They constituted the mainstream, dominant formula within what was, then, the country's largest film industry, based in Bombay. This is not to say that the Hindi feudal family romance was the only available genre. By the end of the 1920s, in Bombay at least, exhibition had become stratified, with films released first in the up-market theatres of Grant and Lamington Roads, and then traded off to suburban and mill-area halls. Whereas "socials" were seldom passed down the line, other films were.[2] In this way the Hindi feudal romance co-existed with mythologicals, devotionals, historicals and pseudo-historicals, thrillers, stunt, detective and horror films, in Hindi and other languages, as well as with foreign features, primarily from the US, Europe and, later, from Hong Kong. The display of physical energy, the "action" ingredient, has featured in Hindi cinema since the beginning in each of these types of film, including in the feudal family romance. In the 1970s, perhaps as in the 1930s, films featuring and emphasising fights and various other stunts began to be seen to deserve (critical) attention. Unlike in the 1950s, when the feudal family romance set the industry's agenda, in the 1970s films emphasising the action ingredient became constitutive of the Hindi mainstream.

Film historians have dealt with this situation in a confused way: on the one hand, the Hindi action film as it first surfaced in Bombay's first-run theatres with Amitabh Bachchan in the lead role is discussed as the outcome of a script-based production practice that, within the Indian film industry, was new and unique; on the other, these action films are understood to owe their existence, specificity and success to their star.[3] This circular argument is not unique to Hindi film historians.[4] Evidence shows that with regard to the 1970s Hindi action films and their star this is a historically incorrect account that takes its cue from a historicist model of cultural periodisation — one generic series succeeding the earlier one, one star the next. Action film and "popular culture" historians transpose onto "the star" that subliminal quality of final instance that 1960s film theory ascribed to "the auteur" or film director, initially exclusively of art cinema and then also of selected Hollywood films. Whether as *auteur*-director or as film star, within this "biographical" historical model one element of production is singled out and endowed with extraordinary powers of determination, as if above or outside the very set of tensions in which he or she, along with other elements of production, is caught. Underpinning this frame of analysis is therefore a humanist concept of the individual as independent from the historical conditions that overdetermine subjectivities, and also a notion of culture as pertaining to a different realm than the material conditions of which cultural items are the products. Since, as Peter Bürger has argued, the latter notion of culture was historically overdetermined by the rise of the bourgeoisie out of the ashes of a religiously sanctioned aristocracy,[5] the question worth asking is whether the critical shift from director to star answers a new phase in the development of capitalism and, within it, of the industrialisation of culture.

Apparently oblivious to such an eventuality, film historians remain caught in, and lend legitimacy to, the circular discourse of the film industry's marketeers, where star-value sells films and films sell star-value. Accordingly, in the literature the qualities of the star and his hero are projected onto that particular "audience" who is understood to be the films' intended market. The Amitabh Bachchan hero is "lumpen proletarian" and so, we are told, is the films' most dedicated public. Again, there is no evidence that this was indeed the case. Rather the contrary; whatever evidence there is indicates that what sets Amitabh Bachchan's action films apart from pre- and coexisting films containing or emphasising the action ingredient is precisely the fact that his films were exhibited in first-run venues patronised also by the middle-class and traditionally reserved to the mainstream melodramatic fare. Which is why Bachchan's action films, unlike contemporary, cheaper films also containing the action ingredient, made their way into respectable magazines for the English-speaking, middle-class public such as *Film World.* The invocation of "the public" in place of specific marketing strategies allows critics a further displacement into a dichotomy — "the People" and "the State" — that, especially in the context of Indian cinemas (but not only there), has been tested out *ad nauseam* in discussions of the melodrama. At this point, critical positions come to blows between those (the populist) who endow "the public" with an active, culture-producing and transgressive role, and those (the orthodox) who see the same "public" as the passive target of a monolithic notion of ideology. With criticism caught between "State" and "the public", the processes most immediately determining the films are nominally acknowledged (through the short-hand term "formula film") and dismissed (ditto). As an eminent cultural historian puts it, the film industry is "merely" handling already circulating sentiments and fantasies.[6]

This refusal to engage with even the most basic processes of cultural production and circulation while simultaneously projecting them to the circumscribed terrain of the nation is baffling, not least because it hovers around, without addressing, a tension between, on the one hand, geographic, social and political specificity, and, on the other, economic networks unproblematically assumed to be "global". Film studies has remained caught in an analytical framework that, having developed alongside specific European and US cinematic traditions, has tended to emphasise the national dimension of the cinema at the expense of the local and transnational interconnectedness of its many forms. This is the analytical framework that is still deployed today in film studies departments in universities across the world. But action cinema, however defined, emerged as a category of the mainstream sector world-wide and more or less simultaneously. It is a highly hybrid, transnational category, the national and regional forms of which retain distinctive characteristics. This is particularly true of the Hindi action cinema of the 1970s, and there may well be good reasons for critics to regard the Indian State as one of the factors determining the shape of Hindi cinema, as most do. Yet, when it comes to action cinema, as opposed to melodrama, film historians explain its emergence in India in terms of "global" influence, where the "global" is restricted to Hollywood. This is also the line of argument that was adopted in the 1970s by most film trade magazines, even if US pressure was not a factor unique to those years. The customary emphasis on Hollywood appears, in turn, to rule out other influences — such as the Italian western and the Hong Kong martial art film — the impact of which on the 1970s Hindi action film is, as I show below, far more evident than that of US films. A better understanding of these interconnections requires an examination of the material circumstances determining the production and circulation of films in India that takes into account the broader economic context, criss-crossed, as always, by local, national and transnational pressures.

INDIA'S RESPONSE TO THE 1970S FIRST WORLD CRISIS

As a consequence of the reduction of trade barriers at the end of the 1950s, from the early 1960s the growth of global trade accelerated spectacularly and unexpectedly. Finding its markets, at home and abroad, under increased pressure from the lower cost, lower price exports of the developing blocs, the US redirected its economy towards the FIRE (finance, insurance and real estate) sectors. Manufacturing remained the foundation of the new capitalist order, but it turned global. Firstly, the crisis of profitability in First World countries created an over-abundant liquidity – liquidity, that is, which was recycled as loan capital on highly favourable terms to Third and Second World countries. Secondly, the new economic regime enabled the US to run large deficits in its balance of trade and to reflate effective demand and investment, which, in turn, created an expanding demand for imports of those industrial products that North American businesses no longer found it profitable to produce. As a result, during this decade, relative to First World countries all Third World regions increased their degree of industrialisation and urbanisation to a far greater extent than they improved their GDP per capita. Unlike in the post-war period, throughout the 1970s this expansion was financed by borrowing on the international money market.[7] In addition, the US economy's historic reversal split world regions into two groups: those that, for historical and geographical reasons, had strong advantage in competing for a share of the expanding North American demand for cheap industrial products, and those that did not. East and, to a lesser extent, South Asia belonged to the first group; Sub-Saharan Africa and Latin America to the second.[8]

In the 1970s, Indian economic growth underwent a small but significant acceleration. Manufacturing increased; trade, commerce, and, more generally, the tertiary sector also grew significantly. Indeed, by far the most important economic measure of this period was Indira Gandhi's nationalisation of the fourteen largest commercial banks in 1969. At the time, the agrarian and the industrial bourgeoisies opposed this radical measure, so much so that it helped precipitate the first split in the Congress Party. In retrospect, however, the centralisation of credit and its administration through government-controlled institutions (such as the Industrial Finance Corporation, the Industrial Development Bank, and the Industrial Credit and Investment Corporation) established the crucial financial infrastructure for the systematic industrial development of the country. They also led to a huge expansion of the tertiary sector, of central administration and red-tape.[9]

Credit centralisation was part of a broad programme of economic and political centralisation which responded to the rise of finance capital in the US by sheltering India from its pressures. Indira Gandhi's administration, not the IMF, took full control of the country's capital outflow. By the 1980s, India's industrial manufacturing and overall economic performance was bettered only by China and South Korea. Unlike South Korea, whose total long-term debt services rose from 3.1 percent of GNP in 1970 to 10.2 percent in 1986, India's total debt services over the same period, like those of China, barely changed (1.1 in 1970 and 1.6 in 1986). Debt centralisation had huge repercussions on the shape of the Indian industry and finance that grew under the State's protectionist aegis. Until the mid-1990s, the Ministry of Finance controlled the five most important financial institutions in the country. These institutions played a key role in inter-corporate wars by helping one monopoly house or another to benefit at the expense of the rest, through mergers and acquisitions as well as through government red tape. As a result, unlike in the First World, in India industrialisation has tended to comprise large, government-run companies providing public services and agricultural development, a few large private corporations, such as the Tata and Birla groups, and small-scale industrial units, which constitute by far the vast majority of all Indian industrial units.[10]

In the mid-1960s, when the state of Maharashtra came into existence, major changes in the structure of Bombay's economy occurred. The struggle for the city of Bombay brought to the surface the contradiction between the dominant interests in agriculture — the rich and middle class farmers of Maharashtra — and those in industry — the non-Marathi controllers of commercial and industrial capital. In the end, the demand for a Marathi state was granted only when the Maharashtra Congress Party persuaded the national leaders that it could guarantee that the interests of industrial capital would be fully safeguarded while the dominant rural interest would be given its appropriate share of state resources.[11] In this context, the underside of state-sponsored private capitalist development, an "underworld", began to expand so as to enable a capital moored in local, clientelist networks to circulate unhampered by the controls of an increasingly centralised state apparatus. Indeed, the sector that grew most as a direct result of the 1970s centralisation of finance was the so-called "black" economy. The large body of work produced by historians on this particular feature of the Indian economy has tended to agree on two points: that the "black" economy — which first emerged during World War Two — has grown and is growing, and that the boundary between the "black" and the official, or "white" economy is anything but clear.

As Achin Vanaik has observed, in India, this "black" economy is closely integrated with the "white" economy:

> Black savings flow into the capital market and into bank deposits (with few questions asked), thus providing resources for investment. [...] A black economy is not unique to India, but its size — conservatively estimated at 40-50 percent of the recorded economy in 1990 (and growing) — is almost certainly significantly larger than in other industrialising countries, such as Brazil, South Korea and Mexico, if only because of the array of Indian government controls.[12]

From the early 1970s, with the nationalisation of the banks, a spiralling share of Indian capital found a parallel and, on the whole, cheaper channel of circulation in the film industry. This fact, and the type of small-scale, labour intensive mode of production upon which Indian capital works as a result both of credit centralisation and of localised networks' resistance to it, are responsible for the form and content of the Hindi action cinema produced in Bombay in the 1970s.

THE INDIAN FILM INDUSTRY AND HOLLYWOOD

In the 1970s, foreign films entered the Indian market through four legal channels: the Motion Picture Export Association of America (MPEAA); Sovexport Film; the National Film Development Corporation; and non-resident Indian importers. With the radical shifts in the US economy briefly outlined above, cinema became one of the US's few remaining domestic industries and exports, along with military technology. The MPEAA was set up as a body separate from the Motion Picture Producers and Distributors of America in 1945. It acted as a cartel to secure distribution of its members' films on an exclusive basis in territories where severe currency shortages existed. Once the market was secure for US films, the MPEAA would leave distribution to individual member companies.[13]

Like much of US industry, between 1966 and 1968 Hollywood underwent an over-production boom that landed the industry in a crisis that lasted until 1971.[14] Overseas markets became temporarily more important for the US majors during this period, and certain kinds of films — World War Two epics and disaster films — were designed with an international cast specifically to appeal to foreign audiences. When the 1970s began, as much as 50 percent of rental income came from abroad, and 80 percent of that from Europe. By the end of the decade, however, the resurgence in the home market (led by agents and their financial backers) restored the domestic-foreign ratio to 60/40, with the largest overseas share going, for the first time, to Japan.

While the shift from Europe to Japan may indeed prove that Hollywood's foreign fortunes did, at that point, take a turn to the "East", India was barely on the majors' map. English is one of India's official languages, but the Indian market as a whole has a poor purchasing power. The 10 percent who do have adequate purchasing power, many of whom are also the English speakers, equal a third of the US market, but in the eight years from 1955 to 1962 gross revenues of the MPEAA companies in India grew from under US$2 million to just over US$3.2 million. That is, compared to MPEAA earnings worldwide, as well as in terms of the average Hollywood budget, the Indian market was then, and remains to a large extent today, insignificant. From 1955 to 1962 the total revenues of the MPEAA members from the Indian market increased, as a percentage of foreign revenues, from 0.65 percent to 1.08 percent; compare this to the 80 percent of foreign revenues represented by the numerically smaller market of Europe.

During the late 1960s and early 1970s US imports in India decreased, while Indian production rose significantly. The single main factor behind these changes was not the US or its film industry, but Indira Gandhi's economic policy. By 1963, MPEAA companies in India were earning profits of US$1 million. Like every other foreign company operating in India, the majors were restricted to converting (i.e. to send back as hard currency profit to the US) only US$400,000 annually. The remaining accumulated funds, in Indian rupees, or "blocked funds", had grown to US$6.5 million by 1971. Again, the figure, by Hollywood standards, was minimal. Less so by Indian standards: the MPEAA pushed to repatriate these funds, while the Indian government, short of hard currency, refused to allow it. A further bone of contention between the MPEAA and Indira Gandhi's government was the issue of reciprocity. Many film-producing countries had demanded trade reciprocity from the MPEAA on a voluntary basis. Instead, perhaps because of the size of Indian film production as well as of the actual and potential markets for Indian films abroad, the Indian government demanded reciprocity as part of a trade agreement. The MPEAA members' 16mm distribution networks would have absorbed the Indian films at no great loss for the majors, but the MPEAA refused because it would have set an undesirable precedent. This situation led to an MPEAA embargo, which lasted from 1971 to 1975. Incidentally these are also the years which saw the appearance of a Hindi action cinema in Bombay's first-run houses.

In 1975 diplomatic intervention resulted in a new agreement. The number of imported films was lowered from a maximum of 150 to 100. In addition, all imported films were to be "canalised" through the National Film Development Corporation (NFDC), a new, centrally controlled body that, as a result, became the sole provider of raw stock and foreign films in India. Thirdly, gross revenues earned by the US majors could be spent for operating expenses, for remittances abroad, and for "other" designated expenditures. Under the latter, allocations were made for production and co-production of films in India, script review, and interest-free loans to *any* government-sponsored body, returnable after five years in hard currency.

Compared to the fate of other US companies in India during Indira Gandhi's regime, Jack Valenti had arrived at a relatively good deal for the MPEAA: the US majors succeeded in repatriating the to them insignificant sum, albeit with a delay of five years; unlike Coca-Cola, they also managed to retain a foot in the Indian market, which they "flooded", within the very low import limits, with cheaply priced prints so as to incur lower importation fees. Italian westerns and Hong Kong-made martial art films constituted a large share of these imports. As to the Indian contingent, the NFDC became one of the several institutions to be set up during this period to control capital circulation.[15] Added to those of other, similarly treated foreign companies, the majors' "blocked funds" enabled the Indian State to contain its foreign debt and reduce dependency on First World financial institutions to levels comparable to those of China.

THE HINDI FILM INDUSTRY: A HISTORICAL PERSPECTIVE

The problems caused by film historians' habit of ascribing Hollywood undue reverence are not confined to action cinema. Irrespective of whether they see the cinema in India as overdetermined by US influence or the Indian State, film critics and historians have tended to transpose the categories and industrial practices obtaining in Hollywood cinema to analyses of Indian cinemas. As a result, superficial parallelisms with US action cinema are used to sustain the assumption that some Bombay cinema of the 1970s is indeed "action cinema". Somewhat similarly, that some Hindi action cinema should contain elements that resonate with Hong Kong martial art films is ascribed to vague notions of generic transferrals the actual circumstances and reasons of which are left, on the whole, unexplored.[16] An understanding of the factors that led to an indigenous action cinema in India in the 1970s being made for release in first-run theatres has to begin with a better understanding of the film industry's modes of operation, their history, and their rationale in the Indian context. There is no doubt that generic forms circulate, but stylistic permutations to and fro between diverse cinema formations can be better understood if examined as dynamics constitutive of the specific film industry under consideration — so long as the latter is viewed in the broader context of the global movement of cultural value. In other words, the question is less that Amitabh Bachchan's type of action echoes kung fu, but rather why Hong Kong kung fu was deemed a suitable mode of action for an Indian hero.

A domestic film industry was at work in India by the 1920s. Its growth from the mid-1930s has been narrated as a struggle between two co-existing tendencies: concentration of production around three main studios on the one hand, and "regional" or "independent" decentralisation on the other. In reality, the focus on production is misleading and the term "independent" ahistorical. The 1930s saw the formation of what became by far the most common mode of film finance and production throughout the 1940s, 1950s and 1960s. Unlike Hollywood, where, by the 1930s, a small number of production studios endowed with revolving credit facilities controlled a large share of the domestic market, most Indian cinema, and certainly the majority of the films made in Bombay until the mid-1960s, resulted from what is known as the "minimum guarantee policy" system. A financier-exhibitor advances the money for production under an agreement that assures the producer a minimum return on each film, after which the revenues are shared between exhibitor and producer. The amount that is fixed as the minimum guarantee for the producer is usually the amount loaned during the making of the film. Madhava Prasad has observed that, "As a result, the producer often gets no revenue from a film after production because the minimum return has already been given in the form of loans".[17]

In Hollywood too, producers, distributors and exhibitors share what remains after production, distribution and exhibition costs and fees are met, either as part of an externally (agent) stipulated agreement, or because production, distribution and exhibitors are integrated departments within the same studio. That in the Bombay system the producer should get no additional revenue on top of the minimum return is no fault of the "minimum guarantee policy" itself, but of a different equilibrium between production, distribution and exhibition than that at work in Hollywood. Whereas in 1950s Hollywood the economic priority and operational emphases were on production, in Bombay, before and after the 1950s, exhibition and distribution have dictated over production,[18] as they began to do in Hollywood in the 1970s under the growing power of agents first, and corporations later. In short, it is not a matter of whether one industry is integrated or not, but of the different nature of the integration. In India, the exhibition sector has, so far, remained in control, and constitutes the industry's cohesive force, its locomotive.[19]

Distributors of Indian films hardly existed in the 1920s, when producers dealt directly with exhibitors. Due to the misleading emphasis on production and its effect on research agendas, it is unclear as to whether, with the coming of sound, distribution grew in importance. Distributors may have become more important after the coming of sound, and, from the mid-1930s, they grew in number. By 1948 there were no less than 887 distributors across India. Again, their role and function is not altogether clear, but they are certainly not comparable to Hollywood distributors.[20] To this day, an Indian producer may approach exhibitors directly; a distributor may be independent or little more than the employee of a large producer or exhibitor. By contrast, after 1947 the Indian domestic market was organised into five exhibition territories or circuits.[21] Unlike exhibition, distribution and production have remained fragmented, low capitalised sectors, with industrial structures based on small operational units.

In the 1930s, the expansion and fragmentation of the market across regional networks relied both on language and, perhaps as heavily, on a calculation of the role of the star in the success of a film. At the time, under colonial rule, star exploitation owed much of its function within the Indian film industry not simply to the fact that, as in Hollywood, a star could guarantee box-office revenues, but also to the possibilities it offered in colonial India for links with a "black" economy which was historically rooted in the fabric of early Indian capitalism — that is, of a capitalism that emerged out of, and against, a set of economic and political measures aimed at inhibiting its development. In the 1930s, and with the open support of the nationalist Congress, film stars were offered a sizeable share of their salary in the form of under the table money. Part of it would be "(colonial) tax free", and its reception considered a nationalist act.[22] Then, and to a degree after 1947, the Indian film industry has functioned as an ancillary circulation belt for undeclared money and, more generally, as a means to make capital "work" through financial speculation. The star has played a crucial role in this respect, not only because part of a star's salary is undeclared, that is, paid with free-floating, un-taxed money, but also because casting a star requires the producer to borrow a greater amount of money from the exhibitor-financier, which in turn allows the latter to circulate a greater amount of money. In addition, a share of the total sum borrowed by the producer during the making of the film can, and often does, consist of last-minute loans conceded at extortionary rates of interests and necessitated by unanticipated shooting delays. Often, a major reason for such delays is the star's involvement in several productions simultaneously.

Until the mid-1960s, at least in the Hindi cinema, the feudal family romance dominated the mainstream market. In his seminal *Ideology of the Hindi Film: A Historical Construction*, Prasad has argued that the rise and consolidation of the feudal family romance in the 1950s was an effect of the fact that films were conceived as single units put together by an *impromptu* combination of financier-producer-director-stars, a rented studio and a large number of underpaid, *ad hoc* extras and technical staff. The feudal family romance owed its dominance to its narrative frame's capacity to subordinate other genres internally — by incorporating from them disparate ingredients, and externally — "by reducing the number of films with a distinctly different generic identity and/or by relegating them to the more provincial or subcultural exhibition outlets".[23] The feudal family romance's generic conventions were symptomatic of the films' function as a means to circulate capital which was generated within a "passive revolution", that is, in a context where a modernising centre ruled on the basis of a compromise with a reluctant and powerful landed bourgeoisie still very much entrenched in localised, regional financial networks.

Production centres in the South, like Madras, made a steady stream of feudal family romance films and other genres, which were not, as a rule, seen in the first-run houses across rest of the country, even if Madras grew to boast the best production facilities available to the whole of the Indian film industry. By contrast, a (Bombay produced) Hindi film might have some exposure in each of the five exhibition circuits. As a rule, however, and unlike, say, US exploitation cinema, Hindi feudal family romances were not exhibited intensely across the national territory. They were expensive and glossy productions, at times with extremely long turnover times, so that producers, depending on district-based exhibition networks, remained more or less confined within the allocated linguistic and financial district belt.

THE 1970S: SYMPTOMS OF CHANGE

In 1949 the Indian government appointed the S. K. Patil Film Enquiry Committee to write a report on all aspects of cinema. The report, published in 1951, accompanied its critique of the industry's mass-cultural product with recommendations for major State investment in film production, for the setting up of a film finance corporation, and the opening of a film institute and archive. The report was ignored by Nehru's administration for more than a decade, and direct State intervention in the film industry was confined to the Film Advisory Board.[24] While little was done on the part of Nehru's government to inflect features production, exhibition was especially targeted by heavy taxes and the practice of compulsory, taxed screening of "approved films" — both practices inherited by the Raj.[25] In 1960, nearly a decade after the report's publication, the Film Finance Corporation (FFC) was launched under the Ministry of Finance to provide low interest loans for feature production. The stated aim of the FFC was to assist the mainstream industry "by providing, affording or procuring finance or other facilities for the production of films of good standard". In 1971, the FFC directive was written into its official objective: to turn cinema into "an effective instrument for the promotion of national culture, education and healthy entertainment". In 1980, the FFC was merged with the Indian Motion Picture Export Corporation (IMPEC) to become the National Film Development Corporation (NFDC).

The Indian State's operation in the domain of cinema in the 1970s has been interpreted as a real or perceived impingement on the Indian film industry's sphere of action.[26] In reality, with the partial "withdrawal" of the MPEAA from the Indian market, the NFDC became the sole "provider" of foreign films, in the sense that no foreign distribution company was allowed into the Indian market without an operating agreement with it. The Indian State has used this policy well into the 1990s to limit the number of imports into the country, and thus to promote the domestic film industry through a form of protectionism it had never benefited from before the 1970s. Secondly, in contrast to the earlier government, which froze the construction of new cinemas, Indira Gandhi's administration promoted exhibition through a state governments-based financing scheme offering low-interest loans and subsidies to private entrepreneurs willing to build and maintain exhibition venues. Above all, and in spite of these schemes, the Indian State promoted the film industry by failing, or refusing, to disturb its existing exhibition networks.

The NFDC was not a threat to the film industry's operation, if one takes the latter to be film production. There is no doubt that low interest loans by the State to both production and exhibition ventures were attempts to break the monopoly of exhibitors and their hold on production. After all, historically, this monopoly and the mode of film production that resulted from it have been instrumental to the workings of the "black" economy, while the FFC, as part of a larger project of finance centralisation that included the nationalisation of the fourteen largest Indian banks, could have been in an ideal position to hijack that link. The FFC, however, failed; as Madhava Prasad has argued convincingly, the FFC was a nominal concession, a lip-service strategy to contain actual State scrutiny and intervention into the film industry's financial operations.[27] Pulled by a cohesive exhibition sector, from the 1970s the film industry grew significantly stronger as an ancillary mechanism for the circulation of undeclared capital, precisely *because* of credit centralisation. It is not a coincidence that in 1970, one year after the nationalisation of the banks, Hindi productions doubled,[28] fuelled by the sudden increase in credit that became available as it sought to flee State control. This mechanism was allowed to remain in place and expand, unhampered by the operation of the US majors, by other foreign companies, or by the Indian State itself, despite and even because of, the heavy taxation on exhibition.

The sudden recovery of the Hindi cinema in the domestic and Hindi markets in the 1970s, and the rise of exports, coincided with a massive increase in production costs. Costs of all inputs, such as sets, equipment rental, and the salaries of technical personnel did rise; the significant increase, however, was in stars' salaries, raw stock (all of which is imported) and print and publicity costs. The cost of colour raw film rose due to the devaluation of the Indian currency against the US dollar. A star's salary, on the other hand, increased 400 percent between 1975 and 1985 (from RS 1.5 million to 6 million).[29] Whereas in 1970 the average Hindi film was produced for under RS 1 million, a star studded film for about RS 5 million, and a low budget film for RS 150,000, by the late 1980s, the average Hindi film required about RS 7.5 million, a star studded film may cost between RS 20 and RS 30 million and a low budget film may come close to RS 2.5 million. All-India publicity for a big budget film cost RS 1.2 million in 1975 and 3 million ten years later.[30]

In spite of these rises, and in comparison to the average Hollywood and other major national cinemas' budgets, these remain small sums. Today, the rate of failure within the Indian film industry is very high: of the 132 films made in Hindi in 1983, only 17 were reported to have recovered their negative cost, while for every film that recovered its cost in 1985, 8 incurred a loss. According to Manjunath Pendakur, "it is widely believed in the industry that more films [were] not recovering their investment [in 1989] than was the case ten years [earlier]".[31] The fact is, none of these figures are reliable because most of the industry's operations go unrecorded. It is also a fact that, in spite of the apparent unprofitability of film-making, the number of films produced has increased significantly. Since it is estimated that in the late 1980s 2,500 million rupees were invested annually in film production, and that in 1985, for instance, the sector incurred estimated losses in the range of 1,200 million rupees, and given that there was no drop in the number of productions in following years, it would seem that the expansion of the Hindi film industry has taken place not "in spite of" but, because of, the phenomenal increase in declared "production losses".

For the exhibition sector, which constitutes the industry's locomotive and whose financial activities are sheltered from direct government control, these are not, strictly speaking, "losses". Rather, they are good indications that the industry's links with, or rather its function *as*, a "black" economy is a growing formation, in which "production losses" constitute a different type of capital gain. It is common knowledge that a Hindi film star receives most of his/her salary "off the record". While this was already the case in the 1930s, if the rise in stars' declared salaries in the 1970s is anything to go by, it would seem that during that decade the cinema's operation and production were further organised in such a way as to fulfil primarily the function of evading central credit control and facilitating "black" capital circulation, irrespective of whether such capital is generated within or without film production. Which is why the Indian government, determined since 1969 to centralise finance, has insisted on imposing high taxes on film exhibition.

In the early 1970s, centralisation of finance made a larger amount of credit available for productions, but, in spite of this, the production sector did not expand in a cohesive manner: smaller, *impromptu* productions proliferated instead. Exhibition also expanded and, at least initially, it also did so in a fragmented way. As a result, and for a short while only, the already disproportionately high number of distributors managed to infiltrate exhibition networks previously closed to them. So, Southern productions, which until the late 1960s had marginalised Hindi cinema locally for some time but had hardly been visible on the mainstream circuits of the North, began in the early 1970s to be more visible in the North as well, and particularly in Bombay, the home territory of Hindi cinema. These changes registered enough with the Bombay public for film magazines of the period to recurrently complain about the Southern and foreign "invasion" of Bombay theatres, that is, of first-run outlets traditionally dedicated to the Hindi melodrama fare. James Bond, Hong Kong martial art movies and Italian westerns formed a large share of all imports into India, but, targeting a fundamentally different section of the market, these films never featured in the English-language film magazines addressing the small Indian middle-class public. From the early 1970s onward, foreign films featuring action-type heroes gradually began to replace foreign *auteur* cinema (the only type of foreign cinema previously covered by English language magazines). Increasingly covered were also Indian remakes of James Bond, martial art films and Italian westerns. Initially, the magazines' take on these films was spiteful, and any Indian film adopting "proven elements" alien to the Hindi melodrama was not only seen to slavishly borrow from imports, but was also reviewed negatively for wanting — as the magazines put it — "to make a fast-buck". In 1980, a magazine would retrospectively refer to this kind of films as "the Crude Wave".[32]

Indeed, a further factor to be taken into consideration is censorship. Following a series of reforms, the early 1970s saw a massive drop of censored films, from 114 in 1972 to 38 in 1973 and 26 in 1974.[33] These changes, which are all the more remarkable for having being implemented during one of the most oppressive regimes India has ever seen, facilitated the industry's growth under the aegis and priorities of an expanding and faster-moving exhibition sector seeking to absorb greater sums of Indian capital fleeing centralised control. This is the context that framed the incorporation of Hong Kong martial art elements, and determined their function, in the Hindi action cinema of the 1970s.

THE AMITABH BACHCHAN ACTION FILMS

The label "the social", as used to refer to the Hindi feudal family romance, is more an effect of the Indian cinema's relation to the State and its project of social and economic modernisation, than a meaningful characterisation of specific generic bundles. A "social" could treat "contemporary issues", that is, issues of "modernisation", by presenting them in a historical or mythological idiom, as a modern romance or as a thriller. Most socials were a combination of these and other strands and big film stars remained, on the whole, versatile. In the Bombay film industry stratified exhibition had applied since the end of the 1920s, with first-, second- and third-run cinema houses showing a variety of Indian and foreign films. Socials, however, were rarely passed down the line. In the 1950s, for all its orientation towards exhibition, in the then melodrama-dominated mainstream Hindi cinema, strict generic distinctions did not obtain, so long as musical spectacle and stars guaranteed the exhibitor-financier's capacity to circulate capital as "production value". Socials, and especially late examples of feudal family romance, were big budget productions with lavish sets and extremely high turnover times. *Mughal-e-Azam* (K. Asif 1960) and *Pakeezah* (Kamal Amrohi 1971) took respectively nine and thirteen years to make. Given the shortage of cinemas throughout India, in the 1970s, the expansion of the industry led not simply to a growth and temporary fragmentation of exhibition, but, as exhibition priorities fed back into production, to the kind of film that could be made and circulated at a much faster pace than the glossy melodramas of the 1950s and 1960s.

In comparison to late feudal family romances, *Zanjeer* (Prakash Mehra 1973), the film that, along with *Sholay* (Ramesh Sippy 1975), catapulted Amitabh Bachchan, the barely known actor, to "Amitabh" the film superstar, was a cheap production with poor sets, no star value and poor quality film processing, but with narrative ingredients that, until then, had been deemed to appeal exclusively to a larger but unofficial market, the "lower end". In that sector, *Zanjeer's* story of personal revenge, police action and corruption already circulated in the form of James Bond films, Italian westerns and Hong Kong martial art movies — which constituted the bulk of Hollywood's export strategy, targeting primarily those markets (the "lower end") not prioritised by the Indian mainstream. As far as *Zanjeer* is concerned, the only unusual investment was in the script, a practice that was then, and remains today, very uncommon in the Hindi mainstream cinema. Nor was this investment significant: after *Zanjeer*, scriptwriters Salim Khan and Javed Akhtar came to be referred to as "the team" but, at the time, they were quite unknown. Their script was symptomatic of the industry's new direction and strategies for expansion: the incorporation, into the mainstream, of the ingredients that had proved popular in the large but so far untapped "low-end" of the market. The Salim-Javed formula provided the narrative template that still holds today for what has since become the "Hindi action cinema", in spite of the array of different directors, stars and producers that have since come to occupy it.

In 1972, when *Zanjeer* was being produced, many stunt actors were available in the low end of the market. Bachchan was not one of them. With Bachchan, a former stage actor and radio announcer, the Hindi mainstream cast a relatively unknown, unsuccessful actor who had previously had minor roles in mainstream films — from war movies to romantic stories about middle-class couples — alongside (and possibly thanks to) his wife, NFDC acting school graduate and film star Jaya Bhaduri. Stars of the 1950s stars were, on the whole, versatile, and the likes of Dilip Kumar could play romantic characters as well as more active roles involving some action. However, crossovers between the mainstream and the lower end of the market were not admitted. By the late 1960s, when the boundaries between the two sectors began to blur, film magazines for the English-educated public took to the habit of warning established melodramatic stars against the risk of being "typecast" whenever the stars acted in a film containing a measure of action. The opposite — that is, the possibility of being "typecast" in melodramatic roles — was not perceived as such, but as a step forward in the actor's career. Unlike existing stars, in 1972 Bachchan had very little to lose indeed. Prior to the release of *Zanjeer*, Bachchan is practically absent from film magazines; the rare mentions consist of sniggering one-liners consistently dismissing his performances as "sleepwalking".[34] Unlike well known mainstream stars such as Dilip Kumar and, to a lesser extent, Dharmendra, who were often referred to as "thespians", Bachchan was deemed a "bad" actor because he lacked their melodramatic capacity to emote on stage. Bachchan was cast because, as an ordinary actor devoid of melodramatic skills, he was male flesh, and cheap flesh at that, as cheap a body as already available within the mainstream.

Sholay (Ramesh Sippy 1975), also scripted by the Salim-Javed team, went a step further in combining the box-office ingredients of cheap productions (which include, to an extent, *Zanjeer*) with the narrative and production-value sensibilities of a mainstream public addicted to feudal family romances. The longest running film in the history of Hindi cinema, *Sholay* was a feature that relocated *Zanjeer's* urban story in a rural setting heavily inscribed with notions of national modernisation. Rare in the mainstream Hindi cinema for its few songs, and cheaper for that — since the composer, lyricist, and playback singers' fees and rights represent a significant share of a film's budget and revenues — *Sholay* could be less easily marketed through the pre-release campaign of songs (played on national television, on the radio and available as music cassettes) that habitually accompanied mainstream melodramas. After its phenomenal box-office success, however, recordings were released with extracts from the film's dialogue. Dialogue pre-release has since become common practice for all Hindi action films. In addition, Dharmendra, then an established star, was cast in the lead role; Bachchan as the star's sidekick. The allocation of action activities between star and sidekick in the film is clear: Bachchan, the cheaper actor, performs the more "dangerous" stunts and his character covers exclusively "action" ground; Dharmendra's character, on the other hand, is granted a romantic interest, while his action is confined to more stationary, and, on the whole, safer gimmicks.

Sholay set the template for a new marketing and distribution strategy, the "multi-starrer" (the Hindi version of the blockbuster), where the industry's new priority — to expand exhibition capacities by tapping into a larger market with a faster cycle — was fed back into production through a script that reinscribed that "lower" market's proven ingredients into, or *as* the mainstream's formula. As a consequence, and unlike less celebrated Hindi action actors, such as Feroz Khan, who featured in Indian remakes of Bond films and Italian westerns, throughout the 1980s Amitabh Bachchan retained the versatility of the 1950s stars. He was available for action films and for romance. The son of a famous poet whose family was closely connected to the Nehrus, unlike other unknown or established action actors, Bachchan could be just "a body" and simultaneously project an image imbued with the status expected from a star in the then melodrama-dominated mainstream. In every action film he has made Bachchan has played "the underdog"; as a critic has observed, however, he "operated with the symbols of poverty visually inscribed on the body and the codes of an upper class upbringing projected through his gestures and posturing".[35] Salim Khan and Javed Akhtar's script worked with acting material that was cheap, non-melodramatic, or "blank", and, simultaneously, not "vulgar". Accordingly, whereas in 1972 lack of facial expression or emotional charge was regarded as a lack of acting skills, one year on from *Zanjeer* reviews of Bachchan's performances elevate the same lack of expression to a quality: the skill of looking unperturbed, steely, cool and invulnerable were built into the image of the mainstream star, thus radically altering the mainstream's generic stock.[36]

THE MARTIAL ART FACTOR

In spite of melodramas such as Guru Dutt's *Pyaasa* (1957) — a Hindi film that, ten years after independence, voiced a trenchant critique of the State for its failure to meet promises of social modernisation — historians of the Indian cinema have tended to read any 1950s social as no more nor less than Nehruvian State ideology. *Awara* (Raj Kapoor, 1951) is a textbook case of the social melodrama that addresses issues of social reform as formulated by the Congress before and during the time of Jawaharlal Nehru. The film tells the story of Raj (R. Kapoor), the son of a strict judge who is forced to move to the city with his mother when, the latter having been kidnapped by low-life Jagga, she is repudiated by her husband and thrown out of the family home.

The story, which dwells on Raj's struggle to survive in the city's slums, where hunger and the need to support his ill mother push him into Jagga's world of smuggling and crime, is partly told as the judge's flashback. Called in to judge the hero, whom he does not recognise as his own son, the judge and father is instead invited to the witness box by Raj's defence lawyer and sweetheart, Rita (Nargis). The judge's testimony, prompted by Rita, unwittingly reveals that petty crook Raj is, in reality, the judge's son. The reformist streak of the plot verges on discounting the judge's lineage-based belief that the son of a criminal will also be a criminal. However, if the story, so far, stages a compromise between notions of family lineage and individual civil rights in a manner typical of the Hindi melodrama of the 1950s, on closer inspection *Awara's* core dichotomies produce a tension at the level of narration which, while also part and parcel of the genre's reformist agenda, has tended to be ignored in the literature on the subject because film criticism has itself remained caught in a nationalist frame of mind. Whereas part of the story is told in the court of law as the judge's flashback, called forth by Rita, herself voicing the reformist agenda of the Nehruvian State, the remaining part of the story is revealed by the criminal, Jagga, who abruptly interrupts the trial sequences to address the spectator directly (as a non-diegetic jury) from his shelter in the city's slums. Jagga's narrative is a story, not of reform, but of revenge: a petty crook because he is from a deprived background, Jagga has been a victim of the judge's unforgiving and merciless law. In revenge, Jagga kidnapped the judge's wife to make him believe, wrongly, that he has raped her and that she will thus give birth to a criminal son. When the destitute Raj arrives in the city, Jagga proceeds to disprove the judge's system of belief by turning Raj, the judge's own son, into a small-time crook.

The narrative tension at work in *Awara* is a function of the film's reformist discourse, of which Rita and Jagga are the two complementary sides. The protagonist, Raj, is contended by two perspectives that confirm each other, and the struggle thus staged is designed to pull the sensibilities of a moderately reformist, middle-class public whose interested benevolence and mercy for "the outlaw" are no more than strategies aimed at containing social unrest. *Awara* confronts the latter possibility as a threat, the potential proliferation of evil crooks like Jagga. By the time of *Zanjeer* and *Sholay*, the reformist perspective of "the social" has not been abandoned. However, the State and its institutions, the court of law, can no longer be seen to embody it. Jagga's perspective, on the other hand (the perspective of the outlaw from the slums) acquires a new dimension: dissociated from the structures of the State, the original reformism and the notion of social justice implied therewith are transformed in Amitabh Bachchan's action films into a discourse of social and economic aspiration the terms of which are dictated by notions of brotherhood and family honour, that is, by lineage, rather than democratic State's law. At one level, the shift from a modern notion of law to a code of honour changes the temporality of narration: the Amitabh Bachchan action hero is not driven by romance, as Raj is by Rita, but by revenge, the contract binding the judge and Jagga, the representatives of the previous generation. At another level, whereas in the Hindi melodrama reform is presented as a lesser evil, the cure against the emergence of a social underworld, the same threat provides the point of departure of the 1970s action film.

Following the nationalisation of India's fourteen largest banks under Indira Gandhi, the Indian film industry emerged as a privileged network for capital seeking to evade central controls on the circulation of finance. This was not an entirely novel development, for the Indian film industry had fulfilled this role since the 1930s. However, in the 1930s the evasion of colonial taxes and administration was part and parcel of the discourse of nationalism, whereas after 1947 the "black economy" became a network pitted against the independent Indian State. Having been excluded from the government's programme of economic development and thus from direct government control ever since Independence, with credit centralisation in 1969 the film industry emerged as a privileged site for the negotiation of an ambivalent relation to the State — simultaneously benefiting from central control and seeking to evade it. To reduce its operation to that of the State, whatever the latter's persuasion, would be a mistake. The action cinema that emerged as a result mediates first and foremost this tension.

In the melodrama of the 1950s the hero moves between village and city. The Bachchan action hero too moves from village to city, but his is an irreversible journey to the place that, in the melodrama, stood for corruption and moral dissolution. The narrative motive — a wrong suffered by the family, or, more specifically, by the father, in their native village — functions as a device to dwell on the film's core preoccupation, the interruption of a patriarchal lineage that it will be the hero's task to restore. In the process, a patriarchal order is redefined, displaced and translated onto an urban setting. In *Zanjeer*, Vijay's parents are gunned down in front of his eyes; in *Sholay* the entire family of Baldev Singh is massacred; in *Deewar* (Yash Chopra 1975), Vijay's father, wrongly accused of theft, deserts the family, which is forced to face immense ordeals to survive; in *Amar Akbar Anthony, Naseeb, Coolie,* and *Mard* (Manmohan Desai 1977, 1981, 1983 and 1985) happy homes are torn asunder and the family members separated. The melodramatic hero of the 1950s was not an entirely secular character, but a project of modernisation committed to secularisation made him a subject endowed with a personal dimension. By contrast, in *Amar Akbar Anthony* and *Naseeb* the heroes restore the original dismembered family against the odds of fate; in *Coolie*, the action hero is simultaneously urban and aided by the heavens, as he is in *Mard*, where the goddess Durga intervenes to assist him in her customary shape of a tiger. The Hindi action hero embodies an independent vision of the individual and conquers villains through a combination of physical and moral strength, but also and simultaneously, through his mother's blessings and divine benediction.

In order to make sense of this contradictory set of ingredients, it is important to recognise the significant overlap between the Hindi action film and the melodrama of the 1950s, with the latter attached to discourses of the modernising State, and the former, the action film, within and, simultaneously, at a remove from the same discourses. Notions of destiny, of Hindu mythology and of status as caste are evidence of the action film's distance from the discourses of the (nominally) secular State. More pertinently here, these notions link the genre to localised Indian networks and, indirectly, to the Hong Kong martial art film, where the hero's skill is also embedded in ideas of status as proximity to the imperial head, of spiritual integrity and Chinese mythology. However, it would be a mistake to assume that with the mainstreaming of ingredients at work in the lower end of the market, elements of the Hong Kong martial art film were automatically incorporated in, and adapted to, the Hindi mainstream cinema. Rather, of all the material that circulated in India as imports from the US, the Hong Kong martial art films were deemed a suitable source of inspiration for the Hindi action because, through this genre, the industry was reshaping itself so as to better function as a medium for the circulation of capital — a capital rooted in localised, lineage-based networks that sought to evade a centralising, secular State.

To recognise that Indira Gandhi forcefully centralised credit in response to, and as a defence against, the globalising pressure of US finance capital, in order to promote the Indian economy and thus redefine the country's role as a provider of cheap industrial goods for export also to the US, is not to say that Hindi action films can be justifiably read as Hollywood imitations. More than the MPEAA embargo itself, which coincides with the production and release of the two landmark Hindi action features *Zanjeer* and *Sholay*, it is the template of the Hindi action film which disproves such claim. Firstly, the Salim-Javed action formula has come to be known as the "anti-hero" film because the Hindi action hero operates outside the law, against a corrupt system that he seeks to replace with the notions of honour that he embodies. Yet, for all its economic and narrative opposition to the State, the Hindi action cinema reveals, to this day, a strong melodramatic component which the films derive from the Hindi feudal melodrama also staging (but not exhausted by) the agenda of the modernising State. Secondly, none of the mythological and hierarchical connotations at work in the Bachchan films play any significant role in US action productions. It follows that to read Hindi action films as Hollywood remakes is as misleading as to reduce them to "voices" of the Indian State. Thirdly, mythological and hierarchical connotations connect the Bachchan action films to the Hong Kong martial art cinema. And while here notions of status, spirituality and mythology attaching to the action hero in India and Hong Kong do resonate, differently specific modes of circulation underpin their meaning and function in the Hindi and in the Hong Kong cinemas.

Nowhere is the complex relay of pressures constitutive of the Hindi action film more evident than in the hero's body and mode of action. The bodies of Indian stunt actors and stars of the 1930s, or of Hindi stunt star Dara Singh in the 1950s, were relatively static, chubby bodies that conveyed a sense of pampered status because they were inflected either by Indian notions of the *yogic*, balanced body, or by wrestling (in India a very popular sport, the training and sponsoring of which draws on caste-based, religiously-defined networks), or by both. Alternatively, stunt actors had athletic bodies, as in the case of Raja Sandow, in the 1920s. A fourth model also available to Indian and Hindi stunt actors was provided by the more muscular bodies of circus strongmen, from whom Raja Sandow, with a reference to the popular strongman Eugen Sandow, derived his name but not his body shape. The Bachchan body combined the first three sets of influences, the *yogic*, the wrestling and the athletic body, but not the fourth, the muscular body. In contrast to US action films of the 1980s, or to the Italian peplums of the 1960s, the Bachchan body was a status-endowed, slim and long-legged body entirely devoid of muscles and displaying a very limited amount of bare flesh. Well into the 1990s and, with a few exceptions (such as Sunny Deol and Sunil Shetty) also later, the performance of the Hindi action star has been more about mastery, equilibrium and self-control — expressed as (awkwardly performed) acrobatics and a capacity to endure physical abuse — than about sheer muscle power. Again, the resonances with the Hong Kong martial art film are striking. When compared to earlier Indian stunt heroes, it becomes evident that in the Bachchan body the martial art techniques that had become available because the Hong Kong produced films formed a significant share of the US imports, were added as a further, fifth layer, to be combined with indigenous notions of physical mastery and social status.

The resulting action body can be read as a map, laying out the trajectory of the Hindi film industry in the following two decades. Action cinema emerged in India in the 1970s, just as it did in the US, in Hong Kong and in other countries, but differently. In that decade, in India as elsewhere, the circulation of finance was heavily impacted by changes in the US that had global repercussions, but that impact in India was equally heavily mediated by the Indian State. Unlike other national formations, Indira Gandhi's government took the bull by the horns, which is why the Hindi cinema, even as it was formulated on the basis of ingredients (e.g. action) that would enable it to become one of the strategies by which finance capital could circulate outside the networks monitored by the State, simultaneously retained a strong narrative and formal link with the Hindi melodrama. In this context, the Hindi film industry borrowed from, and radically transformed, the available narrative stock. The Hong Kong martial art mode of action was one such stock element. Uniquely attached to the export operation of the US majors, it presented itself to Indian film-makers as a way to further expand their market — in the process securing the Hindi film industry's role as a parallel network for the circulation of "untaxed" capital. Paramount to sustaining this role was the film industry's capacity to reshape its operation so as to better fit in a broader, but specifically Indian, industrial context characterised by small, little capitalised and labour intensive production units.

In the Hindi action film "technology" is not, as a rule, conceived as weaponry or military-scientific gadgetry, as it is in US action or Bond films, or, for that matter, as according to the agenda of the Hindi right, but as *transport* — that is, the kind of technology associated with the Nehruvian State. Interestingly, never is the Nehruvian technology of the Hindi action film attached to the hero's body, or in any other way seen to enhance his physical might, as it does in US action and Bond productions. From the early 1980s, films such as *Qurbani* (Feroz Khan 1980) indulged in ostentatious displays of cars and similar gadgetry, as well as of sexy women, in a somewhat Bond-like fashion. Yet, even then, when it comes to fighting, the action hero resorts to body stunts and punches, or, at the most, a knife. This is also the case in the more militaristic features, such as *Tiranga* (Mehul Kumar 1992). In this respect, the films' mode of action has remained more or less the same as it was in the 1930s and Homi Wadia's stunt films with Fearless Nadia, even if in the latter films the combination of choreographed circus acrobatics and balanced physical bulk is unambiguously attached to a notion of "the law". Modern Hindi action heroes occasionally mix choreographed acrobatics and physical bulk, where acrobatics borrow both from indigenous fighting techniques, such as wrestling (*Zanjeer; Ghatak*, Raj Kumar Santoshi 1996; *Ziddi*, Gaddu Dhanoa 1997), and from (Indian ideas of) "kung fu" (*Sholay; Deewar; Coolie*). Some films may pay lip service to the display of muscles (*Khalnayak*, Subash Ghai 1993), but never do muscles and a sense of pure physical strain take priority over acrobatics. The Hindi action body is, on the whole, a body oblivious of sheer physical energy and of modern technology as a means of enhancing it. Instead, what appears to be envisaged is an ideal "acrobaticity", the choreography of which presents physical mastery and equilibrium as acquired, modern techniques.

To conclude, in the 1970s and 1980s Hindi action film the influence of the Hollywood or of the peplum's muscled body is nowhere to be seen (and it will not appear until well into the 1990s), whereas acrobatic mastery resonating with Hong Kong martial art films is combined with indigenous ideas of status and physical equilibrium. However, having been incorporated in order to sell more films on the Hindi film industry's traditional domestic and foreign markets, the Hong Kong martial art reference in the Bachchan action films is twice refracted: (a) by the Indian film industry's oblique relation to American "globalisation", heavily mediated as it was by the Indian State, and (b) by the Indian film industry's resistance to State control. That the connection between the 1970s Hindi action and the Hong Kong martial art film is relayed and far from direct becomes particularly evident if attention is paid to the narratives lending verisimilitude to the body in space.

I have described at length those narratives obtaining in the Hindi action films. Other narrative concerns and mixes inevitably play in the Hong Kong martial art film, even as similarities seem to connect the display of human physical energy in the two types of film. Outlined here are some of the economic relays by which presentational elements of Hong Kong martial art films were incorporated into Hindi action films. Given the state of historiography on Indian cinemas, they have been offered here as much as a way towards a line of enquiry, as an agenda for future research – that is, a truly comparative and critical approach to the cinema that, precisely as "comparative", gives their due to the concrete processes by which films come to be, in all their complexity. The instance of martial art in the Hindi action cinema gives good indications as to the historically specific and complex ways in which generic forms circulate. The consolidation of some of these forms as a distinct action genre in India, and the specific characteristics the genre assumed in that formation suggest that cultural similarities and permutations across national borders can be best explained not as instances of synchronicity within vague notions of "global culturisation", nor as monolithic effects of "State ideology", but as a dialectic between the global circulation of finance and the activities of the State as the agency regulating the movement of capital within the nation. Here I have tried to map the trajectory by which one action body, in a specific manifestation of that dialectic, acquired value.

9

Let's Miscegenate:[1]
Jackie Chan and His African-American Connection

Laleen Jayamanne

> *"Our failure to diversify our mode of address is catastrophic"*
> — Meaghan Morris[2]

> *"... tailor for the object a concept appropriate to the object alone, a concept one can barely say is still a concept, since it applies only to that one thing"*
> — Gilles Deleuze[3]

Who Am I? I am an Australian-Sri Lankan who discovered Jackie Chan in 1996 thanks to Charlie Chaplin and Meaghan Morris. I had read a paper on Chaplin's mimetic mode of performance at a conference in Sydney when Morris asked me what happened to that tradition of slapstick in Hollywood. I said it died with silent cinema and the death of vaudeville. She said I had to see Jackie Chan's *Project A* (Jackie Chan 1983) and then lent me her copy of Chan's great 1978 success *Drunken Master* (Yuen Wo-ping). At that time it was not easy to get either of these films on video in the local shops, unlike now. I love *Drunken Master*, use it in my teaching, and some years ago wrote an article about it for an art exhibition catalogue.[4] In that essay the link with Charlie Chaplin was what really interested me in terms of kung fu slapstick's mimetic mode of activating bodily impulses.

I have followed Chan's career on and off and I must confess that *Drunken Master* is still my favourite Chan film. Here, however, I want to focus on four of his recent films that have either an African or African-American connection: *Rumble in the Bronx* (Stanley Tong 1994); *Who Am I?* (Benny Chan Muk-sing and Jackie Chan 1998); *Rush Hour* (Brett Ratner 1998); and *Rush Hour 2* (Brett Ratner 2001). I want to place them within the context of Chan's move into Hollywood the second time round, after his initial failed effort in the early 1980s. By "Hollywood" here I also mean a cinema where digitized, special effects-driven film is the most globally marketable form of mass entertainment.

Let me return to Chan's first encounter with Hollywood as recounted by him. Chan made three films in Hollywood in the early 1980s: *The Big Brawl* (Robert Clouse 1980), *Cannonball Run* (Hal Needham 1981), and *The Protector* (James Glickenhaus 1985), all of which bombed at the box-office. After *Rumble in the Bronx* became a hit in the US he was asked what had changed, and Chan replied:

> It's all a question of timing, when I came to America first time, it was really tough. With the press it was like:
> "Who are you?"
> "Jackie Chan."
> "Jackie who? / Where you from?"
> "Hong Kong."
> "Is that part of Japan?"
> "No, it's part of China."
> "What do you do?"
> "Martial arts."
> "Oh, Bruce Lee."
> "No, I'm different."
> It was really tough. After that [I] just want to come back to Asia.[5]

I will have Chaplin's film career in mind as I think of Chan's career moves (which also entail a varying of his "mode of address"), as a way of understanding the pressures that Chan faces in a changing technological environment of global film making in the late twentieth and early twenty-first centuries. Chaplin, as we know, was the first truly global film star, a status he reached in the 1920s and consolidated through his second world tour in 1933, when he travelled not only to Europe but also to Ceylon and other Asian countries. My father remembered that trip and his love for Chaplin is one of the few things we had in common, something we passed on to the third generation in a casual sort of way. I imagine that my father and other colonized people embraced this chameleon-like figure as their own, as a kind of third world hero. I have theorized this intuition elsewhere in the following way:

> Chaplin galvanized a global audience (in a way that Buster Keaton, say, did not), perhaps because he offered a glimpse of an alternative modernity to the peoples of the world who would come to western

modernity always already a little too late, almost as though always already a little retarded. To such an audience (of which I am a descendant), Chaplin's famous walk (the lateral, duck-like move while going forward) would offer something like a mimetic cipher of differential rhythms and movements in the very heart of the infamous 'homogeneous empty time' of the capitalist-industrial everyday.[6]

Similarly, what Chan means to Hong Kong is no doubt very different from what he offers to a non-Hong-Kong audience. However, Chaplin's career, too, spanned major technological revolutions such as the coming of sound and the transformation of Hollywood itself from a cottage industry to an oligopoly leaving very little room for independent artists like Chaplin and Buster Keaton. It was Chaplin's great business sense, artistry and internationalism (which are all related) that enabled him to keep on making films from 1914 well into the1950s, unlike Buster Keaton who didn't make a successful transition into sound cinema. Chan, who has had a privileged relationship to the Hong Kong production company Golden Harvest for many years, has in the 1990s been highly aware of the global changes in film production due to the new digital-technology-driven Hollywood cinema and the local effects this has had on the Hong Kong industry.[7]

THE "TRANS" IN TRANSNATIONAL

I want to take up the idea of a "transnational imagination", one of the terms that framed the conference that gave rise to this book, by emphasising movement, the *trans* in "transnational", as a movement *across*, including not only the actions of characters but also those of the camera and other cinematic forces and powers that enthrall us. This means that I will privilege "any-instant-whatever"[8] that tapped my imagination, enabling me to address that rare event within cinema and cultural studies, a truly international/ transnational gathering of scholars: rare, because "international" to us Australians usually means having two Americans at a local conference, not scholars from many parts of the world. I will return to the idea of an "any-instant-whatever" presently.

Movements across can be dizzying, trance-inducing, in that they derail smooth sensory-motor movements which (like those of the happy Bergsonian cow who moves from one green patch we call grass to another) take a familiar trajectory following the main characters and their problems. But most films, even the most impoverished, in their proliferation of movements do move in odd ways that would, if we were to follow them, derail our cow-like mode of recognition of the familiar that is of interest to us. How might one open up one's own intellectual interests and habits to an outside and make an unforeseen connection or two?

Gilles Deleuze's *Cinema 1 — The Movement-Image* releases a perception and conceptualisation of movement which in my opinion is gothic in its vitality. Despite this, however, I gather that it is *Cinema 2 — The Time-Image* that has sold the most copies for its English publisher. Is this an Anglo-Protestant tendency to identify the good book and the bad book? *Cinema 1* is mysterious and wondrous because of the proliferation of lines of movement that are not simply governed by the sensory-motor schema of actions and reactions. The restless dynamism of the gothic lines of the book is forever differentiating, resisting, surmounting, going this way and that and in any-which-way rather than in straight lines, going into the second volume and returning. It may even be a broken line, hence a supple line, sometimes almost imperceptible, so you may sense it but it may not be visible. A "transnational imagination" may, I reckon, be activated on such a line because the coordinates of such a volatile encounter cannot be given in advance; they have to be invented on a moving line.

Such a process happened many a time during the "Hong Kong Connections" conference. The idea for the following section was in fact generated from what I heard there the first day, enabling me to incorporate it into my paper — a truly daring and nerve-wracking thing for me to do as I am usually most comfortable with a fully pre-written though not necessarily a "well-made" paper. This change to my usual mode of address meant that I was able to speak to the conference rather than read, and this I felt gave me greater flexibility and stimulated a capacity to improvise (in a limited manner), no doubt spurred by the improvisational moves central to the great slapstick tradition of performance common to both the Western and the Chinese opera tradition. I especially remember the screening of a film clip at the conference demonstrating a Chinese opera "gag" consisting of a table and chair routine.[9] This instantly made it clear where Chan's skill with any-object-whatever[10] comes from.

TO AMERICA, SECOND TIME; GENERIC KINSHIP NETWORKS

It is clear that in order to keep working, Chan has to work with Hollywood. (At the risk of bathos, may I draw an analogy with those of us writing on international cinema in Australia? If we wish to be heard then we have to get our work published in either Britain or the US. For career advancement purposes, it certainly is better if our publications are with overseas presses.) The image of Chan hanging, high above the road, onto a street sign marked "Hollywood" in order to get out of a tight spot on a bus, marked this necessity through a simple gag in *Rush Hour*; he has to hang in there somehow. Though this time round he has worked on his entrance rather well, it seems. Take the cluster of films, *Rumble in the Bronx*, *Who Am I?* and *Shanghai Noon* (Tom Dey 2000). It seems to me that in these films Chan has made for himself a transnational kinship group by creating filial networks with familiar generic types.

The generic family networking begins with *Rumble in the Bronx* where, to the surprise of the Chan character (who has just arrived from Hong Kong to help his uncle guard his shop in a mean Bronx hood), his elderly uncle marries a not very young African-American woman. The uncle reassures an astonished Chan with a cryptic "this is America", implying that miscegenation is now cool. Within the history of American cinema (hanging on to the idea of generic filial networks of a long *durée*) and going back to the founding father D. W. Griffith, this marriage between two "untouchables" of that cinema resonates with a particular force. I am thinking of Griffith's *Birth of a Nation* (1915) and *Broken Blossoms* (1919). In *Birth* the emancipated African-Americans who dare to cross the race line (those who do actually touch white skin) are played by white actors in blackface (as though in a zone of contact blacks should not touch whites), recalling the performative traditon of blackface minstrelsy. In *Broken Blossoms* the Chinese man places the white girl on a pedestal and worships her, and her father batters her to death for activating this illicit desire for miscegenation. The desire for miscegenation wreaks havoc in an America conceived as paradise in *Birth*, or in the case of *Broken Blossoms* the attraction across race lines has to be sublimated and then made untenable with an extraordinary violence. The comic couple in *Rumble in the Bronx* (blithely unaware of such a dense history) goes off on their honeymoon dressed in identical clothing leaving the rumblings in the Bronx for Chan to deal with. Now it seems that Chan has the proper Asian sanction of an elder to cross phobic ethnic boundaries and tap diverse markets at the same time.

In *Who Am I?* he gets the okay from a tribal African community as well when they christen the amnesiac Chan persona "Whoami" because he has forgotten his identity and keeps asking them "Who am I?" Indeed it must be a question foremost in his mind as he has to reinvent himself across the various technological and industrial divides. The "I" of course needs a "you" and implies the problem of a mode of address, the need to invent it each time, and amnesia is an apt conceit for that.

When Chan told the parochial American journalist that he was not Bruce Lee, thus asserting his difference, he reminded us that he did so by inventing a slapstick kung fu genre and a set of comic moves that has also had to change over the decades. One remembers Chaplin belatedly bidding farewell to the tramp in *Modern Times* (1936). Belatedly because Chaplin had resisted the technology of sound for nearly a decade after its arrival in 1927, knowing full well that though "actions speak louder than words", (a pointed inter-title from *Modern Times*), his time for speaking or at the very least becoming a singing waiter was long overdue. Chaplin's ability to play with time, his mimetic skills, as well as his good business sense (he had his own studio and an ownership interest in United Artists, the distribution company he co-founded in 1919), meant that he could enter sound on his own terms and in his own time.

With *Shanghai Noon* Chan makes sure that he arrives in America by traversing the Western frontier, like the great pioneers, creating kinship ties not only with a lonesome cowboy played by Owen Wilson but also a whole tribe of native Americans who ensure his victory this time around. They, after all, know the taste of defeat and are there to help him. These generic moves by Chan create an odd extended family of sorts, and it is in *Rush Hour* that he really begins to reap the benefits of being so well connected.

BLACKFACE MINSTRELSY[11]

In striking up a partnership with the African-American comedian Chris Tucker in the two *Rush Hour* movies, Chan has tapped a deep vein in American popular culture, the blackface minstrelsy which goes back to the mid-nineteenth century when whites painted their faces black with burnt-cork and gave themselves the license to mimic the African-Americans who were, at that time, slaves. The history of this form of fascination (really an attraction-repulsion dynamic) with the other, culminating in a mode of performance, has a long history in American cinema and other media as well, and recently Spike Lee has explored the complexity of African-Americans taking on blackface in his daring film *Bamboozled*. Of interest to me here is the way Chris Tucker is perceived by some Americans to be *playing at* being in blackface, as someone who exaggerates the racial stereotypes that have branded African-Americans. Tucker came to prominence in the 1990s and at a time when it seems that just about everybody wants to be black, or, let's say, when it is now cool to "wanna be black", and it seems an embarrassment to some that Tucker is harking back to a mode of performance that is less than cool in a post-hip-hop era of African-American youth culture.

Chan's partnership with Tucker creates a comic duo in that one is a master of comic action and the other is known as the big mouth — "7/11" is what another African-American (who has become Chinese) calls Tucker in *Rush Hour 2*. So we have two highly marketable modes of performance brought together in this odd pair who don't want to be professional partners. In a *Newsweek* cover page advertisement, Tucker stands for the West and Chan for the East, and "West" here is really America — and so at last an African-American stands as an emblem of America in a special Asian issue of an American news magazine.[12] This is good marketing because African-Americans, who have been devotees of Hong Kong cinema since at least the 1970s, constitute a significant group in box office terms in the US.[13] In sociological terms, however, friends who know more than I do about the politics of ethnicity in the US tell me that the Chinese and African-American communities don't really mix as merrily as they do in the Chan films. So it seems to me that these films are creating new kinship lines.

The way Chan (as Inspector Lee) arrives in America in this film is more formal than in *Rumble in the Bronx*, where he just slips into the shot from the side unannounced. In *Rush Hour*, in contrast, he arrives in a private plane, in a centred shot, and descends quietly while Tucker (as detective Carter) impatiently waits for him on the tarmac, beside his black sports car. As Chan thanks the Chinese crew Tucker strides up to him and starts his "Do you understand-a English?" routine of using language as a weapon of derision. Chan's response to this is a tentative smile. And from then on there is a running gag on linguistic misapprehension. Tucker assumes that Chan assumes that he is the chauffeur and the scene plays with the idea of the gag in its literal sense as something stuffed in the mouth making speech impossible; here it is the "big mouth" who "gags" the other with his torrential minstrelspeak.

A SILENT FACE; WHAT CAN IT DO?

What is striking about the first moments of the meeting between Chan and Tucker is that the man of action is silent and still and the big mouth doesn't stop talking. Even more striking however, is not the silence itself but what the silence makes visible; Chan's face framed by the jet black of his suit and of the black surface of Tucker's sports car. His familiar body is framed-out, highlighting his face. While Chan's iconicity usually includes his dazzling smile at the camera, this time round there is no reason to smile as yet so he simply sits and listens to the torrent of words pouring forth from Tucker's mouth as they drive through L.A. This goes on for a while (making Tucker think that Chan does not know "American"), and as the moment of silence expands one begins to pay attention to Chan's face; he is tired, no doubt, as he has just crossed the Pacific, but his face is now lined, marked by time and it is his silence and stillness, framed by the black of the car and his suit that really makes one notice all these micro-details of a familiar, lovable face. It is also very beautiful, a kind of beauty present in a face that abandons the necessity to produce social and psychological signs; he does not emit phatic signs of listening, such as a nod or even a "hmmm". It is hard to get there (Robert Bresson's strategies for reaching this beyond of human sociality through his "actors" flit past, though I am not at all suggesting that Chan gets there or even wants to). But to encounter such a micro-instant in a comic action film is truly wonderful. And I am beginning to feel that this trans-Pacific action comedy is taking me on a strange ride.

The comic gag of the three-way face-off between Tucker, Chan and a white American cabby played by Gene LeBell (also known as Gene "Judo" LeBell[14]) is, while comically unpredictable, also a lovely set piece reprising the John Woo move from *The Killer* taken up by Tarantino. As Chan gets his partner out of this deadlock the hitherto silent Chan comes up with a beautiful set speech which knocks Tucker off his guard and yet he is game enough to appreciate it, so that he starts mockingly imitating Chan's flawless English speech, adding gestures to it, as they get into his car and drive off.

Now instead of following them the camera makes a strange gesture of its own, tracking and panning the car then letting it go out of frame and staying with the large mural of African-American musicians painted on a wall against which some of the previous action has been performed. The background now comes to the fore when the moving camera tracks across the faces (in large close-ups) of the greatest — Duke Ellington, Louis Armstrong, Ella Fitzgerald and others — to rest at the right hand corner for an instant, on the face of Nat King Cole. And instantly I hear him purring "The night is mighty chilly and conversation seems pretty silly ..." from Robert Aldrich's great 1950s B noir, *Kiss Me Deadly*, also set in L.A. I am most intrigued. Why does the camera rest on one of the favourite singers of my Ceylonese youth in the 1950s? And then I remembered how Cole's music was criticised for watering down black sound to make it palatable to white ears; a tributary of blackface minstrelsy so to speak. The long *durée* of this history suddenly opened up, in a Benjaminian flash, one might say, in the virtual any-instant of a painted black face on a brick wall. This virtual instant was made perceptible through the film's attentiveness to a silent face in counterpoint to a chattering mouth. These are fine micro-lines that appear and disappear almost imperceptibly and if we don't catch them, well, it's just too bad, the loss is ours.

The more explicit moves are announced and performed so wonderfully that *Rush Hour* became a major box office success. One of the high points of such cross-cultural mimetic generic movement happens when Tucker and Chan exchange kung fu moves and African-American dance moves with hip-hop street origins. And in *Rush Hour 2*, there is another great set piece on miscegenation. Chan and Tucker, looking for vital clues, visit the "Chinese Soul Food" restaurant where the African-American owner has made himself Chinese, dressed in traditional garb with a long pigtail. When an altercation leads to a fight Chan steps in to find his "Chinese–African–American" opponent highly skilled, and not only in kung fu: he is also able to talk to him in Chinese and joke about Tucker. The fighting technique he uses turns out to be one taught to him by the brother of the famous master of the technique who has clearly migrated to America. The gag thus becomes a zone of violently funny contact producing unpredictable flows of movement and information and kinship ties. The climax of the gag is quiet, the camera just shows us the Chinese-African-American family of "Chigroes" recalling the infamous Dr No and the Chigroes of the Caribbean in the James Bond movie of that name.

A less predictable move happens as they ride through L.A. in *Rush Hour*. To Tucker's fury Chan quite innocently changes the radio station on Tucker's car to catch the Beach Boys, his favourite American sound. So Tucker changes back to his station and does a series of gestural dance moves to the beat of his own favourite black sound that transforms his image as a "blackface simulating blackface minstrelsy" into a threatening energy that you don't wanna fool around with. In his previous films Tucker is used as a comedian, speaking in a falsetto register, camping up the humour.[15] This is the only time to my knowledge that he modulates his performance into a register that makes him seriously scary for an instant. So it seems that the partnership is working precisely because there is a new energetic field activated by their simply being together that does not really belong to either in their familiar star image. Part of the dynamism of this process is that this energy moves in unpredictable ways.

As Rob Wilson points out, these trans-Pacific moves happen within the narrative framework of a "transnational assembly line of criminal financialization".[16] And in *Rush Hour 2*, fake American $100 bills are produced in Asia, shipped to L.A. for distribution and laundered in a faux-Chinese casino in Las Vegas. I want to focus finally on Tucker's performance at the gambling table in this casino. Here the action runs in two parallel lines with Chan in action mode tracking down the Chinese super-criminal while Tucker moves into his most outrageous blackface minstrel routine as a way of distracting the attention of the guards from the main action of his buddy Chinese cop.

This is the truly aberrant speech line to end all aberrant lines: Tucker begins with the famous Martin Luther King speech "I have a dream …" and improvises on it, culminating in the punch line "everyone (even Chinese people) has the right to gamble". The film cuts to a Chinese couple at that moment and King's great speech is brought down to a bathetic level: nothing is sacred to the comedian. Remember Chaplin's drawing laughs from World War I in *Shoulder Arms* (1918): while the whole scene in the casino is an elaborate verbal gag, Tucker takes upon himself the licence to say stuff that is uncool. This power of the comedian to violate norms or express their violence with licence is made possible through that simulation of blackface minstrelsy with which Tucker is certainly not "stuck", thanks to these two films. He knows that he is in a game where masks are a useful means to get what you want. And because it is Tucker's own face that does this, one never really knows when he is sincere and when he is not. The gleeful abandonment of the African-American sincerity and rectitude (think of the star images of Sydney Poitier, Morgan Freeman and Denzel Washington) that is now a proper strand of Hollywood cinema helps Tucker to bring a certain improper playfulness into the serious realm of race relations, and Chan, his buddy by now, has made this possible. Such are the moves available to the powerless, one hears Chaplin whisper across the decades of cinematic history.

Here we may also listen again (and we should do so at length) to Ralph Ellison's fine analysis in his brilliantly illuminating and humorous essay "What would America be without blacks":

> If we can revisit for a moment the temptation to view everything having to do with Negro Americans in terms of their racially imposed status, we become aware of the fact that for all the harsh reality of the social and economic injustices visited upon them, these injustices have failed to keep the Negro clear of the cultural mainstream; Negro Americans are in fact one of its major tributaries. If we can cease approaching American social reality in terms of such false concepts as white and nonwhite, black culture and white culture, and think of these apparently unthinkable matters in the realistic manner of Western pioneers confronting the unknown prairie, perhaps we can begin to imagine what the U.S. would have been, or not have been, had there been no blacks to give it — if I may be so bold as to say — color.

For one thing, the American nation is in a sense the product of American language, a colloquial speech that began emerging long before the British colonials and Africans were transformed into Americans. It is a language that evolved from the King's English but, basing itself upon the realities of the American land and colonial institutions or lack of institutions, began quite early as a vernacular revolt against signs and symbols, manners and authority of the mother country. It is a language that began by merging the sound of many tongues, brought together in the struggle of diverse regions and whether it is admitted or not much of the sound of that language is derived from the timbre of the African voice and the listening habits of the African ear …

Whitman viewed the spoken idiom of Negro American as a source for a native grand opera. Its flexibility, its musicality, its rhythms, freewheeling diction and metaphors as projected in Negro American folklore were absorbed by the creators of our nineteenth-century literature even when the majority of blacks were still enslaved …

Without the presence of Negro American style, our jokes, our tall tales, even our sports would be lacking in the sudden turns, the shocks, the swift changes of pace (all jazz shaped) that serve to remind us that the world is ever unexplored and that while a complete mastery of life is a mere illusion the real secret of the game is to make life swing.[17]

And oh boy, don't they swing! That's what Tucker offers Chan, this power to swing, to vary, to modulate to differentiate himself from within, so to speak, and Chan too has done "likewise, likewise".[18] Though he gets beaten up for doing "likewise" in the "what's up my nigger" routine in the pool hall scene in *Rush Hour*, he does learn something about idiom and gesture, that simple imitation is not enough, that the moves have to be internalised and that some gestures may just not be negotiable. But I do think this is the first time we have had a glimpse of a soulful Chan and a seriously awesome Tucker.

"WHAT'S THE PLAN?"

Whenever Owen Wilson and Jackie Chan are in a jam in *Shanghai Knights*, Wilson asks Chan: "What's the plan?" I take it that for Chan the "catastrophe" of failing to diversify his mode of address (entailing also internal differentiation)[19] will be the loss of a career, which also means a loss of the power to invent in the face of formidable odds — digital technology and an aging body come to mind as two key factors. As for us academics, our catastrophe might be more banal, simply the very real possibility that nothing much will happen and we will have a lot more of the same, just two Americans constituting for us our sense of the "international", thus disabling unpredictable transnational moves, our chance to swing.

In a scene referred to earlier, in *Rush Hour* when Chan tries to change Tucker's radio station Tucker says something that I have puzzled over for a long while, he says: "I Michael Jackson, you Tito". Who was Tito, I wondered — unlike most Americans and some Australians who would most certainly know the reference. Recently the *Sydney Morning Herald* newspaper had a spread on the Jackson Five, focusing on Michael's recent arrest, and it is through this that I learnt that Tito was Michael's younger brother. So, well before they become buddies Tucker accepts Chan as his (younger) brother, even as Tucker takes on the persona of the pop icon whose identity is visibly in flux, "taking on" a white mask; strange minglings indeed. It is as though the neuralgia and fascination of black face minstrelsy as a backward or retarded image has returned to haunt us with added force; for now we have blacks in white-face as well and it is difficult to pinpoint and nail someone down with his or her identity based on skin colour as indelible sign of authenticity or inferiority. The *Rush Hour* films offer an odd, mobile image of a kin group where black-face and white-face (through plastic surgery and/or disease), converge to create a divergent link, incorporate a brother into the fold, so to speak. The membrane thus stretched and folded is truly flexible enabling leakages across tightly guarded phobic boundaries.

It is this flexibility and quick wittedness that makes me imagine that Chaplin, Chan and Tucker are brothers of sorts, slower than others around them (because of a physical impediment in Chaplin's case, because of being in a foreign culture whose codes are unfamiliar, in the case of Chan, and because of Tucker's "black-face" in the two *Rush Hour* movies); they are somewhat retarded and also faster than everyone else. Tucker, verbally and through gesture, and Chan and Chaplin through gesture and action can take "any-object-whatever" whether language or a thing, and make them swing in Ralph Ellison's sense. Tucker and Chan's partnership was certainly a "good plan" economically and its success suggests that the qualities we scholars need to be intrepid travelers in culturally phobic zones of contact are a certain daring to appear or be foolish (retarded), agility, and above all humour. And by the way — I also learned the art of relaxed listening from my Chinese colleagues at the Lingnan conference and have decided not to be so tightly wound up (in typical South Asian fashion), every time I see red.

10

The Secrets of Movement:
The Influence of Hong Kong Action
Cinema upon the Contemporary
French Avant-garde

Nicole Brenez

PREAMBLE

My conviction and endeavour are dedicated to the hope that film studies in universities do not become a "registration office" administering the corpus imposed by the industry. This means that we have a duty (urgent to the point of becoming an emergency) to seek out and to comment on what I would call "free-films", that is to say, films made outside the industry for ethical, political, economic or purely aesthetic reasons. Nowadays it appears that fewer and fewer films are made by the industry, because more and more films are the same film under different titles — like those in the pornography market. There are fewer and fewer films to watch because there are more and more prints of the same movie on regular screens (when I left Paris for Hong Kong in January 2003, 80 percent of the screens were taken over by *Harry Potter and the Chamber of Secrets*). And nowadays more and more "free films" are appearing because of the proliferation of tools for making images, and because of the moral and political necessity to escape from economic censorship. This is why I will analyse in this paper three modest, unknown, and unique French experimental films.

INTRODUCTION

What can be exchanged or transmitted between one national-geographical cinema and another? First of all, products, people, and skills can be traded, including capital, filmmakers, actors, tools and so on. Second, stylistic figures can be traded such as, for example, the art of speed Hong Kong has offered to the rest of the world. Third, figurative problems can also be traded; for example, the aesthetics of the phantom that goes from Jean-Pierre Melville to John Woo and is systematized in the opening credits of Antoine Fuqua's *The Replacement Killers*. ("Phantom" here does not mean the shadow of the divine, fantasies of power, or the dead, but ways of dealing with a deep melancholia.) Lastly, cinematic problems about the meaning of basic constituents can be traded, and the conception of these problems can differ greatly from one visual culture to another as with, for example, the relationship between continuity and discontinuity.

There is seemingly nothing more remote from the action cinema of Hong Kong than French avant-garde cinema. One is an industrial, hierarchical cinema, organized by laws of iconography. It's a cinema of archetypes, fit for universal acceptance and universally loved. The other is an artisanal cinema, composed of singular initiatives, devoted to questioning and criticizing all and every cinematic law. It's a cinema of prototypes, globally unacceptable and deliberately unreconciled ("Not Reconciled", following the title of Straub's and Huillet's film). There should be no connection between these two continents of cinema.

Nevertheless, one cannot but see a deep, strong and dynamic relationship between them, an unexpected link which is like an ultimate testimony to the vitality of Hong Kong action cinema. This cinema is known and admired by several cinephile French experimental filmmakers like David Matarasso, Stéphane du Mesnildot, Agathe Dreyfus, Xavier Baert, and Othello Vilgard. Among them, Agathe Dreyfus knows by heart the works of Zhang Che (Chang Cheh), John Woo and Tsui Hark, Xavier Baert considered devoting his thesis to Wong Kar-wai, and now they are all fascinated by Johnnie To. David Matarasso wrote probably the first piece in France about Fruit Chan's *Made in Hong Kong*.[1] For these filmmakers, in contrast with previous generations of the avant-garde, the political and aesthetic choice to work in the experimental field does not mean a global rejection of industrial cinema. It rather expresses the demand for a deep knowledge of the cinema accorded all its possibilities, and a refusal to subscribe to any economically determined ideological divisions. For this new generation, Tsui Hark's *Time and Tide* is a much more experimental film than the hundredth imitation of Jonas Mekas's diaries. And in the industrial field, nothing now seems closer to experimental research than the action cinema of Hong Kong.

Why is this so? My hypothesis is this: Hong Kong action cinema supplies French experimental cinema with a liberating lever to reconstruct the problem of movement — that is, the problem that structures cinema itself. What is the function of this lever, what does it displace? It allows the cinema to slip from a *kinematic* conception of movement to a *kinetic* one. These two apparent synonyms in fact derive from two different branches of science. Kinematics belongs to mechanics and is the study of the movement of material bodies disregarding the forces determining that movement, while kinetics belongs to physics and is concerned with theories of energy. Among the various forms of energy, let's just mention "potential energy" and "resonance or radiation potential energy" for their magnificent theoretical virtualities.[2] Translated in a cinematographic imaginary these two spheres of movement broadly correspond, *mutatis mutandis*, with Western (kinematics) and Eastern (kinetics) conceptions of movement. The original research of Etienne-Jules Marey and his assistants Georges Demenÿ and Lucien Bull, a project of systematically describing the material motions of bodies, was inscribed in a rationalist, positivist framework of the objectification of movement. It was designed with a precise purpose: dressage, a training of bodies to gymnastic functionality.

An important book by Christian Pociello, a historian of sport, has recently established that the birth of cinema participates in what he calls an "anthropotechnie". This is a term referring to a canonical modelling of human gesture, the financial and historical origin of which may be found in the military subsidies that created the "Station Physiologique" for Marey in preparation for an inevitable new war against Germany.[3] In France, the cinema emerged as a massive and collective training for death. The scientific program of the Station Physiologique was to investigate highly practical matters: to find out the maximum weight a man could support, the maximum length a man could walk, and the "best", i.e., the most economical, way to put a foot on the ground to move forward. Here "man" precisely means "soldier", and indeed all of Marey's actors were on loan from the French army. This also explains why the first slow-motion films made by Lucien Bull are visual studies of the ballistics of bullets, shells, and human bones exploding. These visually sublime films, made mainly between 1903 and 1912, between a war lost and another largely conducted for revenge, are the first real action films.[4]

In France, the invention of cinema as a technique for de-composing movement is clearly inscribed in a "history of the social control of the body", as Marta Braun, following Michel Foucault, has written so well.[5] This is an almost unknown phenomenon that has not yet been thought through in terms of original sin, but which constitutes, however, a kind of original unconscious repression that contemporary experimental cinema is now beginning to question.

The recourse to Asian concepts, whether scientific or spiritual, opens up other paths for filmmakers to work on motion. For example, in chapter 23 of *Zhuang-zi* we read: "man has a real existence, but this has nothing to do with his position in space; he has a real duration, but this has nothing to do with its origin or end in time". According to the American historian Joseph Needham, *Zhuang-zi's* foundational scientific thinking from ancient China is shocking from a Western perspective in that Chinese "traditional scientific thought was deeply attached to ideas of continuum and remote action", allowing for various conceptions of causality ("reticulated" and "synchronous", for example) in which a causal event need not always strictly precede its effect in time.[6] For a Western reader, this kind of proposition more immediately recalls Deleuze than Aristotle. What matters most, however, is the recourse to a mode of spiritual thought in which bodily techniques do not take for their purpose either the constitution or the destitution of the Self, as they do in the West, but rather work towards knowledge of the world.[7] Reaching its apogee with Kant, classical Western philosophy puts bodily work at the service of individuation and reason: "physical perfection is the culture of all the faculties for the fulfilment of the purposes given by reason".[8] Eastern philosophy, in contrast, tends towards a fusion between the body and the universe, which gives to its system of representation a great capacity to deal with anthropological symbolic mutations. It is impossible not to simplify such vast issues here but let's say that, in the imaginary of the French filmmakers, movement is not a tool but a value in Asian action cinema. While nobody in France (with the major exception of Robert Bresson) has ever succeeded in creating a bodily syntax of spiritual gesture, for these filmmakers the task of confronting "other" conceptions of movement in their film practice constitutes a critical and, more deeply, a kinetic mode of release — even if those conceptions are reconstructed.

Let us now consider three different solutions to the problem of representing movement as essayed in, respectively, *Samouraï* by Johanna Vaude (2002, 7 minutes), *Révélation/Chunguang Zhaxie* by Xavier Baert (2001, 7 minutes), and *Lighting* by a collective under the direction of Othello Vilgard (2002, 7 minutes).

SAMOURAÏ BY JOHANNA VAUDE

Let me first explain how *Samouraï* was made. Technically speaking, the process can be described in five steps: Johanna Vaude chose the music (by Photek, an experimental group); she refilmed in Super 8 a selection of shots from other films and details in the shots; she pre-edited in Super 8; she refilmed this first editing with a digital camera and then she reworked the editing on a computer, to diversify as much as possible the speed of the shots and the gestures. The films chosen by Johanna Vaude are Japanese with a touch of Hong Kong: *Sugata Sanshiro, Rashomon, Kagemusha, Seven Samurai* and *Yojimbo* by Akira Kurosawa, *Harakiri* and *Rebellion* by Masaki Kobayashi, *Shogun's Shadow* by Yasuo Furuhata, together with *Rain of Light on the Empty Mountain*, and Tsui Hark's *The Blade*. Vaude chose some shots from each film and then, inside these shots, she selected samples of movement, reworking their speeds so as to create new effects of detail, fragment and emblem. All of this iconographic material is edited according to principles of "Hong Kong style", to follow Adrian Martin's formula.[9]

Three motifs can be found in the film: the eye of a child, the lotus (symbol of an "inner quest"), [10] and the gong as shutter release for the rhythm. There is also another, more complicated motif, the duel, produced here by mixing images from about ten films. However, none of these films' narrativity, progressivity, or even symbolic content is retained; all that remains is the motion. But what is this "motion"? The movements are linked as images and matches; no longer trajectories, they are relations and differences of energy. The aim of *Samouraï* is to draw out the energetic substance in the martial movement. Therefore, the fight takes place neither between two characters nor between body and soul, nor does it unfold between abstraction and figuration. It takes place between precision and irradiation, that is, between the absolute instantaneity of the martial gesture and the unending and even cosmic echoing of the energy that gives rise to it. In other words, the fight takes place between, on the one hand, the line, the edge, the operativity and instantaneity of the gesture, and, on the other, the qualitative explosion that this virtuoso "move" provokes as well as the explosion objectified by the chromatic echoes coming from the bodies. The sharp and the blurred, the local and the global, and the unique and the collective can no longer be perceived as oppositional but rather as two faces or aspects of the same kinetic phenomenon.

Certainly, this is the plastic transposition of what the West has understood about martial arts culture. This can be broken down into three phases, as follows:

1.   Physical motion is entirely determined by psychic motion, "spiritual awakening", because the latter has been abolished as a specific form of intentionality. In French popular culture, the classic reference on this is a German short story by Eugen Herrigel, "Zen in the Art of Archery."[11] It concludes with the notion of a "pure act" achieved at

the end of a long process, during the course of which the Western subject learns to relinquish himself in order to conquer the perfection of the gesture.

2.   Psychic motion is wholly informed by ethical and spiritual values. The aim of the gesture is not to accomplish a particular task but to open the path to truth. "Above all, above glory, above victory, even above life, the sword-master sets 'the sword of Truth', the truth with which he experiments and that judges him". [12] At issue here are the seven principles of Bushido, which define the behaviour of the characters of John Woo, Tsui Hark and Johnnie To: truth, bravery, universal love, justice, sincerity, honour and loyalty. For Johanna Vaude the figure of the Samurai, whether Chinese or Japanese, whether in historical or contemporary costume, whether depicted by Kurosawa or John Woo, represents the chivalrous qualities of the demanding creator at work in every man.

3.   This culture of spiritual motion opens up for Westerners an extraordinary formal freedom allied with the experimental attitude. Both refuse normative divisions, usual paradigms, and even mechanistic dialectics. What is perceived *a priori* as a figurative paradox (e.g., the shooting without aiming in John Woo's *Hard Boiled*) is simply the result of an inner journey dedicated to rectitude. To outline the spiritual grounds for this shedding of identity, it would no doubt be necessary to return to Lao Tseu's *Tao-tö King* [Lao Tzu's *Tao Te Ching*]: "To walk well is to walk without leaving a rut or a trace. To close well is to close without bar or bolt, and then nobody can open. To tie well is to tie without rope or string, and then nobody can untie". [13]

It is not surprising that Johanna Vaude chooses *The Blade* as exemplary of the editing process. In France, *The Blade* marks a new era of editing. Among its many innovations in rhythm, movement and cutting, one special moment is particularly exciting. It's in the final fight when we can feel, rather than see, that the protagonist's body is multiplying by its own force. If one watches the character's movements carefully, we have to suppose that in just one of the shots (lasting about two seconds), three different actors would be needed to accomplish those trajectories at the speed required by the fight. It follows that the imaginary body of the character is totally kinetic and made up of editing. Editing in general is a mobilization of relationship between two phenomena: mobility and immobility, change and continuity, or, the same and the other. But here, at the end of *The Blade*, with the appearance, disappearance, and impossible reappearance of Chiu Man-cheuk's body, editing occurs between the same and the same — being "here" and "there" at almost the same time. The same has become its own other, an other of pure energy and virtuosity; and the most impossible alteration of a body is edited inside the same shot. The figural event is that you obtain the maximal figurative change within an impure continuity. Of course, we must remember that the character here is an emblem of all kinds of mutilation, of a maiming both physical and affective. So he is never whole and intact, being in himself either "too little" (missing an arm, a family and a memory) or, as shown here, "too much", for there is too much movement for one man.

Perhaps this kind of differential intensity in relation to the physical domain is a daily experience for everybody. The body invented here by Tsui Hark cannot but remind us, in and as a popular echoing, of the ancient formula: "Man has a real existence, but this has nothing to do with his position in space; he has a real duration, but this has nothing to do with its origin or end in time". This is indeed the main characteristic of the Hong Kong action cinema body: it can change at every shot, in contrast with the classical Western body, whose energy is devoted mainly to confirming its own identity from one shot to another. This is a structural opposition, between bodies of alteration and metamorphosis, and bodies of confirmation. Whereabouts in cinema can one find precisely the martiality of martial arts? The kinetic principle makes it clear that it is not in the actual move, but in the figurative embrace of impossible motions in a possible body.

Let us now consider the entire logic of Johanna Vaude's film. There is the Japanese martial kinetic art, which treats gesture according to its objective invisibility.[14] There is also the Hong Kong depiction of movement, of which *The Blade* is exemplary, and where all the relations between visibility and invisibility are explored through the diversity of speed and, for the first time, the impurity of continuity. Then there is the French sampling of the internal energy of the Japanese treatment, and the French development of Hong Kong editing through colour and visual echoing. There are thus two connected facts. On the one hand, cinema surely can never really show Martial Art, because it is a spiritual movement. But on the other hand, cinema can always develop many and more ways to describe the non-figurative phenomenon of psychic energy. And this remains a major achievement to be striven for collectively at a time when the cloning of the human body is becoming a reality.

Johanna Vaude's *Samouraï* investigates the Asian culture of martial arts in order to reconfigure the three basic temporal aspects of cinema: mobility and immobility; instantaneity (of the appearance of the image) and accumulation (of the images in the viewer's consciousness); singularity (of one frame) and overlapping (of all the objective images with all the psychic images, the cinema being a floating synthesis of the two). By means of its re-shooting process and its syncretic editing, the film is able to forcefully illustrate these aspects and, through the intercession of martial iconography, to emphasize their spiritual as well as visual logic. *Samouraï* is indeed a manifesto for cinema as a possible chivalric art, forever loyal to the subtlety of all phenomena. Against the Western grain, "loyal" here refers to operativity, which has nothing to do with functionality – and that is precisely my definition of what constitutes a filmic act in action cinema.

RÉVÉLATION BY XAVIER BAERT

Xavier Baert is the author of about ten short essays and his non-exclusive but main subject is dance, for which he invents a new treatment in each film. His *Révélation* (*Chunguang Zhaxie*) is a visual study of Wong Kar-wai's *In the Mood for Love*, a very famous film in France. I will discuss this film only briefly here, since it's not exactly an action film. For Xavier Baert, the immediate purpose of Wong's film is to explore and experiment with superimposition techniques in filmmaking. But his recycling of the trailer of *In the Mood for Love* is a groundbreaking event in the history of recycling found footage, now the dominant trend in the experimental field. For the first time, here the purpose of recycling is not to fetishize, destroy, or analyse the matrix mould (as Joseph Cornell's *Rose Hobart*, Kirk Tougas's *The Politics of Perception*, and Ken Jacobs's *Tom Tom the Piper's Son* respectively do). With *Révélation* we see a film revisit another film passionately to console its characters.

Wong Kar-wai's *In the Mood for Love* depicts an unaccomplished love story. In the film, the two would-be lovers find themselves geographically bound to each other in a small apartment and emotionally drawn to each other after realizing their spouses are having an affair with each other. However, they have to endure double measures of suffering, both from the betrayal and the emerging desire that cannot be fulfilled. Their conservative society, forcefully symbolized by the suffocating mise-en-scène, and the catch-22 situation they are in (they will lose their moral standing to accuse their spouses if they become like them) thus lock them physically and psychologically into a torturing tangential relationship, as they brush against each other's bodies daily in the narrow corridors and stairways with ever increasing longing but without end. Now, thanks to Xavier Baert's superimposition, they appear physically separated in the celluloid space through the encrustation and the explicit rolling of the film, and psychically fusional, since their alternating and mutual transformation in images dreamed by the other affirms their deep belonging to each other. *Révélation* in a way sides with the characters against the melancholy fate that *In the Mood for Love* imposes on them. What more beautiful homage could be paid to the sentimental ascendency that a film like *In the Mood for Love* holds over a critical consciousness? In this sense, *Révélation* is the enactment of a pure passion.

LIGHTING UNDER THE DIRECTION OF OTHELLO VILGARD

The case of *Lighting* is a particularly dynamic and subtle one here, for the director Othello Vilgard is actually saturated in martial arts culture. He has practised karate since he was four years old and later became a karate teacher like his father. Vilgard is also a great connoisseur of Japanese and Chinese literature, philosophy and, of course, cinema. He is also the author of the "Martial Arts" entry in a "John Woo Dictionary".[15] Here it is:

> Often subject to the most foolish idealizations, the martial arts and, more importantly, their deep spirit, constitute a crucial part of John Woo's aesthetics. Beside the dynamic hieratism of a Kurosawa, John Woo delivers in his films a little-known if not invisible form of the martial attitude, which is, moreover, stamped with mythology. The Action becomes a "mise en acte", a relay of the body's general motion towards its total accomplishment, in the eternity of the wound as in the triumph.
>
> The spiritual dimension of the martial arts can be seen more clearly in some minor characters, such as the mercenaries-samurai working for criminal networks, than in the heroes. It's the one-eyed character in *Hard Boiled* and the killer with sunglasses in *A Better Tomorrow II*, both pure warriors, who show the martial ethic in its purity — absolute loyalty and protection of the weak, the latter prevailing over the former as the one-eyed Angel rebels against his boss, who is cruel to his victims. The tool of this art of realising Being is the body, for this is the art of seeing true, of preparing one's own body for the suddenness of a situation, like Chow Yun-fat's total field of vision in *Hard Boiled* when he enters the hospital for the first time. The act has become so precise that it can bypass conscious intention in its accomplishment as a just, true gesture. The way in which Tequila successfully opens the door of the mortuary with a random bullet represents a sublime demonstration of this art of living (and dying).
>
> So if there is a fight, it is always against another self, a double totalising of the forms of the body to be attacked — a principle that allows

Tequila to declare to Tony in *Hard Boiled*: "Your own worst enemy is yourself". The Art of combat is first and foremost one of combating one's own impulses and ignorance in a struggle against the illusion of equilibrium.

His intimate knowledge of the martial way of thinking enables Othello Vilgard to incorporate martial arts in the film structurally and practically instead of through iconographical imitation. Here it is cinema itself, as a practice, that has to become a martial art, so that the film becomes a pure Act. This is why *Lighting* does not *look like* a Hong Kong action film, but rather *is* an action film in its most concrete form. An aesthetic project of this kind implies at least three dimensions:

1. The director has to perform all the filmic operations. Every stage of the creative process depends on his body: Othello Vilgard shoots, develops, and edits the film himself. He has built with his hands his own developmental laboratory within the heart of one of the most productive experimental groups in France today, *l'Etna* — a group which Vilgard co-founded. For him the camera must become the prolongation of the body, exactly as the sword does for a samurai or the gun for Tequila.

2. The director has to work from the inaugural images of the history of cinema, by Albert Londe or Duchêne de Boulogne, because "to make films consists in taking lessons with the masters".[16]

3. The director has to explore the most active aspects of kinetics: the rhythmic, the sensible, and the tactile, as illustrated in *Lighting* through the iconography of the scopic drive, with the purpose of finding pure visual rhythms. For Othello Vilgard, one must "purify according to the rhythm, so that there is nothing left of the image, the editing must be the peril of static images". Or, as he also puts it, one must "follow the spirit of the martial arts cinema and edit as Hong Kong movies do". But the editing isn't devoted exclusively to the combustion of four static images (the inside of an eye, the portrait of a mad man, the breast of a woman, and a seagull, which of course relates to one of the most emblematic motifs of John Woo, the dove). In fact, it generates a fifth image that determines the rhythmics: the fifth motif, which one has to deduce from the whole film, is a photographic rifle, a rifle that would not be held by a French scientist at the end of the XIX° century (Marey in 1882) but by a Hong Kong policeman at the peak of his spiritual energy.

The aesthetic horizon designed by Vilgard's current research has nothing to do with the violence or the scopic predation practised by mainstream industrial cinema; indeed, Othello Vilgard mingles the conjugated influences of Asian culture and the work of Peter Tscherkassky, whose famous "CinemaScope Trilogy" (*L'Arrivée*, 1998; *Outer Space*, 1999; and *Dream Work*, 2001) also proposes a visual critique of the scopic drive. Othello Vilgard's ideal would be to make a film with nothing, a film that would be the ultimate vacuity, not a conceptual work but "something that reverberates the void". Such a cinema obeys the ritual foundations of Chinese culture which, according to the account of the great sinologist Marcel Granet, distinguishes between negative rites ("eliminations, lustrations, confessions, and expiations") and the positive rites of oblation, that is, curative and dynamic suppression.[17] Vilgard's next film aspires to fulfil this ultimate gesture. If you ask Othello Vilgard what his current work consists of, Vilgard will reply, "sketches, trainings"; and if you press him to tell you what his finished films will look like, he would answer: "maybe the same".

Thanks to the three examples discussed in this essay, we can begin to see to what extent Hong Kong aesthetics inspires the French avant-garde — in terms of major formal initiatives instead of mimetic repetition as in French commercial cinema exemplified by Luc Besson or Christophe Gans. With Johanna Vaude, the cinema becomes a manifesto for a figurative ethics; with Xavier Baert a new exegetic genre, the critical elegy; and with Othello Vilgard, like a new Yves Klein, a martial art. This essay is merely an expression of gratitude for the high aesthetic values propagated by the great Hong Kong *auteurs*. I hope it clears away some of the common misunderstandings about excessive violence and simplified figures that are still all too often associated with Hong Kong action cinema.

Translated from the French by the author with the indispensable help of Adrian Martin and Lin Wenchi

11

At the Edge of the Cut:
An Encounter with the Hong Kong Style
in Contemporary Action Cinema

Adrian Martin

> *[A]n inauthentic work has no unconscious. It is not the resolution of any
> inherent problem. It is merely parrotry and antics unless it exploits the
> very procedures of trickery and fascination.*
>
> – Nicolas Abraham[1]

Occasionally, in the middle of a lecture or an essay, one finds *the* great
question of film analysis quietly, anxiously avowed: how to proceed?
Meaning: what level of the film, which exact bits of it demand our attention?
We have often heard the (reassuring) truism that 'analysis constructs its
objects'. But those objects, unfailingly, still manage to resist our best efforts
at corralling them into one specific framework or another. And hence we
are left with the disturbing but inviting temptation to find a method of
analysis that is adequate — I would say culturally and poetically
appropriate — to its object.

The academic world of cinema studies, with its steady tendency
towards producing cookie-cutter templates for analysis, does not always
want to admit this truth: every distinct kind of film — maybe every film in
its singularity — requires a different kind of response, a particular
'shakedown', a special angle of attack. Action films, of all the cinema's
forms, pose this methodological question most acutely.

I recently worked intensively on the first three *Mad Max* films made
in Australia by George Miller.[2] (Sadly, a long-prepared fourth instalment,
Fury Road, was cancelled at the end of 2004.) The more I got into this
adventure, the less interested I became in certain large sections of the films
devoted to ordinary things like plot, theme and character — as well as
more elaborate levels like national allegory, social reflection or the 'subject

positioning' of the spectator. All I seemed to care about as I soldiered on was the action scenes — and, still more fanatically, certain microscopic split seconds of those action scenes. This seemed valid and right to me in so far as, while analysis of musicals always comes to grips with scenes of singing and dancing, many analyses of action films manage to talk about everything *but* the action.

An analytical encounter with action cinema is something that I, as a critic, had long postponed. My files are full of notes, headings and references preparing me for this work, as I dimly and amorphously imagined it might proceed. In the late 1970s, after watching some Clint Eastwood films, I loosely sketched out a piece called "Running the Gauntlet: The Poetics of Action Cinema". Closer to the subject at hand, I was amazed recently to find a computer file from 1991 gamely headed "HK Action Cinema: Some Socially Non-Specific, Mutant-Formalist Notes" — followed by a spray of quotations from an article by Antoine de Baecque on Kirk Wong's *Gunmen* (1988).[3]

Both these pieces remained undeveloped and unwritten. Maybe it's true that, as Raymond Bellour once reflected, "only the imaginary realm of science believes that one always insists on finishing — in a limited period — what one has begun".[4] But whatever synaptic trails my brain hoped to travel when it was poised at those hopeful moments had been broken, lost, forgotten. I look at these sketches for essays like a reader of Walter Benjamin's *Arcades Project* notes, wondering: what on earth was I trying to express, where was I hoping to go? This I do recall, an orientation or aspiration of a roughly Deleuzian kind: a desire to speak of action cinema in terms of forms, shapes, rhythms, intensities, effects in all senses, both technical and emotional — rather than meanings. There was an element of delirium in this, and I have seen the same delirium possess many, in their own, sweet ways, since. How many times in the history of film writing, for how many people, has such a noble reach for unspeakable *intensity* far surpassed any possible grasp, and crashed on the ineffable shores of merely passionate assertion? Perhaps starting a voyage from that sort of binary conviction — up with intensity, down with meaning — is doomed to failure from the start, and maybe that's why those essays of mine from the 1970s and the 1990s never got written.

Composing the *Mad Max* book gave me the opportunity to try to mend this conceptual pathway I had tried, several times over, to walk. Facing this assignment jogged my memory concerning two powerful, formative experiences which filled me with a passionate conviction about action cinema — and the need to not only champion it but precisely describe it. The first formative experience was of a field of analysis that, in those days (the mid-1970s), seemed never to turn its attention to action cinema, but looked ideal for the task: textual analysis, of the kind associated with high-flyers of the period including Bellour and Stephen Heath. I recall, for example, Heath's brief remarks on *Jaws* (1975) — a rare and spectacular moment of high theory colliding in a journalistic context with the latest blockbuster — in which a discussion of the lightning movements of a shark in and out of frame, always involving a derangement of the image and the loss of life and limb, faithfully captured the mercilessly avant-garde side of Steven Spielberg that would be put to even more blissfully sadistic and post-human ends in the *Jurassic Park* series of the 1990s.[5]

The second formative experience was of experimental cinema, which I have come to regard (completely un-perversely) as a special branch of action cinema. In the short *Murder Psalm* (1980) by Stan Brakhage, great sheets of abstract visuals stream, shift and flow; in the middle of all this hypnotically painterly stuff, Brakhage inserts just a few frames of an absolutely legible, representational image, a clip from a primitive cartoon of (as I remember it) a mouse bashing a cat over the head with a baton — and then back to the streaming abstraction. Watching that in a cinema in the late 1980s at an avant-garde event, I had never before seen an audience respond so physically to such a perfectly timed jolt of violent action. The energy and intensity of this content-made-form was palpable: we all jumped in our seats!

During the 1990s, I noted some important developments in the critical literature on action cinema — especially in relation to the infinitely exciting and inspiring productions coming from Hong Kong. I went back and read the special, groundbreaking *Cahiers du cinéma* issue from 1984 on Hong Kong — still an essential, indispensable reference — and followed along the various interview remarks, catalogue notes and occasional writings of several figures associated with that project, like critic-turned-filmmaker Olivier Assayas, current *Cahiers* editor Charles Tesson, and Roger Garcia (whose work in the Hong Kong Festival publications was particularly suggestive and inspiring). Assayas's comments in a 1996 interview (the year of his movie *Irma Vep*) impressed me: what was "innovative or experimental" in mid-1980s Hong Kong cinema, he commented, was "the fast editing, the use of abstract shots that Chinese cinema has always used".[6] Abstraction: was that the magic key, the secret link between action and experimentation … not to mention Deleuzian theory, with its tantalising 'abstract machine'?

The year 1996 is key in this reconstituted history or sentimental education of mine, because it was also the year that a special issue of the journal *Admiranda* appeared, devoted to action cinema and masterminded by Nicole Brenez.[7] For me, this seemed to not only finally bring many threads together — there was Eastwood, and Hong Kong, and Hollywood, and the avant-garde, and even a cameo from Antoine de Baecque — but also move the fine-grain analysis of cinematic action to a new plateau. This collective work is so fertile, so jam-packed and so original that it can leave one exhausted before even beginning any further work along its lines; to adapt a memorable phrase from Meaghan Morris, "the originality of some of its essays … still exceeds our ability to use them on an ordinary day".[8]

It is altogether possible that, in what follows, I am still, personally, only just catching up to where Brenez and her small army of action movie connoisseurs set the bar in 1996. It is worth adding that Brenez herself has kept faith (and pace) with Hong Kong cinema and its mutations since that time — for example, in a text on Antoine Fuqua's *The Replacement Killers* (1998) — but that her own work has come to concentrate more militantly on experimental cinema.[9] This may be precisely because experimental cinema is one realm in which the love of screen action transcends mere assertion and gives rise, creatively, to homages and critiques that are themselves objects, i.e., new films — works that (as Brenez often publicly asserts) embody theoretical insights frequently some way in advance of writing or thought.

I am quite aware that other people's autobiographies of an encounter with Hong Kong action cinema could take radically different paths — through fan culture, for instance, where the joyous cry of Internet chatroom specialists that the genre's bliss is to break every rule finds its true equivalent not in Barthes's avant-garde ideal of the writerly text, but in John Woo's maddening inability to say anything more on the DVD commentaries for his films than that he encourages his cast and crew to 'just go crazy'. Or a more strictly academic formation: through scholarly studies of gender and national identity in Woo, or Wong Kar-wai's Leonesque/avant-garde deformation of the *wuxia pian* tradition in *Ashes of Time* (1994). My own orientation seeks a ground between these two approaches, attuned to cinema's *sensual thought*, the philosophical and cultural action that arises from its materiality.

Why paint this particular self-portrait, tell this tale? It is my way of suggesting, by way of introduction, that what we think of as Hong Kong cinema is in fact much wider and broader than a specific, national case study. For me, Hong Kong cinema starts with *Mad Max*. My perception of what Hong Kong gave to cinema — what potentiality of the medium it actualised — travelled forward through the writings of European, Asian and Anglo cinephile-intellectuals, and backwards into the rediscovered innovations of Brakhage and Orson Welles. Today, with the transnational flows none of us can any longer ignore, Hong Kong action cinema is also Guillermo Del Toro, Robert Rodriguez, and Nam Ki-Woong, among many others.

This is not a strict geo-political or geo-cultural map of influences and borrowings and remakes — it is certainly more of a rhizome. Something in me, which I am compelled to trust, holds to that proud desire to be socially non-specific and mutant-formalist when it comes to the inspirational and generative work of Hong Kong cinema. This is because I resist the twin terrorisms of either a too-specific and enclosed national cinema analysis — which reads everything in a film as a symptom or epiphenomenon of a big-picture history that only local specialists can know — or a too-rigid, empirically minded neo-formalism today associated with David Bordwell and the Wisconsin school. It seems to me that the history of film criticism and theory has knitted for us — if we care to retrace and excavate it, creatively — an open, impure formalism, a mutant formalism, which has a poetic imagination and a taste for the phantasmatic and virtual. This is a materialist approach to cinema which is also ecstatic — and I insist that these two things, materialism and ecstasy, can and do go together.

The following sketch of a rhizome of the Hong Kong style takes its inspiration not from film history, even in its most expanded, inclusive and international sense, but from the Brenzian ideal of a *history of forms* — which is also, in my terms, a history of *impulses*, impulses towards cinema, impulses that take cinematic shapes. A history of forms will always be an experimental history, not an empirical one, because it is aiming at something that animates (often in a subterranean way) the work of filmmakers — some impulse that is going to emerge and develop unevenly, surprisingly, in particular movies or 'runs' of movies. So the impulse towards a certain kind of action-painting in cinema — not driven primarily by literary constructs of character or theme, or ideological processes, but a more abstracted form of action as screen-sensation — is what I am calling the Hong Kong style. In Hong Kong cinema itself it runs (roughly) from King Hu to Johnnie To and has, despite the gloomy prognoses of naysayers, not yet finished evolving.

By contrast, the 'Hollywood action style' would be an entirely different creature, another historical slicing, a distinct impulse. Hong Kong cinema can never be reduced to an inspired exaggeration or distortion of Hollywood's codes, with the latter's moments of edginess or excess (especially in the 1960s and 1970s) taken up and systematised. (This is the argument one hears when, for instance, people claim that Woo's work of the 1980s is simply Michael Mann's TV series *Miami Vice* with still more panache and melodramatic flair.) Here I remember yet another formative moment for me in the late 1970s: an otherwise dull, normative television documentary on stunt work suddenly exploded with a clip from a Chang Cheh film whose title I cannot recall. The whole screen was filled and flattened with men dressed in white charging forth, arranged geometrically, their weapons posing the only contrary pictorial element in shape and colour; and then a cut twisted the entire graphic thrust of scene in another direction, to show the opposing band of warriors in a different colour, at a different angle. Then the sides clashed, the two colour schemes and postural vectors intersecting in beautifully controlled chaos. This is not the sort of action scene that could have come from the camera of Howard Hawks, Walter Hill or even Michael Mann. Still earlier in film history, King Hu's work provides many stunning examples of a new way of conceiving and delivering the play of formal elements in cinema.

The impulse towards cinema involved in this historical experiment is, above all, concerned with the energy of montage, the articulation and interrelation of shot-units and frame-units. It is not enough to lazily invoke, as so many commentators do, 'fast cutting'. The study of montage (in all its forms) has gone backwards in cinema studies since the glory days of Eisenstein and, in another, later era, Karel Reisz's *The Technique of Film Editing*. What we have lost sight of is something that textual analysis brought us to the brink of understanding: the film frame as a concentrated unit of energy — physical and psychic energy — which every inventive or ingenious filmmaker tries to master, whether to control or release.

Why start a discussion of the Hong Kong style with *Mad Max*? There is at least one good historical reason: Miller's film marks a crucial, early moment in the redefinition of the human form in relation to a range of technological objects and processes. It is too limiting to map such a theme only onto the explicit, futuristic allegories of sci-fi cinema; it is in action movies that these changes first registered. The 1996 *Admiranda* editorial suggested:

> An identity crisis begins in the '80s between two poles: the machine as other, and the machine inside the self. In its road accidents, *Mad Max* reveals the operation that brings together the mechanical and the human: it mixes close-ups of eyes and screaming mouths with speedometers, wheels and explosions ...[10]

For my purpose here, the action high-points of *Mad Max* provide a superb model for the way action montage works within the Hong Kong style. There is a formal movement between two stages in the editing. Firstly, Miller constructs what Brian De Palma refers to as a *schematic* — which is not a standard storyboard or decoupage of shots, but a map of the overall formal relations and their evolution in each scene (and, eventually, across the entire film). A schematic is the diagram of a formal shape: will the scene/film move, for example, from high to low, from airy to claustrophobic, from movement to stillness — and back again?[11] I recall Manny Farber's statement of principle, somewhere between a firm sense of film craft and a philosophic abstraction: "a story must ... develop by moving into a more complex space" rather than "perpetually reiterating the same space".[12] Filmmakers including Alfred Hitchcock, Orson Welles and Fritz Lang were meticulous schematists in this fashion, and they gave a practical dimension to film theory's love of lofty things like space and time. In the action scenes of *Mad Max*, Miller's schematics construct relations — thrilling, dangerous relations — of proximity (close or distant), and especially our own imaginary or projective proximity as viewers to the action-screen.

Mad Max's tactic is to inexorably nudge us from side views of the road, then closer and closer to its centre (this theatre of death), then lower and lower down, towards the bitumen. This prepares us, again and again, for the climactic apocalypse: the absolutely primal moment of cinema where two absolutely separated visual fields — one in front of the camera, the other behind — face each other, starkly, in order to then cancel each other out in the short-circuit shock of a head-on collision. It must be emphasised how rare this face-off of fields is in narrative cinema, since most scenographic space is organised within the comfort zone of the one-hundred-and-eighty degree rule, where (even outdoors) the staging of action is confined to a semi-circular area. We need not invoke the slightly loony 1970s reveries about the 'liberation of narrative space'[13] in order to register the jolt to habitual viewing conventions that Miller's three hundred and sixty degree cut-ups entail.

After each seeming breakdown of the filmic system, Miller then sets about rebuilding his schematic relations from scratch. But we must pause within the fine-grain articulations of the head-on collisions in *Mad Max* in order to see what happens when the schematic structure is dissolved, transcended. As the breakdown point is reached, there is an incredible flurry of shots, so fast you can no longer see or grasp, under normal viewing conditions, the montage relations being constructed. At that point it is no longer shots we are talking about, but frames. I call this *distintegrative montage*: the shot-units disintegrate and we are faced with frame-units, a few at a time and sometimes even just a single frame. This kind of montage can create some of the most glorious, sublimely euphoric moments of cinema. The screen seems to disappear, phantasmatically; the action comes right off the screen, in a pure shock or wash or sensation.

To pass from the schematic chain to disintegrative montage — to feel, as a spectator, these relations of sense being built and then instantly dismantled — is to exist, I would say, *at the edge of the cut*: that is the site, the exact point of tension. We physically and emotionally feel the approach of the cut as a *limit-point* in so many ways — a boundary or barrier of the shot or scene that can either be respected (which is what the schematic approach does) or transgressed, taken 'over the edge' as action fans love to say. Where are we, as spectators, when we are 'in' a cut for that split second? We are flying, suspended — and only time tells whether we are about to come down to earth or launch into the stratosphere.

Here a special aspect of the kinship between action and experimental cinema can be noted. At their most intense passages, both types of cinema get down to certain visual and aural phenomena that suggest the most basic and primal set-up of the cinematic apparatus itself: the projection of light upon a screen, and the fact of a viewer seated in front of it. The kind of visual and aural motifs I am thinking of here include: imagery of eyeballs, of shafts of light, stark alternations of pure brightness and absolute darkness, 'flicker' flashes, frozen and refilmed frames, pulsating sheets of sound (mimicking the regularity of bodily breath or machinic rhythms), as well as anything that can evoke the shuttling passage of the individual frames on a celluloid strip through the technology that isolates and transforms them into a single, projected moving picture (from the illuminated defilement of Brian De Palma's train windows to King Hu's cascading streams of bamboo sticks, via a thousand paparazzi photo-bulb flashes and disco strobe-lights). Another aspect of this phenomenon is exploited to the hilt by *Mad Max*: the kineticism (the French have a better word, *cinétisme*) of graphic lines and shapes, such as the shifting horizon, the tip of the road, the tracks and markings on the ground. What thus occurs across all these processes is a 'breaking through' of this bedrock of the apparatus to the surface of an otherwise ordinarily representational film — what Jacques Derrida calls (in relation to painting) "making the subjectile appear as such".[14]

Such breaking through is not a Brechtian reminder of the social fact of film viewing and of the illusion-machine up there on screen — since most of us, not being idiots, don't need that reminder. Rather, it marks an experience where we touch an *unconscious of film*, a filmic unconscious that has the power to go straight in, like an arrow or a bullet, into our viewing unconscious. Of course — and this is what Constance Penley referred to long ago as the 'avant-garde's imaginary' — we actually touch nothing materially in these moments; all that surfaces is another layer of illusion, another phantasm.[15] But what a powerful sensation of 'peeling away' the screen it can be! This seems to me a central arena in which the fantasy figurations and psychic flashpoints in cinema that Paul Willemen speaks of — belonging to the 'other film' under or inside the physical strip of film, theorised by Thierry Kuntzel in the 1970s — can work their ambivalent magic.[16]

Implicit in this argument is my belief that we are not yet and are unlikely to ever be 'beyond' psychoanalysis and into some higher and more materially verifiable realm of analysis in cinema studies. The usefulness of psychoanalysis is as a tool for speculating (beyond the dictates of any one 'school') about that level of the film experience which involves energies, drives and impulses — rather than clear-cut symptoms calling for decoding or interpretation, which tends to return us to the rigidity of literary-thematic or 'subject position' analysis. Much film theory today has banished the unconscious from its inquiries; my big problem with cultural studies as a field (at least in some of its dominant Anglo-American-Australo manifestations) is that it proposes only *fully conscious* subjects who choose their pleasures and make their subversive readings. Whereas true cinephiles crave the living dead — because cinema is, in so many ways, the realm of the living dead, and of the experience of being undead. More on this later.

I would like to turn now to a Hong Kong example — but not an action scene proper, merely a typical clip from a director who treats *every* scene, style-wise, like an action scene. In the jazzy pre-credits montage sequence of *Running Out of Time* (1999), Johnnie To intercuts two scenes and two times: the hero (Andy Lau) making his way to the edge of rooftop, and his visit to a doctor who diagnoses his fatal condition. There are many things worth noting here:

– The use of sound effects as a way not just of dramatically underlining or expressively emphasizing a gesture, but of aggressively *scoring*, sometimes *driving* the action in a highly musical, polyphonic fusion of sound and movement. I refer to those ubiquitous noise effects in contemporary action cinema: the whooshing, wind-like sounds, breathing sounds, runs of glistening bells and chimes — many of them digitally generated and transformed, hence literally unidentifiable as natural or human-made sounds.[17]

–   To's play on spaces, from the biggest to the smallest, from sensations of claustrophobia to vertigo, in bold juxtaposition: hence the breathtaking transition from an impossible crane-shot going over the roof edge and soaring out in space, to a very vulnerable eyeball, delivered to the probing medical gaze, in extreme close-up.

–   Most crucially, To's work with variable speeds or (as it is called in the film industry) *speed ramping* — a nice *Mad Max* touch there in the consonance of movies and accelerating vehicles! — a sudden change of speed *within* a movement or a shot, now very commonly practiced in slick television commercials and music videos.[18] This is a key evolution from the Sam Peckinpah era, when each image might have its own particular speed, but never (or very rarely) fluctuate in speed. Johnnie To explores every possible form of speed ramping: the latest digital manipulations made possible by the AVID editing system, but also older forms, such as jump-cutting (Jean-Luc Godard's *A bout de souffle* [1960], Alain Resnais's *Muriel* [1963]) and skip-framing (the subtle editing-out of particular frames within a continuous motion that render it unreal, as Welles and King Hu practised it). It is important (I note in passing) to not oppose speed ramping as a digital phenomenon to classical means of *mise en scène*: after all, Martin Scorsese revived in *Raging Bull* (1980) the most venerable of all speed-ramping techniques — the hand-cranked camera — and Godard in *Alphaville* (1965) created an electric, whip-like editing effect by simply match-cutting between two takes of an actor who, as someone who never performs the same gesture in the same way or at the same pace twice in a row, is a veritable human speed-ramper: Jean-Pierre Léaud. And it is Scorsese and Godard, precisely, who have found the most artistically apt moments to exploit the newest technologies: *Gangs of New York* (2002) contains select, striking moments of digital speed ramping (as in the fragment where a street gang sets upon its lone victim), and Godard's work on speed in *Sauve qui peut (la vie)* (1980) carries forth his video experiments of the 1970s.

Another example: the climactic scene of the break-up of the houseboat near the end of Scorsese's *Cape Fear* (1991) seems to me very close, in its intensity, to the Hong Kong style (and was probably modelled upon or inspired by moments in Woo and Tsui Hark). What is most central in this scene is the *loss of bearings* it enacts — bearings of orientation, gravity, weight, of the spatial relations between people and objects. A loss of bearings is the supreme pathway to abstraction in the Hong Kong style. What may immediately spring to mind are the many sublime poems to weightlessness within Hong Kong cinema. But we can go a lot further into this particular phenomenon.

I stress the force and bliss of abstraction somewhat as an alternative to David Bordwell's rather classical insistence in *Planet Hong Kong* on clarity, lucidity, legible lines of choreography (and so on) in action scenes, above anything else we might notice.[19] Like Bordwell, I admire this level of achievement in Hong Kong cinema; however, I feel his analysis stalls at the level of the schematic as I have defined it, and this is only half the story. Bordwell derides contemporary Hollywood blockbuster action films (in the Michael Bay vein) for their chaos and confusion — but these elements can be crucial and creative within the Hong Kong style.

Three aspects of such chaos can be noted in the *Cape Fear* sequence. Firstly, the camerawork, which is like a bullet or whip movement, thanks especially to the use of a zoom lens. These movements are extremely strange: one can sometimes not tell what they are pointing at or heading for, exactly. This creates a sort of mechanical delirium specific to cinema, something exploited with brilliance in the comedies of Sam Raimi and Stephen Chiau. Secondly, the equally strange poetry of those moments where the scene deliberately loses its bearings: once into the slow motion ballet of bodies within water sprays, we cannot even say whether the action is in forwards or backwards motion. And finally, the destruction of the set: the houseboat doesn't explode but implodes, folds in on itself slowly, just like in Michael Snow's experimental films, or burlesque comedy.

Compare this to two Hong Kong fight scenes, in *Ashes of Time* (a short scene thirty-eight minutes in) and Tsui Hark's *The Blade* (1996) — the latter described by one commentator as having chaos as both its "subject and manner".[20] Wong's fights are short, elliptical, and easily break into even smaller fragments for scrutiny; Tsui Hark's climax is a sustained, magnificent sequence, surely one of the greatest triumphs of Hong Kong cinema. These two very different masters form a remarkable contrast in styles and inventions.

In *Ashes of Time*, action is subject to a *minimalist disarticulation*: the standard elements of a fight scene are separated, frozen, played out and run through in a disorienting manner. Stephen Chan has offered a fine description of the action in *Ashes of Time*: "A lot is going on, but nothing much is happening".[21] But at the formal level, what is happening? Firstly, an exaggerated use of the technique familiar from Japanese samurai cinema: an illegible flurry of movement is followed by absolute stillness and silence, and then finally we learn who has been struck when we see which fighter topples over dead. *Gangs of New York* renews this mode and outdoes it in the midst of an extremely violent, stylistic chaos: as Alain Masson has remarked, "the principal effect of these 'turnarounds' is to separate an action from its narrative accomplishment".[22] Wong, less grandly, destabilises the Japanese style by using unusual, disorienting close-up compositions in the split-second passages of flurry.

More extremely, Wong works in a very experimental way with stark alternations of extreme light and dark. He seizes upon a key element of the swordplay film — namely, the glistening or dazzling light on steel swords. But look how far he takes it: he gives us an impossible shot which is effectively three shots in one, where an advancing figure is completely dark, then completely bright, then completely dark again. Here, too, we are close to a filmic unconscious or subjectile.

In *The Blade,* Tsui works, like George Miller, with a schematic construction which pops in and out as required within the total movement and rhythm of the climactic scene. Tsui is a master of split-second orientations, or reorientations: the fighter's eye that is suddenly riveted in a certain direction; a camera that flick-pans decisively from one pose or prop to another; the finger or hand that dramatically points ... But Tsui Hark uses this schematic sub-structure as a way to get into furious passages of abstraction. In one of my favourite shots, chaos of movement is translated, paradoxically, by almost absolute stillness in the image (before, and more cleverly than, the 'bullet time' motion made famous by *The Matrix* [1999]): as the two men are locked together in combat, we are no longer certain in what direction they are travelling, whether they are falling or rising, or at what speed. Note again the extraordinary intensities and fluctuations of light in the sequence, and the remarkable flicker-effect created by the endlessly falling, cascading rods. One can see the legacy of Tsui's experimentation in a much more ordinary and 'Hollywoodised' film — but one still distinguished by some remarkable sequences — namely, *The Replacement Killers.* Fuqua, too, moves with dexterity in his action scenes between schematic relations and an ecstasy of abstraction — cued especially by the momentary obscurings of vision prompted by fog, steam, water, tall grass ...

Following on from that reference, I would like to conclude by discussing an example that is deliberately not from the ethereal sphere of masters and masterpieces, but a realm of formal invention that is perhaps more mundane but no less significant or interesting for that. Let's consider James Wong's *The One* (2002) with Jet Li, an underrated movie in my opinion. Taking a cue from the groundbreaking work of Wong Kin-yuen, it is clear that, in the new millennium, all our discussions of speed and movement must deal with the possibilities offered by digital technology.[23]

I am not the first person to call for a digital aesthetics, but unlike many prophets (or hucksters) in this area, I believe we must grow digital aesthetics from the rich history of cinema and its forms.

So I would rather not dismiss *The One* out of hand as a mere MTV/ rock video/martial arts hybrid, a little of everything and a lot of nothing. In it, we can see that new versions of the paradoxes of speed and stasis, motion and stillness, are possible. The slowing down of the environment — that showering/raining motif so characteristic of Hong Kong cinema — tells us that Jet Li's normal speed is in fact super speed (an ingenious variation on 'bullet time'). But the speed ramping allowed by digital technology takes us much further than the physical pause or immobility of a performing body. Speed ramping in *The One* enhances, elaborates, and at certain moments entirely creates, the differential rhythms and energy waves of the martial arts gestures.[24] Especially when a digital image becomes still: then it goes completely dead, even the grain of the image freezes, and we wonder (for the heartbeat of a frame or two) whether that stillness might last for eternity. (Much contemporary Japanese animation also plays on this unusual, formal suspense.) So, this digital mutation of the Hong Kong style takes us to the heart of what theorists including Nicole Brenez and Laleen Jayamanne have described as the issue of 'what a body can do' today, in that interface between life and the screen, between a technology of the body (such as martial arts) and a technology of machines.[25]

I end with a gesture of savage theorising. Across discussions of action cinema we often stumble against, and find ourselves uttering, an intractable binary opposition. We are suspicious of the digital, of technoscience, and in counter-attack we praise — often nostalgically — the supposed realism of the human, performing body filmed in its integrity. This is a position that, fundamentally, owes a lot to André Bazin's notions of 'forbidden montage', and of several decades of mise en scène criticism valuing the long take and the open frame, with their bodies inscribed in real space and time. (Brenez has reminded us that a French film school for many years banned slow motion on Rossellinian grounds!) Even Willemen's intriguing idea that digital cinema requires a reserve of dead labour keeps us within this pessimistic paradigm.[26]

But, in relation to action cinema, this is simply wrong or misguided in so many ways. Firstly, the martial arts-trained body is already technology-in-action. Secondly, the body in cinema has never been whole or authentic: it is always a Frankenstein monster, a living dead body, an agglomeration of bits and pieces stitched together by framing and montage — as George Miller certainly knows when he calls himself a montage director. Film has always been artifice, special effects and technology. In fact, I believe this would be a truly radical, innovative, important thing at this point in the global history of film culture: a theory of film that begins and extends from artifice, not from reality. The cinematic body returns us to our own bodies, to the question of the powers of a body, what a body can do. The Hong Kong style of cinema nudges ever closer now, in its most extreme manifestations, towards animation. But it has always been close to that space, with its zoom lenses and its montages of views, cuts, gestures and frames, not to mention its supernatural fictional conceits. It is we who must now make the magical leap — conceptually, imaginatively, poetically — into this realm.

Part 3

Translation and Embodiment: Technologies of Globalisation

12

Wuxia Redux: *Crouching Tiger, Hidden Dragon* as a Model of Late Transnational Production

Stephen Teo

INTRODUCTION

This essay takes up *Crouching Tiger, Hidden Dragon* (Ang Lee 2000) as an exemplary model of "late transnational" production in the Hong Kong film industry. By selecting *Crouching Tiger* as a prototype, I am investigating, firstly, the concept of genre movies as the most popular channel of transnationalism in the Chinese cinema; and secondly, the *wuxia* genre (the swordfighting martial arts genre that deals with the theme of chivalry) as an archetypal mode of transnational production. *Crouching Tiger* as a *wuxia* model of late transnational production mirrors (but does not duplicate) the stage of early transnationalism at the hub of the Shanghai film industry when the *wuxia* film came into popularity from 1928–1931. The early and late stages of transnationalism revolving around the *wuxia* film and martial arts cinema will be reviewed below.

The development of Chinese cinema and the development of the *wuxia* genre are closely related. The *wuxia* film is one of the oldest genres in the Chinese cinema and has remained popular to the present day. Ebbs and flows characterize its development, but despite this, the *wuxia* genre has remained resilient, bouncing back after each periodic crisis or stage of stagnation, and has quite effortlessly etched itself into the larger fabric of Chinese film culture to become a cornerstone of that culture. The *wuxia* picture followed a populist path of development based on indigenous practices in literature, opera, and the oral narrative tradition known as *tanci* (a storytelling form with musical accompaniment adapted to regional variations). Its origins also stemmed from early genres such as *baishi pian*, films based on popular accounts of history; the *guzhuang pian*, period costume movies; and last but not least, the *shenguai pian*, the fantasy strand dealing with gods and demons, supernatural powers of flight and emission of bodily energy. Fantasy elements from the latter genre were incorporated into the *wuxia* film early on, and the standard way to refer to the genre from the late 1920s onwards was *shenguai wuxia* which has been translated as "sword and sorcery" or "swordplay and magic".

The Hong Kong *wuxia* film is a composite of all these traditional modes. In the second half of the 1960s, the emergence of the Hong Kong Mandarin cinema's "new school" *wuxia* film, as typified by the films of King Hu and Zhang Che (Chang Cheh), and its transference to the Taiwan film industry (through King Hu's productions of *Dragon Inn* and *A Touch of Zen*, which were both made in Taiwan albeit with injections of Hong Kong talent and money) points not only to the continuity of the genre but also the continuity of the Chinese cinema as its production base shifted from Shanghai to Hong Kong, with Taiwan functioning as an alternative base. By "Chinese cinema" therefore, I am really referring to the shifting paradigm of the capitalist industrial mode of production established in Shanghai from at least the 1920s onwards — a paradigm inherited by the Hong Kong film industry and to some extent by the Taiwan film industry. This shifting paradigm illustrates the transnational character of the Chinese cinema.

Transnationalism is also embedded within the genre. In pointing out that *wuxia* originated from traditional sources, I am not suggesting that it is a pristine genre. Indeed, in the 1920s *wuxia* imbibed influences from the medieval European romance, the Hollywood swashbuckler, the western, and the European detective mystery à la the Méliès serials; in the 1960s, there were obvious influences from the sword-and-sandal epic, James Bond spy thriller, Italian spaghetti westerns, and Japanese *chambara*. The absorption of all these influences is a sign of the transnationalism of the Chinese cinema; but it is just as important to note that the Chinese cinema had digested and remade foreign influences into a veritable indigenous form that accommodated the tastes and demands of a diasporic audience.

EARLY TRANSNATIONALISM

Today, the Hong Kong film industry is the most commercially dominant of the Chinese film production centres, earning the honorific "Hollywood of the East", which suggests that Hong Kong has successfully adopted the Hollywood industrial mode of production as well as its practices and strategies of transnational marketing. In fact, Hong Kong inherited its production practices from the Shanghai film industry, which adopted the practices of Hollywood in the 1920s and 1930s: the decades that constituted the stage of early transnationalism in the Chinese cinema.

Early transnationalism also encompassed the production and distribution strategies of Hong Kong's own indigenous film industry in the 1930s. I refer to the Cantonese-dialect pictures, and the Hong Kong film industry's marketing strategies of exporting films to overseas Chinese communities in the Guangdong region, in Southeast Asia and throughout the world. While the southern China region was initially a big market for Cantonese pictures, Southeast Asia became increasingly important as the Chinese government issued a ban on Cantonese-dialect films. The government also banned the *wuxia* genre on grounds that it promoted superstition. These bans affected one major studio in particular, the Tianyi Studio, which pioneered the *wuxia* movie and the Cantonese movie. Tianyi produced the first *wuxia* movie in 1925 and the first Cantonese talkie, *White Gold Dragon*, in 1933. The major factor behind Tianyi's pioneering of both kinds of movies was the need to cater to overseas Chinese audiences.

The cultural impetus of transnationalism is complemented by economic drives. From the late 1920s, Tianyi was engaged in an economic struggle with its main rival, Mingxing, which attempted to monopolize the distribution and exhibition markets through a syndicate formed with five other companies in Shanghai. The syndicate, known as the "United Six", imposed an embargo on Tianyi's products by convincing theatre chains in Shanghai and Southeast Asia to show only United Six products.[1] In a counter-move against the United Six, the boss of Tianyi, Shao Zuiweng, sent two of his brothers, Runme and Run Run, to Singapore in 1928. Armed with a fistful of Tianyi products, their brief was "to recapture the Southeast Asian market (mainly Singapore-Malaya, Thailand, Vietnam) it had lost to its rival Mingxing".[2] The two brothers registered a company, which they named Haixing (Sea Star) that was meant perhaps as a play on Mingxing (which literally means "Bright Star"), and in quick succession built up a circuit of theatres, which gradually developed into the Shaw Brothers Company.

Headquartered in Singapore, the island became a centre for distribution as well as a source of funding for Tianyi films produced in Hong Kong or Shanghai, and later for local films produced by Shaws. Tianyi also registered a branch in Hong Kong in 1934 and after going through further re-structuring and name changes, it gradually evolved into the Nanyang Company and then the Shaw and Son Company. Run Run

Shaw himself came to Hong Kong in 1958 to establish the Shaw Brothers Studio, which became the leading Mandarin studio in Hong Kong. Therefore, Tianyi's move to Hong Kong was a fateful decision that may be seen as the hub of the wheel driving the transnational project of Chinese cinema. Tianyi inspired other Shanghai studios to open branches in Hong Kong and Singapore.

These moves into Southeast Asia and Hong Kong were accelerated by the Chinese government's banning of *wuxia* pictures and Cantonese features, two of the most popular forms of entertainment for the masses of diasporic Chinese (many of whom spoke Cantonese). Early transnational filmmaking was informed by the concept of abstract China as a "diasporic imaginary", to use David Keith Axel's term.[3] In the same way that opera played a role in purveying a Chinese imaginary in the minds of Chinese audiences everywhere, the cinema catered to the psychic needs of the diasporic Chinese to identify, vicariously or nostalgically, with the motherland and its myths — even though many of the overseas Chinese would not have been born in China. Certainly, in the post-colonial era, for many ethnic Chinese of my generation born in the countries of Southeast Asia, Chinese movies made in Hong Kong or Taiwan were often the only means to connect with Chinese culture and language.

The concept of "abstract China" shares a certain affinity with what some writers have referred to as, in Mayfair Yang's words, a "deterritorialized Chinese subjectivity", which Yang defines as a subjectivity that "cannot be contained by the state apparatuses of either mainland China or Taiwan".[4] Yang also analyzes the role of Shanghai in establishing and creating the media by which "transnational subjectivity" is channelled through to the Chinese mind; and she writes about transnationalism drawing on Homi Bhabha's concept of a "third space", in which a mainland Chinese learns about the world at large.[5] Similarly, I refer here to Shanghai cinema's role as an important early conduit of transnationalism but I focus on the *wuxia* film as a genre that epitomizes the sensation of abstract China which can be enjoyed by Chinese outside of China; and in the model of *Crouching Tiger, Hidden Dragon* (Ang Lee 2000), this abstract China has successfully been transmitted to the world and enjoyed by non-Chinese.

The ancient Chinese settings, costumes, and the mythical conceptions of the *wuxia* film are exactly the sort of things that could characterize an abstract China, or a "deterritorialized Chinese subjectivity". I am deliberately putting to one side here the genre of the contemporary melodrama of the early to mid-1930s, which is historically identified as a province of the left-wing. These films, dealing with the social circumstances and urban problems of Shanghai (as a microcosm of China), prevailed after the banning of the *wuxia* genre. While it may be argued that the left-wing cinema was much closer to the sense of a nationalist enterprise (a subject beyond our domain), even the left-wing filmmakers were conscious of the transnational project of bringing social issues — and later, political issues emerging out of the conflict with Japan — to the notice of Chinese in Hong Kong, Southeast Asia and elsewhere; and they were not above exploiting the sense of abstract China in period historical films to function as allegories in order to drum up support among the diasporic Chinese communities during the War of Resistance against Japanese Aggression. To this extent, the left-wing cinema was part of the transnational mode of production in Shanghai. In short, the diaspora was the most important audience, or the most direct recipient, of the early transnational project of the Chinese cinema.

LATE TRANSNATIONALISM

With the onset of late transnationalism in the postwar period, the concept of "Chinese cinema" itself had fractured. The Mainland was isolated as a result of the geopolitics of the Cold War. The Chinese cinema paradigm established in Shanghai was transplanted in Hong Kong and while the transnational project of catering to the diasporic Chinese remained a cornerstone of the industry throughout the 1950s and 1960s, I would say that the process of late transnationalism really began in earnest in the 1970s, when the Hong Kong film industry made strategic moves to penetrate the global market and shift away from the diasporic audience.

David Desser has discussed the subject of the Hong Kong film industry's penetration of the United States market in the early 1970s.[6] I wish only to make the point that the successful push of the kung fu martial arts genre into the global market was a calculated, concerted effort on the part of the two major studios, Shaw Brothers and Golden Harvest. Raymond Chow, the head of Golden Harvest, stated that the "dream of every Chinese producer was that his picture be shown in Europe and America", pointing out that this dream had been translated into reality.[7] Chow listed several factors for success.

1. We are producing better films dubbed into many languages.
2. Our films reflect something special about the Chinese which appeals to the audience everywhere.
3. We have clear-cut story lines with black presented as black and white presented as white. This is what the movie-goer really wants.
4. Our action pictures have a clarity and a rhythm denied to most recent productions.[8]

The tactic of dubbing local kung fu films into English and other languages also meant that the narratives were slightly modified and the often quite bad dubbing practices led to unintentional humour in scenes where such humour may not have been intended. Very often, too, the original titles were changed to accentuate certain themes thought to be more attractive to a global audience: Bruce Lee's *The Big Boss*, for example, was changed to *Fists of Fury*, *Fist of Fury* was changed to *The Chinese Connection*, and so on. Bruce Lee's charisma and popularity also resulted in his spearheading a trend of co-productions between Hong Kong studios and Hollywood, combining kung fu with some element of Western genres or action styles. *Enter the Dragon* (1973), starring Lee, was a co-production with Golden Harvest and Warner Brothers, and successfully combined kung fu with the James Bond-style action genre. Golden Harvest continued along this line in a co-production with Australia, *The Man from Hong Kong* (1975), which starred Jimmy Wang Yu and Sammo Hung to feature the kung fu aspects, and George Lazenby, an ex-James Bond used to evoke the Bond spy thriller aspects, though Lazenby played a villain in the picture.

During the same period Shaw Brothers embarked on a series of co-productions with Britain's Hammer Film Company. Hammer, famous for its horror pictures, conceived a story entitled *Legend of the Seven Golden Vampires* (it also had many other alternative titles) fusing the Dracula legend with kung fu. The picture was shot entirely in the Shaw Brothers studio, combining the talents of Hong Kong actors with British actors under the direction of a British director. The results, when shown in 1974, were highly ambiguous, not because of the mixture of talents, but because of the incongruous mixture of genre ingredients — kung fu did not really sit well with the Dracula legend, and such a combination suggested at the very least that there was a misunderstanding in the West of what kung fu was all about. However, this trend of co-productions intermixing Eastern and Western traditions continued — the first structured signs of postmodernism in the global manner as it related to the Hong Kong cinema.

Significantly, it is in the kung fu cinema that you see clearly the signs of globalized postmodernism entailing changes in the personae of Chinese kung fu stars. Most of the major kung fu personalities in the Hong Kong cinema, Sammo Hung, Yuen Wo-ping, Jackie Chan, Jet Li, Michelle Yeoh, have now worked or appeared in Hollywood movies. And it is interesting to note how these stars change their personalities, if not their action styles, to suit the global audience. Jackie Chan, for example, modified his persona of the indigenous Chinese buffoon in Yuen Wo-ping's *Snake in the Eagle's Shadow* (1978) and *Drunken Master* (1978) to a more amorphous man-about-the-globe persona in his latter films. The scholar Gina Marchetti has observed that Chan's career in the early stages operated within a binary of colonialism versus Chineseness:

> Sometimes, Chan's characters represent bodily the forces of colonialism. He plays royal [sic] Hong Kong police officers and international spies at the service of Western powers. At other times, he appears to be an emblem of authentic 'Chineseness,' chauvinistically celebrating the superiority of Chinese culture and the power of Chinese kung fu.[9]

Chan has quite obviously shifted away from his "Chineseness" in a concession to the forces of late transnationalism in a recent series of movies (*Mr. Nice Guy, Rumble in the Bronx, Rush Hour,* etc), and Marchetti makes the point that Chan now seems to exemplify the "absence of race, ethnicity, and nation found in postmodern theory. He exists at the cusp of the postmodern and the postcolonial, and he can be read as one or the other depending on the circumstances of exhibition and reception".[10]

It could be said that *Crouching Tiger, Hidden Dragon* (Ang Lee 2000) exists on the same cusp of the postmodern and the postcolonial, although I will argue that it is a film more representative of globalization and postmodernism. However, the film's smashing success with the American audience (to date, it holds the record as the first subtitled film to gross more than US$100 million) has raised questions about how the film deliberately panders to a certain Orientalist sensibility in the West — charges made in particular by certain Western critics whom Salman Rushdie, in an article published in *The New York Times,* has decried as those "killjoys who have denigrated 'Crouching Tiger' as a piece of latter-day Orientalism, a Western appropriation of Eastern manner and material".[11] I think the question of Orientalism somewhat muddies the real issues, which I deem to be postmodernism and globalization — both tendencies that determine reception in today's international marketplace. Orientalism in large part illustrates the kind of postcolonial mentality that informs Western analysis of Asian genre cinema along the lines of the "purity" of genres, which is in many ways a spurious argument. I agree with Zha Jianying's point, made in her rebuttal of the charge of orientalism against Zhang Yimou's *Raise the Red Lantern,* that:

> the new Chinese cinema had long been determined by its complicated relation with Western media and techniques, with the tastes of an increasingly international film market and its mainstream audience. To the extent that it never had a chance of escaping these circumstances, 'pure Chinese art' in the contemporary world is merely a fantasy. In this

sense, not only Zhang's personal intention becomes irrelevant, the whole quarrel over 'Orientalism' seems rather simplistic and pedantic.[12]

In the *wuxia* genre, Hong Kong or Chinese filmmakers are conscious of "Self-Orientalism"[13], which is to say that they know that their material is inherently "Orientalist". They choose to exploit this material to portray the quintessence of Chineseness, and they implicitly regard the *wuxia* picture as a "national form" possessing historical and cultural characteristics and attributes of "Chineseness" — all this notwithstanding the foreign influences that have inundated the genre from the stages of early transnationalism to late transnationalism. Salman Rushdie voiced a more affirmative take on the film's success, taking sides with the American audience which saw *Crouching Tiger* as "the arrival of a great, classic film and was simply transported by the movie's brilliance".[14] Rushdie might have had a different response if he had seen the film with a mainland Chinese audience.

Crouching Tiger, Hidden Dragon exemplifies the "crossover" phenomenon, which takes into account the currents of globalization and postmodernism. I use the term "globalizing postmodernism" to refer to the globalizing impulse of postmodernism, as opposed to a postmodernist strategy adapted for local consumption (which may be referred to as "regionalizing postmodernism"). A globalizing postmodernism implies the process where narrative conventions of genre films are reconstructed to take account of a new global entertainment economy. This tendency allows for instant commodification of a foreign culture, where foreknowledge of such culture is not taken for granted. Ang Lee's production of *Crouching Tiger, Hidden Dragon* adopts the approach of cross-cultural methods to transcribe what is culturally specific in order to diminish certain indigenous qualities (while highlighting others) to make them more presentable to a world-wide audience. Shu-mei Shih has written that Ang Lee utilizes the strategy of "flexibility and translatability" in which a national culture (China or Taiwan) is "translated" through processes that allow the West, particularly Americans, to easily decode that culture.[15] This approach differs somewhat from the previous phase of the *wuxia* resurgence, which adopted the strategy of regional postmodernism, and did not achieve the crossover touch necessary for global success though it might have aspired to.

I refer here to the films of Tsui Hark (*Zu: Warriors of the Magic Mountain* [1983], *Swordsman* [1990], *New Dragon Inn* [1994], and *The Blade* [1995]) which set the postmodern tone of *wuxia*: Freudian psychology, allegorical readings relating to Hong Kong's dilemma over the 1997 question, existentialism, and gender politics (the gender bending knight-errant, usually portrayed by Brigitte Lin, being something of an icon of postmodern *wuxia*). In technological terms, more attention was paid to the crafting of atmosphere through production design and lighting, the staging of action choreography became even more elaborate and the field of special effects was revolutionised by the introduction of advanced computer technology. Tsui Hark also introduced the trend of remaking classics of the new school movement of the 1960s, and of blending *wuxia* elements with other genres such as the contemporary action film (cops and robbers, gangster pictures). Although Tsui inspired many other directors to follow suit — one can refer here to the films of Jeff Lau, Wong Jing, John Woo, Ching Siu-tung, Raymond Lee — their mixtures of contemporary genres with *wuxia* conventions underlines the interconnected-ness of genre traditions within Hong Kong cinema rather than a conscious attempt to sell these movies to a foreign audience. Postmodernism in this context underlines the local conditions of film culture, which do not necessarily translate: for example, the 1990s "nonsense" comedies of Stephen Chiau, with their zany mixtures of genres, were considered by some Western critics to be untranslatable[16] (and may still be thought untranslatable given the tardiness on the part of Miramax in releasing Chiau's *Shaolin Soccer* in the US).

Tsui Hark's *wuxia* films — particularly *Zu: Warriors of the Magic Mountain* and the 2001 sequel *Legend of Zu*, as well as *The Blade* — were box-office disasters, as was Wong Kar-wai's *Ashes of Time* (1994). If these films have any appeal in the global market, it is strictly limited to a cult minority audience. Yet *Crouching Tiger* utilizes the same genre elements as all these films and was able to cross over to a global audience. The success of *Crouching Tiger* raises the central question that Emily Apter asks in her article "On Translation in a Global Market"[17]: "How do some works gain international visibility, while others do not?" A whole slew of questions would follow: Was *Crouching Tiger's* success nothing more than a happy accident? Is it a passing fad? or the harbinger of a global phenomenon? Is genre a factor in translatability? In answering these questions, I hope to demonstrate that *Crouching Tiger* was a departure not only from the *wuxia* conventions to which it apparently pays homage, but also from the pattern of late transnational production established by the industry in the early 1970s, beginning with the kung fu craze and the push to export kung fu films to the West. These departures constitute the changed circumstances of late transnational production as the industry steps into the new millennium.

When making *Crouching Tiger, Hidden Dragon*, director Ang Lee was caught in a classic bind. Being a Chinese filmmaker, he had to take into account the intrinsic Chineseness of the *wuxia* genre; he had to appease the proprietary feelings that a Chinese audience would have towards the *wuxia* genre, but at the same time his objective was to make a crossover movie that would appeal to a global audience unfamiliar with *wuxia* conventions. This fundamental contradiction is shown up, indeed encoded within the narrative structure, as I hope to demonstrate; and I would even go so far as to say that Ang Lee consciously implanted such a contradiction because of the conditions of globalized postmodernism that informed the production. As I have stated above, these conditions are quite different from those of the early 1970s, as enunciated by Raymond Chow. The martial arts cinema of the 1970s was presented on its own terms to the West, while *Crouching Tiger, Hidden Dragon* presents a martial arts cinema in terms of the internationalized aesthetics of art cinema.

THE TRANSNATIONAL PROTOTYPE OF *CROUCHING TIGER, HIDDEN DRAGON*

It is worth our while to compare *Crouching Tiger* with the "factors" that Raymond Chow listed as ingredients for success in the global market. These "factors" have changed noticeably in today's environment of globalized postmodernism. Factor number one, about dubbing, appears to be a non-issue since *Crouching Tiger* is not dubbed, but there is in fact an issue here that I will address later. On factor number two, namely that the film should "reflect something special about the Chinese which appeals to the audience everywhere", *Crouching Tiger's* reception in Asia was not uniform. In some territories where Chinese preponderate the box-office takings can only be said to be lacklustre compared with its performance in the West, thus the truism that a Chinese film that appeals to the domestic audience may not necessarily appeal to audiences in the West, and vice versa, still holds. As to factors three and four — "clear-cut story lines with black presented as black and white presented as white" and the "clarity and rhythm of our action pictures" — I would like to concentrate on the film's central character, the female knight-errant Jen, played by Zhang Ziyi, to show how the "factors" have changed since the 1970s. In a sense, Jen must respond not only to changed circumstances around the world but must embody a certain millenarian trait of character.

Jen is an ambivalent character, and this departs from the heroic tradition in the *wuxia* movie that Raymond Chow alluded to as "black presented as black and white presented as white". Jen learns the martial arts from an evil governess — a woman wanted by the law and sought after as an object of vengeance by the Chow Yun-fat character Li Mubai. Jen is also a thief: she steals Li Mubai's 300 year-old sword, the Green Destiny. Jen justifies the theft by considering herself worthy of owning such a fine sword, which should rightfully belong to the knight-errant who has achieved the pinnacle in martial arts skills (Jen has mastered the highest form of Wudang). But Jen shows by her behaviour that she lacks the moral standards of a true knight-errant even though she may aspire to be one. The film's gradual focus on Jen is a sign of the filmmakers' intentions to derail the heroic tradition.

Jen's ambivalence as a character is reflected in the Green Destiny, a slender, elastic sword. The sword's flexible nature and its association with Jen symbolize the quest for *xiayi* (the principle of chivalric righteousness), a quest that Ang Lee poses in terms of an equivocal master-disciple relationship between Li Mubai and Jen. This is another inversion of *wuxia* conventions, as Ang Lee himself points out.[18] In *wuxia* convention, it is usually the pupil who seeks the master but here it is Li, the master, who is seeking the pupil, Jen. Jen has mastered merely the technical aspects of Wudang, whereas Li wants to impart its moral standards to Jen in order to make her worthy of possessing the sword. Their clash in the bamboo forest echoes the psychological dimension of their struggle. Jen flies from treetop to treetop, clinging to a bamboo and bending with it, movements that denote the obliquity of her moral character, which Li Mubai is attempting to sway to his side.

Ambiguity is a part of the film's architecture. This is normally a good thing in a conventional art movie or a genre movie where the director strives to work against stereotypes or clichés. However, this assumes that an audience has foreknowledge of the genre archetypes and clichés. This cannot be assumed in the case of a Western audience vis-à-vis the *wuxia* genre. In postmodernism, such foreknowledge may not be important. *Crouching Tiger's* ambiguity stems not only from the narrative or the plot, but also from the transnational circumstances of production, namely, its complicated globalized financing, the input of an American (James Schamus) in the scriptwriting process,[19] the intermingling of Taiwanese, Chinese and Hong Kong talent, and the conscious effort to present itself as both a pan-Chinese film and a film intended for the global audience. The film's ambiguity illustrates the process by which it was conceived and created as a product of globalized postmodernism, necessitating a reconstruction of the genre's conventions that would be understood by an international audience. This is the process of "translation" in a global market that Shu-mei Shih and Emily Apter have alluded to.

As Lee "translates" the *wuxia* culture, this has the inevitable effect of changing not only its conventions but also its rhythm and clarity — the fourth factor for global success that Raymond Chow spoke of. *Crouching Tiger* may have inspired many in the West to look at the *wuxia* genre, but in many ways, it is a misleading introduction to the genre. A Hong Kong *wuxia* action movie normally starts with an action sequence; one device commonly used in Zhang Che's films, and later in those of Lau Kar-leung (cf. *36th Chamber of Shaolin*), was to stage an action sequence *under the opening credits*. In contrast, the "crossover" ambitions of *Crouching Tiger* require a long passage of exposition designed to familiarize Westerners with the period, the characters, and even the appearance of the sets. The first eruption of action does not occur until fifteen minutes into the film. In his DVD commentary, Lee explains that he needed to show Western viewers *why* the characters fight, because they would not be prepared to take them for granted as generic archetypes, conventional figures as deeply familiar in Asia as the frontier gunfighter is elsewhere. For Lee, "Fighting is an acceleration of repression", and so we are introduced to Yu Shulien (Michelle Yeoh) and Li Mubai not as warriors but as repressed lovers. We see Li Mubai initially as a world-weary hero who wants to give up his sword, the Green Destiny, because the duty it represents weighs upon him too heavily.

The hero-fatigue of Li Mubai is another reversal of the heroic tradition. Even the convention of a heroic death is denied the character, who is killed by a woman and, as Ang Lee points out, "by a very small needle for a very small ambiguous cause".[20] The final shot of the movie, Jen's leap from Mount Wudang, is the kind of open, ambiguous ending that ultimately plays to the Western sensibility of an art house movie rather than to the Chinese sense of a satisfying action movie finale. The final fight, in which Li Mubai kills Jade Fox (Zheng Peipei), is not even the emotional climax of the movie, as Lee himself owns up: "There's yet another fifteen minutes to come", he says, "and above that, when the villain is killed, we don't feel good".

The film's globalizing postmodernist paradigm is further evident in certain techniques adopted for its presentation to a Western audience. The name of Zhang Ziyi's character, Yu Jiaolong, familiar to Chinese readers of Wang Dulu's source novel and from several earlier film and television adaptations, is not denoted as such in the English subtitles. Her Chinese name resonates with two important motifs of the story: her family name, Yu, meaning Jade, associates her with the Green Destiny sword, while her given name, Jiaolong, meaning "tender dragon", identifies her as the

"Hidden Dragon" of the title. Such associations are clearly lost through the use of the name "Jen" in the English subtitles, a pure concoction whose only function is to place the character on a familiar-sounding first-name basis with the Western audience.

Then there is the question of the *sound* of the movie's Mandarin dialogue. Although neither the Hong Kong Cantonese actor Chow Yun-fat nor the Chinese-Malaysian actress Michelle Yeoh are native speakers of Mandarin, the movie was nevertheless shot with live synch-sound, in the Western manner. With the rise of Mandarin-language cinema in Cantonese-speaking Hong Kong in the 1960s, the local film industry adopted the practice of post-synchronization and "voice-doubling". Actors who could not speak "proper" Mandarin were regularly dubbed by those who could. But because Ang Lee chose not to dub *Crouching Tiger*, both of his leading players can be heard on the soundtrack speaking Mandarin with their respective heavy accents. To a Western audience, the result does not sound anomalous but it has a jarring effect on Chinese viewers — which may begin to explain why the film fared poorly on the Mainland.

While some may argue that these issues are just side-effects of the crossover phenomenon and don't really affect the movie's overall aesthetic design, they do point to a shift in the terms of reference for the genre's development in the future. *Crouching Tiger* is not as bold a revisionist genre experiment as certain home-grown products (cf. Wong Kar-wai's *Ashes of Time* or Tsui Hark's *The Blade*), but its "crossover" translation of the *wuxia* movie, necessitating the reconstruction of narrative conventions and the use of accented Mandarin, can be seen as representing an evolving paradigm of the *wuxia* genre as it enters the new millennium. The use of accented Mandarin further points to a shift in the genre's destiny as a pan-Chinese product targeted at the traditional diasporic audience. Filmed in China, by a Taiwanese director based in the US, with money from Hollywood, Europe and Asia, with a cast assembled from Malaysia, Hong Kong, and the Mainland, the film is unusual only in refusing to disguise the transnational circumstances of its production. Lee represents what Shu-mei Shih has called a "flexible subject" who encapsulates both the subject positions of being a transnational (an Asian cosmopolitan) and a minority (an Asian immigrant in the United States).[21] "I can endure accents", Lee says, grafting the spirit of the global melting pot onto a hidebound essentialist genre.

Crouching Tiger's impact upon the world market suggests that Ang Lee may have been on to something. The *wuxia* genre has now gone well beyond the Chinese diaspora. For starters, it has become pan-Asian, as in the Korean production *Musa the Warrior* (2001), a "crossover" *wuxia* imitation featuring Zhang Ziyi as a Chinese princess who finds herself amidst a group of Korean knights-errant in China. Zhang Yimou's 2002 film *Hero* proved to be another attempt to duplicate *Crouching Tiger's* globalised postmodern paradigm: Mainland director, star from Hollywood by way of Hong Kong (Jet Li), co-stars from China (Zhang Ziyi — again) and from the art film wing of Hong Kong cinema (Tony Leung Chiu-wai and Maggie Cheung Man-yuk, the romantic couple in Wong Kar-wai's *In the Mood for Love*).

These ripples stemming from the international success of *Crouching Tiger* represent a *wuxia* resurgence, albeit of a very different kind from the one that swept through Hong Kong cinema in the 1960s. More and more, this resurgence is taking on a transnational character — which also means that the *wuxia* picture is increasingly moving away from its core centre in the Hong Kong film industry, where it has flourished and evolved since the end of the Second World War. The economic malaise still plaguing Hong Kong cinema as a result of the Asian financial crisis, means that the industry must increasingly turn to multi-national financing and co-productions like *Crouching Tiger* and *Hero*. What is not apparent is how the genre will develop when cut off from the nourishing culture of this core centre.

Acknowledgments to David Chute and Cheng-sim Lim

13

Hong Kong Film and the New Cinephilia

David Desser

In her essay, "The Decay of Cinema", Susan Sontag begins by decrying the witless, cynical and decadent state of contemporary cinema.[1] But this polemical, if largely conventional attack on post-1980s Hollywood cinema, makes a more controversial move in claiming that this sad state of affairs does not bespeak the end of cinema, but, rather, the end of cinephilia. For Sontag and others (even those who disagree with her conclusions) cinephilia names a special and particular kind of "love" of cinema, a love which gathered among university students and other young people who fell in love not just with actors but with cinema itself in the 1950s. The primary expression of this cinephilia came through *Cahiers du cinéma* and other film magazines in Euro-America (and in Japan, too). Cinematheques and cine-clubs soon sprang up, the product of what Sontag calls "the feverish age of movie-going". During this period, the 1960s through the mid-1970s, "there were new masterpieces every month". But cinema-as-industry outweighed cinema-as-art and this process pushed out the great mavericks of this other golden age. Along with the death of the cinema-as-art came the death of cinephilia: "the distinctive cinephilic love of movies that is not simply love of but a certain taste in films ... Cinephilia itself has come under attack as something quaint, outmoded, snobbish. For cinephilia implies that films are unique, unrepeatable, magic experiences". Movies may be dead, in fact, even if some very good ones continue to be made, because cinephilia is dead.

There is little of a sustained argument in this essay, especially the abbreviated and Americanized version that appeared in the *New York Times* (which gave the piece its greatest and most prestigious exposure), though it sparked conversation and controversy — the hallmarks of any good essay. But in either version (the quotes in this essay are from the piece as it ran in the *New York Times* and reprinted on the Internet), Sontag's conclusion is that it was the deadening impact of postmodern cinema — assaultive images and their unprincipled manipulation — and the domestication of the film-viewing experience that killed cinema. She claims, "Predictably, the love of cinema has waned ... you hardly find anymore, at least among the young, the distinctive cinephilic love of movies ..." Despite the broad nature of her decrying, one thing which does emerge is the unmistakable twinge of a nostalgia that cannot be contained. It is evident in the phrase "at least among the young" and apparent in an earlier phrase when Sontag says, "How far away that era seems now". Perhaps the inability to lay blame — to decry cinema and cinephilia — stems from this sense of loss that underlies all nostalgia.

Jesse Walker puts his finger on both the nostalgic element of the idea of the lack of cinephilia and points the way toward understanding how cinephilia isn't dead — it's just moved to a different neighborhood. He notes that upon publication of Sontag's essay, "other critics repeated the charge, each evincing nostalgia for the filmgoing culture of the early to mid-1960s, when reviews as well as movies could spark debates".[2] He later claims, however, that cinephilia is scarcely dead. There are fewer film societies but more VCRs, fewer film debates that everyone follows but more film debates in toto ... . The consumption of movies has ... grown more personalized. First video transformed the home into a repertory theatre, and now DVDs have turned it into a school for film archeologists as well. The video-store culture that produced Quentin Tarantino has moved online, where one can find sites and e-mail lists devoted to everything from blaxploitation to Tarkovsky. The invocation of Tarantino is a nice move too, for as I will show, Tarantino's films were instrumental in the shift to a new cinephilia, one intimately connected to video-store culture and online discussions.

Nostalgic cinephilia, a nostalgia, that is, for a certain kind of cinephilia, is also invoked by Peter Hutchings in his thoughtful review of Martin Scorsese's *A Personal Journey*, which he claims is "nostalgic not only for a certain type of cinema — classical Hollywood — but also for a particularly intense kind of spectatorial involvement with the filmic medium".[3] Hutchings does not invoke Sontag's essay on the death of cinema/cinephilia, yet there are eerily clear echoes of her sentiments in Hutchings's analysis of Scorsese's sense of loss, calling Scorsese's tribute to Hollywood cinema "a rather sad book, aware as it appears to be that the desire for cinema that it celebrates is no longer a significant feature of our culture". He, too, invokes Quentin Tarantino, linking Scorsese's memory of stealing film stills out of a book with the famous scene in Truffaut's *Day for Night* where the young boy steals stills of *Citizen Kane* from a movie theatre display, and likening both to Tarantino's "'postmodern' spectatorship" as film geek in the video store.

Scorsese's memory of stealing stills from a film book, linked to a scene in Truffaut's *Day for Night*, reminds us of the importance of "the moment" to cinephilia. Truffaut and Godard, in their influential reviews/criticism in *Cahiers,* often waxed poetic over images and scenes in films. This would carry over into their cinema and helps explain their fondness for cinematic quotation, a particular kind of intertextuality. Perhaps only the cinephile appreciates, at this level, the moment in *The 400 Blows* when Truffaut exactly reproduces the gym-outing scene from Jean Vigo's *Zero de conduit.* The desire to "quote" in cinema finds an even more obvious expression when in Godard's *Vivre sa vie*, Nana (an intertextual, cinephiliac reference itself to Renoir's *Nana*) rapturously engages with Dreyer's *The Passion of Joan of Arc*. Not content as critics simply to praise a film overall or to examine its content, the moment became the privileged point of entry into a film and it was those moments that sparked a desire to write about, to reproduce, to wax poetic over, that moment.

The cinephile occupies an important position historically and at present, between what we might call the film fan and the film scholar. (One is tempted to re-name the latter the "cine scientist" to invoke that moment, post-1968, when semiotics, structuralism and psychoanalysis converged to imagine a science of the cinema that would supercede the mere love of cinema and perhaps go some way toward destroying it.) For we must ask: what is the real object of cinephilia? What is the thing that the cinephile desires, longs for, and wants to possess? The film fan loves movies, loves going to the movies. The cinephile loves the cinema, going to the movies to be sure, but also writing about them, talking about them, and finding precisely those moments that make it all worthwhile. The cinephile is not like the bibliophile. The bibliophile loves books — the object, the physical thing. Does the bibliophile love literature? Not necessarily. The variety of books — their shape, their color, their pages, illustrations, etc. — along with a relative or actual rarity of certain books, that is, of copies — brings value to the physical object. But the cinephile does not necessarily want to own the physical thing.

Here, of course, we are in the realm of Walter Benjamin's still-influential thinking about "the work of art in an age of mechanical reproduction".[4] The worth, the value, of a specific book for the bibliophile lies precisely in its aura, its uniqueness (relatively if not absolutely); the physical object, as much or more than its contents, is precisely what is of value. I can read a great work of literature in a poorly bound paperback copy or, if I could tolerate it long enough, on a computer screen. But what I am valuing is the message, as it were, not the medium. Of course, there are such things as rare films, but once found such rarities can be reproduced, thus rendering the aura of that lone copy less significant. (I am here not interested in smaller scale issues of the "quality" of a copy — the superiority of 35 mm over videotape or the superior visual quality of nitrate over acetate, etc.) By the same token, individual books, regardless of their content, can be superior to others — a leather-bound edition, a quality paperback, etc. But from the outside, so to speak, the actual film stock on which a film resides, is the same: a roll of 35 mm film itself holds no intrinsic value to a cinephile — he/she loves the cinema, not the roll of film (although in the days before video, there was a small species of cinephile known as the collector who prized, precisely, the quality of the copy — 35 mm instead of 16; Technicolor instead of Eastmancolor; rarity over easy availability, etc.). What then, does the cinephile love?

The cinephile loves those moments in the cinema that rise to poetry, that inspire something in the cinephile, something that can only be experienced from the cinema. The intense nostalgia experienced by aging cinephiles may have as much to do with this sense of impermanence, of evanescence, of a fleeting moment of experience and epiphany, as any objective judgment about the decline in cinema and/or cinephilia. Since few cinephiles were actual film collectors (Henri Langlois is the great exception — the true cinephile, called by the New Wave critics, "a great auteur" as the ultimate compliment) there was always something of memory involved in the intermediary nature of the cinephile between text and audience. Given the difficulty of possessing the cinema, even the individual text of a single film, what could be possessed and communicated was the experience. This also involved judgment and discrimination, of course. All films, all texts, could not be equal; time was precious, viewing hours limited, memory fragmentary. Thus the cinephile created a canon, personal though it may have been, and invited others to share in this judgment, this, literally, sensibility. Perhaps the French film critics/would-be film directors of the early 1950s felt they could see what there was to see, to a large extent, and make historical and critical judgments. There was, after all, only 50 years of film behind them, a good deal of it lost. And the concept that films from say, Mexico, Brazil, Argentina, not to mention China, Hong Kong, Korea, Malaysia could potentially have offered those transcendental moments might have been absurd. Today, no one can imagine mastering the entire cinematic past or even a portion of it, let alone keep up with the cinemas across the globe. Thus today's cinephile already works at a distinct disadvantage and the idea of standards, of taste, might itself seem quaint in the postmodern condition. Thus we must speak about a new cinephilia, perhaps one vastly different from the earlier model, but which might, after all, rest on the same concept of moments prized by cinephiles of the past.

Critics have lately come to discuss the increasingly "global" nature of culture, though treating it with ambivalence, mistrust and in contradictory ways. The tendency, too, to treat global culture as an American imposition on Third World or post-colonial sites, remains strong, as does the tendency to link it with transnational capitalism. That is a debate I am hardly qualified to enter and thus will content myself with surveying how an Asian-based center of production, transmission and reception of a transnational and increasingly global culture may be detected. One such model of the dispersion of global culture and the creation of transnational spaces has been put forth by Arjun Appadurai through his notion of "mediascapes" and the consequences for the production of cultural identity, locality and the virtual neighborhood.[5] Aihwa Ong criticizes Appadurai's claims on the basis that "he ignores the political economy of time-space compression and gives the misleading impression that everyone can take equal advantage of mobility and modern communication".[6] Ong may well be right that the poor and, to a still-large extent, women have less access to cultural production and consumption than urban, transnational elites, but I am concerned with the transmission and consequent creation of a pan-Asian film genre and a globalized cinephilia precisely by those "elites" able to take advantage of the machineries and technologies of (post)modernity.

College courses, museum and festival screenings, videotape, DVD, VCD, Internet sales sites, and web-based discussion groups have facilitated the transnational flow of films. In particular, the introduction of the VCR in the early 1980s and the VCD in the mid-1990s may be marked as those moments where the new cinephilia took root. In both instances Hong Kong cinema was at the heart of this new global network of cinephiles. The new cinephilia of which I am speaking began in the late 1980s, when the VCR had sufficiently penetrated the US and the Japanese markets — the world's two biggest economies, unsurprisingly in the vanguard of VCR consumption. Tapes could bypass the official circuits of distribution (Blockbuster Video in particular) and exhibition (film and television), making available, quite cheaply, films and other AV programming difficult to experience otherwise. The Asian grocery store in US cities and towns suddenly took on tremendous importance for cinephiles denied Asian films in theatres or seeking out alternatives to an increasingly routinized Hollywood product.

By the same token, the penetration of the PC into the home market in these two postcapitalist economies must also be considered a subsidiary factor, and for two reasons: the "production" of subtitled videos in the fan network of anime from Japan to the US and the subsequent introduction of Hong Kong action films into this circuit, and the introduction of the internet and World Wide Web which made the PC an even more valuable technology to casual home users. I won't rehearse here the (I hope) well known fact that anime almost completely by-passed official circuits of diffusion into the marketplace. The success of *Akira* in 1989 was not the introduction of contemporary *anime* into the US, but the culmination of long simmering fan-based and anime-club networks. Similarly, the success of John Woo's *The Killer* in 1990 was owed to the videotape success, so to speak, of *A Better Tomorrow* (1986) and Ringo Lam's *City on Fire* (1987). If anecdotal evidence adds anything, let me note my memory of a locally owned video store in Champaign, Illinois purchasing the Japanese laserdisc of Woo's *Hard Boiled* (1992) and renting it to non-Japanese and Chinese speakers with its Cantonese dialogue and Japanese-only subtitles clearly indicated on the label. We are not yet in the realm of cinephilia, to be sure, even the new cinephilia of which I am speaking. Yet something more than mere fandom is at work when self-subtitled videos are being circulated among a select group. And fandom hardly describes the willingness of people to watch a film with neither an audio or subtitle track that they can understand. Typically, the word "cult" is applied to such behavior. Cinephilia adds the level of discourse to this love of cinema going or, in the new case, cinema-viewing. And it is here where the PC and the Internet come into play in the production of a discourse about these movies, not just the numerous fan sites and web pages devoted to actors, directors, anime series, etc., but of on-line film reviews maintained outside the circuit of mainstream reviewing just as the films themselves stand outside the circuit of mainstream exhibition. On the Internet, everyone is a critic, and Internet sites encourage precisely this sort of reviewing, which allows personal expression to those uninterested in, incapable of, or simply unconcerned with, entering into more normative discursive structures such as the daily newspaper, the weekly column, or the academic essay.[7]

The cult popularity of John Woo, in particular, but Hong Kong action cinema in general (the films of Tsui Hark, the star personae of Jet Li, Chow Yun-fat, even Jackie Chan in this period) is, I argue, the driving force of the new cinephilia. But it took the introduction of the even cheaper and more convenient VCD format to solidify this emerging trend toward Hong Kong film consumption and cinephiliac commentary. Simply put, the VCD and consequent web-based sales sites led to the emergence of the new cinephilia:

VCD technology was introduced by Philips and Sony in 1993. With the development of the far superior DVD technology already underway, US OEMs made a technology decision not to develop VCD, but to wait for DVD. Instead of abandoning the seemingly "doomed" technology, Philips and Sony discovered a market in developing Asian countries. They launched VCD in China because it was a technology that was "fit for a poor cousin" in laggard developing countries instead of cutting edge economies, such as the US. Just as they expected, VCD has thrived in China.[8]

The inferiority of the VCD image (no better than videotape) and the 74-minute time capacity per disk doomed the VCD in places like the US and Japan where cutting-edge technology contains its own cultural capital. For the rest of Asia, however, "The 'cheapness' of VCDs — easy to produce, to reproduce, to consume, to exchange, to throw away — makes it a favorite format in Asia, except Japan", say Davis and Yeh, who also point out that the question of video piracy, long associated with the VCD, is also owed to its "inferior" status: "to some extent this allowed VCDs to flourish beneath the notice of international scrutiny".[9] This also meant that there would be much less scrutiny of Internet sites. Since these were Asian films, especially Hong Kong movies, for sale, the FBI and Interpol would be unlikely to take much interest in these sales that did not harm the royalties of Euro-American producers and distributors.

The cheapness of the VCD had advantages in the technologically advanced US where, although it is virtually unknown as a mainstream format, VCDs dominated Asian-cinema Internet sites until recently (the price of DVDs has come down dramatically). VCDs can be played on DVD machines and on PCs, a distinct advantage for the less expensive format since few people in the US purchased VCD players (cheap though they are) but may have balked, until more recently, at the high(er) DVD prices. Easy to mail, to carry, to play, to trade, even to copy to tape or, now, to burn on a PC, the VCD was the perfect format for the new cinephile, perhaps less interested in collecting, but omnivorously interested in viewing. (Here again the anti-piracy features of DVDs come into play, even if they are easy to overcome; there are no such features on a VCD). Simply put, for the American market: "VCDs offer material that is unavailable elsewhere". (8) Davis and Yeh call the VCD a "programmatic technology … one whose use-value is defined primarily by content … a programmatic technology … comes with an agenda; as opposed to mere product differentiation or technical advantages to existing hardware, it differentiates modes of consumption because it taps new audience formations … It satisfies an existing subcultural market while also expanding it into trans-cultural, trans-national areas" (6–7).

This led to a wide-ranging intertextual relay in which a large body of films circulates in a global exchange (sometimes quite literally, with people exchanging tapes and discs completely outside regulated sales.) Similarly, pirated DVDs and VCDs often allow audiences to participate in the simultaneous "release" of blockbuster titles. (Anyone who travels in Asia looking for movies can attest to the availability of brand new or even yet-to-be-released films on often quite acceptable DVDs.) The combination of the inexpensive availability of films on VCD and DVD and the many web-based discussion sites creates not only "cult" figures (Miike Takashi, for instance is more well known than commercially successful) but a new kind of cinephilia. This new cinephilia coalesced around Hong Kong films, in particular the cinema of John Woo, which captured the imagination of a type of white, adolescent male subject in Euro-America who soon found himself identifying with non-white and (outside of John Woo's cinema) female characters. The kinetic montages, sometimes termed "bullet ballets", appealed to the increasing appreciation of fragmentation of the mise-en-scene (not to mention the image itself) and the overt play of cinema stylistics, perhaps, curiously, a recollection of the New Wave playfulness that contributed to the (first) golden age of cinephilia. While Hong Kong cinema has had a huge impact across Asia (of course in a circulation of exchange with Hollywood, French and Japanese cinemas), this appeal to, especially, the largely insular American audience marked a new formation in the appreciation and consumption of global cinema. If the bias in this essay, then, revolves around the cinephilia expressed in English-language web sites, it is partly to marvel at the rejection of the image of the American audience as xenophobic, closed-minded and unwilling to deal with subtitled and "foreign" movies.

With the increased consumption and appreciation of Hong Kong cinema, a more "pan-Asian" film appreciation developed, partly as a consequence of pan-Asian film production, partly because of the influence of Hong Kong cinema on other Asian-based productions, and partly due to an increasing presence of a recognizably pan-Asian culture.[10] This is implicitly acknowledged by the Euro-American fans that avidly purchase Asian films and launch web-sites devoted to their discussion. Sites like Blue Laser, Hong Kong DVD, Poker Industries, Asian DVD, etc. offer films from Hong Kong, Japan, Korea and (in some small number) Thailand, most often, the Hong Kong versions with Chinese and English subtitles. Similarly, fan-reviews regularly compare films from across the region and often little distinction is made as to country of origin: the Japanese film *City of Lost Souls* (Miike Takashi, 2000) is discussed on such web-sites as "Kung

Fu Cult Cinema Review", "Love HK Film Review,' and "Two Degrees of Anthony Wong". That most of the films offered for sale and under review may be grouped into the broad category of Action (or Horror) bespeaks of the global dimensions to contemporary genre films. What is not for sale is no less revealing. One does not find films from mainland China, from Vietnam, Malaysia, or Indonesia, for instance, on "Asian" cinema web-sites. One enterprising site has begun offering Hindi or "Bollywood" films and thus we may conclude that these films are entering what I am calling the new cinephilia of pan-Asian films in terms of both production and reception. The new cinephilia, then, is the product of global communication formations and film production sites centered in global cities, the cosmopolitan centers of cultural production as well as cultural consumption. And the genres favored by the new cinephiliac are those favored by the young Asian and Asianized Euro-American subjects living in these new global cities.

It is Hong Kong cinema primarily that occupies the minds and hearts of the new web-based cinephiliac, the Hong Kong cinema that specializes in the Action and Horror genres favored by globalized youth. That the new cinephiles are young is an important factor. The techno-orientation of the new cinephilia — its combination of digital technology for consumption and retransmission on the web — makes it a particular province of young people at home with these new and emerging technologies. That the Internet is at the heart of this new cinephilia should not disguise, however, its resemblance to the small movie magazine movement of the 1950s to 1970s (a movement which is by no means dead, but which is often "collector oriented", "fan oriented", or academically oriented in various print formats). The Hong Kong-centric nature of these websites may be gauged by the fact that there is a website devoted simply to providing "Hong Kong Cinema Internet Information Sources" (http://www.brns.com/bb3.html). This is a website to lead one to other websites (something apparent for many of the more fan-oriented world of anime, such as "The Anime Web Turnpike", or television shows like *Buffy the Vampire Slayer*). Many such sites are the products of individuals wishing to espouse, inform or pontificate on their feelings about Hong Kong cinema. In addition to the three sites I mentioned a moment ago, we may also surf "City on Fire", "Kung Fu Cinema", "Mr Blues HK Movie site", "The Dragons Den", "A Better Tomorrow", and "A View from the Brooklyn Bridge", among others. Other sites are more open, in particular the very useful Hong Kong Movie Database, which contains capsule reviews submitted by users. The Internet Movie Database does the same thing for all its films, including Hong Kong movies, which tend to be the most frequently commented upon outside of Hollywood films. These websites contain links to other websites thus implicitly offering the kind of dialogue that encourages further discussion. And, of course, there are the very popular "discussion boards" and listservs devoted to Asian film in general and Hong Kong films in particular. Though there is often a slippage between the kind of academically oriented listserv that caters to scholars and teachers and the more cinephiliac ones of which I am speaking, the fact that so many websites exist outside of the rubric of academic or scholarly orientation is precisely the point I wish to make.

It was the combination of film availability in video format (VHS, DVD, VCD) and the Internet that produced not just a new fan base for Hong Kong cinema, but a new cinephilia that had a global impact on film production and film reception. The region-wide circulation of Hong Kong films since the 1960s has long made Hong Kong cinema a major source of cultural influence in Asia and, after 1973, in the US and Europe. However, the domination of Hollywood cinema on worldwide screens that began again in the 1980s has made Hollywood *the* "global" film culture. But just as the cinephilia of the 1950s and 1960s turned away from mainstream products in favor of Hollywood "B" features of the 1950s, Italian neo-Realism, and the "Art" cinema generally, so, too, the new cinephilia found its inspiration in a new cinema, albeit a mainstream cinema in its local context. Just as the French cinephiles of the New Wave rewrote the history of Hollywood cinema in terms of a new canon of taste and sensibility (auteur directors as the standard of value; cinema as a specific medium as the point of entry) so, too, the new cinephilia that emerged in the 1990s prized Hong Kong films precisely for their medium-specific qualities and unearthed a new canon of auteur directors. Hong Kong, long a transnational cinema in terms of its region-wide popularity, its propensity for co-productions, and its use of multi-lingual, multi-national casts, became the center of a global cinephilia in the early 1990s precisely when video availability and web-based discussions enabled it to transcend even the vast borders of Asia.

Just as the cinephile movement of the post-war era ended up impacting the nature and character of film production (the shift in film style and changes in subject matter are virtually all due to New Wave demands), so, too, the new cinephilia has led to the shifts in film style and subject of global cinema that began in the 1990s. The impulse toward cinephilia thus leads to the flattening of difference in the erasure of national origins and boundaries, offering up in their place an intertextual chain of homages, references, borrowings and reworkings. The post-modernist patina of so much of the contemporary Asian action film is thus owed not only to the slick cinematography, urban locales, hip characters and ultra-violence, but also the sense of filmic déjà vu. This may be demonstrated in the movement of one particular sequence from film to film to film, from Hong Kong to Hollywood to Japan.

Arguably the finest moment in Quentin Tarantino's *Reservoir Dogs* (1992) is the three-way, guns-drawn standoff between Mr White (Harvey Keitel), Joe Cabot (Lawrence Tierney) and Nice Guy Eddie (Chris Penn), as Mr Orange (Tim Roth) lies bleeding to death on the floor of the warehouse. It is an extraordinary moment, recalling the three-way gunfight in Sergio Leone's operatic *The Good, the Bad, and the Ugly* (1967), but given its modern-day context and the unusual nature of the scene, it works to create far more tension and seems far more original. And yet it is derived, almost in its entirety, from Ringo Lam's *City on Fire* (1987). For not only does Lam's film similarly feature a three-way standoff, in which Fu (Danny Lee) points his gun at the Triad boss (Fong Yau) who is pointing his gun at Ko Chow (Chow Yun-fat), only to have a gun pointed at him by the second-in-command, it is also motivated by the same plot point — the boss's (correct) belief in both films that Mr Orange and Ko, respectively, are undercover cops. These two scenes do not end the same way — in *Reservoir Dogs* Mr Orange manages to squeeze off a shot at Nice Guy Eddie and Mr White kills Joe, while in *City on Fire* the standoff is interrupted by the arrival of the police. The different endings may be instructive as to the cultural differences between Hong Kong and the US — the latter being more nihilistic and self-contained — but also attests to the creativity of Tarantino, whose film is quite different in structure and approach.

However, it is the visualization of this particular scene which concerns me here, for it is taken up again in Japan's *Shark Skin Man and Peach Hip Girl* (Katsuhito Ishii 1998). At that film's climax we again see a three-way standoff interrupted and brought to head by a fourth party (as Mr Orange and the police may be said to be in Tarantino's and Lam's films). Tanuki points a gun at Samehada's head, while Samehada has one leveled at Tanuki's crotch. Toshiko arrives and she points a gun at Tanuki who then is seen holding a knife to Toshiko's neck. To this standoff is added the uncle who has been more or less pursuing Samehada. This three/four-way standoff is allowed to stand onscreen for some moments in order, I take it, that we may appreciate its derivation from *City on Fire* and *Reservoir Dogs*. It ends differently from the other two films, as Tanuki, Samehada and the uncle all die in simultaneous gunfire, while Toshiko survives unhurt. The multi-character stand-off occurs yet again in the even more anarchic *City of Lost Souls*, in what is actually one of the more low-key moments of this hyper-kinetic film.

Is this repeated use of a multi-character standoff merely a case of homage, as we might understand numerous obvious allusions in contemporary cinema to the cinematic past? Or is something more significant, if not necessarily profound, at work here? *City on Fire* was hardly a film classic by the time *Reservoir Dogs* was made, and thus, unlike the homages to Hitchcock by directors like De Palma and Scorsese, or to Bergman on the part of Woody Allen, a distinctly non-canonical referencing is being promulgated. Tarantino may have "borrowed" from *City on Fire* without attribution (a common enough strategy in any case), but neither is he hiding his references. The Japanese films, in turn, revel in their dual citation, welcoming the recognition of the scene's origins in both Hong Kong and Hollywood. That is, these films reuse what is current, what is specifically of the moment, creating an instant canon rather than relying on the classics which are (obviously) alluded to in contemporary mainstream cinema. Similarly, these moments of overt reworking come in the context of generic play, since more is at work across these films than that one moment of repetition. The transfer from Hong Kong to Hollywood to Japan reflects the migration of more than cinematic quotation, for so many contemporary films contain distinctly and distinctively multi-national casts and their points of origin become increasingly difficult to pin-point, while their locations become increasingly similar. That is to say, to begin with, there is an actual migration of talent. John Woo, for instance, repeats his favored motifs, characters and images from his Hong Kong films in the larger-scale Hollywood films. Hong Kong director Lee Chi-ngai adapting a Japanese novel, filmed in Tokyo, relying on Japanese, Mandarin, Fukienese, etc., used a multi-national cast for *Sleepless Town* (1998), starring Takeshi Kaneshiro. Indeed, Kaneshiro, the Taiwanese-born superstar of the Hong Kong and Japanese cinema, himself of Chinese and Japanese origin, might be emblematic of the transnational character of contemporary Asian cinema and the increasing erasure of national origins and boundaries. He is at home in both the Hong Kong and Japanese film industries simultaneously, and able to work in Cantonese, Mandarin and Japanese. This skill was put to good use in the transnationally postmodernistic film par excellence, *Chungking Express*.

This one moment of repetition, which we might better call replication as Greg Urban understands it, is revelatory of both the new cinephilia and of what, precisely, is new about it.[11] Using Urban's idea of culture and meta-culture, we might note that cinephilia involved the appreciation of cinema (culture) and the creation of discourses about it and discourses inspired by it and, in the case of French and British critics of the 1950s, replicating it in their own films (metaculture). But there was always a necessary time lag between the cultural expression, its metacultural response, and its replication as a new film. Now, in postmodern fashion, the time lag has been compressed, not only in the ability to produce metacultural discourse in a quicker and more accessible fashion (the Internet, most particularly) but in the ability to possess both the cultural object and the meta-cultural discourses simultaneously. That is, what Urban calls "accelerative culture", a culture that is "on the side of futurity, looking forward rather than backward, characterized by newness and novelty, rather than oldness and familiarity"(15), has now been accelerated. Still following on from Urban, we may claim that the new cinephilia is affected both by greater forms of dissemination and by replication. On the one hand, the actual material object is more easily acquirable. Writes Urban: "The relative separation of dissemination from replication means that it is possible to disseminate cultural objects … without replicating them at each step along the way. Therefore, the object created by a single individual or subset of individuals can reach a wide audience … without the need of intervening replication" (213). On the other hand, cinephiliac replications — retellings, reworkings, reimaginings — also act as metacultural discourses, thus both replicating the original cultural idea or moment and creating a new object which is both text and meta-text.

The original reviews of *Reservoir Dogs* make no mention of its indebtedness to *City on Fire*. The vast majority of "official critics" and filmgoers of that year were quite simply unaware of the "original" text upon which the film was in some sense based. When the revelations, so to speak, of its indebtedness to the Hong Kong film became widespread there was something of a backlash against Tarantino, though at that time it hardly impacted on his mainstream reputation, already established by *Pulp Fiction* (1994), whose obvious indebtedness to numerous other films was something of a cinephile's dream — at least for the new cinephilia emerging precisely at this period. I would argue that the very popularity of *Reservoir Dogs* initiated a discovery or an "uncovery" of more of the Hong Kong cinema, allowing Ringo Lam, for instance, into the very small canon of Hong Kong filmmakers known in the West. I don't necessarily wish to privilege Quentin Tarantino, but it is inescapable that *Reservoir Dogs* and *Pulp Fiction* are intimately linked to the cinephiliac appreciation of Hong Kong cinema and to the emergence of something like a global action genre that is the particular province of this new cinephilia. That Tarantino's films emerged in the age of video is no coincidence — see the already-familiar knowledge that Tarantino is a "film geek" who worked at a video store. What is perhaps less remarked or recognized is that the cinephiliac reworkings of *Reservoir Dogs* appeared in the Asian contexts in 1998 and after; i.e. postdating the introduction and wide availability of the VCD, to whose appearance we may thus precisely attribute these cinephiliac returns.

The Euro-American web-based cinephilia that links Hong Kong, Japanese and Korean cinema as equally available for sale or equally available for discussion may obscure cultural or national boundaries. This reflects the especially American inability to distinguish among Asian cultures, flattening them out as simply "Asian".[12] Yet this is also partly attributable, as I have indicated, to the transnational character of Asian film production and the prevalence of multi-national casts. What use might it be to attribute any specific "place" to a film like *So Close* (2002), for instance? With its American financing (Columbia Pictures Film Production Asia, which also financed *Crouching Tiger, Hidden Dragon*, 2000) and featuring Taiwan-born Shu Qi, Mainland star Vicky Zhao Wei, Hong Kong star Karen Mok and co-starring the Korean Song Seung-heon and the Japanese Yasuaki Kurata, does it make much sense to claim any specific place? With famed Hong Kong auteurs like Corey Yuen Kwai and Jeff Lau as director and writer, respectively, certainly one attributes this film, broadly, to Hong Kong, yet given its "three-Chinas" leading ladies and Korean heartthrob romantic interest, not to mention that the film was shot in English (though dubbed into Cantonese in Hong Kong) questions of national origin must take a back seat to what is obviously pan-Asian and even global filmmaking. Film producers and distributors are thus already acknowledging what academics seem reluctant to admit: the transnational character of contemporary filmmaking in Asia.

The dissemination and replication of various specific Asian cultural phenomena across the region (manga, anime, Japanese and Korean TV dramas, Japanese and Korean pop music, etc.) certainly speak to a notion of pan-Asian culture. Yet, in the face of ever-increasing globalization, understood as Americanization, critics remain reluctant to speak of pan-Asian culture. But this should not deter us from recognizing the ways in which the transmigration of peoples and the transmission of culture does create a site of pan-Asian cultural production and consumption. Let us take a statement by Aihwa Ong by way of seeing this ambivalence to claim pan-Asian cultural connections. She states: "I argue that the great appeal of [Jackie Chan's films] for diasporan-Chinese communities lies not only in their action genre; they are also popular because they are a medium for exploring reified Chinese values ... in conditions of displacement and upheaval under capitalism" (162). Does this mean, then, that the enormous popularity of Jackie Chan for non-Chinese audiences is owed to something else entirely? Is it not possible, even likely, that so-called

Chinese values like brotherhood, hierarchized allegiances, and kinship loyalty (162) are values prevalent in other Confucian-based and family-centered Asian societies? And is it not true that other Asian societies faced and continue to face conditions of displacement and upheaval under capitalism? This reluctance to see a kind of pan-Asian culture on Ong's part comes through quite clearly when she dismisses the attitude of former Star TV CEO Richard Li, who once stated that Asians have a lot more in common than they have differences as being "perhaps tongue in cheek" (167).

Yet Star TV continues to promulgate a pan-Asian popular culture through its popular Channel V, a toned-down version of MTV that regularly features Canto-pop, Mandarin-pop, and Korean and Japanese pop as well (and even "Pop from the West".) The popularity of the satellite TV channel and the obvious popularity of Japanese pop and Mandarin-pop in Hong Kong clearly indicate a willingness to import and consume popular culture. That Star TV is based in India, with its news division headquartered in Hong Kong, is reflective of India's increased Asian participation, so to speak, and its desire to enter the realm of cultural transmission, not simply across the vast Indian diaspora. Or take the case of Japanese TV *dorama,* popular in Hong Kong specifically on VCD, according to Davis and Yeh:

> VCD users know that other young Asians are following the same drama in other cities, enjoying the flexibility of VCDs and their slippage out of conventional broadcast nets cast by nation-states. Awareness of other "comrades" in the region (visible through fan clubs, letters, Internet sites) augments pleasure, proximity and domestication of a foreign import, transforming its foreign provenance into not only an imagined, but also an "imaginary," pan-Asian community. (23)

Critics have even defined this community quite specifically: It is the product of an elite, young generation of "Americanized Asian subject(s) ... under twenty-five, (who) watches MTV, wear(s) jeans ... wields a wireless phone, and haunts shopping malls", says Ong (169). I would add only that American Asian subjects have in their turn produced what I have referred to above as Asian-ized Euro-American subjects.

It may be arguable that the Hong Kong cinema entered into its transnational and globalized capacity due in part to the massive Chinese diaspora. With its need to make films that appeal outside the confines of Hong Kong itself — a population base no greater than Sweden's in the 1950s and 1960s, for instance, yet Sweden never produced a globally influential, varied international cinema — Hong Kong was always transnational in funding and marketing. As overseas Chinese communities adapted their culture to the new cultures in which they found themselves, it was inevitable that Hong Kong cinema, needing this market (i.e. these markets) would shift as well. Thus the surprising entry of Hong Kong onto the global scene should be no surprise at all — Hong Kong film culture was well positioned to entertain global audiences. The entry of the Hindi cinema onto the global film scene (its international popularity preceded its belated and long-over-due academic recognition) may similarly be attributed to the vast Indian diaspora. The consumption of Hindi (and Tamil and Telugu) films on the part of Non-Resident Indians (NRIs) encouraged a spill-over into the host communities, while, of course, the values espoused by Indian cinema (with its large component of Muslim talent) was also attractive to North African, Malaysian and other Islamic communities. Just as Hong Kong movies played for some years on the "Chinatown" circuit before breaking into the mainstream, so, too, Indian films may regularly be seen in suburban communities in the Northeast, Midwest and West Coast of the US. In England of late, Hindi cinema has broken out of this ghetto to a greater degree than it has in the US.

Yet we may also note the quite differently positioned, more recent entry of Hindi cinema into the cinephile realm — the offering of Hindi films on web-sites previously the domain of Hong Kong, Japan and Korea. This is owed precisely to the new cinephiliac elements of its cinema, specifically its homages to, borrowings from, and reproductions of, Hong Kong movies. And just as it was John Woo's stylistics around which the new cinephilia emerged and developed, so, too, is Woo an underlying textual relay in the Hindi cinema. One may see this, for instance, in the climax of Sanjay Gupta's *Khauff* (2000). A remake of the Hollywood film, *The Juror* (1996), the ending is derived almost entirely from Woo's *The Killer* and *Face/Off* (1997) (the latter a film in which Woo repeats himself or pays homage to his own sense of loss and nostalgia — another story that).

As usual, while mainstream critics in India (at least the two reviews I have read) missed the cinephilia of Gupta, a web-based reviewer did not, albeit to the film's shame: "Sorry Mr Gupta, but using scenes from *Replacement Killers*, *The Juror* & Endless [sic] John Woo films, and stealing music from *Wild Things*, *Replacement Killers* & *Prince of Egypt* (Yes, I noticed that one in the end, too) will get you nowhere as a director ..."[13] Undeterred by this rejection from a committed cinephile, Gupta entered into the most direct cinephiliac chain I isolated: the *City on Fire/Reservoir Dogs* relay for his hit film, *Kaante* (2002). Critics in India and the US (where, uniquely, it played in some mainstream theatres and was reviewed in the *Los Angeles Times* and the *New York Times*) were quick to note the connections to American films. Where early critics and reviewers were unaware of Tarantino's borrowing from the Hong Kong film, virtually no review failed to comment on *Kaante's Reservoir Dogs* connection. (Shot in Los Angeles, the film hardly disguised its debt to the American film!) When asked about this, the director cagily and perhaps testily replied, "In fact the media has been going crazy saying *Kaante* is a remake of *Reservoir Dogs*. It is not. My film is in the genre of films like *Reservoir Dogs*, *The Asphalt Jungle*, *The Killing*, *City on Fire* … It is a crime film, not a remake of any one film. *Reservoir Dogs* itself is a remake of a Hong Kong … film called *City on Fire*".[14] This is quite a cinephiliac list of references from a director whose own film, arguably, entered the mainstream of Euro/American distribution precisely because of its origins in the new cinephilia.

ACKNOWLEDGMENTS

A portion of this essay appeared in slightly different form in my essay "Global Noir" Genre Film in the Age of Transnationalism" which appeared in *Film Genre Reader III*, Barry Grant, ed., Austin: University of Texas Press, 2003. I would like to thank the participants of the conference organized by Meaghan Morris, particularly Meaghan, Chris Berry, Stephen Teo and S. V. Srinivas, for help in refining this piece, and also Mette Hjort for inviting me to give this paper as a lecture at the University of Hong Kong where it took the basic form it has now, and to the kind audience who heard that lecture and helped me refine it further.

14

Action Cinema, Labour Power and the Video Market

Paul Willemen

Much has been said about the way cinema talks about class. Nothing has ever been said (to my knowledge) about cinema's relation to one of the most fundamental concepts in historical or dialectical materialisms: labour power. Rather than attributing such a surprising omission to a lack of concern or interest, the explanation must be sought in the inadequacies of film theory itself. Consequently, the former problem cannot be addressed without paying serious attention to the latter. It has become, or should have become, a truism to note that the existing corpus of film theory, largely because it has not paid much attention to the historical dynamics which have determined and dictated its agenda, is inadequate, and that these inadequacies are directly connected with the way the cultural dynamics operating in regions of Europe and the US presented themselves in texts, whether these be films, journalistic criticism or academic publications.

Again, this is not a question of whether representations reflect or construct the real. It is a question of how the real, that is to say, history, is present in the very fabric as well as in the organisation of representations. The challenge is not to mimic the Asian-values ploy by adapting cultural theory to contingent cultural formations, but to elaborate a better theory of cinema as a cultural form. Needless to say, this challenge will have to be met collaboratively. Given that historical dynamics necessarily shape and limit the thinkable, it is axiomatic that no individual or any single "national" intelligentsia is in a position to meet that challenge. It necessarily requires trans-national critical collaboration within the framework of an agreed and shared sense of direction: the never-to-be-reached goal being a comprehensive understanding of the way culture (and therefore a social formation) works. However, for reasons of brevity, here I will deal only with labour power in the context of the transformation of action adventure, as a genre, into action cinema as produced by the video industry and fed back into the film industry in the mid- to late 1990s.

GENRE, INDUSTRY, FINANCE CAPITAL

I would like to offer some risky hypotheses concerning the issue of presentation-in-representation by looking at action films and the discussions affixing that label to films. My reason for doing so is that I suspect that hidden beneath this marketing category called action films, there is a kind of cinematic discourse that speaks to us of labour power and of the fundamental dynamics of capitalism in general. Putting it a little more dramatically, the economic histories offered to us by the likes of Robert Brenner[1] and Giovanni Arrighi concern themselves analytically and theoretically with the same issues addressed in the mode of fantasy by action films. The economic historians and action films both address questions of the value of labour power, capitalism's attempts to intensify its exploitation and thus devalue labour power, efforts to extend control over raw materials and labour power though cycles of geographical expansion, and periods in which vast quantities of accumulated capital are destroyed in order to make way for the ascendancy of a new rapacious power-bloc. That is to say, the three main strategies of capital to combat the falling rate of profit can be seen as structuring fantasy pressures in action films: the intensification of the exploitation of labour power, geographical expansion, and the destruction of capital values. Anticipating the rest of my argument, I am suggesting that through the medium of many films currently labeled as "action films", finance capital is giving expression to its concerns and aspirations, whereas in films prior to the 1970s, it was mostly industrial capital doing the talking and the dreaming.

My argument is not that action films are characterised as a genre by this (fantasy) economic discourse centered on the interests of finance capital. If my argument has any merit, then it must follow that this kind of fantasy dimension must be present in all films at some level, however diluted, distorted or otherwise translated. What I do wish to argue is, firstly, that the kinds of films currently lumped together under the label "action cinema" provide more direct or easily detectable evidence of the labour theory of value at work in cultural fantasies; and, secondly, that the modalities in which labour power is inscribed into the films allow us to conclude that it is finance capital which has been the discursive hegemon in Hollywood's cinema since the mid-1970s.

THE GENRE PROBLEM

For the history of what is called action cinema in Hollywood, we have to turn to Hollywood's main trade publication and the American film industry's Bible: *Variety*. *Variety*, published since 1905, makes a significant distinction, not often registered in film studies, between types of genres. The distinction can best be traced in *Variety*'s headline-capsule descriptions of films, that is to say, in the few words or lines printed in bold under the title and before the actual review. These capsules address "the trade" directly, particularly distributors and exhibitors, and provide a thumbnail sketch of a film commodity's two main "images": its generic "image" and its market "image". For instance, Vic Morrow's *A Man Called Sledge* is described as a "violent action western" (*Variety*, 3 March 1971), telling the reader that it is a western which may best be sold on the "action market". Similarly, Andrew V. McLaglen's *One More Train to Rob* (*Variety*, 24 April 1971) is presented in the capsule as a "bawdy western" which is a "suitable entry for the general action market". In other words, although the two "images" overlap, they refer to two different sectors of the industry: production and distribution/exhibition, telescoping the latter two sectors. Roughly speaking, the generic brand image tells us how a film's profit-making potential has been calculated into its very design at the production stage by the way it adheres to or varies from a generic formula, while its marketing brand image advises distributors and exhibitors on how best to realise and maximise that profit. For the time being, let us differentiate between these two generic menus by calling them production genres and marketing genres. The former branding is familiar to film students as the standard generic menu consisting of horror, war film, science fiction, western, gangster, melodrama, thriller and so on. The latter works with categories such as "youth market", "action market", "the drive-in trade" (also called "ozoners" in *Variety*-speak), the "skin trade", the "Black market", the "grind houses" and so on.

Of course, some of these marketing categories will also overlap, but they give an indication to distributors and retailers about the specific niche markets where the product is likely to generate most profits. Geoffrey Reeve's *Caravan to Vaccares* is described as a thriller (sub-genre: an Alistair MacLean thriller) for action markets (*Variety*, 21 August 1974), while Ivan Dixon's *The Spook Who Sat by the Door* is described as "Blaxploitation" but "not for action-oriented fans" (*Variety*, 3 October 1973). Hence, no doubt, the often-noted confusion in generic labels between descriptions of "content" categories such as "western", "gangster" and the like, and categories of audiences (youth market, action market, and so on). The two categories are obviously condensed in a number of widely used generic labels which telescope a "narrative image" with the effect it is supposed to have on an audience that is deemed to regard — or has been disciplined over many years by a number of collaborating institutions ranging from advertising to the written, spoken and televised press to regard — films exclusively as the source of a specific menu of "thrills": horror films, thrillers, weepies and the like.

Prior to the mid-1980s, action was something that happened in films belonging to a wide variety of product-genres. It was not a genre itself in the sense that film studies would use the term: it was merely, like nudity, a characteristic of certain films that some types of audiences might want to pay to see. And just as there were films called "nudies", trading simply on the exposure of naked white bodies as in the many volleyball-in-nudist-camp films or pseudo-sex education movies, so there were some "action pictures" on the fringes of the industry but not actually part of Hollywood's notion of "the industry", in the same way that pornography was deemed to be "outside". For instance, the phrase "action picture" was at times deployed, not in capsule summaries, but in the body of the review of Thai films such as the director-actor Sombat Metanee's *Yeh Nuat Sua* aka *Operation Black Panther* (*Variety*, 8 June 1977) or Chumphorn Tepitak's *Tang Sua Phan* aka *The Tiger's Claw* (*Variety*, 10 August 1977). It was also used for minor Turkish films such as Yavuz Figenii's *Hidir* (*Variety*, 2 August 1978). In other words, the phrase was reserved for films made in countries that the US film industry regarded as barely worth considering. Products emanating from such marginal industrial sectors were treated with extreme contempt if they came from the US or European industries; if they came from and appeared to address some "elsewhere", they were treated with both contempt and racism, as was made clear in a review of Ciro Santiago's *Desert Warrior* (*Variety*, 18 September 1985), one of the many *Mad Max*-imitations described in *Variety*'s review as "obviously designed for [the] foreign action market" because that was the only place where the reviewer could imagine finding "anyone with a low enough IQ to qualify as the target audience".

In the US, action, like nudity or sex, could be added to films, regardless of their generic categorisation, in order to make them more saleable to particular segments of the audience. Genre films could be made with or without that "extra action" ingredient without this affecting the generic classification of the film. There simply was no specific generic product category called "action films", but genre films "with action" could, according to *Variety* — reflecting the industry's experience and priorities — be marketed to some exhibition sectors addressing audiences with a "low IQ".

In spite of the eminently sensible and productive reconceptualisation of the notion of genre proposed by Steve Neale in his pioneering book on genre,[2] the industry's audience-marketing categorisations do not play a role in the way he discusses genres. In fact, as the labelling practice of *Variety* shows, a film may be assigned to different genres depending on which sector of the industry, production or distribution/exhibition, is doing the assigning. A western may be marketed as an action film to "low IQ" audience sectors. Generic categories will thus vary according to the power relations between these sectors of the industry.

Whereas one cannot but agree with Steve Neale[3] and Nick Browne[4] when they discuss genre as a product-design process organising a large set of discourses into recognisable, regulated but dynamically changing interrelated patterns, components of which may enter into various types of generic combinations, it is more difficult to follow Steve Neale or John Ellis[5] when they suggest that genres are discursive constellations where the industry's and the audience's expectations meet. What *Variety's* reviews make clear is that the distribution and exhibition sectors (no doubt aided and abetted by the advertising and journalism sectors) have already *pre-formatted* audience expectations in terms of the ingredients specific audience segments are supposed to be willing to pay for. The result, largely overlooked in cinema studies — even though Rick Altman did draw attention to it as a problem[6] — is that there are indeed two sectors of the film industry which each have their own generic menus: one consisting of the ingredients that are supposed to make up categories of films, that is to say, of genres as we have been taught to understand them, and one consisting of ingredients that are supposed to make up and characterise audiences defined in terms of identity categories. The young urban working class is deemed to be undiscriminating and to have a low IQ; consequently that sector is supposed to want the ingredients a, b and c (for instance, sex, violence and action); middle class suburban youth wants a, b and f (on offer in drive-ins), the black urban working class wants ingredients x, a and z, and so on. What Neale and others refer to as "audience expectations", is in fact, the requirement for individual viewers to find "their" position in relation to both sets of generic-identity labels. And it is the interaction between those two kinds of generic categorisations, between production categories (content genres) and marketing categories, which fails to be taken into account.

MASCULINITY

The case of action cinema offers a particularly striking example of the reigning confusion, which helps to explain why almost all current accounts of action cinema content themselves with noting the obvious: the films concern themselves with issues of masculinity. The problem with such a take on action films is that *all films* made in Hollywood (and by other film industries) are about masculinity in the sense of being "about" the demarcations between genders. Some films may be more about gender definitions than others, but genre has nothing to do with that. It would be absurd to suggest that an action film is somehow more about the definition of masculinity than, say, westerns or war movies or comedies or melodramas, or any other industrially produced generic category. Consequently, claiming that action films are about masculinity amounts to saying absolutely nothing about what differentiates one genre from another.

The available literature on action cinema can be divided into roughly two types. One starts from the assumption that there are clearly identifiable genres in the cinema and proceeds to describe a series of films in a more or less celebratory manner privileging the supposedly defining characteristics of the assumed generic category. This approach merely validates marketing strategies adopted by the industry. As such, these works of "criticism" or "history" are significant and useful elements for a diagnostic understanding of the way cultural production works. On a more personal level, such works at times offer cinephiles useful lists and information, but these are better sought in reference works rather than in "critical" prose.

The second type of writing — also starting from the assumption that the film industry's generic menu contains a specific item called action cinema which is identifiable by internal, aesthetic features of the text rather than by what a group of films says about the industry that markets them under a specific label — discusses the films in an equally celebratory (or condemnatory) fashion on the basis of the way they perform definitions of gender identities.

Some years ago, Lee Grieveson gave a good summary of the main accounts of masculinity in film studies.[7] One line of argument, exemplified by Yvonne Tasker, suggests that an alleged greater visibility of male bodies in the 1980s, especially muscular ones in Hollywood's action films, signalled a splitting of masculinity which thus "performs" a notion of masculinity that encompasses established notions of femininity as well. Tasker called this the re-inscription of masculinity as femininity and vice versa, so that "the male figure in the contemporary action picture often functions in both capacities".[8] In other words, a Hollywood notion of masculinity is not only re-installed as the norm (assuming that this had ceased to be the case), it now also claims that men have absorbed the performance of femininity as well. The absurdities of Jewison's *Kramer vs Kramer* (1979), a film dedicated to the proposition that men make better mothers than women, appear to have been generally accepted and adopted by Hollywood and are now exemplified in action films. Indeed, Schwarzenegger even took up the motif of *Kramer vs Kramer* and demonstrated his maternal excellence in unfunny films presented as comedies.

Of course, this is not to be described as some "splitting" of masculinity. It is the appropriation and integration of femininity into a more totalising notion of masculinity. What is at stake in this move is made clear by the action films themselves: by endowing the testosterone-driven bullies with aspects of a simplistic notion of femininity such as a desire for narcissistic display allied with manifestations of "caring affects", Hollywood has given itself the green light to celebrate brutal aggression as an ideal of masculinity as long as it is done peacock-style by men who possess an appropriate, that is to say, a not too pronounced degree of what passes for caring or nurturing femininity. Here we have the template that allows Bush Jr to declare how much he cares about peace while strutting about in a bomber jacket, arms slightly bent at his side, imitating the stiff-yet-swaggering walk of gunslingers in westerns. One didn't need the 1970s or 1980s action films to come across the type of the sensitive bully or the exemplary male who has allegedly incorporated into himself whatever is deemed worthwhile about femininity all the better to legitimate patriarchal authority. To note that such a mechanism operates in action films as well as in all other films (except maybe in teenage nerd movies, where the features usually allocated to one character are dispersed across a number of characters) is redundant.

A second line of argument, exemplified by Ina Rae Hark,[9] suggests that films such as Kubrick-Douglas's *Spartacus* (1960) dramatise a "fissure" in what has been taken to be a "stable" notion of masculinity. Grieveson sums up by noting that Tasker and Hark exemplify an analysis of the masculine that approaches it as a less monolithic and historically homogeneous essence, demonstrating that it is, instead, an unstable nexus of social and political phenomena. In other words, masculinity must first be assumed to be a stable, homogeneous essence in order then to make the point that it isn't so. The discovery that it isn't so is then projected into Hollywood films where it is duly re-discovered to the greater glory of both

Hollywood and the astute critic. The same procedure can easily be deployed to demonstrate that Riefenstahl's films were demonstrating fissures and instabilities in Nazism.

To discover that masculinity or femininity are social-historical constructions and, as such, unstable concoctions, constantly in need of repair and maintenance, of elements rooted in a variety of political-historical dynamics, is rather like a cyclist discovering the wheel. Of course Hollywood movies, as do movies made anywhere throughout film history, perform notions of masculinity in terms of the requirements of the patriarchal regime within which and to the benefit of which they are made. In order to do this, demarcation lines between the mutually defining notions of masculinity and femininity have to be rehearsed, refurbished and re-drawn. That there are always "contradictions" or, in less political language, "fissures" in such constructions was pointed out some thirty years ago by cultural theorists such as Claire Johnston and many others. Far from signalling a "crisis" in some ideological edifice such as the prevailing demarcations between genders, the fissures traced by the likes of Tasker and Hark are nothing more than the contours of the various elements which the film-texts are stitching together, more or less successfully, in order to achieve (to perform) the simulation of cohesion required if the ideological construct is to have maximum effectiveness. None of this has anything to do with the inscription of an anti- or a non-patriarchal voice into the textual fabric. The notion of femininity detected by Tasker and Hark in Hollywood spectacles and action films is rather like the notion of communism secreted by Senator McCarthy's rants: a necessary "other". That "other" is now constructed a little differently from the way it was done in the days of Rudolf Valentino and Douglas Fairbanks, or Raoul Walsh and Howard Hawks. But talk of a crisis in masculinity when pathological forms of it are being reasserted as the norm in the era of Reagan, Clinton, Bush Sr and Jr, deserves, at best, a hollow laugh.

ACTION ADVENTURE

The closest the Hollywood industry came to "action" prior to the 1980s, was the label "action-adventure", widely used for a whole range of films from westerns to pirate movies and serials, swashbucklers and spy movies, and even some war films. Etienne Perier's *Zeppelin* (*Variety*, 14 April 1971), anticipating the series of disaster movies that were about to be produced, and Peter Yates's *Murphy's War* (*Variety*, 27 January 1971) were both capsuled as "wartime adventure yarns". Action-adventure films constituted a genre in the distribution-marketing sector of the industry and referred to a set of ingredients likely to be found on offer in a range of "genre" products. Steve Neale rightly noted that the term action-adventure as a generic label dates back, at least, to 1927 when it was used by *Film Daily* to describe a Douglas Fairbanks film called *The Gaucho* (Richard Jones, 1928) shortly before its release, and that:

> films in the action-adventure tradition have been a staple in Hollywood's output since the 1910s. With its immediate roots in nineteenth-century melodrama and in a principle strand of popular fiction, action-adventure has always encompassed an array of genres and sub-types.[10]

In other words, it always had referred to a different type of generic categorisation than the main generic labels. Action-Adventure was and remains a marketing category referring to types of audiences who "like that sort of thing", the "thing" being a range of ingredients capable of doing for film-marketing what advertising "extra goodness" in food products could do in supermarkets catering for gullible ("undiscriminating") consumers.

These ingredients were deemed to appeal to audience categories ranging from children and adolescents to young middle class men, while the "heroes" of some of these films could also be used as a sales-pitch to young, half-educated women (which must have included the industry's notion of young-ish married women). Clint Eastwood's *The Eiger Sanction*, a spy film, was capsuled (*Variety*, 14 May 1975) as being for "the adventure market", and George Lucas's *Star Wars* was capsuled (*Variety*, 25 May 1977) simply as an "adventure fantasy", economising a mention of the no doubt all too obvious science fiction product-category into which the film's story was packaged. In fact, most of the films Steve Neale claimed for "action adventure" and which he alleges were "perceived in the 1980s and 1990s to be a new and dominant trend in Hollywood's output"[11] were capsuled in *Variety* as "adventure fantasies".

With the emergence of the action film in the 1980s, the retailing category "adventure", including the "unofficial war" films narrating elaborate "terrorist" commando raids, seems to have lost most of its relevance as a marketing tool. As an ingredient designed to enhance a product's saleability, action-adventure appears to have been split according to age and class criteria, with most of the films being assigned to adult, urban working class audiences by way of the appellation "action film", the rest being allotted to family and other anodyne middle class sectors by way of the phrase "adventure fantasy", regardless of the films' (production) genres. The main victim of this shift appears to have been the adventure film, which nevertheless remained a relevant marketing category referring to a very profitable sector of the market in the wake of the box office success of Spielberg's *Indiana Jones* series starting with *Raiders of the Lost Ark*, capsuled as an "adventure fantasy" (*Variety*, 10 June 1981). Again, numerous sequels and imitations followed: Antonio Margheriti had three imitations released in the US, *The Hunters of the Golden Cobra* aka *Raiders of the Golden Cobra* (released in March 1983), *The Ark of the Sun God*, made in 1983 but released in the US in 1986, as was his *Jungle Raiders*, made in 1984; Bob Schultz contributed *Robbers of the Sacred Mountain* in 1984, Andrew Lane added *Jake Speed* in 1986 and J. L. Agraz *Treasure of The Moon Goddess* in 1987, to cite just a few examples. As noted earlier, *Star Wars* (1977) had also been capsuled as an "adventure fantasy".

"Martial arts" films, which can be seen as a potential sub-category of action-adventure, briefly emerged in relation to the Korean War with John Sturges's *Bad Day at Black Rock* and Sam Fuller's *House of Bamboo* (both 1955), neither of which were marketed as "action films". Films featuring martial arts (seen, like nudity or "action", as an extra ingredient within an established production genre format) resurfaced, in relation to the Vietnam War with Tom Laughlin's *Born Losers* (1967) and *Billy Jack* (1971), two biker movies with the star-director playing a Native American Vietnam vet, and in the context of the double, connected reference to both the Vietnam War and the movement for Black civil rights with Jack Starrett's *Cleopatra Jones* (1973) and Robert Clouse's *Black Belt Jones* (1974), the latter starring one of Bruce Lee's sparring partners, Jim Kelly, well before another sparring partner, Chuck Norris, emerged in Ted Post's *Good Guys Wear Black* in 1978, a belated sub-Bond fantasy set in Vietnam and foreshadowing Stallone's *Rambo* films. However, these films were not (yet) marketed as action or as martial arts movies. That only came about as a result of structural changes in the industry, about which more below.

THE HONG KONG CONNECTION

In *Variety*, by and large, only English language films receive a capsule summary, suggesting that they be regarded as a kind of meta-genre and, subtly or not so subtly, suggesting that real money can be made only with English-language product. Occasionally, when a particular kind of "foreign" film appears to be making serious profits at the American box-office, such films receive capsule summaries. The first relevant example of this, as far as the action cinema is concerned, is the appearance of Hong Kong's martial arts films in Hollywood. *Variety*'s first reaction, which endured for a number of years, was to dismiss Hong Kong films as Chinese combinations of two equally despised "foreign" genres: Italian peplums (called spear-and-sandal movies) and Italian westerns ("Italoaters" or "Spaghetti westerns"). It is clear from the trade paper's reviewing practice that "foreign films" were acceptable only as potential competitors in the art cinema market, where not much money was to be made anyway.

Lo Wei's *Fist of Fury* (1972), later re-titled *The Chinese Connection* in order to squeeze some extra dollars out of Friedkin's *The French Connection* (1971) market, did not receive a capsule and was described in *Variety*'s review as an "Oriental paraphrase of Clint Eastwood's Italoaters", with the added explanation that kung-fu was "a stylised variant on karate" (*Variety*, 1 November 1972). The film's star, Bruce Lee, was presented in contemptuous tones as possessing a "boyish charm" that "could prove appealing to US femmes". However, the Hong Kong films that followed in the wake of the box-office success of the Bruce Lee films did receive capsules. Cheng Chang-ho's *Five Fingers of Death* (actually *King Boxer*, 1972) was described in the issue of 21 March 1973 as "a battering Chinese actioner" with good prospects in US action markets, due, *not* to the success of Bruce Lee's films but to that of ABC-TV's *Kung Fu* series starring David Carradine. The next kung fu film to be released theatrically in the US, Huang Feng's *Deep Thrust — The Hand of Death* (actually *Lady Whirlwind*, 1972, with Sammo Hung as martial arts choreographer) was described in the 23 May 1973 *Variety* as a "Kung Fu actioner", with the added suggestion in the title that customers interested in pornography might wish to see this Hong Kong film as well. The review of the film sneers that the "pic should appeal to unfussy violence seekers, of which there are plenty" while smugly claiming that its "depiction of violence can't compete with, say, Sam Peckinpah's slick slicings". Nevertheless, Lo Wei's next hit starring Bruce Lee, *Fists of Fury* aka *The Big Boss* still went unheralded by a capsule summary in *Variety* despite what the review acknowledged as the "US craze for Kungfu" (*Variety*, 27 June 1973). *Variety*'s reviewer informed his readers that "for sheer mindlessness" the film "competes favourably with the early 60s spear-and-sandal cycle and the late 60s Italian Westerns", grudgingly admitting that Lee did display some "athletic skill and grace". On the other hand, money did begin to talk louder than racism when it came to Lee's next film, the posthumously released *Enter the Dragon*, which was welcomed as "topflight chop-socky" (*Variety*, 22 August 1973).

Admittedly, this return to box-office "visibility" and favour in the eyes of *Variety's* reviewers may well have been facilitated, as far as the American trade went, by the fact that an American director, Robert Clouse, had signed the film. This time, what Lee did was described, not as "stylised karate" for "unfussy violence seekers", but as an "ancient art of Oriental self defence which combines the best elements of karate, judo, hapkido, tai-chih and kungfu", suggesting that the reviewer at least had heard of a number of different kinds of martial arts and that a martial arts "niche market" had emerged to which films could henceforth profitably be addressed. A year later, when Lee's own *Return of the Dragon* (*Variety*, 21 August 1974) was released, also starring Lee's sparring partner Chuck Norris, the trade paper had become still more respectful of the genre's money-making capacities and capsuled it as a "slick chop socky actioner practically guaranteed boff b.o. among devotees". By the time *Variety* reviewed the film, the distributor had already notified them that the film had taken more than US$1.25 million in five days in New York. In deference to that sum, *Variety* almost managed to contain its sneers, still audible, though, in its reference to "devotees".

Contrary to an oft-repeated assumption that the Hollywood action films, especially those deploying gestural choreographies derived from martial arts disciplines rather than from boxing or wrestling, derived from the Hong Kong imports in the early 1970s, *Variety* makes it clear that this was not the case. The perceived and stated genealogy of action films, including martial arts "actioners", connected them to the Italian popular cinema exemplified by Italian westerns, especially the Sergio Leone films starring Clint Eastwood, and the Italian peplums of the 1960s. When Chuck Norris tried to transform himself into a corporate brand capable of selling films, he modelled his film persona explicitly on Clint Eastwood, even hiring some of the directors of Eastwood's films: Ted Post and James Fargo. Moreover, *Variety's* attempt to familiarise its readers with "kung fu" by calling it "a stylised form of karate" suggests that Japanese examples of martial arts films such as Kurosawa's samurai films, especially *Yojimbo* (1961), also played a significant role. Besides, Sergio Leone had made his first "dollar" films as adaptations of *Yojimbo* anyway, which made the Italian "action" cinema doubly important as a conduit for the reconfiguration of Hollywood's products destined for the "non-discriminatory drive-in action trade", as *Variety* specified in its capsule for the American release of Antonio Margheriti's 1965 science-fiction film, *I Diafanoidi Portano la Morte* aka *The War Between the Planets* (17 February 1971), or simply for the "undiscriminating action audience", as Don Siegel's *Dirty Harry* was capsuled on 22 December 1971.

It would be many more years, in fact well over a decade, before Hong Kong-style martial arts films registered a significant presence in American cinema's production sector as opposed to its distribution-exhibition sector, which quickly incorporated cheaply acquired films from Hong Kong and Taiwan, along with Japanese samurai films, into its programmes for the "violence" or "action" markets, that is to say, in its exploitation sub-cinema sector. For aspects of Hong Kong's cinema to register in the mainstream production sector of Hollywood rather than in its exploitation cinema backwaters, something first had to shift within the overall power relations dominating the American film industry: the mainstreaming of exploitation cinema that followed on from the take-over of Hollywood by finance capitalism (as opposed to the studio-system which had worked according to the rules and models of industrial capital) in the 1970s. In spite of the re-structuring of Hollywood in the 1970s, to which I will return a little later, the Hong Kong version of martial arts films did not register in Hollywood until the mid- to late-1990s. Jackie Chan's experiences while shooting Robert Clouse's *The Big Brawl* (1980) and Hal Needham's *Cannonball Run* (1981) confirm that even as late as 1980, the Hollywood production sector knew something about the exploitation of Italian westerns and Clint Eastwood movies, but nothing about Hong Kong films.

The experience was repeated and confirmed by Tsui Hark and Kirk Wong in Hollywood in the late 1980s. Hector Rodriguez's adaptations such as *El Mariachi* (1992) and *Desperado* (1995) together with John Woo's *Hard Target* (1993) and especially Stanley Tong and Jackie Chan's *Rumble in the Bronx* (1996) may be regarded as signalling the arrival of the Hong Kong-variant of action cinema in the heartland of the US production sector. Kirk Wong's *The Big Hit* (1998) extended the series (unsuccessfully) and the confirmation of Hong Kong's presence in Hollywood did not come until the Wachowski Brothers' *The Matrix* (1999), John Woo's *Mission Impossible 2* (2000) and Ang Lee's *Crouching Tiger, Hidden Dragon* (2000), the longer term influence of which remain to be seen. The often mentioned odes to John Woo perpetrated by Quentin Tarantino, as for instance in *Reservoir Dogs* (1992), are merely exotic advertising gimmicks, rather like Brian De Palma's claims that he was inspired by Hitchcock. That may well have been true, but De Palma's movies bear a much greater resemblance to the work of William Castle than to that of Hitchcock, and Tarantino's debut feature merely gestures to one particular scene in a Ringo Lam film. The rest of *Reservoir Dogs*, if it is to be referred to an Asian cinema at all, can best be seen as variations on Japanese *yakuza* movies. In other words, the Hong Kong reference doesn't become genuinely active in the Hollywood production of action films until the mid-1990s.

It is true that by that point, Hong Kong had already been a reference point in the martial arts direct-to-video films, an industrial sector that emerged from about 1983 onwards. But it is part of my argument that the genesis of the generic category "action" has less to do with Hong Kong's influence as exemplified by the Bruce Lee films or even the cross-overs between Hong Kong and blaxploitation films than with the changes brought about in the industry's distribution and marketing sectors as a result of the development of a lucrative video retailing sector.

ACTION FILMS

In the 1980s, there was a change in the way the different sectors of the industry related to each other: a new genre emerged. Already, in the later 1970s, *Variety* very occasionally mentioned "action pix" as a genre in the body of some reviews. However, no film was described as such in its capsule. Indeed, the term "action" appeared fairly seldom in such capsules signalling how and to whom to sell the film, whatever the product-genre happened to be. In 1971, only 21 films of different product-genres were described in capsules as containing the special action ingredient. In 1972, the capsules of only half a dozen titles referred to the action market; in 1973 there were about 18, and in each year from 1974 until 1980, less than 10 films were singled out in this way, in spite of the many titles released which *now* would be classified as "action films". A prominent example might be Gordon Parks's blaxploitation thriller *Shaft*, reviewed in *Variety* of 16 June 1971 and capsuled as a "formula private eye plot". The two main prototypes of what is now regarded as "action cinema", especially with regard to the prominent featuring of extended displays of martial arts skills by the director-star Tom Laughlin, *Born Losers* (*Variety*, 7 December 1967) and *Billy Jack* (*Variety*, 5 May 1971), received no capsule marketing slogans at all, while Dario Argento's slasher-thriller *Cat o'Nine Tails* (*Il gatto a nove code*, 1971) was capsuled (*Variety*, 9 June 1971) as appropriate "for action dualers", suggesting that this horror film or thriller, depending on whether you privilege the plot or the image-sound combinations — a differentiation with class connotations — would best be retailed as part of a double-bill (special offer?) addressed to lower-class (codewords: "undemanding" or "undiscriminating") and generally under-educated (codeword: working class youth or "low IQ") audiences, who are the kind of people who pay to see "action", and sex, and violence. To stress the thriller aspect of Argento's film would have oriented the film towards more affluent, middle class audience niches.

The "adventure fantasy" market category remained, but its companion-label, action, eventually changed from a marketing into a production category. The first designations in the 1970s of a film as simply an "action pic" in a capsule summary confirm that in this period the label is still used as a retailing market strategy. The first explicit designation comes in the capsule attached to Peter Hunt's British blockbuster *Shout at the Devil* (*Variety*, 14 April 1976) apparently costing some US$7 million, a large sum at the time. However, the film is called an "action epic", a category explained later in the review in revealing terms. The reviewer notes that the film has "almost every basic action-suspense ingredient known in the cinema. Exotic tropical settings, man-eating crocodiles, air and sea combat, shipwreck, big game hunting, natives on a rampage, ticking time bombs, rape and fire, malaria, they're all there and then some". In other words, this is an old-fashioned action-adventure movie, an updated version of *King Solomon's Mines* and a forerunner of the "adventure fantasies" later made by Spielberg. The next capsules presenting an "action pic" refer to an obscure Earl Bellamy film about motorcycle racing, *Sidewinder 1* (*Variety*, 27 July 1977) and to George Mendeluk's *The Kidnapping of the President* (*Variety*, 13 August 1980), a film that could just as easily be labelled a political thriller in the vein of William Richert's *Winter Kills* (1979) and other films evoking the Kennedy assassinations.

In the early 1980s, just a few films were capsuled as "actioners", such as the Steve Carver film featuring Chuck Norris, *An Eye for an Eye* (*Variety*, 19 August 1981). By October 1981, *Variety* proclaimed the "death of martial arts in the international market" in its review of the Taiwan-Hong Kong co-production Lam Kwok-tseung and Lee Wing's *Prohibited Area* (28 October 1981). Nevertheless, in 1982, Tom Kotani's *The Bushido Blade* aka *The Bloody Bushido Blade* (3 February 1982) was capsuled as a "samurai actioner" while Menahem Golan's *Enter the Ninja* (7 April 1982), Patrick Donahue's *Kill Squad* (9 June 1982) and James Fargo's *Forced Vengeance* (28 July 1982) all were hailed in the capsules as "martial arts actioners". In 1983, only John Badham's *Blue Thunder* was capsuled as an "aerial action picture" (2 February 1983), with John and Beverly Sebastian's *The Delta Fox*, shot in 1977 but not released until October 1983, being summed up as a "dim action pic".

The change in the notion of action cinema started to happen in 1984 when, as *Variety* noted in a review published on 14 November, a "recent phenomenon" started to make a difference with "unreleased feature films finally surfacing for the homevideo market". This trend had become noticeable in 1983 and would continue to gain momentum throughout the second half of the 1980s. Nevertheless, only three films released in 1984 were capsuled as action films: Eduardo Plamos's *Alley Cat*, James Bryant's *The Executioner Part II*, a film shot in 1982 that imitated James Glickenhaus's *The Exterminator* (1980), and Elliott Hong's *Hot and Deadly*. Danny Steinman's rape-revenge exploitation film, *Savage Streets*, was capsuled as being "for action film fans" (*Variety*, 25 July 1984). By 1985, some fifteen films were called "actioners" or "action pictures" and in 1986, the number more than doubled to 33. By 1986, *Variety* hardly ever capsuled films as being "for the action market", instead designating a film's production genre simply as "actioner" or "action picture"; and the label "action film" made its appearance in the capsules, relating, for instance, to Fred Olen Ray's *Commando Squad* (10 June 1987). In 1987 and 1988, the designation became routine, both with and without further indications about its "narrative image", although often accompanied by a statement pointing out that the film was destined to be released directly, or after the briefest of theatrical exposures, to video. The official confirmation of the genre's existence came with Beau Bridges' *The Wild Pair* (23 December 1987) which was directly designated as belonging to the "action film genre". Henceforth, the genre had acquired an industrially consecrated name.

Around September 1987 *Variety* changed its editorial practice. Instead of emphasising the "guidance-to-distributors and exhibitors" function of the film reviews (in the case of the English language films most likely to interest their trade subscribers) in the layout through the use of brief, at times even one-word capsule-judgements in bold at the head of the review, a more conventional journalistic practice was adopted. Henceforth, the consumer-guidance aspect addressed to specific sectors of the film industry was to be less explicit and the reviews were presented in a format analogous to the way many newspapers presented reports of events: by printing the first, summarising paragraph of the review in bold, the first word nearly always indicating the location where the reports were supposed to be "from". This may have been part of a strategy to expand the range of subscribers, to enhance the general sense of cultural "authority" that the trade paper sought to achieve or to disguise self-serving commercial assessments by and for the American film business as "objective reporting". Probably all three factors played a role. However, the function of the reviews as exemplified by the approach taken to the films remained the same: the summarising paragraph efficiently indicated the type of film and what its box-office potential might be in specific markets. The differences between cultural genre and market genre were maintained, but the label "action film" had changed from being a market category to being a product design label. In other words, by the mid-1980s, the action film had become a genre just like the musical or the western.

What *Variety*'s reviews in the 1970s and 1980s make clear is that the action film, as a genre, emerged in terms of a shift from retail marketing to product-design, that is to say, through a kind of feed-back process in which a retail marketing category is re-inscribed into product presentation. Based on its experience of promoting different kinds of genre films to the "action market", the industry appears to have selected a number of characteristics deemed responsible for a film's profitability in that market. Producers then redesigned a range of their products to fit more closely with that consumer-profile and marketing category.

The interesting thing about this shift is precisely that it relates primarily to the emergence and practices of video stores. *Variety* also recognised this as it eventually began to run a special reviewing section devoted to "home video" releases alongside its film, television and theatre reviews. It is blatantly obvious that the growing video market created the type of films subsequently designated as action films.

In many respects, the video market benefited from the film industry's deliberately created product shortage in the 1960s and 1970s. Independent producers and exhibitors had tried to remedy the situation, but the majors managed to maintain their monopoly control over exhibition. Existing inner-city and even suburban exhibitors, part of the run-clearance zone distribution system (see below), were forced out of business, making way for the ambitious multiplex-building programme in shopping malls, a sector directly under the majors' control and constituting a tailor-made exhibition sector designed to exploit the new kind of one-off blockbuster product which, after the success of Tom Laughlin's saturation re-release in California of *Billy Jack* in 1971, was adopted on a national scale with Spielberg's *Jaws* in 1975. As a result of the engineered product shortage, which had been a crucial move in the production sector's re-appropriation of the exhibition sector, and the new saturation release practices a glut of films remained stuck in the pipeline with nowhere to go. This is what *Variety*, as early as November 1984, called a crisis of "over-production", that is to say, there were far too many films stacked up waiting for a release. The only outlet for this product was cable television and the video store.

Many of the films that are now classified as action films were not so designated by the film industry when they were released or offered by distributors. They acquired the label as a consequence of the way video stores arranged their wares, using very rough-and-ready generic distinctions between their different sections. The most common way of organising the shops was to divide films into categories such as: children, adults, comedies, drama, horror (or fantasy), war, action, occasionally adding a section for "foreign films" and "new releases". As a result, many students and even critics who have only the dimmest memory of cinema prior to video, follow the video stores' lead and retroactively incorporate films into a genre that, in effect, was invented by video stores and fed back into the production sector.

On the other hand, too much importance should not be attached to results obtained from a systematic perusal of *Variety*'s reviews over two decades. In fact, such an investigation does not yield much more than a snapshot. Nevertheless, it does allow the conclusion to be drawn that the main trade journal of the American film industry did not recognise the existence of action cinema as a genre until around 1985, when the genre was named. No doubt, some people used the label before 1984–85. Even *Variety* did so on occasion, but when it did, the term referred to a market sector rather than to a production genre. What matters is to note the gradual shift in the industry's main trade paper, accelerating rapidly from 1983–84 onwards, from action being seen as a sales ingredient to becoming an autonomously named film genre, and the fact that this labeling shift coincided exactly with, firstly, the video boom, and, secondly, the video stores' system of categorising the products on their shelves. In effect, action film as a genre was born in the video stores and adopted by the film industry within a year or so. Almost a decade later, in 1993, the genre finally received its first book-length academic legitimation with Yvonne Tasker's *Spectacular Bodies: Gender, Genre and the Action Cinema.*[12]

FINANCE CAPITAL

However, the video stores on their own do not provide a sufficient explanation for the current dominance in the mainstream film industry of "action films". The interaction between Hollywood and the video industry may explain the timing of the naming of the genre, but it doesn't explain why the films classified in that manner by video stores came to dominate film production. For a broader account of the dynamics involved, one must turn to David Cook's recently published analysis of the way Hollywood was restructured in the 1970s.[13]

In the 1960s, Hollywood, along with much of the rest of the US economy, tried to boost profits by way of massive investment in off-shore production. The majors at that time had almost ceased production and had turned themselves into investment-management and distribution companies. However, a combination of factors, including bad management decisions and cultural-political disorientation, reduced profits and led Hollywood's financial backers to hire a new generation of managers, drawn from the talent-agency and real estate rackets and from financial institutions. As Cook notes:

> Veteran industry leadership had been replaced by a melange of agents, lawyers, bankers, and business executives who saw filmmaking primarily as an investment strategy, not unlike commodities trading, which combined the risks of high-stakes speculation with a virtually limitless potential for corporate tax-sheltering. ... Formerly, banks and other lending institutions had negotiated revolving credit agreements with the studios, leaving the companies free to allocate the funds themselves, but in 1971 banks began to extend loans on a picture-by-picture basis, with the films themselves as collateral.[14]

The new managers set about restructuring the business. They intensified the existing policy of blackmailing exhibitors into submission by creating a product shortage while persuading the US Government to disgorge vast quantities of subsidies (estimated at about US$1 billion) to the film industry by way of changes in the tax legislation. Cook astutely observes that the representatives of finance capital also brought the stylistic and marketing practices of exploitation cinema into the mainstream. During the Nixon-Reagan years of "free enterprise" in the 1970s and early 1980s, studio bosses no longer had to account to their backers on the basis of annual production schedules and profit plans. Now that finance capital had put its own henchmen in charge of each individual production decision, the much-complained-of rule of the accountants had begun. The "run-clearance zone" system of distribution was ended and the simultaneous mass-release of "blockbuster" films began, enabling a major increase in ticket prices. In 1975, *Jaws* extended the *Billy Jack* exploitation strategy with a saturation release, including suburban shopping mall cinemas, preceded by eight months of marketing. This was followed by *The Deep* (Peter Yates 1977) and, also in 1977, *Star Wars*. In addition, as finance capital's gambling syndicates took over the film business, costs exploded (between 1972 and 1979 they increased by 450 per cent), individual films were replaced by franchises, with a series of films acting as the central advertising engine for a wide variety of business ventures, a strategy pioneered by the James Bond series. Marketing costs mushroomed to the point that by the late 1990s, the *average* cost of releasing a film in the US was estimated by the Motion Pictures Association of America to be some US$76.8 million while the *average* marketing budget amounted to some US$100 million per film.

Cook shows how and why the characteristics of what had been a marginal and disreputable sector of the industry, exploitation cinema, and its marketing and exhibition priorities, gradually came to be adopted by the mainstream of the Hollywood film industry. The mainstreaming of exploitation cinema, including the recourse to that sector's main product genres (horror, science fiction, action-adventure with added sex'n'violence), were facilitated by changes in censorship regulations, subsidies, a restructuring of exhibition and the attendant changes in marketing practices, such as the "bringing into line" of the "informal" advertising sector consisting of newspaper reviews, television programmes, film magazines and publishing. The quickening of "play-off" rhythms forestalled any possible interference in the advertising campaign from critical word-of-mouth; interviews with stars were strictly controlled in order to guarantee positive publicity; advertising was withheld from magazines or newspapers that tried to retain some independence from the marketeers; extracts were refused to television stations that had shown similarly alarming tendencies not to toe the marketing line.

The restructuring of Hollywood under new FIRE management (the finance, insurance and real estate sector of the economy) had caused a return to the "cinema of attractions" which had dominated the industry prior to the development of cinema as narrative. As Cook notes:

> The direct sensory stimulation (the delivery of spectacle and shock) became a key element of spectatorial pleasure. ... By the 1970s, the collapse of the studio system, with its vertical and horizontal monopolies on all three industry tiers, produced a return to the original industry structure in which production, distribution, and exhibition were all separated, but financial and marketing power was concentrated in the distributors (or, as they were still called, the *major studios*). ... Given this reversion to its pre-World War I industrial configuration, it is no anomaly that the American film industry would revisit the cinema of attractions as its economic mainstay.[15]

LABOUR POWER

When I was first prompted to think about action cinema as a possible genre, it soon became apparent that the core structure of the system comes into view when we compare the 1950s and 1960s Italian peplums (mostly films set in some version of antiquity and featuring musclemen performing feats of strength) with films such as *Robocop* (Paul Verhoeven, 1987) by way of the James Bond films of the mid-1960s. However, it is important *not* to see the trajectory from Hercules to James Bond and then to Robocop as a chronological sequence. All three types of figurations were there from the beginning of cinema (and probably also in the two or three decades before cinema, as the late-nineteenth-century preoccupation in Europe with automata and scientific gadgetry would suggest). For my purposes, the three main figurations can be described in terms of three types of bodies, Hercules, James Bond and Robocop, which relate to each other in a way that suggests the elaboration of a fantasy about the value and uses of labour power as the dreams of industrial capital gradually give way to those of finance capital.

The Hercules body emerged most notably with Pietro Francisci's *Le fatiche di Ercole* (1958), starring Steve Reeves. It is a muscle-bound, bulky and weighty device with a well-defined musculature denoting its energy-producing mechanisms. In that respect, the Hercules-body is a modernised, machinic version of the equally bulky but un-defined mass of the pre-modern wrestler or strongman. It is a body that a lot of work has gone into; a body built in gymnasia and displayed for its energy potential. The Hercules-body is an eroticised fantasy of labour power. Simply comparing it to actual working-class bodies makes the point sufficiently. It bespeaks immense amounts of leisure time spent in gyms and is (over)fed on special diets, carefully groomed and oiled to be put on show. It is much too impractical to be a working body. It is a showcase of labour power.

The Italian peplums of the 1950s often filmed the Hercules-body (also called Maciste, Samson, Goliath, Ulysses and a number of other names) with a static camera showing the muscleman straining while performing an act of strength. Often the camera lovingly caressed the body with slow pans and tilts detailing the sweating torso, the arms and biceps, the bulging, hairy thighs, and so on. The actor, if he moves at all, does so slowly, signifying the expenditure of massive quantities of energy. Incidentally, this slow-down of movement as a way of signaling the expenditure of excess energy was later repeated in the US television series *The Six Million Dollar Man* (the pilot film directed by Richard Irving was shown in 1973). In that respect, the Hercules-body does not (yet) speak of efficiency, as does, for instance, Jean-Claude Van Damme's inscription into action stories. For the latter, the productivity of labour power is measured in terms of the efficiency of its deployment: maximum impact energy applied in short bursts. The distance between Hercules-Steve Reeves and Van Damme is a historical one: while Reeves's body is valued for its labour power potential, Van Damme's relates to a subsequent period of capitalism when the falling rate of profit and competition from low-wage economies required the available labour power to be exploited with greater efficiency.

Similarly, it is instructive to compare the Hercules-body with its antecedent figurations, which range from the turn-of-the-century boxing films (the male equivalent of the many striptease or "dance-of-the-seven-veils" nickelodeon films) to the wave of nationalist Italian films starting with Enrico Guazzoni's *Quo Vadis* (1912) and especially the role of Bartolomeo Pagano as the black slave Maciste in Pastrone's *Cabiria* (1914).[16] The history of the Hercules body in cinema remains to be written. Suffice it to say that it is a fundamentally different body from the athletic Fairbanks-body, suggesting that the Hercules body and the athletic body each crystallised out of different historical pressures, although overlaps and fusions are always possible in specific texts, as, for instance, in the eulogies of modernity in Italian futurist manifestos written by Marinetti around 1912 and in the *Manifesto Ardito-Futurista* of 1918, where machinic efficiency and athleticism are telescoped together. The athletic body is part of the discourses of expertise, speed and geographical displacement, while the Hercules body is part of a discursive constellation emphasising the static expenditure and management of labour power. The statically filmed muscular body is a figure in fantasies about the transformation of agricultural labourers into factory labourers, valued for the quantity of labour power at their (and therefore the factory owner's) disposal. The mobile athletic body is more part of a militarised labour power available for the territorial expansion of capitalism and, as such, still contains many elements associated with Imperial-aristocratic bodies to which skill rather than great strength has been attributed. This, at least, has been the case in Western countries since the breakdown of the feudal order, which attributed "maximum positives" to the top of the social hierarchy: wealth, wisdom, beauty, strength and so on. The static labour body is predominantly part of stories marketed as myths and epics; the flexible athlete is more characteristic of stories marketed as "adventure".

The history of the athletic or acrobatic body remains to be written as well.[17] Any such history will have to be able to account for the fact that, for instance, in Hong Kong martial arts and sword-fighting movies, the energy-impact of gestures is displaced onto the soundtrack: it *may* be signified through editing, but it is *always* on the soundtrack through greatly intensified sound-effects. When watching Shaw Brother movies, it is striking how visually fluid movement is constantly accompanied by percussive soundtracks, as if the almost ethereally speedy gestures needed an aural supplement to signify the quantity of expenditure of physical energy. In that respect, Hong Kong's way of inscribing martial arts bodies, at least since the mid-1960s (King Hu's *Come Drink with Me*, 1965, is a notable milestone in this history) can be seen as a compromise formation orchestrating the encounter between, and the inter-mingling of, both archaicising and modernising currents within the texture of the films. Ng

Ho noted a similar mixture in aspects of Hong Kong's martial arts comedies when he pointed out that:

> The protagonist in kung-fu comedy is conventionally a bright but hopelessly lazy kid who lacks both the staying power needed for martial arts training and respect for his *sifu* [master]. … Often, after suffering a defeat, he will muster the perseverance to train in martial arts more seriously, and will eventually reach the point where he surpasses the skills of his *sifu*. … This emphasis on individual achievement and on outdoing one's own master undoubtedly parallels the ethos of capitalism.[18]

Other aspects of Hong Kong's complex cinematic martial arts genres also need a great deal of further analysis. For instance, how is it that notions of tradition come to perform the function which, in James Bond movies, is performed by the addition of gadgetry to physical productivity. There is a suggestion in the Hong Kong films that the absorption of a historical-cultural tradition by a body (usually under the guidance of a *sifu* as the marker of social reproduction) constitutes a way of incorporating know-how accumulated through historical tradition.

The James Bond body is a complex figure where labour power (physical strength) is enhanced by technological gadgetry, that is to say, by quantities of stored dead labour. Only weakly present in *Dr No* (1962) — mainly in Bond's relation to his Aston Martin — the Bond-stories came to emphasise this fusion more and more as the series continued, with a corresponding rise in the cult status of the Q character played by Desmond Llewellyn. The display of quantities of physical energy no longer suffices in these fantasies of national competition and transnational corporations. At the same time, the Bond-body is part of fantasy scenarios dramatising not only the globalisation of Anglo-American capital represented and policed by its enforcement institutions, it also features increasingly the orgiastic spectacle of the destruction of capital values in the course of international competition. The labour body (the Hercules body) is still part of the figuration, but it has become more sexualised, eroticised: Bond displays his bare torso or other parts of his anatomy, but his main displays of energy are in his ability to handle machinery. His productivity is governed by the combination of physical strength and plant, that is to say, it is enhanced by putting large quantities of dead labour at his disposal, a power-position that is also supposed to enhance his sex appeal. The Bond-body is part of transnational monopoly capitalism's dream-world, a decidedly Post-World War II configuration. The combination of labour power with corporate technology deployed on an international scale animates fantasies that go beyond the simple accumulation of wealth and power through which national bourgeoisies sought to acquire dominance at the level of the nation state. Transnational corporate capitalism also requires the destruction of capital values accumulated "elsewhere" in order to clear the ground for new markets. The spectacular explosions and conflagrations that form part of the Bond-fantasy scenarios are barely disguised implementations of world-bank urban renewal and industrial development policies involving large-scale projects simultaneously causing large-scale destruction.

In Paul Verhoeven's *Robocop* (1987), the Robo-body offers an electronically redesigned version of labour power, again imbricated in fantasies about the way social relations should be enforced. Here, labour power is not conjoined with the dead labour stored in machines: the machines are fused with the body to form a single unit capable of both massive quantities of labour power and equally massive information processing capacities. Verhoeven's film is quite explicit in this respect: the story is presented as the drama of transition from "old Detroit" (the rustbelt version of industrial capitalism) to a "New Detroit" which is, in fact, Los Angeles merged with Silicon Valley. The film concerns itself with the kind of social authority and organisation that would have to accompany the rule of a triumphant transnational corporate capitalism anxious to control the flows of credit and to ensure the "correct" distribution of surplus capital (financial power). What appears to be at issue in the deployment of Robo-body fantasies is the fact that, once industrial capital has imposed its transnational control, another sector of the bourgeoisie appropriates the resulting flows of super-profits: the financial bourgeoisie becomes dominant — hence the emphasis on the importance of instantaneous omnivorous information processing. The Robo-body characterises finance capital fantasies and betrays the way they address industrial capital: in *Robocop*, finance capital tells industrial capital how it must reformat social relations and systems of governance in order to ensure maximum profit-flows.

The story told by the different modalities of the inscription of physical energy and its relations to gadgetry and, later, to information processing, is a story of the way, in different places and at different times, capital dreams of ways of increasing profitability through the intensification of the exploitation of labour power, and of the social risks attached to such a move. The story can be presented as a chronological sequence, except, of course, that the chronology relates to the (non-linear) development of the relative dominance at any given time of a particular sector of the bourgeoisie. First there are the fantasies of the transformation of pre-modern, mainly agricultural and artisanal labour into industrial labour power, signalled by way of fantasies of muscular bodies disposing of enormous quantities of energy; then the corporate phase of capital mobilises large quantities of dead, stored labour to enhance productivity, and lastly (to date) we get fantasies of re-engineered cyber-bodies capable of serving both as sources of energy and as enforcers of global discipline by virtue of the combination of bodies with gadgetry *and* information processing technology. These latter labour power fantasies have need only of particular, specialised bits of bodies capable of being combined with the required mechanical and electronic technologies.

Part and parcel of these fantasies of capitalist development is their diagnosis of the impediments obstructing perpetual increases in profit. Robert Brenner has argued, convincingly, that the post-war, relentlessly deepening crises in capitalism are due primarily to a structural-historical feature of the development of industrial capital.[19] The organisation and building of large-scale industrial plants with huge amounts of expensive but not-easily adaptable machinery condemned to remain in fixed locations becomes a handicap for the heartlands of capitalism when they succeed in opening up global markets. The globalisation required by capitalism also results in increased manufacturing competition from low-wage regions. As a consequence, the investment represented by large industrial factories or industrial parks in the historically older (advanced, higher wage) capitalist areas turns into an expensive, insufficiently mobile millstone around the bourgeoisie's neck. The need to de-industrialise, difficult in practice because of the immense social costs and risks involved, is fantasised in the form of the orgies of capital value destruction in so-called action movies (but also in disaster movies, spy films, war films, post-apocalypse science fiction films and so on). In other words, movies do indeed talk to us of capitalism's fundamental systemic aspects: they do so in the form of fantasies of labour power and stored "value"; and they do so at times by way of the fantasy scenarios represented, or by way of the technological means deployed in the making of the films (such as digital effects), or by both at the same time. The place where these fantasy discourses can be heard loudest, for the last two decades or so, is in the films marketed under the "action" label.

15

Spectral Critiques: Tracking "Uncanny" Filmic Paths Towards a Bio-Poetics of Trans-Pacific Globalization

Rob Wilson

> *The experience of Latin America [photographing migration sites and displaced peoples] made the sprawling cities of Asia seem strangely familiar ... . Yet at times I would forget where I was. Cairo? Jakarta? Mexico City?*
>
> – Sebastiao Salgado, *Migrations: Humanity in Transition*[1]

Under the space-time compressions of globalization, time all too often seems harried, frantic, out of sorts; place all but lost into a matrix-like hologram of flux, speed, and mixture; the self coded into a trans-local semblance of inter-connection, multiplicity, and pseudo-power.[2] "Thank you for activating your Bank of Trans-America credit card. You may now use it at any one of 19 million locations worldwide", a voice-message from God-knows-where comforted me, as I used my not-so-bottomless credit card to purchase an electronic ticket to jumbo-jet across sixteen times zones from San Francisco to Hong Kong. As if to glaze over everyday instability, 'globalization' becomes trumpeted and installed via a discourse of achieved "globality".[3] This seamlessness brings no relief: crossing trans-Pacific vastness, we feel like the Manifest-Destiny-crazed Whitman who is haunted by *lack* at the end of "Facing West from California's Shores" — "the circle almost circled [on the Passage to India] ... (But where is what I started for so long ago?/And why is it yet unfound?)".

These "global souls" of transnational mobility, as Pico Iyer has named more fortunate citizens of the "postglobal order" like himself — in passages echoing Ralph Waldo Emerson abolishing selfhood in a 747 cabin over the Pacific, as the Postcolonial Oversoul (as it were) enters some "duty-free zone" of transnational "deracination" on route (and working as travel-writer for Time Inc.) to write-up Hong Kong and Asia/Pacific — do remain uneasy in their offshore abodes.[4] Such "global souls" are never fully at home in the jetlagged speed and rhizomatic newness of global modernity, Iyer's travelogue does help show. These cosmo-global citizens are (like Whitman's trans-imperial Oversoul) somehow 'in and out' of those globalization processes, "watching and wondering" at them.

From Taipei and Paris to Los Angeles and Seoul, everyday citizens of such global-cities (in the process of becoming what the Indian/British/ American Pico Iyer calls "fellow in-betweeners" of global rootlessness),[5] become disoriented, restless, haunted by the postcolonial uncanniness ('un-homeliness') of a world driven by the dynamism of neo-liberal values that go on uprooting local identity and primordial ties of location, yet riven all the more so by irruptions of spirit presences and place-hauntings that techno-science cannot abolish, undo, nor calibrate.[6] In the 1930s, Walter Benjamin was drawn to invoking a passage from Marx's *Eighteenth Brumaire* to the effect that the "feverishly youthful pace of material production" in the mid-nineteenth-century United States was being driven by the creative-destructive temporal dynamics of capitalist technologies like the railroad, steam engine, phototype, hydraulic mining, and telegraph (embraced as quasi-poetic achievements of US Manifest Destiny by Whitman and the past-liquidating Emerson et al.).[7] These dynamic forces of relentless production, spatial expansion, and global waste, as Marx read this global-industrializing America, "'had neither time nor opportunity … to abolish the old spirit world.'"[8]

So lyric poets under high capitalism have anxiously wandered the malls, crowded sidewalks, dried-up rivers, and residual back alleys of the global city in search of some lost aura or spirit-shining, as alienated into the commodity form, cultural sign, or material technology, as if looking back (in spectral terms) to the diminished maker/flaneur of global production as "profane illumination". This lyric "shock" is all too ephemeral or fleeting ('unreal city' lamented Eliot of modernizing London) ever to disrupt the feeling of *not-being-at-home*. For Baudelaire, in a famous prose-poem on the cusp of Euro-global modernity in *Paris Spleen*, the poet had lost his vaunted aura of lyric productivity in the Parisian mud; for Poe, in the hurrying city crowd of Philadelphia which treats urban-dwellers like fellow-paranoid ghosts; for Whitman, the US-as-global poet squandered the afflatus of high-seeing and sublime selfhood in the sea-drift and dirty muck of Long Island Sound or displaced such attributes into the euphoria of the electro-dynamo or the Brooklyn Bridge. But we are on the other side of Hiroshima as a hegemonic "shock and awe" instance of the US sublime. Postmodern thinkers of narrative "dissensus", like Lyotard, would disrupt the reign of neo-liberalism's master-narrative claiming to produce the enrichment of global humanity through the progress of capitalist technoscience, in effect, by decentering the deformed spaces and mediatized genres the liberal subject inhabits as life-world. "We are like Gullivers in the world of technoscience: sometimes too big, sometimes too small, but never the right size", Lyotard warns in his trope of uncanny world-dispossession.[9] The worlding-world of neo-liberal globalization can have this broadly uncanny, ever-morphing, or unevenly syncopated effect.

Global cities daily register this uncanny circulation and mix of locals, strangers, and non-locals; they are becoming "translocalities" of semiotic interface all the more unbounded and open than the nation-state and its border-stalking citizenship criteria called (in the US) the Patriot Acts of un-Americanization. As Ien Ang describes discrepant versions of this rooted/routed mix of fluid "Chineseness" via portraying her diaspora from Indonesia to Amsterdam to an ever-anxiously "Asianizing" Australia, the global city "is [becoming] one large and condensed contact zone in which borders and ethnic boundaries are blurred and where processes of hybridization are rife", and diasporas are undone.[10] The very intensification of globalization flows in such border-crossing spaces has often led to the felt necessity to elaborate "an intensified version of the local situation" at the global/local interface, thus expressing "both/and" linkage.[11] "Best thing about Brooklyn? All the countries of the world are here. Worst thing about Brooklyn? None of us get along", concludes an elderly black man in the Wayne Wang/Paul Auster movie *Blue in the Face*.[12] At some Pacific Rim neo-extremity of race war, uneven development, New Age euphoria, pornographic simulacra, and lurid catastrophe, the "noir" Rim city of Los Angeles nestles within such a globalizing "ecology of fear" from *Chinatown* and *Blade Runner* to *Mulholland Drive*.[13]

The banal anguish of not fully belonging to this modern life-world, that uneasy state of being outside modern space-time coordinates, takes away self-attunement to urban discipline and globalizing locality, but gives the possibility of an uncanny rupture of the spirit world and its alien utterances. "In Angst one has an 'uncanny' feeling", is how Heidegger describes this in the influential modernist ontology of *Being and Time*. The fretful feeling of being-thrown into ever-new forms of modernity is disrupted by the "nothing and nowhere" feeling of "not-being-at-home" in the presence of dislocated, subliminal, or traumatized being. Such dis-attuned anxiety, in its full range of terror, trauma, and wonder, "fetches Da-sein [Being] out of its entangled absorption in the 'world'"; as phrased in the un-homely terms of Heidegger, the uncanny approaches, irrupts, and dismantles the taken-for-granted security of everyday space-time horizons and the threat of placelessness of life in the modern city.[14] The global effect can be exactly that sense that place and city is morphing into the future-imperfect.

Mike Davis has pointed out, in his uncanny analysis of the World Trade Center going up in flames, that the imaginary of global terrorism and war-from-above hitting the Euro-American city was long dreamt of, imagined, if not luridly posited, in Hollywood action films and science fiction during the 1980s and 1990s, as well as in darker modes of German expressionism and Spanish surrealism from contexts between the wars. The catastrophic event thus had that "uncanny effect" of disrupted modernity (Davis quotes Freud and echoes Zizek on the ideological power of the Hollywood uncanny), "as when something that we have hitherto regarded as imaginary appears before us in reality".[15] Reaching some nodal point of global/local materialization in the World Trade Center's vanishing into the smoke and debris of instant ruins in 9/11, the resulting "globalization of terror" and daily specter of new security-threats and disease has become a shared affect of the global city, from Taipei and Paris to New York and Seoul. In structural terms of North/South dialectics, as more people get born into poverty and are made more vulnerable to the effects of an interdependent economy of weaponry, spectacle, state security, identity theft, bio-disease, and terror, "global violence [becomes] the hard core of our existence" as Sven Lindquist outlines in the long-duree of global violence-from-above.[16] The Bush II administration of global empire and techno-perpetual war-machinery, all hailed under the hegemonic sign of "shock and awe", seems to take a special paranoid-pleasure in the return of the security-state apparatus from cold war storage and the reinstalled binary discourses of a global-civilizational East/West antagonism between us/them.

Given this hegemony of globalization forces, the uncanny effect all the more circulates in the global technologies of post-modernity, as in cinema of the fantastic or the magical-realist novel, haunts them, and gives them some exploratory efficacy in the aesthetic and bio-poetic mapping of the real, however broken or incomplete the languages, images, or frames. In *Modernity at Large*, Arjun Appadurai is pointing to such a large-scale shift in this global "technoscape" of interactive narratives and border-clashing "ideoscapes", as the imagination takes on the force of a new social practice and becomes an emergent site of figuring collective agency crucial to "the new global order" of mix, rupture, and flow.[17] Unsettling this neo-liberal regime of foreign globalization, Derrida has called this bursting out of spectral media-effects in neo-liberalism some kind of global *hauntology*, "the ghost that goes on speaking" in our technologies and languages from the future if not across the borders of our modern nation-states.[18]

Such modes of alien "hauntology" and ghost-threatening otherness might have a peculiar pungency in a divided Pacific Rim country like Korea, for example, haunted by a Marxist alter-reality and Confucian simulacrum to the North, and the cold war remainder of what American President Bush has recently re-demonized (like some lost Nazi kernel) as our new and abiding "axis of evil".[19] The media of representation, like photography or film, can barely keep up with, tame, or register the new global conditions of migration, urban saturation, aesthetic shock, and transnational flight. As this paper will aim to flesh out, the cinemas of Pacific Rim sites like Korea and Hong Kong have been in the vanguard in mapping these spectral sites and using these technologies of global hauntology to offer images, genres, and narratives of spectral critique.

What Derrida lambasts as the "euphoria of liberal democracy and of the market economy" is thus haunted in South Korean films throughout the 1990s by "spectral effects", as I will discuss, and narrate and image forth an alternative geopolitics of blasted trees, haunted temples, restless tombs, blind soothsayers, possessed beds, the returning horror of the ruined and dispossessed. Such a triumph of capitalist modernity is challenged, bereaved, if not threatened with catastrophe amid all too manic watching of the dot-com-dot-gone-dot-con calculus of the globalizing market. As Derrida puts the claim for the "strange familiarity" of unhomely spectral forces of globalization like mounting homelessness or the return of postcolonial citizens and migrant workers ("the visibility of the invisible" at home in the 1990s) to the global-imperial city, "Haunting [by the uncanny] belongs to the structure of every hegemony".[20]

Haunting by spectral critique belongs all the more so, I would suggest, to a neo-liberal state like South Korea (if not a postcolonial city-state like Hong Kong) which has increasingly pushed towards an enlightenment-based abolishment of the pre-modern and, as it were, oriental allure of its own Buddhist ghosts, Confucian echoes, and rural paths. This Buddhist alternative path to national enlightenment via an ascetic renunciation of urban wealth and the worldly world haunts the geopolitical cosmology of a Korean art film like Bae Yong-Kyun's *Why Has the Boddhi-Dharma Left for the East?* (1989), for example, which uses Seoul city to represent the allure of market accumulation, disorientation and fury, if not the blindness of the poor to such a fate (as captured by the blind mother the priestly son has abandoned). Beautifully filmed to the point of Asiatic sublimity, the film shows only a tattered temple and a broken male-centered genealogy of succession, ash, and ascetic anguish as some kind of dead end. The film gestures towards an alternative path to globalization, an alternative Buddhistic cosmology for Korea, but it is one that goes on wandering as in some anti-modern void?[21]

In a 1996 Korean horror film directed by Kang Che-Gye (also known as Jacky Kang in Hong Kong distribution), *Gingko Bed*, the scientific and artistic orders of contemporary Seoul are disrupted by the uncanny entry of a spirit-laden wooden bed returning from the pre-modern order of feudal relationships which threatens the cigarette-and-laughter modern relationship of the woman doctor and her art-lecturer lover. The jealous class-rivalry between a general and a court musician over the preternatural Mi-Dan acts as an uncanny catalyst and works its way, from a "love felt over a thousand years" in the spirit world by General Kang, into the relationship of the present-day couple, ruining their careers, their homes and offices, burning up their horizon of banal everydayness. The cash-nexus of the ordinary city is put out of joint, de-familiarized in Seoul. Some stunning visual effects add symbolic credibility to the cinematic spirit-conjuring as needy ghosts flit in and out of contemporary bodies and disrupt the medical and artistic technologies for measuring the line between life and death, self and other, body and soul, reality and spirit. The Korean uncanny at times becomes luridly theatrical (showing the hokey spectrality of special effects, as it were), but, in its reach back, aims to hook into the political unconsciousness of abolished spiritual beliefs and debts adhering to the past. Released from the market of commodity exchange and returned to the fetish world of Korean spiritual-political-romantic force, the gingko bed here becomes a kind of commodity-in-reverse, "a 'thing' without phenomenon, a thing in anti-modern flight that surpasses the senses" in its uncanny spectrality disturbing the homey bedroom.[22]

The out-of-the-body experience of *Gingko Bed* is rendered everyday via the quasi-Buddhist horizon of metempsychosis, souls of a romantic triangle reincarnated into two gingko trees and a hawk. The Korean middle-class couple is finally restored to everyday modernity, but not before the comforting boundaries of modern reality and the space-time coordinates of techno-capital (which seemingly have abolished the spirit-world in its rationalized calculus of instrumentalized profit) have been luridly challenged with the blood and terror of vengeful ghosts, vampiric murders, heart captures, resurrections, spirit unions, and a large-scale exorcism symbolized in the end by the burning of the gingko bed. No less bold in its visual hyperbole, Kang later reached into the global uncanny via his trans-Asian blockbuster of spectacular effects and cold war retro-plottings, *Shiri* (1999).

We have to wonder, with the innovative Korean scholar and filmmaker Kim Soyoung, if "uncanny" effects like this circulating in such Pacific Rim techno-films of the 1990s have not surfaced to re-visit present-day South Korea to remind the county of what has been lost in the furious making of the postwar modern city and capitalist nation. In an interview with Kim Soyoung, Chris Berry has called attention to the recent "resurgence of the fantastic mode in various [Korean] box office hits" such as the horror films *The Quiet Family* and *Whispering Corridors* in the anti-globalization climate of 1998, which became popular "just when entry to the OECD and democratic politics seemed to have secured middle class prosperity".[23] Pushing this return of the repressed back before the Asian currency crisis of 1997 had called into question South Korea's bond to the neo-liberal discourse of wall-to-wall globalization, Kim Soyoung links the "brutal sweep of the modernization project" under the earlier regime of Pak Chun-hee to the ongoing rise of using Korean cinema as "liminal space" and uncanny irruption within Asian modernity.

The Korean uncanny indeed has a long trajectory in postwar Korean cinema and surfaces, again and again in differing contexts, as a ghostly imagery of what we could call *fantastic,* or better yet, *spectral critique.* Kim calls attention to the "re-emergence of the fantastic mode" in such new wave late 1990s films as *Gingko Bed, Nine Tales Fox, Soul Guardian* and *Yongari.*[24] Beyond this, Kim Soyoung has exposed the cold war traumas and all-too-reactionary geopolitics returning to haunt the Korean blockbuster mode of pseudo-Hollywood production in films like *Phantom: The Submarine* (1999), *JSA (Joint Security Agreement)* (2000) and *Shiri* (1999). We might recall Pak Chol-Su's alluring film *301/302* (1995), where two apartment dwellers act out female symptoms of over-eating and under-eating in cleanly modern spaces, haunted by traumas of childhood abuse and a claustrophobic marriage, evacuating the seeming prosperity and stylized success of a well-ordered life. As Kim summarizes the generic promiscuity and trans/national imaginary of such Pacific Rim films, "Ghosts seem to exist not only in the horror film but in the propaganda film, historical epic, and action and espionage genre. Korean cinema is becoming the liminal space of apparitions."[25] These Korean films pursue a "discrepant hybridity", and in so doing, "pursue the politics of the possible by articulating the discrepant, the non-normative, the traumatic, and the scandalous in the films' rendition of the Asia/Pacific" as an uncanny trans-Pacific region haunted by ghosts, ghouls, and motley dead or ex-colonial figures who "have yet to die".[26]

Chunhyang and her undying love for Mongryong is by no means a ghost story, but her force as intertextual construct and interpellative legacy in Korean patriarchal culture gives her much-filmed narrative a haunting quality as blasted allegory coming down from the pre-modern past of the Chosun Dynasty to call upon and constrain the globalizing nation-state present and its concert-going (or Hollywood-enchanted) audience. From

Yu Chin-Hahn's Chinese-character version in 1754 to the popular-tradition-entrenched novel of 1955, *Chunhyangjun*, not to mention more recent joint performances of the *pansori* (folk opera) folk tale by South Korean and North Korean artistic groups performing in Pyongyang, the Chunhyang narrative stands at the core of Korean folk culture, conveying an inter-textual archive of attitudes, beliefs, pieties, mores, and modes. As Kim Soyoung notes of myriad Korean melodramas fetishizing suffering women as a way of narrating "the inscription of the new patriarchal order in rapidly shifting society", one of the earliest Korean films, *Chunhyangchon* (*The Story of Chunhyang*, 1923), enlisted a renowned contemporary courtesan to play the lead role of virtuous wife and thus gave the film-commodity an early courtly aura and cross-over of traditional prestige for modern culture.[27] Haunted by class tensions and the gender codes and sexual morality structuring a Confucian-based social order, "*Chunhyangjon* is a text apt for an ideological interpretation" by Korean filmmakers both in the North and the South, as Hyangjin Lee has argued, whereby globalizing Koreans can work through a heritage of colonized subjectivity and preserve residual feudal values of face-saving, ethical idealism, and the patriarchal gaze.[28]

A vast intertext of cultural uses and implications haunts any contemporary retelling of the Chunhyang story, creating discrepancies of meaning between local, national, and international audiences. As film director Im Kwon-Taek has noted of this story, this beloved Korean folktale of forbidden passion and sublimating romance crossing class lines had been filmed fourteen times before his own version became the first Korean film to compete at the Cannes Film Festival and the first of his own films to go global beyond an art-festival film venue. By way of pushing this reflection on a distinctively Korean path to trans-Pacific globalization to a close, I want to interrogate the global/local dynamics of this Chunhyang figure of Korean nationhood in Im Kwon-Taek's recent mini-blockbuster film, *Chunhyang* (2000), if only to call attention to the uncanny localism of this period-piece film which actually once again tracked a distinctive Korean path to globalization.

Here I am invoking an argument I made in the journal *Inter-Asia Cultural Studies* outlining a more sweeping analysis of Im's films from *Mandala* (1981) to *Sopyonje* (1993).[29] There I defended Im's use of "strategic localism" as long as Pacific Rim film production more and more confronts, as a global-structural condition, "the larger global/local plight of entrenched locality and nationality as such under global endangerment". Employing over 8,000 extras and 12,000 costumes and carefully researched and filmed with impeccable cinematic detail, *Chunhyang* emerges as

"Korea's largest cinematic production ever" the Dream-Suite Productions website boasts in Demille-like terms of the spectacle-sublime. More on the localist mark, Ryan Motteshead, in an *indieWire* interview with *Chunhyang's* director, has called attention to "Im's stubborn Korean-ness" in his use of the pansori voice-over narrative, not just as context but as perspectival device.[30] It seems fair to contend that the weirdly "caterwauling ... barking and yowling and shouting" voice of the pansori singer, here played by Cho Sang-Hyun, is what gives the movie its uncanny Korean power and defamiliarizing frame: its turn to represent (in aural and visual disjunctive modes coming in and out of narrative synch) an alternative mode of narration, linking the audience of the performative context (shrouded at first in black, later brought into the diegesis via call-and-response towards the film's ending) to contemporary Korea.

"Who knows what will happen after the story's end?" the pansori narrator taunts the aroused audience with the seemingly happy ending, suggesting that the portrayal of exploitative rulers "fattening their pockets" and "impoverishing the poor" may continue into the patterns of crony-capitalism and trickle-up economics haunting modern-day Seoul and its rural peripheries like Cholla province where the film is set and where Im comes from. The ideology of class status uttered by the corrupt Governor Byun — "class has a natural order and cannot be violated" — gives way to a discourse of human rights and a sacrificial vision of gender equity. The fidelity to principles of a Confucian state and the scholar-centered patriarchy ("serving two husbands is like serving two kings" Chunhyang laments to the point of self-sacrifice) are given postcolonial ratification via cinematic spectacle that borders on epic in its vistas and *Citizen Kane*-like perspectives upon power seen from afar and from below.

Pondering the uneven situation of local globalization in which (to quote Im Kwan-Taek from the *indieWire* interview) "Korean films have yet to establish their own identity for international audiences", and furthermore having faced the relative inattention of international film criticism due to what Tony Rayns sees as "extreme specificity in references and commitment to a kind of activism deemed passé in the west", Korean films are beginning to forge their way into the international circuit by a distinctive and scrappy, if belated, way.[31] As I contended in my *Inter-Asia Cultural Studies* essay, "Korean film at times seems torn between the quite culture-based extremities of these two transnational film genres: (a) the diasporic one [followed by Ang Lee and many Hong Kong film makers] portraying international hybridity, global flux, and cultural impurity, versus (b) the other deftly self-orientalizing one using an ethnographic gaze backward, imagining some damaged trait as a national essence or enduring cultural trait" (315). *Chunhyang*, in my opinion, heads down this latter path toward globalization, portraying, with ethnographic mastery and sumptuous visual detail, enduring Korean stories and genres, if not cultural traits.

When asked by Motteshead what he thought American audiences could take away from watching this film version of *Chunhyang*, director Im replied, with grim humor: "American audiences may very well not be interested, because I am not well known in the United States. So it may be very natural for audiences not to come to see my films. (laughs) However, I am not too worried about it".

Such is the power of the Korean uncanny to make its way through the transpacific circuits of globalization, laughing, seemingly oblivious to a superpower whose genres, outlets, forms and codes often define the very global in terms of its own neo-liberal particulars, though American film thankfully is by no means the worlding-world of globalization.

Global productions would send the transpacific local culture offshore and worldwide, resolving the tensions of imperial history and global imbalance into mongrel fantasy, soft spectacle, and present-serving myth. Given the reach and impact of an "increasingly globalized popular culture", we have to wonder (with Paul Gilroy) if such works are not engaged in creating "racialized signs" of cultural difference and, with all the liberal good-will of a corporate multiculturalism gone cosmopolitical and sublime, spreading "commodified exotica" under the myth of authenticity.[32] Solidarities evoked around blood or land crucial to the sovereignty claims and precolonial ontology of native peoples in the Pacific, are superseded by the pop-culture community of Elvis Presley music, beach-going, and the pleasures of multicultural mixture as in Disney's pro-tourist fantasy, *Lilo and Stitch* (2002).[33] Full of a residual animism and uncanny forces that settler colonialism has not fully displaced or marketed, the Hawaiian islands (for example) may be "the most superstitious place in the world" (or at least the United States), as ex-local Annie Nakao has written,[34] tracing the impact of Japanese *obake*, or ghost stories, and the uncanny hold of Native Hawaiian lore (like the volcano goddess Pele) upon its residents (or driving the contradictions of a mixed-heritage novelist like John Dominis Holt in *Waimea Summer*). While remote or irrelevant to global production, the offshore Pacific (however alternative its vision of Oceania or place) has long served as such a testing space for global fantasy and the transnational reach of "Americanization" stories, where nuclear weapons, imperial wars, contact phobias, cultural mutations, and (nowadays) the multicultural hyperbole of transnational community can work themselves out with romantic dreaminess, narrative immunity, and the (ridiculous) postcolonial sublimity of historical oblivion.[35] The full force of these trans-Pacific displacements — ecological, financial, semiotic and cultural — demand the scrutiny of de-orientalizing tactics, for the "uncanny" Pacific of transnational globalization remains haunted by historical injustice, social unevenness, and racial phobias coming back from the postcolonial future.

Looking back to John Huston's close-to-war-propaganda film, *Across the Pacific* (1942), the Pacific was portrayed as a deceptively romantic, uncanny, and ultimately phobic space full of inscrutable oriental forces (and their subversive white allies) harboring imperial designs and an array of anti-US forces as they gather to undermine the US hegemony over the Panama Canal just before the attack on Pearl Harbor. Sydney Greenstreet plays a huge strategizing white man who is a Japanese spy and double agent, a karate expert who breathlessly recites haiku and is sickened by the weak-willed and drunken white rancher in Panama, where the Japanese hide the attack planes. Even a second-generation Asian American "nisei" character from California is shown to be part of the international takeover move by the Japanese axis — this all had to be decoded and stopped by the counter-espionage Humphrey Bogart character (and his hotel-owning Chinese ally), who thwart the Japanese air attack just in time in a kind of lone-gun, stealthy, and pragmatic bit-by-bit way. Such works of cinema helped to provide the perceptual apparatus to reclaim, fantasize over, and integrate the Pacific as an American-dominated space, as Paul Virilio has written: "For the Americans, the abstractness of their recapture of the Pacific islands made 'cinema direction' a necessity — hence the importance of the camera crews committed to the [Pacific] campaign".[36]

"The Pacific is the white man's ocean" as William Randolph Hearst proclaimed in response to the Pearl Harbor air attack, and Huston's movie works to provide a geopolitical rationale and, even more, what Verilio calls the "perceptual arsenal" of cinema to keep it this way.[37] This phobic Pacific as space of peril and threat is recognizable in an array of war-era poems by Robinson Jeffers, as in "The Eye" which shows an ocean full of blood, scum, and filth, and the "world-quarrel of westering/ and eastering man, the bloody migrations, greed of power, clash of faiths". Or in Robert Frost's west-coast poem "Once By the Pacific" where the ocean grows apocalyptic with yellow peril forces and God's Jehovah-like wrath, inscribed in the trans-Pacific sky and water: "The clouds were low and hairy in the skies,/ Like locks blown forward in the gleam of eyes". In his white-republic diatribe of 1855, *The Land of Gold: Reality versus Fiction*, Hinton Rowan Helper portrayed this *phobic* version of the transpacific as a mongrelizing site of swarming immigrants like "the solemn Chinamen, tattooed [Pacific] islander, and slovenly Chilean" coming in across the ocean from alien sites of bad blood and cheap labor, thus creating a "copper Pacific" as threatening politically as the chattel slavery and miscegenation of the Black Atlantic. "Our population was already too heterogeneous", Helper writes of life in the free-soil American state of California, "before the Chinese came; but now another adventitious ingredient has been added; and I should not wonder at all, if the copper of the Pacific yet becomes as great a subject of discord and dissension as the ebony of the Atlantic".[38] Exclusion acts would soon be enacted to try to keep this ever-coppering Pacific white, and to keep Pacific coastal states like California the exclusive domain of so-called "native" white labor.

Globalization discourse inscribes a very different trans-Pacific, one full of motion and mixture and interconnection to Asia and the Pacific. This globalization "discourse implies concurrence" and would push the globe towards some transnational fusion.[39] The dream of global fusion goes on recuperating an Asian origin of transpacific synthesis dreamed of in Whitman's "Facing West from California's Shores" (1860) when "the house of maternity" in Asia's civilizations and wisdom-traditions would meet hard-headed European technologies, "the circle almost circled," Columbus or Emerson settling down to meditate in Bombay.[40] Globality achieved, as if in the eternal image of wholeness and completion and fusion-culture. But this US-dominated globalization across the Pacific is all the more threatened these days by a new-world order of anxieties, disrupted space-time coordinates, and everyday fears, and perhaps it is best to keep this war-era and Cold War Pacific of clashing imperialisms, civilizational divides, and racial antagonisms lurking in mind as we push to map a contemporary array of uncanny forces and emergent forms that give the lie to the end-of-history triumph in marketization.

Less critique than a symptom of the large-scale Pacific Rim globalization patterns we are living through, as temporal dislocation and spatial disorientation, and embracing, as identity-mix, Pico Iyer's *Global Soul: Jet Lag, Shopping Malls, and the Search for Home* offers a privileged postcolonial travelogue written around a set of haunted global/local paradoxes: the more market unity we have, the less the "global soul" feels it belongs. Uprooted into cosmopolitan flow, the transnational self all the more longs for a sense of home, some psycho-geography of postmodern belonging, and bond to place (which Iyer feels, finally, at a Buddhist spirit-lantern site in Nara Japan, his own home in Santa Barbara gone up in flames). The more unity we have on certain levels of commodity-exchange and media flow, the more tribal, fragmented, and divided we remain as civilizations and cultures. Embracing the global adventure, Iyer searches through the East/West and North/South hybridity-effects of paradigmatic sites for globalization: Los Angeles Airport (LAX) as Disney-like site of multicultural mixture and border-crossing flux and fear; Toronto as global city of managed cosmopolitan interface; London as site of periphery-to-center reversals and ex-imperial transformation into Cool Britannia; Atlanta as site of Olympics brotherhood and terrorist threat. The threat of residual tribalism gives way to the mongrel mix and unity of global commensurability. But for Iyer the site of maximal globalization where the global soul feels most (temporally and spatially) disoriented, lost from place, lost into "the global marketplace" of commodified identity and the self becoming a PIN number, credit card, and phone card, is Hong Kong.

While in the globally paradigmatic city of Hong Kong, Iyer portrays his "global twin", a British friend (fellow student of Eton and Oxford) named Richard (now working as a management consultant for an American firm "in a global market that asks him to move as fast as it does" [84], although his ancestors had served as governor-generals in India [100]) who lives in an expensive flat furnished with suitcases, laptops, modems, cell phones, and Delta business class toilet kits for "people passing through" (82). Life at One Pacific Place has become a space of flows and transient comforts, a "permanent hotel" that flows into a shopping mall and an airport for leaving and returning, a place to use 12 phone cards and live as if "in midair" like some ex-imperial air-plant. Richard's life as "flex-executive" lackey to high-capitalist exchange is so accelerated, so tied into the nexus of global markets, flows, and 24-hour exchanges, that at times he gets so jet lagged he does not know who he is or where he is. In Hong Kong, Iyer realizes the digitalized comfort of belonging in some de-materialized way: "You could live on the plane, I realized, or on the phone — or, best of all, on the phone on the plane" (85).

Pico Iyer's postcolonial life of luxurious displacement on the Pacific Rim, like Richard's, nonetheless becomes a compound of time lag, culture mix, zone shift, "living out of displacement" (86). On the cusp of the Chinese handover in 1997, Iyer finds not a "uniculture" but remnants of "generic" British colonial style (in Hong Kong's Central district, spotting an Anglican church) that make him feel not just like being in Singapore or Bombay (where his father is from), but as if "I was in England, on a gray November morning" (90). Amid the transience and mongrel flux of globalizing and postcolonializing Hong Kong with its share of boat people and migrant domestics Iyer barely engages with via his ever-present hybridity tropes of surface mix, the space will also "accommodate a thousand kinds of homesickness" (93) and lead to gazing at those diasporic paradoxes of "'white coolie' waiters from Britain and Australia who'd taken over the menial jobs in Hong Kong now that the lines of power were being redrawn" (105). That Hong Kong is now filled with "abode seekers" from mainland China only adds to the pathos of this uneasy mix of privileged nomads with less fortunate refugees and labor diasporas of the global flow. Losing his soul into a more privileged version of what Bruce Robbins calls the "sweatshop sublime", Iyer's self-doubling Richard ends up lost into the more digitalized or cyborg sublimity of global capitalism: he leaves Iyer with phone numbers for an office in Tokyo, home and fax numbers in Hong Kong, an 800 number for voice mail, mobile number, fax numbers, his mother's number in London, and a toll-free number for calling voice mail from Japan. "Somehow, that left no room in my address book for his name" Iyer ruefully concludes (112). Only displaced back into a trans-Pacific Japan glutted with global products and yet still staunchly itself as locality and culture, can Iyer claim to feel at home, as if enacting some uncanny repetition of Thoreau at Walden Pond. But this time the transcendental market release into the illusion of autonomy takes place in Nara, Japan, with a woman who speaks little English and Iyer himself speaking less Japanese, as if in entering into semiotic immunity and de-racinated into the global oversoul: "I read Thoreau on sunny Sunday mornings, as Baptist hymns float from across the way, and think that in our mongrel, mixed-up planet, this may be as close to the calm and clarity of Walden as one can find" (296). Pico Iyer, rather obsessively, now stages the cultural fantasies and psychic needs of a latter-day American Transcendentalism, but finds a home for them not at Walden Pond, but in Nara and Kyoto, fronting the Pacific Rim interface of transnational encounter.

In a related cross-cultural travelogue set on the Pacific Rim, *The Lady and the Monk: Four Seasons In Kyoto*, Iyer takes his essential copies of Thoreau and Emerson to Kyoto this time, where he searches for moments of Zen intensity and romantic self-abolishment in temples and inns. Finding a secret Japan within its globalizing corporate culture, one closer to the libidinal desires and blasted lives of Tsushima Yuko's feminist fiction, Iyer self-ironically situates himself in the lineage of writers like Pierre Loti, Lafcadio Hearn, and Kenneth Rexroth, for whom the Zen mystery of Japanese otherness and aesthetic epiphany is embodied in a quest for Japanese women.[41] Again, the travelogue is a brilliant acting out and critique of this post-orientalist symptom and transnational romance. Iyer becomes the monk haunted and consumed by romance, here staged as an American ontological obsession with cultural difference.

In *Global Soul*, the American transcendental imaginary of Iyer's global-oversoul has been brought as spiritual cargo along with Starbucks, Costco,

America Online, and Mister Donut across the Pacific and transplanted into a Japan full of "Western things (played out, as it were, in katakana script) [283]". Iyer realizes (in his last chapter, called "The Alien Home") that "a sense of home or neighborhood can emerge only from within" (282). Ever mobile yet longing to belong to the brave new world of techno-driven globalization, Iyer sets roots down in postmodern Japan amid the uncanny disruptions of everyday life where "minglings are more and more the fabric of our mongrel worlds" (292), writing transcendence into Japan amid the anxiety-laden space-time co-ordinates of globalization for the offshore global soul.

Pico Iyer's path to East/West or transpacific globalization is a quite recognizably American one, to be sure, linking up and down to local differences while at the same time disavowing traces of imperialism or transnational expansionism in the drive to install (translate different cultures into) a neo-liberal American version of universal liberation at LAX: "And so half-inadvertently, not knowing whether I was facing east or west, not knowing whether it was day or night, I slipped into that peculiar state of mind — or no-mind — that belongs to the no time, no place of the airport. … I had entered the stateless state of jet lag" (59). Or, better said, Iyer has re-entered the uncanny myth-engine of a US-centered global capitalism on its latest Passage to Cathay, where Pacific Rim expansion is recoded as self-loss and the globalization dynamic is read (translated downward) as a victory of the local culture over the regime of global time-space.

Against Pico Iyer's vision of a hyper-globalizing Hong Kong always already given over to "The Global Marketplace" (this is what Iyer calls his chapter on Hong Kong in *Global Soul*), we would have to unpack contemporary Chinese national tensions, British legacies, US incursions, and global/local dynamics in a more situated and inventive way to understand the global/local dialectics of "always already transnationalizing" Hong Kong. This more localized Hong Kong of cultural production needs to be deciphered as a cultural-political space wherein a trenchant localism recodes, translates and deforms the global, as in the poetry of Ping-kwan Leung in *Travelling with a Bitter Melon* and *Foodscape* for example.[42] Arguing that "a trend of transnationalizing of the local was evident in [Hong Kong-made] *kung fu* movies early in the 1970s", Kwai-cheung Lo has affirmed a globalized dialectic in which "the meaning of the Hong Kong local is always already overdetermined by the framework of the transnational that structures our perception of its reality".[43]

This global flow from capitalist culture is (like the unhomely ghost of William Holden in Peter Chan's *Comrades, Almost a Love Story* [1997]) settled into the Hong Kong local in complex, fluid, and inventive ways that challenge easy binaries. For, as Rey Chow summarizes the poet Leung's uncanny poetics building up Hong Kong localism around grasping the tensions of global capitalism and 1997, "Against the oft-repeated moralistic indictment that Hong Kong is a place driven exclusively by materialism and consumerism, Leung's work, through cohesively nuanced self-reflections, forges an alternative path to the materialist and consumerist world [of globalization] that the poet, like any other person, inhabits".[44] Leung's "foodscape" poems like "Salted Shrimp Paste" or "Eggplants" help to provide alternative mappings of Hong Kong's global-local dialectics, where local culture abides within and resurfaces against looming forces of globalization and appropriation without being reified into timeless essence or some unchanging "Chinese" trait.

If this Hong Kong localism is "always already over-determined" by transnational frameworks and the drive to globalize its cultural products for export and appropriation beyond city-state and Chinese or trans-Asian regionality, the ghost of globality (as it were) that haunts this uncanny localism may be a mode of deconstructive parody, embraced inauthenticity, anti-essential secondariness, a kind of blessed belatedness to the global popular culture that (in the transnational era) one can build something new upon if not decenter, disturb, and topple. "The only global cinema comes from America", David Bordwell contends, reminding little "Planet Hong Kong" (as well as regional peripheral powers of filmic Asia like Bollywood) that however kinetic, hybrid, and splendidly ecstatic its action cinema is, it has never really ever become a global Planet Hollywood (even if in these bankruptcies of transnational scale, the star-studded restaurant named Planet Hollywood has already gone bust). "A truly global cinema", by this capitalistic measure of transnationalized production and distribution is, Bordwell tells the rising inter-Asian cultural satellite, "one that claims significant space on theater screens throughout developed and developing countries", and in this respect, "1980s–1990s Hong Kong films did not constitute a global cinema".[45] Need we accept such bottom-line centered claims? Hasn't this Hong Kong uncanny localism worked its way into Hollywood streets and genres, uprooting classical gestures and heroic mores, toppling white mythologies, contaminating genres and codes?[46]

In his 1990's rush to globalize Hong Kong success stories and localized forms, for example, Jackie Chan all but doubles and deflates the global power of Bruce Lee and Hollywood, even as counterfeit currencies and gangster corporations haunt the forms of urban prosperity and everyday well-being of Pacific Rim spaces like Los Angeles and Hong Kong. Such global/local fusions spaces all but collapse into one borderless space of transnational criminality in *Rush Hour* (1998) and *Rush Hour 2* (2001), films that Hong-Kong miming director Brett Ratner built around the US multicultural/transnational buddy-cop team of Jackie Chan and Chris Tucker. "The fastest hands in the East [Chan] meet the biggest mouth in the West [Tucker]" and combine black/Asian forces and global-popular stylistic codes (like the Beach Boys, Michael Jackson, Snoopy, Godzilla, Little Kim, the Police, and Kobe Bryant, who a wizened Chinese granny mistakes Chris Tucker for in her apartment hallway). Such cultural mixtures serve the reinvention of the ever-globalizing cities of Hong Kong and Los Angeles as transpacific fusion/Confucian-confusion spaces of wealth/crime, belonging/flight, localism/globalism, heroic action/comic deflation.

In these "rush hour" spaces of traffic jams, car jackings, interrupted meals, ever-present cell phones, gouged eyes, art theft, and frenetic profit-seeking cum cross-border expansion, every local fortune (as Brecht reminded us in the 1930s where socialist alternatives still seemed possible) is haunted by global crime, counterfeiting, fraud, and theft. Miming transnational selfhood and border-crossing codes of expansion, Jackie Chan is haunted not only by the local-global ghost of Bruce Lee, whose heroic style he often inverts into drunken slipshod accomplishment and hyperbolic parody (as in the wondrous *Drunken Master 2* [1994]); he is also haunted by the modern mimicry of Buster Keaton, Charlie Chaplin and Harold Lloyd, whose neurotic ticks and absurdist feats of soaring and ducking emanate from rubbing against the specters of capitalist technology/Fordist modernity in "modern times" that are about to crush and maim them. Endearingly, and with great poetic abandon and sublimely masochistic pleasure, Chan mimes the transnational expertise and a kind of post-Fordist multicultural selfhood necessary to survive in these becoming-borderless spaces where identity is a fusion, an ephemeral invention, a lost originality, a miming of multiple codes and flights. Performing his own stunts and feats of de-materialization, Jackie Chan puts his body on the transnational assembly line and becomes the fast hands and tireless mind of late-capitalist production. Jackie Chan helps to image forth a whole nervous biopoetics of global survival tossed and turned inside-out by the globalizing borders and image-empires of the Pacific Rim as some kind of Hollywood-Hong Kong nexus zone.

By being so fully unhomely and uncanny in his globalized localism, this trans-localized "global soul" from Hong Kong named Jackie Chan charts a path forward to the haunted spaces and times of excessive globalization where authentic culture will give way to mongrel creativity and the fusion of global imagery and authentic sign into local motions that have trans-Pacific efficacy. "I'll bitch slap you back to Africa" becomes Chan's expressive revenge upon the black-authenticity claims to self-presence of Chris Tucker, who had earlier threatened this out-of-place and English-mangling "Chung King detective" from Hong Kong by saying he would "bitch slap [him] back to Beijing" for the cultural miscue of "touching a black man's [car] radio" to play his beloved Beach Boys music.

Fusing Hong Kong modes into New York problems and distant snow-capped Vancouver settings, *Rumble in the Bronx* (1996) mimes this un-building of America, delighting in the dismantling of a grocery store and hard-working immigrant spaces of the Bronx into uncanny wrecks where bathtub, toilet, shop window, and sofa fly back into the violence laden streets of multicultural gangs and transnational syndicates. Hong Kong meets America and applies its transnational tactics of diasporic unsettlement and offers its post-cultural embrace of absurdist transience. Here, everyday commodities go uncanny and fly into reverse, becoming weapons, junk, unidentified flying objects, and kung fu props: pool cues, shopping baskets, pinball machines, TV sets, refrigerators, soda cans, crutches, wheelchairs, car antennas, all are comically activated and relentlessly de-familiarized by Jackie Chan in the mission of urban dismantlement, dislocating the built-up local New York City (which still had its lofty twin towers) and national immigrant forms into a global hodge-podge of creative-destruction. The Bronx homeland becomes unhomely as the little convenience shop is demolished into the multicultural New York City streets, and diamond thieves turn urban-jungle motorcycle gangs into boy scouts. The streets of Africa, Latin American and Asia flow into the American living room bringing a multi-ethnic array of immigrants and thugs into the space of comfort, as garbage and wrecking energy flow back into the ordinary form.

In another take on Pacific Rim outreach which New Line brought from Golden Harvest for world-wide distribution, the diasporic Chan does the glocal-wacky same for urbanized and immigrant-rich Australia in Sammo Hung's *Mr. Nice Guy* (1997) as a Chinese noodle-chef reverts back into a martial artist to dismantle Melbourne in the process of undoing a transnational cocaine ring. Chan becomes now and again what Steve Fore calls "an amorphous, disembedded faux-global identity", a "globe-hopping design professional".[47] That is, Chan becomes an agent of global/local skills who can mime and de-mint the global codes of action cinema into a reverse-commodity and counter-flow. Diasporic cultural production across the Pacific for Jackie Chan offers New York (and Hollywood) a way of dismantling the stable forms of Chinese values and heroic action culture too, as the uncle marries out and the filial pieties and social respect of nice-guy Chan seem woefully inadequate to the transnational mongrel mix. An American audience often bursts out laughing when they hear Jackie preach, with Confucian nostalgia "Don't you know you are the scum of society?" or "Dad, watch over me". *Rumble in the Bronx*, with its destruction of urban streets and rolling over of White Tiger on his suburban golf course, repeats the urban demolishment and anti-architectural sublime of Melbourne violence in *Mr. Nice Guy,* in which Chan wipes out a global syndicate of cocaine dealers and local thugs with an earthmover put to broader uses. Desacralizing ex-white-settler colonial spaces, Chan helps turn American, British, and Australian spaces "like 'home' into something less familiar and less settled".[48]

Counterfeit money and a transnational syndicate of crime, drugs, and illegitimate profit haunt the murky blue spaces and filial codes of Hong Kong in John Woo's *A Better Tomorrow* (1987), where crime seems a transnational given and masculinist *mise-en-scène* of post-national globalization, which Jingle Ma carries over with anti-macho verve into Japanese urban spaces in *Tokyo Raiders*. In another brashly successful Chan-vehicle *Rush Hour 2*, the Los Angeles cop mandate to "follow the rich white man" to the origin of the crime leads willy-nilly to the cognitive mapping of a transnational assembly line of criminal financialization. Here, "superbills" of fake "Benjamins" (US hundred dollar bills) are produced in Asia, shipped for distribution to Los Angeles, then laundered in huge faux-Chinese casinos in Las Vegas where a Chinese cop turned super-criminal (John Lone) and his orientalized cast of kung fu thugs and dragon-goddesses (including the foot-stomping heroine from *Crouching Tiger, Hidden Dragon* [Ang Lee 2000]) take on the US secret service and Hong Kong police until he finally meets his match in father-avenging Jackie Chan. "I'm from Los Angeles, you can't tell me anything about gangs, we invented gangs", says African-American sidekick Carter, as if to absorb and fuse Hollywood gangster plots with Hong Kong mores and solutions. The uncanny space of postcolonial Hong Kong fuses into the uncanny offshore periphery of Los Angeles and Las Vegas to create signs of the Pacific Rim as harbinger of a post-national culture of adventure, excess, and profit-seeking risk.

By way of summary, let me provide an overview of some of my broader claims which gravitate around the need to generate trans-Pacific circuits of production and circulation as well as emergent cultural forms/genres that can challenge centrist globalization or American-centric versions of the mongrelizing global/local Pacific. Under the regime of capitalist globalization, time has become accelerated and space shaken by cross-border flows of signs, goods, outside forces and modes. Refracting these everyday forces, global cities (like Seoul, Hong Kong or Los Angeles in my analysis here) are becoming paradigmatic sites — "translocalities"

— that can figure forth the over-saturation of space-time codes as well as generate uncanny feelings and forms to disrupt, double, and dismantle the global-modern through what I am calling "spectral critique".

This global-uncanny takes a melancholic or neo-gothic turn in the contemporary Korean movies I have examined, including *Gingko Bed* and *Chunhyang*, as if the modern space-time forms of the city are haunted by the return of the repressed from the pre-transnational and rural-vanquishing past. Whereas in the contemporary Hong Kong films of trans-Pacific globalization I have looked at, the tone and modes are much more comical, gleeful, and absurdist, as if doubling and undermining the reign of globalization by cranking up its creative-destructive and cyborgian energies to some ludic breaking point, as in *Rumble in the Bronx, Mr. Nice Guy*, or the Cantonese/English collage of *Rush Hour* and *Rush Hour 2*, where the transnational assembly line implodes into fraudulent excess and counterfeit affluence even as the global city dissolves into site of insecurity and mongrel inventiveness.

In such filmic works of trans-Pacific cultural production, we can begin to see that, as I have claimed earlier, this fully uncanny Pacific of transnational globalization remains haunted by historical injustices, social unevenness, and racial phobias coming back from the postcolonial future. If the luxurious displacements and cosmopolitan excess of the postcolonial travel writer Pico Iyer, for example, ends up being just another brand of American transcendentalism where the consumption of cultural difference becomes a higher ground of ontological unity and a universalizing version of geo-political empire, then the action films of Hong Kong (through the mongrel creativity of global/local forces like Stephen Chow in works like *Shaolin Soccer*) do help local/global audiences across the Pacific to envision and generate a new imaginative way forward: a mode of living with and inside Asia/Pacific globality and Hollywood influence where the succession of high-speed action scenes and transnational finales need not be another mode of living-death or neo-colonized capitulation to market forces and Anglo-global values.

16

Technoscience Culture, Embodiment and *Wuda pian*

Wong Kin-yuen

In this era of new technologies in which posthuman forms of human energy are emerging, and in which humans themselves will soon, according to Jean-François Lyotard, reach a "material point" at which the complexification of materials is such that our perceptual, experiential and cognitive rhythm will be unable to describe or represent it,[1] cultural or film critics are suddenly witnessing the unique phenomenon of Hong Kong style *wuda* (武打)[2] impacting on the film industry almost everywhere in the world. Not only is the traditional Chinese *wuxia* novel a unique genre in the sense that it seems to be the only fictional discourse on human movement and the embodied capacity of human energy ever formulated within a still classical "technoscience culture", but the *wuda pian* produced in Hong Kong and elsewhere can be considered one of the major artistic forms within pop culture to have at least tried to reach for what Mark Hansen calls "embodying technesis", that is, "technology beyond writing".[3] It is as if the *wuda* Hong Kong style has achieved universal recognition as an ideal marriage between bodily movement and its aesthetic, expressive dynamics of energy flow on the one hand, and, on the other, visual culture, comics, video and the technological advancement of the cinema towards digitalization and special effects. In what follows, therefore, I would like to suggest that *wuda pian* reminds us not only that "technology is us", but that it was technology which created humans as humans in the first place. These films can certainly be one way of preparing ourselves for technological "shock", as Walter Benjamin puts it, by providing us with what Hansen calls a "robust *posthermeneutic realism* concerning culture and technology" (p. 213).

That Chinese martial arts discourse has always been closely related to technoscience culture is widely accepted and discussed by critics. Medical science, *qigong*, mathematics, *jingmai* (經脈 acu-points on the human body) are the scientific elements one usually finds in the *wugong* discourse; and the term *shu* (arts) within *wushu* (the martial arts) already shows its relatedness with all kinds of *techné* in classical Chinese culture such as dance *wushu*, technical skill *jishu*, archery *sheshu*, etc. However, an aspect of the combination between *wugong* and technoscience that may have escaped attention is the weaponry the martial artists use; this artisanal artifice (an integral part of the *wugong* discourse) has a good deal to do with metallurgy and with the mythic, fantastic, spiritual representation of, say, the kind of "sword" a kung fu master has in his/her hand. At this point I foresee the objection that the *techné* embedded in kung fu is very different from the kind of technology used in making cinema; however, my argument will be that to a large extent it is technology *per se* which undergoes an evolution in the history of artisanal artifice — cycles following cycles within what Timothy V. Kaufman-Osborn calls the projection/reciprocation dialectic.[4] There is no need to point out that training our body's strength and technique is a technological act, and that actual technological devices have been used since the beginning of time in most cultures to help enhance bodily movement and energy; one thinks of the rumors about the excessive use of technical devices (drugs included) connected to the untimely death of Bruce Lee.

My interest in weapons and metallurgy in kung fu discourse can be further pursued in terms of the technoscientific embeddedness of matter in the human body. The stick, for example, has undergone millions of years of evolution in the projection/reciprocation dialectic, beginning from its use for gathering fruit that hung beyond the reach of the human hand, and from its role in Greek mythology where it is, in the Sphinx's riddle, the "third leg" that the aged animal/human relies upon; it has become part of the human body in, say, Chinese Daoism (Taoism), when we see a butcher amazingly skilled with his knife, or an old man masterfully catching cicadas with his sticky pole. The hunchback explaining his "way" to Confucius and his followers says that he could "hold his body like a stiff tree trunk and use my arm like an old dry limb". What matters here is the Daoist idea that "when Body and Vitality are flawless for one another, this brings forth the ability to move" (形精不虧，是謂能移).[5] To move is also to transform; it implies not simply a movement of the body, but the body's capacity to transform (into) its tool (or matter or weapon, for that matter), to establish a "nuanced" relationship with its technological device, the movement itself being technological through and through.

Since most swords are made of metal, their relationship with the fighters in martial art is best explained through the Deleuzian notion of the "machinic phylum", or "the flow of matter" as illustrated by the "metallic or metallurgical".[6] When they develop this notion in *A Thousand Plateaus*, Deleuze and Guattari are concerned with "nomadism" as a process of following contingencies or the *haecceities* (events) of matter. In *Cinema 1: The Movement-Image*, however, Deleuze uses the idea of the "non-organic life of things" to describe the first principle of Expressionism which, like the pre-war French school, effects "a break with the organic", but does so with a type of montage which plunges into "the vital as potent pre-organic germinality, common to the animate and the inanimate, to a matter which raises itself to the point of life, and a life which spreads itself through all matter".[7] In the former book, Deleuze and Guattari also assert that "the living thing has an exterior milieu of materials, an interior milieu of composing elements and composed substances, an intermediary milieu of membranes and limits, and an annexed milieu of energy sources and actions-perceptions" (*ATP*, p. 313). Discussing the Deleuzian notion of virtuality in nonlinear causal relations within "feedback loops" (a term reminiscent of Kaufman-Osborn's projection/reciprocation dialectics), Manuel DeLanda refers to nineteenth-century Western metallurgy to illustrate how blacksmiths go about their trade:

> For the Blacksmith, "it is not a question of imposing a form upon matter but of elaborating an increasingly rich and consistent material, the better to tap increasingly intense forces" [*ATP*, p. 329]. In other words, the blacksmith treats metals as active materials, pregnant with morphogenetic capabilities, and his role is that of teasing a form out of them, of guiding, through a series of processes (heating, annealing, quenching, hammering), the emergence of a form, a form in which the materials themselves have a say. His task is less realizing previously defined possibilities than actualizing virtualities along divergent lines.[8]

This rings a bell for those familiar with Chinese kung fu discourse both in novels and in films. Whereas one does not find much elaboration given in the West to the mysterious relationships between the swordsman (his hand) and his sword (with the possible exception of King Arthur and his Excalibur), in Chinese culture fantastic narratives abound in which "the sword", being itself as full of Life and consciousness as any human being, is very much part of the swordsman (or swordswoman, since there are, I would say, a lot more women sword-users than in the West). Leaving novels aside, we can surely remember many moments affirming this in films; for example, when Lord Beile in *Crouching Tiger, Hidden Dragon* (Ang Lee 2000) admiringly takes up the "Green Destiny" and says, "Swords need to use people in order to be alive, the way of the sword is the way of humanism." In Tam Ka-ming's *The Sword* (1993) (*Mingjian*), a blacksmith, who is also a connoisseur, announces in the very first scene that the "Cold-star" (*hanxing*) is an evil sword, full of hatred in its heart. Towards the end of the film Cold-star's owner, having been slightly wounded in the chest by another companion-sword, called "All Things Equal" (*qiwu*, a direct allusion to *Zhuang Zi*), receives his fatal blow from the stolen "Cold-star" in exactly the same place he was wounded. It is as if the earlier wound itself urges the action on by its own volition and calls upon "Cold-star" to "strike home". In *Hero* (Zhang Yimou, 2002), the technology of swordplay is equated with calligraphy, and the pair of swords owned by Broken Sword (*canjian*) (what a name for a swordsman!) and Flying Snow (*feixue*) are also referred to as lovers. Even the Emperor Qin in the film points out that "Swords are humans and humans are swords".

More interesting for our discussion here is the reed stick that Broken Sword uses when he first appears in the film, practicing calligraphy on the sand. Standing upright, much like the cicada catcher in *Zhuang Zi's* tale, the calligrapher holds a reed stick instead of a brush, moving it steadily on the sand in front of him, apparently absorbed in the process of training himself in calligraphy at the same time as his kung fu. Sand is an intriguing aspect of this sequence because, unlike other surfaces such as bark or bamboo plates, sand's materiality is such that it spreads and swells easily and loosely, but will immediately slide back and mesh, particle after particle, just as easily and spontaneously. Besides, a lot depends on how deeply the reed stick reaches into the sand, since a different quality of force will be needed for different layers with different textures of sand. (In Chinese theories of calligraphy, papers have different textures and ways of absorbing ink, hence their different expressive characteristics.)

While this is clearly a matter of "moving-in" (trans-formation) or embodiment, I would also suggest that the calligraphy/swordplay analogy in this sequence can be explained by the Deleuzian concept of a tension (or balance) between "striated space" (rules of calligraphy) and "smooth space" which, as Thomas Lamarre observes, enables the calligrapher/ swordsman to achieve "juxtapositions, overlays, inlays, complications, alternations that create new resonances". [9] Using this pair of concepts, Lamarre also differentiates the "imperial line" from the "abstract line", the former belonging to the "center of gravity" and the latter to the "center of motion" in Chinese calligraphy (p. 158). From here it is not difficult for us to relate calligraphy to martial art in general, since the tension between rules (imperial line) and creative repetition (smooth motion, force, floating, hovering) can also be found in *Hero*. In Chinese calligraphy brushwork "has the potential to come close to the virtual; it strives toward that moment of inclusive disjunction" (p. 159). Whatever the brush can do, the reed stick in Broken Sword's hand can do better, and it can do *more* in oscillating and flickering, in creating nuances of forceful intersection between materials and matters, in summoning a nomadic line that martial artists are always looking for.[10]

Swords also play an important role in Tsui Hark's new *Legend of Zu* (2001). First, the "Heaven" and "Thunder" swords, respectively used by a male and a female disciple of Omei, are the most precious and powerful weapons, following a tradition in kung fu discourse that Yin/Yang complementarity generates a tremendous power that exceeds a simple combination of two swords. In this film the swords have to be "united" in a rather fantastic manner: the two disciples must fly towards each other, rather like Superman and Superwoman, along two colorful lines of "sword-chi" (*jianqi*). When the mystical union fails, a young boy is "recomposed" by the Grand Master to prepare for another attempt, with the eventual addition of a "third element" to make it complete and successful. At this juncture we are presented with an initiation narrative in which the young boy is supposed to be "enlightened" to attain a cosmic memory, and to be equipped with the power of the "Heaven" sword, which now takes the form of a rusty, ugly piece of crooked metal stuck to the rocks. What follows is a detailed description of how the sword transforms itself, non-organically and molecularly, in that process which DeLanda describes as "the emergence of a form in which the materials themselves have a say". The opening of one's mind and the reaching back to a pure memory are here an integral part of the emergence and transformation of the sword, which, now full of spirits and power, literally (that is, visually on screen) sheds its outer rusty skin like a snake. I would argue here, that "embodied capacity" is as much attended to in *wuda pian* as in classical Chinese Daoism and kung fu novels. By "embodied capacity", remember, Kaufman-Osborn means our body's ability "to engage in projection" which can "itself be projected into an artisanal artifact" (*Creatures of Prometheus*, p. 41). Using a hammer as his example, Kaufman-Osborn observes that it can be "one vehicle by means of which a body projects its transformational capacities into the world", when "that body's good sense is immanent within its skilled habits" (p. 44).

Strangely enough, such an "embodied capacity" may not be represented in *wuda pian* in concrete visual images of bodily movement.

As the post-Bruce Lee period of kung fu performance on screen increasingly comes to rely on high-tech or digitalized special effects, it has become obvious that authentic martial arts skills are being replaced by technology itself — or, to put it another way, machine technology is increasingly being substituted for bodily techniques of action and movement. Of course, die-hard admirers of Bruce Lee's triple kicks or Jet Li's smart and powerful moves (deliberately retained by constructive editing) lament that such feats of action are disappearing and that special effects have become the superstar instead. I certainly understand this sentiment; I was one of the admirers present at the first screening of *The Big Boss* at Queen's Cinema in 1971, yelling out in the middle of the movie, in unison with many other viewers, that "those kicks were real". However, I still want to argue that maybe, just maybe, digitization and special effects might have something to do with rendering possible other dimensions of bodily movement and action congenial in a mutually reinforcing way both to kung fu and to cinema as technological art. The move away from the so-called "authentic" human capacity for movement and action may have been a response to precisely the kind of "embodied complexity" initiated by the advent of modern technologies that Mark Hansen discusses (*Embodying Technesis*, 28–29). For Hansen, our way to understanding "the rich corporeal dimension of technology's impact on embodied experience can only be opened by a fundamental exhaustion of the epistemological perspective", that is, by "a thorough critique of '*technesis*'" of any kind (p. 29). For the purpose of explication I propose to use a number of films which feature the action of *running* to show how this relational structure between human action, machine action and cinema action can be discussed in the light of the embodying technology of the twenty-first century.

The first film of interest which foregrounds running as one of its thematic and formal concerns is the German film *Run Lola Run* (1998). The opening sequence of the film is immediately puzzling to viewers; its bricolage of images, sounds and shots doesn't really come together to establish any narrative logic. The use of super 8 (faster than the usual 24 frames per second), animation, black and white TV-show flashbacks, a map shown from a bird's-eye view, snapshots of criminals, the soccer ball thrown up in the air by a policeman, the glasses of passers-by: all these refer back to the initial remark in the voice-over that "Man is probably the most mysterious species of our planet". What ensues is a portrayal of an in-between time where bodily movement meets with modern technologies, creating what Brian Massumi calls "a gap of suspended animation following the preparation of the (filming) event but preceding its culmination".[11]

Here, Lola's running is presented three times in real-life footage, and in each of the runs it is interwoven with a cartoon or animated world featuring a superwoman figure that stands for Lola. Even though the act of running itself is at no time "enhanced" or manipulated by digital technology, there is no doubt that this act cuts across different worlds and that digital technology is the connection between them. For Lev Manovich, the digitization of film brings us back to animation, the plasticity of the moving image enabling us to go along with its refusal of any mimetic relation to the real.[12] *Run Lola Run* differs from classical "lens-based" mimetic films in its attempt at bringing the computer graphic back to the screen, a kind of painting on film in "the fluidity of multiplane animated perspective". [13] It is as if the director were rehearsing the different forms or texts to best "represent" the predicament of Lola and her boyfriend with the repetitive structure cutting back and forth between forms or texts, experimenting with computer games and soundtracks together with life-like human bodily action. This is therefore a film about the technologizing of film-making itself.

Run Lola Run is not a kung fu film, but my next example, *The Matrix* (1999) is more immediately relevant to our discussion. It also opens its narrative with a running scene, but this time the bodily capabilities on screen are closer to *wuda* visuals. This running sequence is preceded by a show of high-tech artifacts such as computer interface, a Nokia mobile phone, and the powerful weapons of agents and police. Confronted by the police, a woman dressed in black displays her dexterity in kung fu technique; she can even perform the impossible by raising her whole body in the air like an eagle before she delivers her kicks, and during the shoot-out sequence she starts running on the walls. Then the action is cut to a chase on the rooftops, reminiscent of video game combats on the one hand, and the Chinese style of *qinggong*, the discipline of bodily swiftness and weightless leaps, on the other. Compared to *Run Lola Run*, where the process of cutting across different media remains visible, *The Matrix* assumes suspension of disbelief by virtue of its genre and tries to smooth over the highly technologized feats, maintaining continuity in the manner of conventional realism. We later discover that the rebels must train themselves in martial art in order to cope with the ferocity of the avatars in power within the virtual reality of the matrix. Even Keanu Reeves's hand-to-hand combat training relies on computer programmes (we have a glimpse of the Chinese "Drunken Fist" and a couple of tai chi moves) before he proclaims that "I know kung fu". We have now come full circle in the embodied experience of technology. For the purpose of resisting the authoritarian regime of a fully technologized posthuman world, the rebels resort to this rather traditional technology of body training so they can overcome their colonizers in cyberspace. Here, the way to parry the de-humanizing technological shock is to go back to an embodied technology of human action. It is as if the virtuality of bodily capacity is being tapped into in order to resist the tyranny of virtual reality, along with, of course, the help of other high-tech weapons and computers.

Returning to the chase sequence in *The Matrix*, we can say that the acrobatic feats performed by the woman warrior and the agent have little to offer except that the technological atmosphere is foregrounded so obviously. This is reminiscent of several running scenes in *The One*, in which we see that the ever-energized Jet Li is capable of out-running police cars. Personally, I would select the two chase sequences in *Crouching Tiger, Hidden Dragon* as by far the most aesthetic and appealing to date in the eyes of *wuda pian* fans, at least as far as Chinese "weightless leaps" are concerned. The first sequence comes right after Zhang Ziyi steals the Green Destiny and Michelle Yeoh gives chase. The chase is presented in an intensely visual way: we see step-by-step, foot-over-foot details of the bodily movement, interlaced with fist-countering-fist, palm-confronting-palm *quanshu* (拳術). In the sequences of kicking, climbing, pulling down of a foot, whenever the action stops it is at a point when the pair are preparing for another round of attack. This is of course a product of "digital compositing", which, according to Lev Manovich, means "assembling together a number of elements to create a single seamless object" (p. 139), with the object here of creating the effect of a *seamless effort* of leaping and running on walls, rooftops and so on. The sequence depicts a series of intense moments of escaping and catching, but the effect is stunning in that the actions are presented almost in unison, and the fluidity of the camera enhances a fluidity of bodily movement in perfectly uninterrupted continuity. For the viewers, it is simply "pure poetry of the body as it exceeds the expectations of normal physical reality",[14] a new aesthetics of body-in-motion choreography seamlessly merged with the virtual interface of a digitalized technological apparatus.

The second chase and swordplay exchange is even more visually spectacular. Again holding the Green Destiny, Zhang Ziyi literally flies in a long take from behind some houses onto the water of a lake (an action clearly modeled on a famous *qinggong* move called "dragonfly pointing on water" (*qingting dianshui*), to be followed, of course, by Chow Yun-fat doing the same. Then the chase cuts to a beautiful forest of luxurious green foliage and bamboo. The graceful movements of whirling around, embracing the trees, standing on the tips of the shafts, balancing, swinging in perfect accord with the mechanics of the bending branches burdened by their weight, are then cut by a zoom-in on the faces of the couple, moving and gazing, short of breath but retaining their serenity. Sword-moves are then exchanged, all the while in harmony with the natural "forces" borrowed from the swinging movements of the shafts and bamboo, making up a milieu of interrelationships between living things and their environments.

Here, body movements, the sword, and the forest merge into each other in an interconnectedness expounded by the Chinese concept (also used in kung fu) of "in accordance with the *shi*", or *shun shi* (順勢). It seems to be an everyday concept to the Chinese but like many other concepts it has its root in Daoist teachings. There are in fact numerous passages in *Zhuang Zi* which deal with this *shi* (which I would translate as "moving structure") in the myriad forms of life and things in nature, pointing to non-linear kinds of life-tendencies — particularly in terms of the relational ontology of forces and the differential rhythms of intensity among them. This sequence in *Crouching Tiger, Hidden Dragon* is certainly a showcase of what digital composite can do visually to realize such a concept in the Chinese aesthetics of bodily movement, and particularly of how it can be related to the bio-philosophy of Daoism itself.

We have now examined different relational processes embracing bodily movement and technology as embodied experience. In *Run Lola Run*, it is the cinematic technology of shooting a film concerning running against time that is at stake. Sharp cuts between real bodily action, comics, and animation are made thematic throughout. In *The Matrix*, fantastic human action is being disciplined by machines, and what we have is a full circle feedback loop in the projection/reciprocation evolution of the human/machine interface, where a classical technology for enhancing bodily capabilities is being used in modern high-tech programmes for the purpose of resisting a still more powerful virtual world — demonstrating clearly that reciprocations by rule always exceed their earlier projections. With *Crouching Tiger, Hidden Dragon*, not even a "suspension" of disbelief is required of the audience. This is because digital composite and kung fu discourse (in the fictional rendering of flying swordsmen) reinforce each other, rendering a poetic performance of beautiful human action possible by having it seamlessly merged with its background environment: the two fighters supported and swaying (by the springing up and bending down of bamboo shafts in the sequence) while swinging their swords.

Having drawn out the Daoist concept of *shi* in kung fu discourse, I want to turn now to one of the most salient features of kung fu performance on screen, namely, the "rhythm of pause/burst/pause" as described by David Bordwell.[15] These so-called "instants of stillness" or "moments of pure stasis" are of course related to the Peking opera (*liangxiang*) tradition, but they also go back at least to the Daoist bio-philosophy of the mutuality and reinforcement of stillness/movement in all lives. Long a fundamental component in poetry, painting, and calligraphy as well as martial arts, the concept of "*dongjing xiangsheng*" suggests that stillness is the ultimate source of all energies. This is amply demonstrated by tai-chi, which emphasizes circular movements *beyond* the specific moves of one-move-one-form (*yizhao yishi*), and which maximizes energy flow not by confronting force with force, but by borrowing the opponent's power in the *shun shi* manner I have just described. Bordwell's observation that pauses intervene between speedy bursts of attack of course recalls the kung fu idea of gathering up your *shi* to a bursting point, as in the phrase *xushi daifa* (蓄勢待發), action in ferment or folding in on itself. *Shi* is a very common word which can be combined with various other words to make compound nouns such as form/structure *xingshi*, tendencies *qushi*, denoting a double-bind situation or a stillness/movement dialectic. The idea is that crouching within things or matter which are supposed to be still are dynamic forces of intensity, ready to burst out at a moment of utmost disequilibrium. One only has to look at the term mountain-move-structure *shanshi* to understand this concept, mountains being very "still" to the naked eye, but in fact, full of intense energy — volcanoes, for example, within. We are reminded here of the common practice in kung fu pedagogy of making novices learn to set their horse-like form *zama* in perfect stillness — like a mountain — before any other lessons can begin.

The pauses in *wuda pian* that Bordwell discusses, and the Chinese concept of *shi* or tendencies, as I said, can be traced back to Zhuang Zi's idea that all lives are the result of the intensive transformation under the sky and on earth (*tiandi zhi wei he ye* 天地之委和也). The word *wei* refers to snake-like turns and whirls, describing the self-opening of the Lathe of Heaven (天機自張) when all lives are at a point of emergence within an intensity of differentiation before their forms are individualized. Here Zhuang Zi is presenting a tacit but intensive process of qualitative change between life-forms, their environment, weather, vapors and light within a structure of mutual affordance. Such a natural tendency toward affordance is exactly what is meant by "embodied capacity" as expounded by Manuel DeLanda who, basing his studies on a Deleuzian geo-philosophy, develops the idea that "a biological population may exhibit attractors (and thus be defined in part by the *tendencies* with which these singularities endow it) but in addition its members will typically display complex *capacities* for interaction".[16] When Lao Zi in *Tao-te Ching* talks about the appearance of the two animals *you* and *yu* (猶 and 豫, which later combine to form a compound noun *youyu* meaning "hesitation"), one seeming "Cautious, like crossing a frozen stream in the winter", and the other "Being at a loss, like one fearing danger on all sides" (*Wing-Tsit Chan*, 126), he is granting a primitive authority to kung fu practitioners who develop action programmes modeled on the careful and attentive "pause-and-action" movement practiced by animals in the wild. One is reminded here that in many action sequences, including those of Bruce Lee, we see numerous zooms in on feet shifting and moving, sometimes inch by inch, right at the point of an emergent attack or defense. It is as if the fighters' bodies were, in Deleuze's terms, in an "infolding" of a pressing multitude of incipiencies, right at a critical point between a germinal state and the act of selecting a form of movement. The point here is that the significance of these patterns of pause-burst-pause does not stop at martial arts aesthetics in films, but goes a long way towards a bio-philosophy of affordance of all lives; and this may partly explain why martial artists are fond of modeling their moves on those of animals, or rather, using Deleuze and Guattari's term, why they are prone to becoming-animals.[17]

Another way of explaining this pause-burst-pause kung fu screen action aesthetics, one that brings us closer to our discussion of the technology of cinema, is through the Deleuzian notions of *interval* and *duration*. This aspect of Deleuze's philosophy in general begins with his Bergsonism and culminates in the "time-image" elaborated in his *Cinema 2*, absorbing Bergson's radical thinking about images, perception, time and becoming, and holds that *duration* and *interval* are the key concepts around which body action and cinema can be combined towards a new artistic way of thinking the concept itself.[18] In the opening chapters of *Matter and Memory*, Bergson devotes himself to an overall discussion of images in which, first, everything including our brain and eyes can be conceived of as images, and second, all images are thought of as moving images. He writes: "I am in the presence of images, in the vaguest sense of the word, images perceived when my senses are opened to them ... all these images act and react upon one another in all their elementary parts ...".[19] It follows that isolated images are a fiction and it is up to our perception to "freeze" them, at which point the flow of time is spatialized. This is important for our discussion of human action, since, as Pearson points out, Bergson is arguing that "the body, as a living centre, is first and foremost a centre of action and not a house of representation".[20] I get to know my body through its movement and affections from within: "I examine the conditions in which these affections are produced: I find that they always interpose themselves between the excitations that I receive from without and the movements I am about to execute ..." (*MM*, p. 17). From images to action, we have now a theory of the "interval" which can be useful for further understanding kung fu's patterning of stillness and movement:

> [E]very affection is conditioned by a dual movement that itself contains a multiplicity. Each and every affection is situated at the "interval" between a multiplicity of excitations received from "without" and the movements about to be executed. The movements about to be carried out arise because each affection contains an invitation to act as well as the permission to wait to act, or not to act at all.[21]

Now, we have all witnessed many a scene in kung fu movies where the two opponents, having exchanged a series of moves, simultaneously stop, swords raised high at eye level, with the free hand (also raised behind the head) forming a so-called sword-sign (*jianjue* 劍訣). (I am describing here a typical sequence between Yeoh and Zhang in *Crouching Tiger, Hidden Dragon*). Then, with this sudden stop we cut to the moving feet, usually as the two opponents circle and gaze at each other, before another burst of action. This animal-like movement of caution and intensity is, of course the "interval": interference, cutting-in, a negotiation between excitation and affect, a form-like tension between tendencies toward singular movement on the one hand, and, on the other, a multiplicity of choices (that is, between different moves in response to the moves from without). We call this an intense moment simply because the fighters are thrown into a "duration" extending towards a virtuality of capacities — in Deleuze's bio-philosophy, a kind of "creative explosion" or threshold effect.[22] Duration is eventful movement and continuity within the differential rhythms of intensity, a fluidity which temporalizes itself without being frozen by perception. Action in duration is action of quality-change. It is, as it were, the crouching of tigers and the hiding of dragons waiting for a moment of projection into a series of tendential movements and intertemporal moments of shock and pulsative life-force rhythms. The Chinese phrase "to use stillness to overcome motion" (*yijing zhidong* 以靜制動) is exactly a recognition of that durational fluidity which makes real change possible. Intervals in duration point towards an embodiment of interaction within an undivided continuity of forces. They are important in kung fu discourse because kung fu, like classical Chinese philosophy, emphasizes intuitional creativity at crucial moments during combat, through an embodiment of an intensive difference (whether to regain strength after being ferociously attacked, whether to resume positionality for another set of moves), which is truly innovative in quality. We have only to remember King Hu's *Come*

Drink with Me (1966) (recently reissued on DVD/VCD) to discover that nearly one third of the film's fighting sequences are devoted to confrontational stillness, either from one side of the combat or from both. It is King Hu, we should also remember, who likes to depict fighting scenes in which kung fu masters (Cheng Pei-pei in *Come Drink with Me* is a case in point) remain very still while fighting, making only minimal movements with their arms.[23] Finally, the most elaborate stand-still appears in *Hero*, where we have Sky (*Changkong*) and Nameless (*Wuming*) apparently not moving a muscle as they confront each other for a long while before the fatal move — the non-movement all the while intensified by music, including songs and strong drum beats.

In one sense Deleuze considers all arts to be about movement of some sort or another, in so far as a series of images is able to move thinking along. Cinema, with its ability to present the moving of movement, is the best art form for Deleuze to deal with bodily movement. For Deleuze, seriality is not the same as succession, since the latter privileges instants along a line of reality-snapshots (in other words, images) frozen into still pictures by perception. Cinema, therefore, represents for Deleuze an art form which can give us "immediate movement", which produces "a shock to thought, communicating vibrations to the cortex, touching the nervous and cerebral system directly" (*C2*, p. 156). Along with the notion of duration, Deleuze emphasizes modern cinema's capacity to "de-frame" images so that an interval is produced in which thought can linger and oscillate; and the time-image is supposed to enact a de-realization, so much so that even cinema is both technoscience and an art providing images of movement vibrating beyond any determining schematism. In his book on the movement-image (*C1*), Deleuze works out an image-ontology by focusing on the interconnectedness between images, and between images and their environment. When he points out that the movement-image exists only in relation to or by virtue of relating,[24] it is not too far-fetched for us in turn to relate this idea to, say, the chase sequences mentioned above in *Crouching Tiger, Hidden Dragon*, where body/movement images interact with their environment in terms of mutual affordance as well as confrontation. There too, as for Deleuze, "every image acts on others and reacts to others, on 'all their facets at once' and 'by all their elements'" (*C1*, p. 58).[25] From the interval derives the "irrational cut" or interstice in cinematography. These all point to a way of cutting or designing montage with a deliberate act of cutting off perception through an aesthetic of force. Bergson had already envisaged a kind of cinematography inside us taking snapshots of passing reality.[26] Cinema as a technological mechanism is seen as adequate to reproducing movement: "movement in action [*se faisant*], *effecting a change in concrete duration*, is replaced by the ready-made (*tout fait*) immobile scheme of the movement covered, in which we can count as many instantaneous views as we like, in an abstract time over space", and this is to use our intelligence to think "the moving via the intermediary of the immobile".[27] From Bergson, Deleuze draws out a concept of seriality which is the time-image proper in *Cinema 2*. Instead of following the sensory motor schemata in the movement-image (which indirectly represents time, indirectly because cinematic technology approximates movement in time), the crystalline structure of time directly presents itself "in a becoming as potentalization, as series of powers" (*C2*, p. 275). Time as series enables us to "witness change or metamorphosis across a sequence of images as the transformation of states, qualities, concepts, or identities".[28] This is carried out by what Deleuze calls "genesigns", which "present several figures ... Sometimes ... they are characters forming series as so many degrees of 'a will to power' through which the world becomes a fable. Sometimes it is a character himself crossing a limit, and becoming another, in an act of story-telling which connects him to a people past or to come" (*C2*, p. 275). For Deleuze, this power of the false effected by art puts the notion of truth in crisis; and such a fabulation of images in series facilitates our thought to become-machinic.

The notion of time as series, rather than as succession, can therefore be adapted to our discussion of kung fu action sequencing. Besides the kind of bodily stillness which takes the form of "positionality" as (in Massumi's words) "an emergent quality of movement",[29] many a time we see "speed" of action on screen is presented by non-speed, that is, speed beyond detection by the human eye. As a young boy in the 1960s I was fascinated by *Zatoichi*, the Japanese blind swordsman series, in which there were often sequences with several bad guys surrounding the blind man, who remains still — except that we can clearly feel that the master-swordsman is listening intently. Then there is a split second's flashing and clashing, before we see, in amazement, another silent moment, the blind man with the tip of his sword still inside its sheath, disguised as the blind man's stick. A few seconds later the bad guys begin to fall one by one, the sword slowly slides back to its place, and only then do we realize that everything is over. King Hu learned from this technique of presenting the unpresentable; a number of times, notably in *Dragon Inn* (1967) (*Longmen kezhan*) and *Come Drink with Me*, a candle is cut and cast into the air, then the next thing we see it is resting stably on the swordswoman's blade, the candle flame still burning. A similar pattern is repeated in *Hero* when

Nameless (Jet Li), in a circle of stacked bamboo scrolls, throws a bowl of water in midair, and leaps around to display his masterful skill and swiftness with his sword, before catching the full bowl on the flat of his blade, and comes to a perfect standstill for a few seconds — then the bamboo scrolls start to break at the stitching and finally collapse in a loud crash.

This deliberate cutting off or interruption of our perception is, of course, initially a way of hiding the inadequacy of technology to represent a speed too fast for the eye to see. But in comparison with the fantastic visuals now enabled by digital composites, where "speed" is shown through multiple exposures, differentiating rhythms and varying speeds of different kinds (as in *The One* [2001], where Jet Li possesses a mode of speedy action which is beyond other characters in other universes or "incompossible presents"[30] shown through a trajectory of multiple exposures, separating slow motion and sped-up motion and then putting them back together, with a perfect matching of sound effects), both *Zatoichi* and *Come Drink with Me* are successful in delinking images so as to open up a gap, an interval of duration or a caesura of the event where the power of falsification institutes what Deleuze calls a "nooshock" to the audience within a pure form of time as change, transformation and unmediated difference of all kinds. Bergson calls this "pure perception", because as "a center of indetermination, the interval is defined as the location of a process bringing ever more numerous and distant points in space into relation with ever more complex motor responses".[31]

So what, one might ask, is the exact content of thought that *wuda pian* provokes, granted that it has the capacity to produce genesigns and nooshocks through intervals of duration? In the context of our concern with bodily movement and the techno-science inherent in Chinese martial arts, I would argue that *wuda pian*, in both its classics and recent experiments with digital graphics alike, provides us with a clue as to "how the true world finally became a fable" as Gregg Lambert puts it in his book on the "non-philosophy" of Gilles Deleuze.[32] The non-representability of bodily movement has a basis in Daoist philosophy as manifested in, say, tai-chi *quan* or tai-chi *jian* where passage precedes position, where isolated moves have to be abandoned for a seamless circling of non-moves which may include a multiplicity of singular moves when needed.[33] Such a refusal to succumb to successive points or instants of spatialized time restores our direct access to the very-"evolving", folding and unfolding temporal flow, tai-chi being movement in which circle overlaps with circle, one being nudged away by another, which is in turn engulfed by yet another. This certainly posits "the simultaneity of incompossible presents"[34] and, translated into a kung fu film, it becomes a duration or event in which an ancient technology of embodying the *force vitale* is juxtaposed with a modern technology for narrating that movement in film. The "dizziness" of swirling around (as mostly felt by the opponent of someone performing tai-chi) issues forth the "irrational cuts" as a new type of narrating technique which deals directly with creating a fable through the power to falsify or to fabulate.

The cinematographic subject (I think) in *wuda pian* takes it upon itself to think with an embodied capacity, outside language, or with technesis as the narrating capability of the camera as a machine. For Eisenstein, it is "in the 'machine' of cinema" that he finds "a means of transcending the mechanisms of perception, opinion ... and cliché in order to invent newer and finer articulations of the linkages between the human and the world". [35] Our goal in re-thinking the kung fu films would be, therefore, to understand how they help create an "outside" for the traditional concept of what human action means. In what way does the modern technology of cinematography push the boundary of humanism in general, so much so that we may begin to open ourselves to, say, posthumanist thinking or even machinic thinking? How does the new digital magic inspire us towards accepting something like a co-evolution of human and machine? Mark Hansen advocates a "robust post-hermeneutic realism concerning culture and technology" to go beyond semiotics (p. 213) and in the wake of Benjamin he finds a possible solution to our (re)embodying technology as *Erlebnis* in a bodily capacity to receive the image, through tactility, as "shock" (p. 248). I would argue that this so-called "corporeal mimeticism" finds another potential version in *wuda pian*, which opens up a sensorium for both human and artificial forces to meet in our age of the "technological real". By technological real, I mean an ability or rather a capacity to parry, adjust or even embody modern technology without objectifying the machine (or the digital composite for that matter). In this time of facing a "general emergent series of cultural phenomena [of virtual reality or 'VR'] as machinic phylum",[36] we had better think through these phenomena on an interface where the virtual interacts with realities. Deleuze and Guattari point out in *What Is Philosophy?* that a body "proceeds by a cascade of actualizations" (p. 123), and that "bodies are new actualizations whose "private" states restore matters of fact for new bodies" (p. 154), and in Deleuze's geo-philosophical system movements made by humans, animals, atoms and mountains are basically the same, and "the behavioural patterns of sub-atomic particles have no more or less significance than a film plot".[37] On this point, Stephen Zagala records that during the informal seminar conducted by Deleuze at Vincennes in the early 1970s topics "'would range from Spinoza to modern music, from *Chinese metallurgy* [my emphasis] to bird-song, from linguistics to gang warfare ... The rhizome would grow. (Deleuze and Parnet 1987, xii) Artistry, in this general sense, is concerned with creating new modes of existence".[38]

Finally, I would reiterate that more and more *wuda pian* afford us with both the virtual and the actual as we experience an ever increasing degree of material complexification. They provide us with differential operations at the threshold between an ancient technology of body capabilities and a digital or virtual technology specializing, as cybernetics does, in movements of all kinds. Through the performance of body mechanics in humans and machines we are given to understand that "bodies are intensifications of relations".[39] Therefore, should anyone succeed in being unoffended by the idea that non-organic things have life — that the sword and the hand holding it are one and the same thing, that the human/machine interface is on its way to being our reality, that humans are evolving together with other species in a process of symbiosis in the concept of posthumanism — then this person would begin to like *The Matrix* more than before; she would have not been all that disappointed with Jet Li doing too little in *The One*; and she would definitely have been more generous with Tsui Hark's new *Legend of Zu*. From a humanist viewpoint, the new *Legend of Zu* has many flaws simply because the characterization is thin, the thematic statement clichéd at best, the imported influence in its design is too obvious and perhaps too much digital composite technology is used for technology's sake. From a posthumanist perspective, however, Tsui Hark has done something unrivalled in the history of *wuda pian*. That the visuals are innovative and stunning is not to be denied, but the experimentation with digital visuals in creating a mountain beyond mountains, a heaven outside the heavens, is a real attempt at presenting the "outside" for thought.

Here we can see human bodies becoming real but abstract, and their concreteness and embodying capacity have reached a kind of incorporeality that belongs to the dimension of the virtual. From the perspectives of myths, legends, fantastic tales, magical universes, the "forever changing universe" of *Legend of Zu* is a world of becomings, of transformations, and of rhizomatic growth at that. It could be a film which pertains to freeing "human life from fixed or 'moral' images of what humanity is, and opens thought up for a future".[40] One striking group of visuals gives the general tonality of "chaosmos" in a cosmic dynamism.[41] Many sequences start with chaos, a pre-formed, pre-individualized but creative disorder of fire, light, heat and particles. Everything is wrapped up at first in a nebulosity of the enveloping micro-perception; and here we have mind/universe/materials/regeneration as the film's overall composite; these forces are combined in a chaotic way so as to pass even through human bodies for regeneration. Cosmic (essential, pure) memories are to be acquired by forgetfulness, and dualistic structures of cosmic forces are shattered and have to join forces with the third element of power in order to restore order and good cause. The whole film is what Rodowick calls a posthuman "figural", meaning, "the force of difference" as "the secret and power of ... virtuality".[42] To me, Tsui Hark's film has a mythical setting which comes close to Deleuze's notion of "milieu" where all life species, human and nonhuman, interact between elements, compounds and natural forces in an immanent world of constant change. From here I venture to suggest that the very futurity in the recent development of *wuda pian*, according to the Bergsonian-Deleuzian concept of time, is the future of the past where virtuality projects itself in full force.

Notes

INTRODUCTION

1. See David Desser's analysis of the Ringo Lam example in chapter 13 of this volume.
2. See, for example, Davis Miller, *The Tao of Bruce Lee* (London: Vintage, 2000).
3. Anthony C. Y. Leong, *Korean Cinema: The New Hong Kong* (Victoria, BC: Trafford Publishing, 2002).
4. The quotations here are from Nix, "Ong-bak Muay Thai Warrior (2003)"; www.nixflix.com/reviews/ongbak.htm/. See also the comments by Ng Kai Chong in MoovGoog Movie Blog (www.mallasch.com/movies/review.php?sid=110).
5. Joel Quenby, "Ong-bak. First Action Hero", www.movieseer.com/. Accessed 11 June 2004.
6. Indicative here is José Arroyo's *Action/Spectacle Cinema: A Sight and Sound Reader* (London: BFI Publishing, 2000), a useful collection of short pieces on Hollywood blockbuster action which offers a "John Woo Interlude" (Section 3, pp. 59–80) and a review of *The Matrix* which does not mention the choreography of Yuen Wo-ping (pp. 259–261).
7. See n. 3 above. Other examples of works on national cinema are Lathia Gopalan, *Cinema of Interruptions: Action Genres in Contemporary Indian Cinema* (London: British Film Institute, 2002); Karl G. Heider, *Indonesian Cinema: National Culture on Screen* (Honolulu: University of Hawaii Press, 1991); Krishna Sen, *Indonesian Cinema* (London and New Jersey: Zed Books, 1994); and Rolando Toletino (ed.), *Geopolitics of the Visible: Essays on Philippine Film Cultures* (Manila: Ateneo De Manila University Press, 2001). A regional survey is Lee Server, *Asian Pop Cinema: Bombay to Tokyo* (San Francisco: Chronicle Books, 1999).
8. Significant critical works that explore or refuse this division include Eric Cazdyn, *The Flash of Capital: Film and Geopolitics in Japan* (Durham, NC:

Duke University Press, 2002); Joel David, *Wages of Cinema: Film in Philippine Perspective* (Diliman, Quezon City: University of the Philippines Press, 1998); Madhava M. Prasad, *Ideology of the Hindi Film. A Historical Construction* (Delhi: Oxford University Press, 1998); and Paul Willemen, *Looks and Frictions: Essays in Cultural Studies and Film Theory* (London and Bloomington: British Film Institute and Indiana University Press, 1994). At the other extreme, the UK-based TV critic Clive James made his own media career in the 1980s by sampling "weird" Japanese game shows on British TV.

9. Ding-Tzann Lii, "A colonized empire: Reflections on the expansion of Hong Kong films in Asian countries", in Kuan-Hsing Chen (ed.), *Trajectories: Inter-Asia Cultural Studies* (London and New York: Routledge, 1998), pp. 122–141.

10. I owe this observation to Mandy Thomas.

11. See the website on "Hong Kong Action Film at the Frontiers of Cinema" (http://www.cscsban.org/Hongkong_Action/) conceived by S. V. Srinivas, and his essay "Hong Kong Action Film in the Indian B Circuit", *Inter-Asia Cultural Studies* 4:1 (April 2003): 40–62. See also chapter 7 of this volume.

12. Esther Yau (ed.), *At Full Speed: Hong Kong Cinema in a Borderless World* (Minneapolis: Minnesota University Press, 2001), p. 25. I discuss this issue in more detail in "Transnational imagination in action cinema: Hong Kong and the making of a global popular culture", *Inter-Asia Cultural Studies* 5:2 (2004): 181–199.

13. The ground-breaking discussion of these themes was Yvonne Tasker, *Spectacular Bodies: Gender, Genre and the Action Cinema* (London and New York: Routledge, 1993). See also Steve Cohan and Ina Rae Hark (eds), *Screening the Male: Exploring Masculinities in Hollywood Cinema* (London and New York: Routledge, 1993); Sherrie A. Inness, *Tough Girls: Women Warriors and Wonder Women in Popular Culture* (Philadelphia: University of Pennsylvania Press, 1999); Susan Jeffords, *Hard Bodies: Hollywood Masculinity in the Reagan Era* (Rutgers: Rutgers University Press, 1994); Neal King, *Heroes in Hard Times: Cop Action Movies in the U.S.* (Philadelphia: Temple University Press, 1999); and Chuck Kleinhans, "Class in Action" in David E. James and Rick Berg (eds), *The Hidden Foundations: Cinema and the Question of Class* (Minneapolis: University of Minnesota Press, 1996), pp. 240–63.

14. See Toby Miller, Nitin Govil, John McMurria and Richard Maxwell, *Global Hollywood* (London: British Film Institute, 2001) and Steve Neale and Murray Smith (eds), *Contemporary Hollywood Cinema* (London and New York: Routledge, 1998).

15. Lo Kwai-Cheung, "Double Negations: Hong Kong's Cultural Identity in Hollywood's Transnational Representations" in Esther M. K. Cheung and Chu Yiu-wai (eds), *Between Home and World: A Reader in Hong Kong Cinema* (Hong Kong: Oxford University Press, 2004), p. 76. See also Jackie Chan's comment: " Honestly, I don't like *Rush Hour*. I didn't like *Shanghai Noon* … Why? Because I really don't understand the jokes". Cited in Leon Hunt,

Kung Fu Cult Masters (London and New York: Wallflower Press, 2003), p. 168.

16. Yau's *At Full Speed: Hong Kong Cinema in a Borderless World* includes innovative studies in transnational reception: see Jinsoo An, "*The Killer*: Cult Film and Transcultural (Mis)Reading" (pp. 95–113) and Bhaskar Sarkar, "Hong Kong Hysteria: Martial Arts Tales from a Mutating World" (pp. 159–176). Other examples are David Desser, "The Kung Fu Craze: Hong Kong Cinema's First American Reception", in Fu and Desser (eds), *The Cinema of Hong Kong: History, Arts, Identity*, pp. 19–43; May Joseph, "Kung Fu Cinema and Frugality" in *Nomadic Identities: The Performance of Citizenship* (Minneapolis: University of Minnesota Press, 1999), pp. 49–68; Vijay Prasad, *Everybody was Kung Fu Fighting: Afro-Asian Connections and the Myth of Cultural Purity* (Boston: Beacon, 2001); and Yvonne Tasker, "Fists of Fury: Discourses of Race and Masculinity in the Martial Arts Cinema" in H. Stecopoulos and M. Uebel (eds), *Race and the Subject of Masculinities* (Durham and London: Duke University Press, pp. 315–36.)

17. Miller, Govil, McMurria and Maxwell, *Global Hollywood*, p. 172.

18. See chapter 7 of this volume, p. 111.

19. Thomas Elsaesser, "The Blockbuster: Everything Connects, but Not Everything Goes" in Jon Lewis (ed.), *The End of Cinema as We Know It: American Film in the Nineties* (New York: New York University Press, 2001), p. 13. Elsaesser is referring to the name of the Stephen Spielberg, David Geffen and Jerry Katzenberg studio, "DreamWorks".

20. The citations in this paragraph are from Elsaesser, pp. 20–22. Of course, the category "blockbuster" for Elsaesser encompasses more than action movies, notably including Disney's fantasies and fairy tales.

21. See Poshek Fu, "Going Global: A Cultural History of the Shaw Brothers Studio, 1960–1970" in Law Kar (ed.), *Border Crossings in Hong Kong Cinema* (Hong Kong: Hong Kong International Film Festival, 2000), pp. 43–51; and Steve Fore, "Golden Harvest films and the Hong Kong Movie Industry in the Realm of Globalization", *The Velvet Light Trap*, 34 (Fall 1994): 40–58. The term Hong Kong "ecumene" (for "a 'region of persistent cultural interaction and exchange'") is derived by Fore from Ulf Hannerz, *Cultural Complexity* (New York; Columbia University Press, 1992); Fore, p. 56.

22. This idea derives from Georg Lukács, *The Historical Novel,* trans. Hannah and Stanley Mitchell (Lincoln and London: University of Nebraska Press, 1962); first published in German, 1955. See my "Transnational imagination in action cinema: Hong Kong and the making of a global popular culture" (n.12 above), and "Cultural Studies, Critical Theory and the Question of Genre: History in Action Cinema" in Joyce C. H. Liu (ed.), *Visual Culture and Critical Theory* (Taiwan: Rye Field, forthcoming 2005) (in Chinese).

23. See Tasker, *Spectacular Bodies: Gender, Genre and the Action Cinema.*

24. Lee Server, *Asian Pop Cinema: Bombay to Tokyo*, pp. 9–10 ; David Bordwell, *Planet Hong Kong: Popular Cinema and the Art of Entertainment* (Cambridge, MA, and London: Harvard University Press, 2000), p. 96.

25. Hunt, *Kung Fu Cult Masters*, p. 184.

26. Stephen Teo, *Hong Kong Cinema: The Extra Dimension* (London: British Film Institute, 1997). See also Law Kar (ed.), *Border Crossings in Hong Kong Cinema*; the Hong Kong International Film Festival retrospective catalogue, *Cinema of Two Cities: Hong Kong — Shanghai* (1994); the Hong Kong Film Archive's *50 Years of the Hong Kong Film Production and Distribution Industries (1947–1997)* (Hong Kong: The Urban Council, 1997); and, particularly interesting on the complicated cultural and linguistic geographies of competing Chinese cinemas, Wong, Ain-ling (ed.), *The Cathay Story* (Hong Kong: Hong Kong Film Archive, 2002).

27. Lisa Odham Stokes and Michael Hoover, *City on Fire: Hong Kong Cinema* (London and New York: Verso, 1999), p. 30.

28. On "the national", see Willemen, *Looks and Frictions: Essays in Cultural Studies and Film Theory*, pp. 206–19. On the issues posed by this model in India, see Ashish Rajadhyaksha and Paul Willemen (eds), *Encyclopaedia of Indian Cinema* (London and Delhi: Oxford University Press and British Film Institute, 1994).

29. Poshek Fu and David Desser (eds), *The Cinema of Hong Kong: History, Arts, Identity* (Cambridge: Cambridge University Press, 2000), p. 5.

30. Law Wing-Sang explores the history of the "undercover" motif in his paper "Hong Kong Undercover: An Approach to Collaborative Colonialism" delivered to *Urban Imaginaries: An Asian-Pacific Research Symposium*, Lingnan University, Hong Kong, May 22–24, 2004. Publication forthcoming.

31. For example, Sheldon Hsaio-Peng Lu's substantial edited volume *Transnational Chinese Cinemas: Identity, Nationhood and Gender* (Honolulu: University of Hawaii Press, 1997) remains overwhelmingly focussed on mainland Chinese issues, with two and a half chapters out of fourteen devoted to Hong Kong.

32. Cheung and Chu (eds), *Between Home and World: A Reader in Hong Kong Cinema*, pp. xxi–xxii (my emphasis).

33. These terms are suggested by, respectively, Fu and Desser, p. 5; and Stephen Teo, "Local and Global Identity: Whither Hong Kong Cinema?", in Cheung and Chu, p. 103.

34. Bordwell, *Planet Hong Kong*, pp. 82–83.

35. Bordwell, p. 96.

36. Cheung and Chu, p. xxiii.

37. Bordwell, p. 96.

38. The literature on this interactivity is now extensive. Some of the best empirical and critical work on the transnational "making" of Hong Kong cinema is to be found in the Hong Kong International Film Festival publications edited by S.-H. Lau, *A Study of the Hong Kong Martial Arts Film* (Hong Kong: The Urban Council, 1980) and *A Study of the Hong Kong Swordplay Film* (Hong Kong: The Urban Council, 1981). On the way in which local issues and affects invest Hong Kong cultural texts that have a much wider circulation,

see the essays in *Cultural Studies* 15: 3–4 (2001), a special issue on "Becoming (Postcolonial) Hong Kong" ed. by John Nguyet Erni.

CHAPTER 1

1. Society for the promotion of Chinese culture (*Zhongguo wenhua xiejinhui*) (ed.) *Guangdong wenwu* (Hong Kong: *Zhongguo wenhua xiejinhui*, 1941), p. 792.

2. Yung Sai-shing, Sau-yan Chan, *Rong Baotian (Alice Yung), Mai Xiaoxia (Mak Siu-ha), and Xue Juexian (Sit Kok-sin)*, unpublished manuscript, 1996.

3. Yu Mo-wan, *History of Hong Kong Cinema (Xianggang dianying shihua)*, Vol I (1896–1929) (Hong Kong: Subculture Press, 1996), pp. 167–168.

4. Nowadays only a very limited number of Cantonese Opera actors still know how to perform the "southern style" martial arts. According to the renowned actor Luo Pinchao (1912–), the "southern school" is characterized by its beautiful gestures and movements. Originating from the martial arts of the Shaolin Temple, its mode of performance emphasizes quick actions of the body, particularly the movement of the arms. This marks a difference from Peking Opera which emphasizes the skills of the legs. See Luo Pinchao, "The traditional art of the southern school in Cantonese opera" ("*Yueju nanpai chuangtong yishu*"), in Li Jian (ed.), *An Oral History of Cantonese Opera in Hong Kong (Xianggang yueju koushushi)* (Hong Kong: Joint Publishing Co., 1993), pp. 3–11. Also see Huang Zhaohan, Zeng Yingjing (ed.), *Detailed Talks on Cantonese Opera: Essays and Letters on Cantonese Opera by Chen Tie'er (Xishuo Yueju: Chen Tie'er Yueju lunwen shuxinji)* (Hong Kong: *Guangming tushu gongsi*, 1992).

5. Hong Kong Film Archive, *The Making of Martial Arts Films: As Told by Filmmakers and Stars* (Hong Kong: Hong Kong Film Archive, 1999), "Biography", p. 96.

6. This poster is preserved in the Chinese Opera Information Centre, Department of Music, Chinese University of Hong Kong. I would like to thank the Director of the Centre, Professor Sau-yan Chan for allowing me to use these historical materials related to Sit Kok-sin and Mak Siu-ha (Mai Xiaoxia).

7. Chen Feinong, *Sixty years of Cantonese Opera (Yueju liushi nian)* (Hong Kong: n.p., 1982), p. 7.

8. Yu Mo-wan, "The most regrettable things of Xin Ma Shizeng" ("*Xin Ma Shizheng zuiyihan de shiqing*"), *Ming Pao,* 26 December 2002.

9. Lai Bojiang, *A History of the Artistic Life of Sit Kok-sin (Xue Juexian yiyuan chunqiu)* (Shanghai: *Shanghai wenyi chubanshe*, 1993), pp. 33, 41, 45, 98–99, 103–104.

10. Hu Peng, *Wong Fei-hung and Me (Wo yu Huang Feihong)* (Hong Kong: n.p., 1995).

11. Interview with Yuen Wo-ping, 20 January 1999, Oral History Project, Hong Kong Film Archive. I am grateful to Ms Wong Ainling for sending me the transcript.

12. Ibid.

13. Hong Kong Film Archives, *The Making of Martial Arts Films*, p. 71. I have slightly revised the English translation based on the Chinese text.

14. Ibid., p. 71.

15. See Lau Shing-hon's interview with Han Yingjie, in his "Three Interviews", *A Study of the Hong Kong Swordplay Film* (Hong Kong: Urban Council of Hong Kong, 1991; 2nd Edition, 1996), p. 211.

16. Ibid, p. 73.

17. Ibid.

18. The content of this table is based on Yu Mo-wan, *Tantan xianggang dianying de wushu zhidao* (Martial Arts Directors in Hong Kong Cinema), Hong Kong Film Archives, *The Making of Martial Arts Films*, pp. 80–86.

19. See Sau-yan Chan, *Ritual theaters in Hong Kong (Shengongxi zai Xianggang)* (Hong Kong: Joint Publishing, 1996).

20. David Bordwell, "Aesthetics in Action: Kungfu, Gunplay, and Cinematic Expressivity," in Esther Yau (ed.), *At Full Speed: Hong Kong Cinema in a Borderless World* (Minneapolis: University of Minnesota Press, 201), p. 78.

21. Ibid.

22. In the contemporary Chinese opera, the "drunken step" is often used in the excerpt "The Eight Immortals Cross the Sea". The story goes that the Eight Immortals, a well-known immortal group in Chinese legend, have gotten drunk, and the eight actors perform this special step when they enter the stage. In the movie, the full name of the "drunken fist" is known as the "Drunken Eight Immortals", which is composed of eight sections. Each section is named after a member of the Eight Immortals.

23. Interview with Yuen Wo-ping, 20 January 1999, Oral History Project, Hong Kong Film Archive.

24. Newspaper clipping, nd. In the "Alice Yung Collection", Chinese Opera Information Centre, Department of Music, Chinese University of Hong Kong.

25. Lai Bojiang, *A History of the Artistic Life of Sit Kok-sin (Xue Juexian yiyuan chunqiu)*, p. 51.

CHAPTER 2

1. David A. Cook, *A History of Narrative Film,* 2nd Edition (New York: W.W. Norton & Company, Inc. 1990), p. 778.

2. The well-known *wuxia pian Dragon Gate Inn* (1967, King Hu) was released in Hokkaido in 1968. However, it was regarded as a Taiwanese production and, despite its success in Southeast Asia, *Dragon Gate Inn* did not succeed commercially nor did it arouse any critical attention during its first release in Japan.

3. Lau Shing-hon, "Introduction", *A Study of the Hong Kong Martial Arts Film,* ed. Lau Shing-hon (Hong Kong: The Urban Council, 1980), p. 3.

4. Tadashi Nishimoto and Isamu Kakita were employed for the sake of upgrading the Eastmancolor and wide-screen photography at Shaw Brothers. Their work was under the shared Chinese pseudonym 'He Lanshan' in Hong Kong.

5. The boom in *huang mei* opera filmmaking was started by Li Hanxiang's *Diau Charn* in 1958, and *The Kingdom and the Beauty* in 1959.

6. Toshiaki Sato, *Japanese Film 1955–1964 Vol.1*, ed. Black & Blue (Tokyo: Neko Publishing, 1999), p. 48.

7. Tomo Uchida's version includes five sequels, namely *Miyamoto musashi, Hannyazaka no ketto, Nitoryu kaigan, Ichijoji no ketto,* and *Ganryujima no ketto,* in which the hero was played by Kinnosuke Nakamura.

8. The producers of *A Fistful of Dollars* were sued by Akira Kurosawa over its violation of the copyright of *The Bodyguard.* The issue was resolved with compensation to the Japanese party consisting of US$100,000, the distribution rights to *A Fistful of Dollars* in Japan, Taiwan and Korea, as well as 15% of the total box-office in the world.

9. "Theatres in Hong Kong", *Hong Kong Film Pictorial,* June 1968, p. 48.

10. Cheuk Pak-tong, "The Characteristics of Sixties Youth Movies", *The Restless Breed: Cantonese Stars of the Sixties,* ed. Law Kar (Hong Kong: The Urban Council, 1996), p. 73.

11. Sek Kei, "The Development of Martial Arts in Hong Kong Cinema", *A Study of the Hong Kong Martial Arts Film,* ed. Lau Shing-hon (Hong Kong: The Urban Council, 1980), p. 27.

12. Law Kar, "Crisis and Opportunity: Crossing Borders in Hong Kong Cinema, its Development from the 40s to the 70s", *Border Crossings in Hong Kong Cinema,* ed. Law Kar (Hong Kong: The Urban Council, 2000), p. 121.

13. Kentaro Yuasa was the martial arts instructor for *Three Samurai* (Hideo Gosha 1964).

14. Han Yingjie was a former Peking opera actor who appeared in *The Adventure of the 13th Sister,* and worked as Lin Dai's stunt double in *The Swallow Thief.* Elevated to the role of martial arts instructor in *Lady General Hua Mulan* (Yue Feng 1964), he acted in and helped choreograph King Hu's *wu xia pian* including *Come Drink with Me, Dragon Gate Inn* and *A Touch of Zen* (1971). He signed with Golden Harvest as martial arts instructor and actor in 1970, contributing to Bruce Lee's *The Big Boss* (Lo Wei 1971) and *Fist of Fury* (Lo Wei 1972).

15. Lau Kar-leung and Tong Kai were the leading combination in Hong Kong martial arts choreography. From collaborating on the Cantonese film *South Dragon, North Phoenix* (Wu Pang 1963), the pair went on to work in one of the earliest new-style Mandarin *wu xia pian, The Jade Bow* (Fu Qi and Zhang Xinyan 1965). They joined Shaw Brothers together in 1965. During the next ten years, they worked on most of Zhang Che's martial arts films.

16. King Hu, Koichi Yamada, Koyo Udagawa, *King Hu Bukyo Denei Saho* [The Martial Arts World of King Hu] (Tokyo: Soshi-sha, 1997), p. 92.

17. Zhang Che, "Creating the Martial Arts Film and the Hong Kong Cinema Style", *The Making of Martial Arts Film — As Told by Filmmakers and Stars,* ed. Hong Kong Film Archive (Hong Kong: Hong Kong Film Archive, 1999), p. 11.

18. Under the Chinese pseudonym Gong Muduo, Yukio Miyaki also worked on Zhang Che's *The Invincible Fist* (1969), *Dead End* (1969), *Have Sword, Will Travel* (1969), *Vengeance!* (1970), *The Heroic Ones* (1970), *King Eagle* (1971), *The New One-Armed Swordsman* (1971), *The Duel* (1971), *The Anonymous Heroes* (1971), *Duel of Fists* (1971), *The Deadly Duo* (1971), *Boxer from Shantung* (1972), *The Angry Guest* (1972), *The Water Margin* (1972), *Trilogy of Swordsmanship* (1972), *The Blood Brothers* (1973), *Heroes Two* (1974), *The Savage Five* (1974), *Shaolin Martial Arts* (1974), *Na Cha the Great* (1974), *Five Shaolin Masters* (1974), *Disciples of Shaolin* (1975), *The Fantastic Magic Baby* (1975), *Marco Polo* (1975), *Spiritual Fists* (1976), *Seven Man Army* (1976), *The Shaolin Avengers* (1976), *Shaolin Temple* (1976), *Magnificent Wanderers* (1977), *The Brave Archer* (1977), *The Five Venoms* (1978) and *Life Gamble* (1979).

19. Zhang Che, *The Hong Kong Cinema Retrospective in Thirty Years* (Hong Kong: Joint Publishing Co., 1989), p. 51.

20. According to Yu Mo-wan, the first Hong Kong kung fu movie is Hong Zhonghao's *Fang Shiyu's Battle in the Boxing Ring* (1938), with Xinma Shizeng as the leading hero. Yu Mo-wan, *The Hong Kong Film History, Vol. 2, 1930–1939* (Hong Kong: The Sub-culture Co., 1997), p. 182.

21. *Zhang Che — Memoirs & Film Critics*, ed. Wong Ainling (Hong Kong: Hong Kong Film Archive, 2002), p. 68.

22. Sek Kei, "The Development of Martial Arts in Hong Kong Cinema", p. 33.

23. Rokuro Kurata, *Hon Kon Denei Hyakka* [The Encyclopedia of Hong Kong Cinema] (Tokyo: Yoshiga Shoten, 1984), p. 126.

24. Kazuo Kuroi, "*Fist of Fury* — The Aesthetics in Bruce Lee's Movies", *Kinema Junpo*, ed. Yoshio Shirai (Tokyo: Kinema Junpo-sha), July 1974.

25. Kazuo Kuroi, "The Boom of Karate Movies", *Kinema Junpo*, ed. Yoshio Shirai (Tokyo: Kinema Junpo-sha), April 1974.

26. Koyo Udagawa, "From the Appearance of Bruce Lee to the Hong Kong Handover", *Hon Kon Denei Mankan Zenseki* [The Full Course of Hong Kong Cinema], ed. Nobukazu Uegusa (Tokyo: Kinema Junpo-sha), March 1997, p. 106.

27. The famous Japanese action star Shinichi Chiba [Sonny Chiba] has been involved in Hong Kong cinema since a Japan-Hong Kong co-production called *Golgo 13* (1977, Yukio Noda). One of his recent Hong Kong films was *Stormriders* (1998, Andrew Lau), in which he played the title role opposite Aaron Kwok and Ekin Cheng.

28. Another Japanese action star, Yasuaki Kuruta made his first appearance in a Hong Kong movie in 1972, when he played the title role opposite David Chiang and Di Long in Zhang Che's *The Angry Guest*. He has claimed that the film career of the *Nunchuk* (two pieces of wood attached by a string), a weapon from Okinawa, had its beginning when he gave a pair to Bruce Lee as a gift.

29. This series included *Gekitotsu! Satsujinken* (Shigehiro Osawa 1974), *Satsujinken II* (Shigehiro Osawa 1974), *Gyakusyu! Satsujinken* (Shigehiro Osawa 1974) and *Kozure satsujinken* (Kazuhiko Yamaguchi 1976).

30. This series included *Cyokugeki! Jigokuken* (Teruo Ishii 1974) and *Cyokugeki jigokuken daigyakuten* (Teruo Ishii 1974).

31. Kazuji Hagiwara "Japanese Cinema in Showa 30s", *Japanese Film 1955–1964 Vol. 1*, ed. Black & Blue (Tokyo: Neko Publishing , 1999), p. 9.

32. "Creating the Martial Arts Film and the Hong Kong Cinema Style", *The Making of Martial Arts Films — As Told by Filmmakers and Stars* ed. Hong Kong Film Archive (Hong Kong: Hong Kong Film Archive, 1999) p. 18.

33. Gu Long's works were broadly adapted by director Chor Yuen in the 1970s, with such films as *Killer Clans* (1976), *The Magic Blade* (1976), *Clans of Intrigue* (1977), *The Sentimental Swordsman* (1977), *Pursuit of Vengeance* (1977), *Clan of Amazons* (1978), *Legend of the Bat* (1978) and *The Proud Twins* (1979).

34. Leung Cheuk Fan, "The Lure of the Exotic — Hong Kong Cinema in Japan", *Border Crossings in Hong Kong Cinema,* ed. Law Kar (Hong Kong: The Urban Council, 2000), p. 156.

35. Rokuro Kurata, "The Top 15 Box-office among the Hong Kong Movies Released in Japan 1973–1983", *Hon Kon Denei Hyakka* [The Encyclopedia of Hong Kong Cinema] (Tokyo: Yoshiga Shoten, 1984), p. 132.

36. Yeung Yin Lin, "Understanding the Japanese Market of the 1980s — Interviewing Peter Lam and Lau Fong", *Border Crossings in Hong Kong Cinema,* ed. Law Kar (Hong Kong: The Urban Council, 2000), p. 150.

37. Yeung Yin Lin, p. 150.

CHAPTER 3

1. The title of one of Leo Ou-fan Lee's Chinese works is *Xiandaixing de zhuiqiu: Li Oufan wenhua pinglun jingxunji* [The quest for modernity: selections of Leo Ou-fan Lee's cultural criticism] (Taipei: Rye Field, 1996).

2. *The Pierre Berton Show,* Canadian Broadcasting Corporation, aired in Hong Kong, 1971.

3. The battleship *Yamato* was re-imagined in a hit sci-fi anime *Uchuusenkan Yamato* [Universe Battleship Yamato] by the famous Reiji Miyamoto (the TV series premiered in 1974, the film version in 1976). In this connection, it is worth recalling that in Steven Spielberg's *Empire of the Sun* (1987) the expatriate English boy trapped in the foreign enclave of Shanghai during World War Two precisely fetishizes the Zero, not the Hurricane or the Spitfire.

4. This comparative study will require full-scale research. It is often fruitful to compare and contrast the historical and cultural experience of China and that of other Asian countries in our attempt to understand our modern history.

Many historical studies have compared China's mid-nineteenth century Self-Strengthening Movement with Japan's Meiji Restoration. I have elsewhere examined the representation of the traditional "family" in a modern Chinese novel and a Japanese novel both bearing the same title "The Family": see my "The 'Family' Under Western Threat: (Dis)continuity of Cultural Tradition in Ba Jin's *Jia* and Shimazaki Tôson's *Ie*." *The Comparatist* 19 (May 1995): 114–33.

5. All translations from movie dialogue are my own. I base my translations on the original Cantonese track and render them as literally as possible for the purpose of critical analysis.

6. For further elaboration, see Siu Leung Li, "Kung Fu: Negotiating Nationalism and Modernity." *Cultural Studies* 15:3/4 (July 2001): 515–42.

7. Ibid.

8. According to Sek Kei's review of *Matrix Reloaded* in *Ming Pao,* 26 May 2003.

9. For Wong's account of technological thinking in and through kung fu, see his essay in this volume.

10. A remark made at the international conference *Hong Kong Connections: Translation Imagination in Action Cinema,* 6–9 January 2003, organized by the Department of Cultural Studies, Lingnan University, Hong Kong.

11. I owe this idea to Professor Laleen Jayamanne.

12. Stephen Teo, "The True Way of the Dragon: The Films of Bruce Lee." *Overseas Chinese Figures in Cinema* (Hong Kong: The Urban Council, 1992), 70–1 (emphasis added except last).

13. Jackie Chan said in a radio interview that the special effects of *Stormriders* "belonged to the kindergarten level" [*shu youzhiyuan jishu*]. This was reported by every major newspaper in Hong Kong. I am quoting from the entertainment news coverage in *Apple Daily* and *Wenhui Bao* of 23 August 1998. Chan's remarks incited much debate in the media and on the Internet.

CHAPTER 4

1. See, for example, the famous recollection by the former director of the Xin Hua News Agency (Beijing's official representative) in late-colonial Hong Kong after his defection to the US: Xu Jiatun, *Memories of Xu Jiatun,* 2 vols. (Taipei: Lian-ching, 1993).

2. Marilyn D. Mintz, *The Martial Arts Films* (1978; reprinted Rutland, Vermont and Tokyo: Charles E. Tuttle, 1983), p. 171–2.

3. Mintz, p. 172.

4. Mintz, p. 172.

5. Chen Mo, "Reconsiderations of the Early Chinese *Wuxia* Cinema", *Contemporary Cinema* (No. 1, 1997).

6. Chen Mo, p. 38.

7. Mintz, p. 145.

8. See, for an excellent introduction to and discussion of Tsui Hark's hybrid narration about the national identification of Hong Kong people: Stephen Teo, *Hong Kong Cinema: The Extra Dimensions* (London: BFI, 1997), pp. 162–74; also see Teo, "Tsui Hark: National Style and Polemic", in *At Full Speed: Hong Kong Cinema in a Borderless World*, ed. Esther C. M. Yau (Minneapolis and London: University of Minnesota Press, 2001), pp. 143–58.

9. Huang Xilin, "The Integration of Spectacle and Nationality: Traditional Nationalist Culture in Hong Kong *Wuxia* Cinema", *Journal of Wuzhou Teachers College of Guang Xi* 14.3 (Oct. 1998), p. 40.

10. Mintz, p. 208.

11. Lau Tai-muk, "Conflict and Desire: Dialogues Between the Hong Kong Martial Arts Genre and Social Issues in the Past 40 years", trans. Tsang Hin-koon, in *The Making of Martial Arts Films as told by Filmmakers and Stars, ed. Hong Kong Film Archive* (Hong Kong: Provisional Urban Council, 1999), p. 33.

12. Mintz, p. 181.

13. Zhang Che, "Creating the Martial Arts Film and the Hong Kong Cinema Style", trans. Stephen Teo, in *The Making of Martial Arts Film as told by Filmmakers and Stars*, p. 21.

14. In a *Ming Pao Monthly* article published in May 1998, titled "Hong Kong's Anti-Establishment Movies and the Mass Movement", Law Kar wrote: "Zhang Che's movie characters are young swordsmen, assassins, martyrs and death-defying fanatics. His heroes are tragic men who defy authority and the establishment. 'At the time, people called my movies "violent" and "bloody". I always thought this was a very shallow way of looking at my movies'" (pp. 21–22) (My translation).

15. See Barbara Ryan, "Blood, Brothers, and Hong Kong Gangster Movies: Pop Culture Commentary on 'One China,'" in *Asian Popular Culture*, ed. John A. Lent (Boulder, San Francisco, and Oxford: Westview Press, 1995), pp. 612–76. "It is significant that these posings are characterized by male-male intimacy and by the desire for friendship — and that they always end up with their heroes bathed in [the] brothers' bright red blood" (p. 74).

16. For a detailed reading of *Ashes of Time*, see my "Figures of Hope and the Filmic Imaginary of *Jianghu* in Contemporary Hong Kong Cinema", *Cultural Studies*, 15:3–4 (2001), pp. 486–514.

17. Michael Hardt and Antonio Negri, *Empire* (Cambridge, Mass. and London: Harvard University Press, 2000), p. 45.

18. Mintz, p. 85.

19. Mintz, p. 187.

20. "The better framework, then, to designate the distinction between the global and the local might refer to different networks of flows and obstacles in which the local moment or perspective gives priority to the reterritorializing barriers or boundaries and the global moment privileges the mobility of deterritorializing flows. It is false, in any case, to claim that we can (re)establish local identities that are in some sense *outside* and protected against the global flows of capital and Empire" (Hardt and Negri, p. 45).

21. Johan Fornäs, "The Crucial in Between: The Centrality of Mediation in Cultural Studies", *European Journal of Cultural Studies*, 3.1 (2000), p. 54. "What texts do is certainly as important as what they say, but what makes the discursive work of text specifically *cultural* is that it is mainly fulfilled precisely by their signifying force of saying something to someone. *The power of culture is anchored in a capability to induce meaning, which makes interpretation the clue to critique*" (p. 49, original emphasis).

22. See Stephen Teo's essay in this volume for a full discussion of the issue.

23. Law Kar, "Who's Afraid of Hollywood?", *Film Art* (*Dianying yishu*) 2 (2001), pp. 30–32.

24. For another discussion of some such works in Hong Kong cinema from a similar perspective, with a special focus on female action, see my article "Burst into Action: The Changing Spectacle of Glamour Heroines in Contemporary Hong Kong Cinema", *Cultural Studies Review*, 10.1 (2004), pp. 11–26.

25. Mintz, p. 139.

26. The editorial commentary published in the *Oriental Daily* (8 November 1996), signed by "The Oriental Tea House" entitled "Long Live the Chinese" reads:

    We have to ask … why the Americans could put up their national flag on the Moon about 30 years ago, and it is still there, and the Chinese couldn't even put up their own/our own flag in a place so close to home; it only stood there [at Diao-yu Islands] for 10 minutes? [We want to have 10 years, 10 centuries!]

    National super-star BRUCE LEE made the film *Fist of Fury*

    In the (1972) film (called *The Chinese Connection* when released in USA) he smashed the board with the words "The Sick Man of East Asia" into pieces with his famous Bruce Lee kicks. We need to think hard about why such a scene can appear only in the kung fu movie, while in real life, whenever we have a chance to fight a war, the opposite SCENARIO would often be seen … [If *good old Bruce Lee* were alive today, what would he have to say?] (My translation)

27. "(King) Hu once said: "I've always seen the action part of my films as dancing rather than fighting … A lot of people … have remarked that my action scenes are sometimes 'authentic', sometimes not. In point of fact, they're always keyed to the notion of dance".

28. For a schematic outline of the local, national and transnational as constituents in an analytical framework for Hong Kong culture, see my discussion first presented in "Mapping the Global Popular in Hong Kong: Re-Articulations of the Local, National and Transnational in Contemporary Cultural Flows", in *Re-Inventing Hong Kong in the Age of Globalization*, eds. Yee Leung et al. (Hong Kong: Chung Chi College & Faculty of Social Sciences, The Chinese University of Hong Kong, 2002), pp. 47–52.

29. Law Kar, "Who's Afraid of Hollywood?", p. 31.

30. The now well-known notion of the "political unconscious" has been given

a definitive treatment by Fredric Jameson, *The Political Unconscious: Narrative as a Socially Symbolic Act* (Ithaca: Cornell University Press, 1991).

31. Cf. Miriam Hansen's view on modernity in her remarks on Benjamin's aesthetic as the doctrine of perception: "What he sees as the major struggle in modernity is the struggle for the integrity, the functioning and the ecology of the human senses as the main political organ that we have, that society has ... So in that sense the aesthetic for Benjamin was deeply political". Hansen as quoted in an interview by Laleen Jayamanne and Anne Rutherford, "'The Future of Cinema Studies in the Age of Global Media': Aesthetic, Spectatorship and Public Spheres", *UTS Review: Cultural Studies and New Writing*, 5.1 (1999), p. 107.

32. There are, to be sure, a few great moments of exception to this general tendency: the support for the Beijing students by over a million Hong Kong people marching on the streets in June 1989, the outbreak of atypical pneumonia (or SARS) in the spring of 2003, and the massive demonstrations by approximately 500,000 of the population on 1 July (the HKSAR anniversary day) in both 2003 and 2004.

CHAPTER 5

1. Mainland film people call Hong Kong action movies "Tsui Hark Films", because on the Mainland in the 1980s the view was that the director played the main creative role in shaping a film. Even granting the truth of this view, however, the name is not quite appropriate. Only a few of the films associated with Tsui Hark were actually directed by him; for most he was a screenwriter, a producer, or an adviser. Nevertheless, Tsui Hark was a leading force in the new and dynamic Hong Kong action movies in the late 1980s and early 1990s.

2. Wang Shuo, "My Way of Looking at Hong Kong and Taiwan Cultures", in *Fearless Are the Ignorant* (Beijing: Huayi chubanshe, 2000).

3. In martial arts novels, such necessary suffering usually follows one of two models: 1) the protagonist is framed or misunderstood, and therefore is rejected by his martial arts master or other good people; 2) the protagonist is seriously injured and captured because of a promise or commitment to a just cause, and his injury affects his martial arts skills. Either way, in the end the protagonist meets a grand master during his suffering; and through hard training under the grand master the protagonist finally achieves glory as a martial arts hero.

4. Here I am referring to the new martial arts movies, which are not re-adaptations of traditional martial arts fiction. Films based on the rewriting of martial arts novels, such as those by Jin Yong, still maintain certain masochistic elements in the portrait of the suffering of the main protagonist.

CHAPTER 6

1. Chuck Stephens, *Village Voice,* March 27, 2002.
2. Sigmund Freud, 'The Uncanny", in *The Standard Edition of the Complete Psychological Work of Sigmund Freud,* ed. trans. James Strachey, vol. xvii (London: Hogarth,1953), pp. 217–56.
3. W. E. B. Du Bois's model of double consciousness appeared in *The Souls of Black Folk* (New York: Bantam, 1989). He discussed African-American people's sense of double consciousness as a sense of looking at one's self through the other's gaze. I borrow this term to connect with Benedict Anderson's notion of doubled vision (specter of comparisons); see n.4 below. The double vision interestingly overlaps with the Freudian "uncanny" in a sense of the oscillation between the familiar and the unfamiliar.
4. However, the relation of the Korean series to the Japanese model so influential in Hong Kong was more oblique for reasons I discuss below.
5. Benedict Anderson, *The Spectre of Comparisons: Nationalism, Southeast Asia and the World* (London and New York: Verso, 1998).
6. Anderson, p. 2.
7. Unlike China and Japan, Korea has not had a long history of a group-based or private soldiering or martial arts training since the beginning of the Choson dynasty, because the first Choson king forbade private soldiering out of fear of a revolt similar to that he had successfully launched against the Koryo dynasty. The disciplined bodies trained in fighting and soldiering were governed only by the state. This partly explains the absence in Korea of novels and stories that would be equivalent to the *wuxia* swordplay novels and samurai stories that provided the material for *wuxia* swordplay films and samurai films.
8. Mary Louse Pratt, *Imperial Eyes: Travel Writing and Transculturation* (London: Routledge, 1992), p. 6.
9. Nick Browne, "Preface", in Nick Browne (ed.), *Refiguring American Film Genres* (Berkeley: University of California Press, 1998), p. xi.
10. Linda Williams, "Melodrama Revised", *Refiguring American Film Genres,* Ibid. p. 42.
11. The Continental *Hwalkuk* produced male stars like Chang Donghui, Hur Jangkang and Hwang Wang Hae from the mid-1960s on, stars who would later appear in 1970s action movies as middle-aged fighters.
12. The auteur cinema was led by filmmakers like Yu Hyonmok, Kim Ki-young and Shin Sang-ok (Simon Sheen).
13. I thank Kim Kihyon for alerting me to this.
14. According to King Hu's filmography he made two films (*Raining in the Mountain* and *Legend of the Mountain*) in 1979 that overlapped with the production date of *Wandering Monk*. Since these two films were shot in Korea, one could speculate that *Wandering Monk* was shot in line with them.
15. It should be noted that a number of productions relating to Hong Kong were

made both before and after the 1970s. Examples include *SOS Hong Kong* (1966), and *Fist of Fury* (1981). But an action movie fan-turned-filmmaker, O. Seunguk warns us that most of the so-called Hong Kong–Korea co-productions were fakes. To procure permission to import foreign films, Korean film companies used existing clips from Hong Kong action movies in their films as proof of co-production. This resulted in incredibly incoherent action movies that suddenly change locations and major characters.

16. In 1999 *Shiri*, a blockbuster in the Korean mode, repeated some elements from *Golden 70 Hong Kong Mission* — the partition-provoked espionage, the affair between the South and North Korean agents, the cosmetic surgery and resultant mistaken identities, and the final elimination of the North Korean female agent. *Golden 70 Hong Kong* is an obvious displacement of the tension between the two states (the North and the South) onto the city of Hong Kong, where the alleged rivalry between China and Hong Kong and that between the North and the South finds its mediator in the form of America. Contemporary action movies in the Korean blockbuster mode are mostly set in the present. The regionalism of *Paldo Sanai* in the 1970s is reworked in *Chingu* (*Friends*, 2000). Commercially unsuccessful action movies such as *Phantom: The Submarine*, *Musa* (2001), and *Lost Memories 2009* (2002) indicate that movies harking back to the past do not succeed in the market. The ambivalence of the uncanny double consciousness seems to disappear in the era of the global, which is characterized by the blockbuster in the Korean mode.

17. I thank Stephen Teo for sharing his insight.

18. Whereas action movies set outside South Korea largely function to provide a space of decolonization, it is melodrama that responds more directly to the industrialization process. *The Prime Time of Yongja* (Yongjaui Jonsongshidae) is a 1970s hostess melodrama. It includes a scene where the protagonist Yongja loses one arm while working as a bus conductor. Unlike the one-legged man, who becomes an enhanced hero after losing his leg, she ends up in the sex industry, which rapidly proliferated in the 1970s under the euphemistic slogan of the "3 S" (sex, sports, and screen). As the textile industry based upon female labor was the leading industry of the time, it was melodrama that depicted the female migrant workers' downfall into the sex industry.

19. *Snake Crane Flying Fist*, a.k.a. *Sahak Palbo*, *Snake and Crane Arts of Shaolin Sau Hok Baat Biu*, Dir. Chan Jeung Wa, 1978.

20. The martial arts actors of the 1970s often note that the most memorable moments of their career as action stars were spent in beautiful places like Sorak Mountain, where the Korean action star Jung Dong Sub recalls acting with Wong Ho, and Pulkuk Temple in Kyongju, recalled by Cho Chun.

21. As a minor footnote, it should be noted that the choreography of the Snake and Crane martial arts technique and other techniques do not involve a recognizably Korean taekwondo style. Thus, in terms of unconscious optics, the landscape becomes more interesting than the style of action.

22. Cho, Jeonghwan, "Vitality, Power, and Violence", in *Jayul Pyungron* (Self Regulating Criticism), 1(3), 12, 2002.

CHAPTER 7

1. The Telugu film industry is the second largest (after Hindi) in India. The Telugu-speaking state of Andhra Pradesh is the largest market for film, including Hong Kong film, in the country.

2. David Bordwell, *Planet Hong Kong: Popular Cinema and the Art of Entertainment* (Cambridge, Mass and London: Harvard University Press: 1999), p. 178.

3. I have suggested elsewhere that this influence is not limited to film but also includes popular print literature and went on to argue that the neighbourhood martial arts school is to Hong Kong film what the film star's fans' association is to Telugu film. See S. V. Srinivas, "Hong Kong Action Film in the Indian B Circuit", *Inter-Asia Cultural Studies* 4:1 (2003), pp. 40–62.

4. Interestingly he does not recall the name of the film (probably *Enter the Dragon*), which resulted in the epiphany (Srihari, interviewed by G. L. N. Reddy, 27 February 2003, Hyderabad).

5. This is not to claim that the narrative is the indigenous core of the cinema in India. The strange sense of familiarity I have had with a number of films by Wong Jing, even as I watched them for the very first time, suggests to me that the typical "Indian" commercial film may not be so unique after all. My point about the narrative and borrowings however holds good.

6. Van Damme's close association with films that are more or less directly inspired by the Hong Kong action film is of course well known; see for example, Meaghan Morris, "Learning from Bruce Lee: Pedagogy and Political Correctness in Martial Arts Cinema" in Mathew Tinkcom and Amy Villarejo, eds., *Keyframes: Popular Cinema and Cultural Studies* (London and New York: Routledge, 2001), pp. 171–86.

7. As with a number of film industry categories, the English phrase "mass-film" or "mass-chitram" (film) is used to refer this generic entity. There are obvious difficulties in calling the mass-film a "genre" since the category of the mass-film includes a variety of tendencies that might themselves be termed genres: certain "action" films, ruralist melodramas, the occasional western and costume drama. Insofar as it is a supra-generic entity, rather than a genre in the usual sense of the term, the mass-film is similar to the category of the "social", which in Indian cinema has served as the broad category for describing a whole range of films set in contemporary times and dealing with "social issues". Madhava Prasad argues that the social effectively *prevented* the development of individual genres at a time when the industry was interested in ensuring that the audience was not disaggregated; see his *Ideology of the Hindi Film: A Historical Construction* (New Delhi: Oxford

University Press, 1998, 117–37). The crucial difference between the social and the mass-film is that in the recent past the latter has begun to resemble a conventional genre with the Telugu film industry preferring increased product differentiation. The social, in contrast, disappears with the emergence of generic distinctions.

8. Paul Willemen, "Action Cinema, Labour Power and the Video Market", this volume. It is, however, doubtful whether Indian film industries are *industrialized* enough to be able to predict the profit-making potential of a film or even able to successfully predict the final outcome of what is being put together. This takes us back to the question of whether we have genres in Indian cinemas. Nevertheless Willemen's category of "production genre" is useful to understand how the mass-film might differ from other generic formations/tendencies.

9. NTR established the Telugu Desam Party in 1982 and was elected chief minister of Andhra Pradesh in 1983. Andhra Pradesh thus became the second state in southern India, after Tamilnadu, to be governed by a film star turned politician. There has been much discussion on cinema and politics in south India. For the most insightful cinema-centred argument yet, see Madhava Prasad, "Cine-Politics: On the Political Significance of Cinema in South India", *Journal of the Moving Image*. No. 1 (Autumn, 1999). pp. 37–52.

10. Prasad, *Ideology of the Hindi Film*, pp. 138–59.

11. A section of the film industry sought to engage with the question of linguistic identity by incorporating what the industry calls *nativity*. The English term itself is used to connote a range of attempts by the south Indian film industries to create a diegetic space that is at once distinct from and related to the (Indian) "national" one. Nativity is a crucial site for the often-difficult negotiation between linguistic identity and particularity of the local and the larger Indian nation-state. Nativity is closely associated with a certain variety of realist melodrama in Telugu and Tamil cinema of the 1970s and 1980s. Arguments have been made about nativity being an important source of realistic presentation. However, nativity is also used to denote a less contested and more loosely defined notion of the local (scenes of rural life, for example).

The two modes of dealing with identity — one founded on the deployment of the male star and the other relying on themes and settings — had emerged as distinct tendencies, at times in direct conflict with each other. Simultaneously there was a division of labour with reference to the mandate to represent "Telugu-ness". Mass-film was thus seen as being devoid of nativity, which was left to the middlebrow "class film". This despite the fact that nativity has been an important consideration even in the mass-film. In an examination of Tamil cinema, Sundar Kaali makes a distinction between the "Old Nativity Film" and the "Neo-Nativity Film"; "Narrating Seduction: Vicissitudes of the Sexed Subject in Tamil Nativity Film" in Ravi S. Vasudevan, ed., *Making Meaning in Indian Cinema* (New Delhi: Oxford University Press, 2000), pp. 168–90.

Although Kaali's argument is interesting, it is not of direct relevance to my analysis of the mass-film. Suffice it to say that nativity is historically specific and has undergone substantial changes over the years.

12. Ashish Rajadhyaksha, "Viewership and Democracy in the Cinema" in Ravi S. Vasudevan, ed. *Making Meaning in Indian Cinema* (New Delhi: Oxford University Press. 2000), p. 283. Emphasis original.

13. In an amazing attempt to construct a spectator in the know, the film *Big Boss* (Vijay Bapineedu, 1994, no connection with the Bruce Lee film of the same name) has a lengthy sequence in which the hero of the film (Chiranjeevi) is "mistaken" as the star himself by a petty shopkeeper who plays the role of a fan of the star Chiranjeevi!

14. I am grateful to Meaghan Morris and the other participants in the Hong Kong Connections conference for drawing attention to what seemed to be an obvious preference on the filmmaker's part.

15. The petty crooks, played by Mallikarjuna Rao and Kota Srinivasa Rao who are both famous for their comic roles, transform themselves into sidekicks of Bhadrachalam in the final segment of the film. Crucially, they become diegetic spectators of the hero's transformation.

16. More often in the early part of the film but also throughout the film, a variety of techniques are deployed to address the spectator in rather direct ways. The male star is generally privileged to look at the camera, to wink at it, to salute it, wave at it and even talk to it at crucial points in the film.

17. I am grateful to Paul Willemen for pointing out the true significance of the sequence to me.

18. When a mass-film is screened in the cinema hall the whistles of viewers greeting the star upon his first appearance actually begin a few seconds *before* the star can be seen on screen.

19. The argument is best demonstrated by citing an example from the devotional film, a genre that was revived around the time the mass-film went into a decline. A more detailed discussion is not possible here but see for example *Ammoru* ("Mother Goddess", Kodi Ramakrishna 1995), in which the goddess intervenes in the spectacular climax in precisely the manner that the mass-film's star-protagonist does, not merely by performing a similar role — saving the heroine — but also responding to the spectator's expectation.

20. I advance the argument about Hong Kong cinema hesitantly because the version I have access to might differ substantially from those that circulate in other parts of the world. In the unlikely event that there is a substantial difference, my argument degenerates into a statement of the obvious since the Indian version is certainly modelled on what is locally available.

21. Ng Ho, "Kung-fu Comedies: Tradition, Structure, Character" in *A Study of the Hong Kong Martial Arts Film*, 4th Hong Kong International Film Festival (Hong Kong: Urban Council of Hong Kong, 1980), p. 43.

22. S. V. Srinivas, "Telugu Folklore Films: The Case of *Patala Bhairavi*", *Deep Focus: A Film Quarterly* 9:1 (2001), pp. 45–51.

23. *Snake in the Monkey's Shadow* (Cheung Sum 1979), remarkably similar in terms of plot to *Snake in the Eagle's Shadow*, has a similar credit sequence in which the hero is shown exhibiting his expertise in kung fu by beating three other fighters. Here too it is not till much later that the hero masters kung fu.
24. Ashish Rajadhyaksha, "Viewership and Democracy in the Cinema".

CHAPTER 8

1. The term "martial art film" is here deliberately vague because, for reasons that will become evident below, it refers to Indian perceptions of martial arts in Asian cinemas, rather than to specific types of martial art schools and Hong Kong film traditions.
2. Kaushik Bhaumik, *The Emergence of the Bombay Film Industry 1913–1936* (Oxford: Ph.D. dissertation, Oxford University, 2001), p. 28.
3. See, for instance, Kishore Valicha, *The Moving Image. A Study of Indian Cinema* (Hyderabad: Orient Longman, 1988), p. 67; Fereeduddin Kazmi, "How Angry is the Angry Young Man? 'Rebellion' in Conventional Hindi Films" in Ashish Nandy (ed.), *The Secret Politics of Our Desires: Innocence, Culpability and Indian Popular Cinema* (Delhi: Oxford University Press, 1998), p. 139; Ashwani Sharma, "Blood Sweat and Tears: Amitabh Bachchan, Urban Demi-god" in Pat Kirkham and Janet Thumin (eds), *You Tarzan: Masculinity, Movies and Men* (London: Lawrence & Wishart, 1993), pp. 169–71. These studies dedicate no more than a *pro forma* paragraph to the socio-economic context of the Bachchan action films, the remaining several pages focusing entirely on the star and the hero. Even in Rashmi Doraiswamy, "Les Genres dans le Cinema Indien" in *Cinem-Action: Panorama des Genres du Cinema* (1993–1994); in Siddharta Basu, Sanjay Kak and Pradip Krishen, "Cinema and Society: A Search for Meaning in a New Genre" in *India International Centre Quarterly* vol. 8, no. 1 (1980); in Wimal Dissanayake, "The Concept of Evil and Social Order in Indian Melodrama: an Evolving Dialectic" in *Melodrama and Asian Cinema* (Cambridge: Cambridge University Press, 1993); and in Wimal Dissanayake and M. Sahai, *Sholay: A Cultural Reading* (Delhi: Wiley Eastern, 1992), where the writers attempt more systematic approaches to generic patterns, the focus remains the hero and the star, who are compared to earlier types and actors (Doraiswamy and Dissanayake) or provide the starting point for the identification of narrative structures (Basu, Kak and Krishen, and Dissanayake).
4. David Desser, "The Martial Arts Film in the 1990s" in Winston Dixon Wheeler (ed.), *Film Genre 2000: New Critical Essays* (Albany: SUNY Press, 2000), uses the starring of acknowledged martial artists as distinguishing criteria between US action and martial arts. The artist's role as the star is seen by Desser to have an impact on the narratives, settings and motifs of the films themselves.

5. Peter Bürger, *Theory of the Avant-Garde* Translated by Michael Shaw (Minneapolis: University of Minnesota Press, 1984), and, by the same author, "Some Reflections upon the Historico-Sociological Explanation of the Aesthetics of Genius in the Eighteenth-Century" in *The Decline of Modernism* (Cambridge: Polity Press, 1992), pp. 57–69.

6. Sudhir Kakar, *Intimate Relations: Exploring Indian Sexuality* (Chicago: The University of Chicago Press, 1989), p. 28.

7. Giovanni Arrighi, "World Income Inequalities and the Future of Socialism" in *New Left Review* 189 (1991), pp. 39–66. See also Robert Brenner "The Economics of Global Turbulence" in *New Left Review* 229 (1998).

8. Giovanni Arrighi, "The African Country: World Systemic and Regional Aspects" in *New Left Review* 15 (2002), pp. 5–32.

9. Partha Chatterjee, "Indian Democracy and Bourgeois Reaction" in *A Possible India: Essays in Political Criticism* (Delhi: Oxford University Press , 1997), pp. 35–57.

10. Achin Vanaik, *The Painful Transition: Bourgeois Democracy in India* (London/New York: Verso, 1990).

11. Jayant Lele, "Saffronisation of Shiv Sena: Political Economy of City, State, Nation" in *Economic and Political Weekly* (24 June 1995), pp. 1520–1528, p. 1521.

12. Vanaik, Op. cit., p. 36. See also Heather Joshi, "The Informal Urban Economy and Its Boundaries" in *Economic and Political Weekly* (March 1980), pp. 638–644.

13. See Manjunath Pendakur, "Dynamics of Cultural Policy Making: The US Film Industry in India" in *Journal of Communication* 4 (Autumn 1985), pp. 52–72. Although dated, Pendakur's remains one of the most informed accounts of the US presence on the Indian market.

14. David A. Cook, *History of the American Cinema* Vol. 9: *Lost Illusions: American Cinema in the Shadow of Watergate and Vietnam, 1970–1979* (Berkeley, CA: University of California Press, 2000).

15. Manjunath Pendakur, Op. cit., argues that a share of the US majors' "blocked funds" was used by the NFDC to sponsor Indian national film production. In reality, the funds' "true" nationality is irrelevant: for all intents and purposes "blocked funds" were monies at the disposal of the Indian government to use as it saw fit, including, but not exclusively, the centralised distribution of foreign films and the production of Indian films.

16. Recent work by S. V. Srinivas has gone a considerable way towards mapping the interchanges between South Indian action and Hong Kong martial arts films. See S. V. Srinivas, "Hong Kong Action film in the Indian B Circuit" in *Inter-Asia Cultural Studies*, Vol. 4, No. 1 (2003), pp. 40–62.

17. Madhava M. Prasad, *The State and Culture: Hindi Cinema in the Passive Revolution* (Pittsburg: Ph.D. dissertation for the University of Pittsburgh, 1994), p. 68; published as *Ideology of the Hindi Film: A Historical Construction* (Delhi: Oxford University Press, 1998).

18. The S. K. Patil Film Inquiry Committee would thus observe that the producer's dependence on distributor and exhibitors for financing the film "led the producer to concentrate on the particular aspects of the picture which would appeal to the distributors and help in securing a quick sale or a good price. […] distributors make 'suggestions" in regard to the story and sometimes about the song and tunes. Considering the financial relation between producer and distributor, such 'suggestions' are generally taken as mandatory by the producer. […] Distributors appear to have been ultimately responsible for the temporary success of some 'stars' […] [and] appear to have been at least partly responsible for the establishment of certain 'cycles' in film-making, resulting in the production of a dozen different variations of a theme." (*Report of the Film Enquiry Committee,* New Delhi: Govt. of India Press, 1951), pp. 116–17.

19. For an account of the importance of exhibitors in the early days of Indian cinema, see Bhaumik, Op. cit.

20. Erik Barnouw and S. Krishnaswamy, *Indian Film,* Second Edition (New Delhi: Oxford University Press, 1980), p. 145.

21. Ibid. p. 145.

22. Ibid. p. 57.

23. Prasad, Op. cit. p. 88.

24. The Film Advisory Board held the monopoly of raw stock and produced educational documentaries, war propaganda and the newsreel *Indian News Parade.*

25. Entertainment tax was introduced by the British Raj in 1922 and first levied on exhibitors in Calcutta and Bombay, then the two centres of film production. Subsequent tax rises were introduced in 1944 and again by Nehru's independent government in 1949. Finally, in 1969 Indira Gandhi's Information and Broadcasting minister, I. K. Gujral, announced that the film industry's ongoing demands for reduction of entertainment tax would be considered seriously if the industry was willing to pay a "social tax" instead (Prasad, Op. cit. pp. 227–28). Until the 1990s entertainment tax amounted to an average of 60 per cent of a film's revenues, with lower peaks in regions where the state government undertook efforts to promote the local film industry. Entertainment tax is levied on the basis of tickets sold. It is common practice for exhibitors to sell a ticket twice, thus effectively halving the amount due as tax.

26. See, for instance, Prasad, Op. cit.

27. Prasad, Op. cit., gives an illuminating account of the industry's mixed reaction to government intervention and to FFC-NFDC policies.

28. In 1971 India produced 433 feature films, making it the world's largest film producer. Throughout the 1970s exports to the Middle East, Africa, Asia, the USSR, Latin America and the UK rose significantly: gross revenues from export of feature films grew from RS 55 million in 1973 to RS 150 million in the peak year of 1980, after which they started to decline. Although no breakdowns are available as to the share of Hindi films in all Indian exports, most Indian films

available abroad are Hindi films. See Manjunath Pendakur, "India" in John Lent (ed.), *The Asian Film Industry* (London: Christopher Helm: 1990), p. 239.

29. The salary of a top director rose by 300 per cent (from RS 1 million to RS 3 million) and that of a top music director from RS 400,000 to RS 800,000. Action choreographers saw the biggest relative pay increase (from RS 15,000 in 1975 to 100,000 in 1985) but remain still significantly lower than that of stars. By contrast, extras received RS 22 a day in 1975 and RS 37 in 1985. Ibid. pp. 231–32.

30. Ibid. pp. 231–32.

31. Manjunath Pendakur, "New Cultural Technologies and the Fading Glitter of Indian Cinema" in *Quarterly Review of Film and Video* Vol. 11 (1989), pp. 69–78, p. 70.

32. In a feature review entitled "A Poor Crop", *Cinema Vision India* wrote: "there was this 'germ', carrying on almost clandestinely. Now it has become an epidemic seemingly out of control. It could even destroy the Punjabi cinema! Crudities, vulgarities and double-meaning dialogue [...] abound in Punjabi films today. These films have gathered a fan-audience that includes the uneducated urban-class, drop-outs, idlers and loafers. These kind[s] of films not only debase public taste, [but] corrode society and morals. These films have alienated the educated Punjabi, the older generation, families and the women-audience who otherwise flocked to theaters screening Punjabi films." *Cinema Vision India* Vol.1 No. 3 (July 1980), p. 55–57.

33. Ashish Rajadhyaksha and Paul Willemen (eds) *Encyclopedia of Indian Cinema* Revised Edition (London and New Delhi: British Film Institute and Oxford University Press, 1999).

34. "Amitabh Bachchan walks across the screen like Alice in Wonderland" in *Film World* Vol. 8 No. 3 (May 1972); "Amitabh is lifeless." in *Film World* Vol. 8 No. 7 (September 1972); "Amitabh looks like a patient of insomnia." in *Film World* Vol. 8 No. 8 (November 1972).

35. Ranjani Mazumdar, "From Subjectification to Schizophrenia: The 'Angry Man' and the 'Psychotic' Hero of Bombay Cinema" in Ravi Vasudevan (ed) *Making Meaning in Indian Cinema* (Delhi: Oxford University Press, 2000), p. 247.

36. A similar dynamic can be traced around the stardom of Clint Eastwood, whose performances Pauline Kael criticised as "wooden".

CHAPTER 9

1. Miscegenation has a specific history in Hollywood cinema: the Production Code introduced in the early 1930s prohibited the representation of sexual relations between whites and other races. The memory of this racist rule is important to this essay written at a time when the mingling of races is an emerging characteristic in global culture. This essay is concerned with minglings that have a neuralgic component.

2. "Who Needs Cultural Research?" Lingnan University — Centre for Cultural Research (UWS) Joint Workshop, University of Western Sydney, Parramatta Campus, 22 July 2002. See "Comparative Cultural Research: Hong Kong/ Western Sydney Exchange", http://www.uws.edu.au/research/ researchcentres/ccr/partnerships/lingnanuniversity/.

3. Gilles Deleuze, "Bergson's Conception of Difference" in *The New Bergson*, ed. John Mullarkey, Manchester, UK: University of Manchester, 1999, p. 43.

4. Laleen Jayamanne, "Above and Beyond One's Cultural Heritage; Jackie Chan and his Drunken Master", in *Above and Beyond: Austral/Asian Interactions*, ed. Michael Snelling, Brisbane, Australia: Institute of Modern Art, 1996, pp. 12–16.

5. Lynette Clementson, *Far Eastern Economic Review*, 159/11, 14 March 1996, p. 46.

6. Laleen Jayamanne, "A Slapstick Time: Mimetic Convulsion, Convulsive Knowing" in *Toward Cinema and Its Double: Cross-Cultural Mimesis*, Bloomington: Indiana University Press, 2001, p. 183.

7. See Steve Fore's "Life imitates entertainment; home and dislocation in the films of Jackie Chan" in *At Full Speed: Hong Kong Cinema in a Borderless World*, ed. Esther C. M. Yau, Minneapolis: University of Minnesota Press, 2001, pp. 115–41, for details on Chan's astute transnational production moves, especially in the mid to late 1990s.

8. See Melissa McMahon's "Beauty; Machinic repetition in the age of art" in *A Shock to Thought: Expression after Deleuze and Guattari* ed. Brian Massumi, London: Routledge, 2002, p. 6, for an elaboration of this Bergsonian-Deleuzean concept.

9. I am referring to Yung Sai-shing's chapter "Moving Body: The Interactions Between Chinese Opera and Action Cinema", included in this volume.

10. "Any-object-whatever" is my idea in response to Chan's ability to transform objects into something other than what they were meant for by misusing them. This notion was developed by thinking of the Deleuzean idea of "any-space-whatever" and the Bergsonian idea of "any-instant-whatever". See Gilles Deleuze, *Cinema 1: Movement Image*, Minneapolis: University of Minnesota Press, 1986, pp. 111–22.

11. The archive on blackface minstrelsy is vast and dense and I have but glanced at it so as to be able to talk about what Chris Tucker has done in the *Rush Hour* films.

12. July–September 2001; "East Meets West" is written in bold lettering over the cover page image of Tucker and Chan and a smaller caption says "Asia teams up with the rest of the world" and a still smaller line, "A Chinese Century?".

13. David Desser, "The Kung Fu Craze: Hong Kong Cinema's First American Reception", in *The Cinema of Hong Kong, History, Arts, Identity,* eds. Poshek Fu and David Desser, Cambridge, UK: Cambridge University Press, 2000, pp. 19–43.

14. My thanks to Michael Carmody for the esoteric piece of information that Gene LaBell was a Judo champion.

15. *Fifth Element* (1995), *Money Talks*, (1997), and *Jackie Brown* (1997), are the only other films of Tucker's that I have seen.

16. See this volume, "Spectral Critiques: Tracking 'Uncanny' Filmic Paths Towards a Bio-Poetics of Trans-Pacific Globalization".

17. *Time*, 6 April 1970, pp. 32–33.

18. See Jackie Chan's autobiography *I Am Jackie Chan: My Life in Action*, New York: Ballantine, 1998, 342, for an account of a funny incident back stage during the Oscar ceremony to which Chan was invited after the success of *Rumble*. He didn't know the expression "likewise" that the Hollywood stars were using to return a compliment, so he asked his mate what it meant and then kept saying "likewise, likewise" whenever someone came up to him and said he was a fan of his.

19. Henri Bergson's concept of the *élan vital* as internal differentiation or duration is well explained in Keith Ansell Pearson, *Germinal Life: The Difference and Repetition of Deleuze*, London and New York: Routledge, 1999, pp. 65–66.

CHAPTER 10

1. See David Matarasso, "Dossier: Hong Kong fin de siècle: Udine 1998", *Positif* 455 (January 1999), 78–81.

2. See E. B. Uvarov and D. R. Chapman, *Dictionnaire des Sciences* (Paris: Presses Universitaires de France — PUF, 1956), p. 51.

3. Christian Pociello, *La science en mouvements. Etienne Marey et Georges Demenÿ (1870–1920)* (Paris, Presses Universitaires de France — PUF, 1999, p. 26). The Station Physiologique or "Physiological Research Station" was the laboratory set up for Marey in which he could photograph human movement.

4. [*Editors' note*: the wars referred to here are, respectively, the Franco-Prussian war of 1870 (won by Prussia) and the First World War of 1914–1918.]

5. Marta Braun, "Marey and Demenÿ: The Problems of Cinematic Collaboration and the Construction of the Male Body at the End of the 19th Century" , in *Marey/Muybridge pionniers du cinéma* (Rencontres Beaune/Stanford: Beaune/Stanford, 1995), pp. 72–89.

6. Joseph Needham, *La science chinoise et l'Occident (le grand titrage)*, trans. Eugène Jacob (Paris: Seuil, 1973), p. 151. First published as *The Grand Titration: Science and Society in East and West* (London: Allen & Unwin, 1969).

7. For an outline of Michel Foucault's work on these matters, see his "Les Techniques de soi" (1982), in *Dits et Ecrits*, vol 4 (Paris: Gallimard, 1994), p. 783–813; see also *Technologies of the Self: A Seminar with Michel Foucault*, ed. by Luther H. Martin, Huck Gutman and Patrick H. Hutton (London: Tavistock, 1988).

8. English translation by the author from Immanuel Kant, *Métaphysique des mœurs — Doctrine de la Vertu*, trans. A. Philonenko (Paris, Vrin, 1968) VIII;

Immanuel Kant, *The Metaphysics of Morals,* trans. Mary Gregor (Cambridge and New York: Cambridge University Press, 1991).

9. See Adrian Martin's essay in this volume.

10. Johanna Vaude, interview with the author, Paris, 14 November 2002.

11. French edition: Paris, éd. Dervy, 1997. See Eugen Herrigel, *Zen in the Art of Archery* (Pantheon Books/Random House: New York, 1981) [1953].

12. Herrigel, p. 126.

13. Lao-Tseu, *Tao-tö King,* French trans. by Liou Kia-hway (Paris: Gallimard, 1967), p. 61.

14. See the essay by Kinnia Yau in this volume.

15. "Woo's Words. Lexique pour l'œuvre de John Woo", *Positif* no. 455, January 1999. I give here the complete text, of which *Positif* published only the second paragraph. English translation forthcoming in *Rouge,* www.rouge.com.au/.

16. Othello Vilgard, interview with the author, 27 December 2002. The following quotations also derive from this source.

17. Marcel Granet, *Danses et légendes de la Chine ancienne* (Paris: Presses Universitaires de France — PUF, 1994), p. 57. [1926]; *Festivals and Songs of Ancient China* (New York: Gordon Press, 1975).

CHAPTER 11

1. Nicolas Abraham (trans. B. Thigpen and N. T. Rand), *Rhythms: On the Work, Translation, and Psychoanalysis* (Stanford: Stanford University Press, 1995), p. 130.

2. Adrian Martin, *The Mad Max Movies* (Sydney: Currency Press, 2003).

3. Antoine de Baecque, "Le feu d'action", *Cahiers du cinéma* no. 434 (July/ Aug 1990).

4. Raymond Bellour, *The Analysis of Film* (Bloomington: Indiana University Press, 2000), p. 195.

5. Stephen Heath, "*Jaws,* Ideology and Film Theory", *Framework* no. 4 (1976), pp. 25–27; reprinted in Bill Nichols (ed.), *Movies and Methods II* (Berkeley and London: University of California Press, 1985).

6. Helen Bandis and Adrian Martin, "The Cinema According to Olivier Assayas", *Cinema Papers* no. 126 (August 1998), p. 35.

7. Nicole Brenez et. al. (eds.), *Admiranda* no. 11/12 (1996). The issue is titled "Fury: Contemporary Action Cinema".

8. Meaghan Morris, "On Going to Bed Early", in Peter Craven (ed.), *Best Australian Essays 1999* (Melbourne: Bookman Press, 1999), p. 346.

9. Nicole Brenez and Sébastien Clerget, "Mitraille formelle en milieu Hollywoodien, *The Replacement Killer's* [sic] d'Antoine Fuqua", in Jean-Pierre Moussaron and Jean-Baptiste Thoret (eds.), *Why Not? Sur le cinéma américain* (Pertuis: Rouge Profond, 2003).

10. Brenez and Clerget (et. al.), "Introduction: ode à la nitrocellulose", *Admiranda* no. 11/12 (1996), p. 15 (my translation).

11. The most relentlessly schematic director in contemporary cinema is Spielberg. Every scene in *Catch Me If You Can* (2003) is diagrammatically constructed: from overhead to ground-level camera set-ups, from wide shots to shot/reverse shots, from gliding movements to concentrated stillness — and always ending with a movement (whether through montage, camera, *mise en scène* or all three) into the brooding face of a central character.

12. Jean-Pierre Gorin et. al., "Manny Farber: Cinema's Painter-Critic", *Framework* no. 40 (April 1999), p. 45.

13. Cf. Stephen Heath, *Narrative Space* (London: Macmillan, 1981); for a critique of this notion, cf. Andrew Britton, "The Ideology of *Screen*", *Movie* no. 26 (1978), pp. 21–22.

14. Paul Patton and Terry Smith (eds.), *Jacques Derrida: Deconstruction Engaged — The Sydney Seminars* (Sydney: Power Publications, 2001), p. 40.

15. Constance Penley, "The Avant-Garde and Its Imaginary", *Camera Obscura* no. 2 (1977), pp. 3–33.

16. Cf. Willemen's essay in this volume; Thierry Kuntzel, "A Note Upon the Cinematic Apparatus", *Quarterly Review of Film Studies* vol. 1 no. 3 (August 1976), pp. 266–275.

17. For more on this, cf. Adrian Martin, "Silence and Cry: Notes on Sound Design in Some Recent Films", *Rouge* (forthcoming 2006), http://www.rouge.com.au/.

18. For a useful discussion of this phenomenon, cf. David Cox, "Speed Ramping", *Otherzine* no. 5 (2002). http://www.othercinema.com/otherzine/otherzine5/pspeedramp.html/.

19. David Bordwell, *Planet Hong Kong: Popular Cinema and the Art of Entertainment* (Cambridge: Harvard University Press, 2000).

20. Jean-Etienne Pieri, "*The Blade* de Tsui Hark: du chaos comme sujet et manière", *L'Art d'aimer* no. 6 (November 2002), http://lartdaimer.free.fr/num/6/index.htm/.

21. Cf. Chan's essay in this volume.

22. Alain Masson, "*Gangs of New York*: Au Coeur de la mêlée", *Positif* no. 504 (February 2003), p. 6.

23. Cf. Wong's essay in this volume.

24. The extensive information about digital effects processes provided on the DVD of *The One* is instructive in this regard.

25. Cf. Brenez's and Jayamanne's essays in this volume.

26. Cf. Willemen's essay in this volume.

CHAPTER 12

1. On the competition between Tianyi and the "United Six", see Gongsun Lu, *Zhongguo Dianying Shihua* [*Conversations on Chinese Film History*] (Hong

Kong: Nantian Books, n.d. but probably 1961), vol. 1, pp. 175–83; Du Yunzhi's *Zhongguo Dianying Qishi Nian* [*Seventy Years of Chinese Cinema*] (Taipei: Republic of China Film Library Press, 1986), pp. 65–71. See also Li Suyuan and Hu Jubin, *Zhongguo Wusheng Dianying Shi* [*A History of Silent Chinese Cinema*] (Beijing: China Film Press, 1996), pp. 208–9.

2. Poshek Fu, "Going Global: A Cultural History of the Shaw Brothers Studio, 1960–1970", *Border Crossings in Hong Kong Cinema* (24th Hong Kong International Film Festival catalogue: Leisure and Cultural Services Department, 2000), p. 43.

3. See David Keith Axel, "The Diasporic Imaginary", *Public Culture*, vol. 14, no. 2 (Spring 2002).

4. Mayfair Mei-hui Yang, "Mass Media and Transnational Subjectivity in Shanghai: Notes on (Re) Cosmopolitanism in a Chinese Metropolis", in Jonathan Xavier Inda and Renato Rosaldo (eds.), *The Anthropology of Globalization* (Malden, Mass.: Blackwell, 2002), p. 341.

5. Ibid.

6. David Desser, "The Kung Fu Craze: Hong Kong Cinema's First American Reception", in Poshek Fu and David Desser (eds.), *The Cinema of Hong Kong: History, Arts, Identity* (Cambridge, UK: Cambridge University Press, 2000), pp. 19–43.

7. Raymond Chow, "Chinese Pictures in World Market", *Jiahe Dianying* (*Golden Movie News*), no. 14 (May 1973), p. 23.

8. Ibid.

9. Gina Marchetti, "Jackie Chan and the Black Connection", Matthew Tinkcom and Amy Villarejo (eds.), *Keyframes: Popular Culture and Cultural Studies* (London and New York: Routledge, 2001), p. 154.

10. Ibid., p. 156.

11. See Salman Rushdie, "Can Hollywood See the Tiger?", *New York Times*, 9 March 2001.

12. Jane Ying Zha (Zha Jianying), "Excerpts from 'Lore Segal, Red Lantern, and Exoticism,'" *Public Culture*, 10, vol. 5 no. 2 (1993), p. 332.

13. The term "self-orientalism" is referred to in Leo Ching, "Globalizing the Regional, Regionalizing the Global: Mass Culture and Asianism in the Age of Late Capital", *Public Culture*, vol. 12, no. 1 (Winter, 2000), see footnote, p. 239.

14. Ibid.

15. See Shu-mei Shih, "Globalisation and Minoritisation: Ang Lee and the Politics of Flexibility", *New Formations*, no. 40 (Spring 2000), pp. 86–101.

16. See Tony Rayns, "'Cultural Abnormalities': A Distant Perspective on Hong Kong Cinema in the '80s", *Hong Kong Cinema in the Eighties* (15th Hong Kong International Film Festival catalogue: Leisure and Cultural Services Department,1991), p. 67.

17. Emily Apter, "On Translation in a Global Market", *Public Culture*, vol. 13, no. 1 (Winter 2001), p. 2.

18. In his audio commentary on the DVD of *Crouching Tiger, Hidden Dragon.*
19. For an account of the film's financing and Schamus's travails in writing the script with the two Chinese writers, see James Schamus, "The Polyglot Task of Writing the Global Film", *New York Times,* 5 November 2000.
20. All quotes by Lee are taken from his audio commentary on the DVD of *Crouching Tiger, Hidden Dragon.*
21. Shu-mei Shih, op. cit.

CHAPTER 13

1. Susan Sontag, "The Decay of Cinema," *New York Times,* 25 February 1996. Rpt: http://film.sm.to/sontag1.php/.
2. Jesse Walker, "Everyone's a Critic," Reasononline, June 2002, http://reason. com/0206/cr.jw.everyones.shtml/.
3. Peter Hutchings, review of *A Personal Journey with Martin Scorsese Through American Movies. Scope: An On-line Journal of Film Studies,* http://www. nottingham.ac.uk/film/journal/bookrev/persjour.htm/.
4. One of the most frequently anthologized essays of the twentieth century, it can be found, among other places on the World Wide Web at: http://comcom. kub.nl/driel/bieb/classic/benjamin.htm/.
5. Arjun Appadurai, *Modernity at Large: Cultural Dimensions of Globalization* (Minnesota: University of Minnesota Press, 1996).
6. Aihwa Ong, *Flexible Citizenship: The Cultural Logics of Transnationality* (Durham, NC: Duke University Press, 1999), p. 11. Further references in parentheses in the text.
7. The "user comments" devoted to John Woo's *Windtalkers* is a perfect example of what is right and wrong with the democracy of the Internet: "could of been better. Not wasteing much of my time of this film but all i got to say is the battle scene was alright but way over the top its trys to be an action film more then a war film and its only a 2 hour film felt like over 3 hours. 3/10 really only giving the film 3 mostly because of the music Oh John Woo don't ever make a war film again." http://us.imdb.com/CommentsShow?0245562/.
8. R. Todd King, "The VCD Industry in China," http://www.rtoddking.com/ mit912_execsum.htm/.
9. D. W. Davis and Emilie Yeh Yueh-yu, "VCD as programmatic technology: Japanese television drama in Hong Kong" (manuscript), p. 5. Further references in parentheses in the text.
10. An index of the centrality of Hong Kong film to a new global cinephilia may be found in the title of a recent work on Korean cinema by Anthony Leong: *Korean Cinema: The New Hong Kong* (New Bern, NC: Trafford, 2003). The publisher's website informs us that the book is meant to appeal to the "many Hong Kong cinema aficionados, who passionately followed the rise of the 'Hong Kong New Wave' during the Eighties and early Nineties, only

to become increasingly disenchanted since then, [and] are now looking to South Korea for Asia's boldest and most innovative films". Most studies of "foreign" cinemas work to domesticate them by recourse to homegrown comparisons: thus Planet Hollywood may apply to David Bordwell's *Planet Hong Kong* (Cambridge, MA: Harvard University Press, 2000) or the Hindi cinema becomes "Bollywood". Inevitably and unfortunately, this "foreign" connection must be recuperated here, too, and thus two of Korea's major stars are reduced to "the Korean equivalents to Tom Cruise (Han Suk-kyu) and Julia Roberts (Shim Eun-ha)". By the same token, author Leong himself may be seen as something of a cinephile, participating in web-based discussion forums before producing this book, which itself arrives outside of the mainstream academic or scholarly presses: "In addition to being a licensed pharmacist and management consultant, Anthony Leong has been a part-time film critic since 1997. Many of his 750+ film reviews and articles have appeared in books, magazines, and entertainment portals all around the world, as well as on his own entertainment web site …" http://www.trafford.com/4dcgi/view-item?item=2449&1760029-3374aaa/ .

11. Greg Urban, *Metaculture: How Culture Moves Through the World* (Minneapolis: University of Minnesota Press, 2001), p. 42. Further references in parentheses in the text.

12. The highly contested terrain of "naming" a cultural or sub-cultural group may be seen in current and vexing issues surrounding the loaded notion of "Asian American". Where diverse cultural groups whose origins may be found in China, Japan, Korea, Vietnam, the Philippines, India, and Pakistan (to name only some) are linked as "Asian American" in the US, obvious problems arise in terms of dealing with these cultures as unique and specific. Yet, alternately, questions of identification, along with the acquisition or seizure of political power work toward erasing difference in favor of solidarity and unity.

13. Internet Movie Database website, "IMDb user comments for Khauff," http://us.imdb.com/CommentsShow?0220596/.

14. Rediff Movies website, "Who is the surprise package of *Kaante*? Director Sanjay Gupta on making a man's film," http://www.rediff.com/entertai/2002/jul/27gupta.htm/.

CHAPTER 14

1. Robert Brenner, "The Economics of Global Turbulence", *New Left Review,* n. 229, 1998.

2. In his book *Genre* (London: British Film Institute, 1980), Neale proposes genres not as corresponding to any fixed menus of ingredients, but as variable combinations of discursive strings, that is to say, as processes of regulation rather than as objectified categories.

3. Steve Neale, *Genre and Hollywood*, London: Routledge, 2000.

4. Nick Browne (ed.), *Refiguring American Film Genres: Theory and History*, Berkeley, CA: University of California Press, 1998.

5. John Ellis, *Visible Fictions*, London: Routledge & Kegan Paul, 1982.

6. Rick Altman, "A Semantic/Syntactic Approach To Film Genre" in Grant, Barry Keith (ed.), *Film Genre Reader II*, Austin: University of Texas Press 1995, pp. 26–40; and his "Reusable Packaging: Generic Products and the Recycling Process" in Nick Browne (ed.), *op. cit.*, pp. 1–41.

7. Lee Grieveson, "Review of Steven Cohan and Ina Rae Hark (eds), *Screening the Male: Exploring Masculinities in Hollywood Cinema*; Paul Smith, *Clint Eastwood: a Cultural Production*; Yvonne Tasker, *Spectacular Bodies: Gender, Genre and the Action Cinema*", *Screen* 35:4, Winter 1994, pp. 400–406.

8. Yvonne Tasker, *Spectacular Bodies: Gender, Genre and the Action Cinema*, London: Routledge, 1993, p. 16.

9. Ina Rae Hark and Steven Cohan (eds), *Screening the Male: Exploring Masculinities in Hollywood Cinema*, London: Routledge, 1993.

10. Steve Neale, *Genre and Hollywood*, London: Routledge, 2000, p. 55.

11. Steve Neale, ibid., p. 52.

12. Published by Routledge in London. Prior to Tasker's celebration of the way finance capital had re-engineered Hollywood, there had been a series of books devoting attention to the alleged "masculinisation" of Hollywood's spectacles, starting with Joan Mellen's *Big Bad Wolves: Masculinity in the American Film* (1977) and A. Douglas's lament, *The Feminization of American Culture*, (also in 1977), followed by Donald Spoto's *Camerado: Hollywood and the American Man* (1978), Antony Easthope's *What a Man's Gotta Do: The Masculine Myth in Popular Culture* (1986), R. Chapman and J. Rutherford's anthology *Male Order: Unwrapping Masculinity* (1988), James Neibaur's *Tough Guy: The American Movie Macho* (1989) and Susan Jeffords's *The Remasculinization of America: Gender and the Vietnam War* (1989), and culminating in the volume edited by Constance Penley and Sharon Willis, *Male Trouble* (1993). These books chart a gradually rising pressure in academic film scholarship as the 1970s theoretical paradigms critical of Hollywood's dominant narrative regimes come to be seen as increasingly out of step with the restructuring of the American film industry's publicity requirements. Tasker's book signaled that film studies should re-align with journalism and advertising, a development also evidenced by the redesign of *Sight and Sound* and other journals in the 1990s.

13. David Cook, *History of the American Cinema*, Vol. 9: *Lost Illusions: American Cinema in the Shadow of Watergate and Vietnam, 1970–1979*, Berkeley, CA: University of California Press.

14. David Cook, ibid., p. 304.

15. David Cook, ibid., pp. 43–4.

16. The development in the 1920s of the strongman (*forzuto*) Pagano-Maciste into a detective relying on physical strength to solve problems later found an echo

in American detective stories, though in an inverted form: the detective's body no longer beats other bodies into the direction of "truth", Marlowe's body is now beaten into its direction by others.

17.   Bruce Lee's body, which participates in both the imperial-athletic body and the industrial-labour body formations, will no doubt require a special chapter in both histories.

18.   Ng Ho, "Kung-fu Comedies: Tradition, Structure, Character", pp. 42–46, in Lau Shing-hon (ed), *A Study of the Hong Kong Martial Arts Film*, The Fourth Hong Kong International Film Festival, 1980, p. 43.

19.   Robert Brenner, op. cit., pp. 23–24.

CHAPTER 15

1.   New York: Aperture Foundation, 2000, p. 11.

2.   On the temporal and spatial alterations of subjectivity under globalization regimes, see Bruce Robbins "Very Busy Now: Globalization and Harriedness in Ishiguro's *The Unconsoled*". *Comparative Literature* 53 (2001): 426–41, and Robbins, "The Sweatshop Sublime". *PMLA* 117 (2002): 84–97.

3.   See Radha Radhakrishnan, "Globalization, Desire, and the Politics of Representation". *Comparative Literature* 53 (2001): 315–32.

4.   Pico Iyer, *The Global Soul: Jet Lag, Shopping Malls, and the Search for Home* (New York: Vintage, 2000), p. 91, p. 284, p. 19.

5.   Iyer, *Global Soul,* p. 19. Further reference will occur parenthetically.

6.   On "uncanny" Aboriginal land and identity struggles in postcolonial Australia, see Ken Gelder and Jane M. Jacobs, *Uncanny Australia: Sacredness and Identity in a Postcolonial Nation* (Melbourne: Melbourne University Press, 1998).

7.   See Anders Stephanson, *Manifest Destiny: American Expansion and the Empire of Right* (New York: Hill and Wang, 1995).

8.   The spectral Marx is invoked as such in Walter Benjamin, *Charles Baudelaire: A Lyric Poet in the Era of High Capitalism*. Trans. Harry Zohn (London: Verso, 1989), p. 52.

9.   See Jean-François Lyotard, *The Postmodern Explained: Correspondence 1982–1985*. Trans. edited by Julian Pefanis and Morgan Thomas (Minneapolis: University of Minnesota Press, 1992) p. 79 and p. 17.

10.   Ien Ang, *On Not Speaking Chinese: Living Between Asia and the West* (London and New York: Routledge, 2001), p. 89.

11.   See the introduction to Rob Wilson and Wimal Dissanayake, eds. *Global/Local: Cultural Production and the Transnational Imaginary* (Durham, NC: Duke University Press, 1996), p. 5.

12.   This is used as an epigraph to the globalizing-sport city of Atlanta chapter in Iyer, *Global Soul,* p. 174.

13.   See the quasi-apocalyptic ruminations in Mike Davis, *Ecology of Fear: Los Angeles and the Imagination of Disaster* (New York: Vintage, 1998).

14. Martin Heidegger, *Being and Time: A Translation of Sein und Zeit.* Trans. Joan Stambaugh (Albany: State University of New York, 1996), p. 176. Heidegger's disturbing closeness to "mystical raciological ideas" and quasi-fascist resolutions to the flux of global modernity are critiqued by Paul Gilroy in *Against Race: Imagining Political Culture Beyond the Color Line* (Cambridge, Mass.: Harvard University Press, 2000), pp. 163–16. Gilroy warns that this romantic notion of some organic "Lebensraum (living space)" was appropriated by German fascism into a place purified of mongrel bloods and mixed cultures, p. 39.

15. See Mike Davis, "The Flames of New York". *New Left Review* 12 (2001): 34–50. For a related discussion of the cinematic uncanny, see Slavoj Zizek, "Welcome to the Desert of the Real!", *South Atlantic Quarterly* 101 (2002): 385–89.

16. Sven Lindquist, *A History of Bombing*, Trans. Linda Haverty Rugg (New York: The New Press, 2001), p. 186.

17. Arjun Appadurai, *Modernity At Large: Cultural Dimensions of Globalization.* (Minneapolis: University of Minnesota Press, 1996), p. 31.

18. See Jacques Derrida, *Specters of Marx: The State of the Debt, the Work of Mourning, & the New International*, Trans. Peggy Kamuf (New York and London: Routledge, 1994), pp. 31–32 and p. 51.

19. By 'Confucian simulacrum to the North,' I am alluding to the hyper-culturalist argument of Hyangjin Lee in *Contemporary Korean Cinema: Identity, Culture, Politics* (Manchester and New York: Manchester University Press, 2000) contending that the films of North and South Korea, especially those from the 1980s, share a core of residual Confucian values that endure despite ideological divisions of capitalism in the South and socialism in the globally de-linked North: "Confucian tenets on social hierarchy and family life are widely incorporated into the films from both areas. The five adaptations of *Ch'unhyangjon,* for example, invariably stress the time-honored Confucian family ethic based on harmony, unity, and loyalty among its members" (191).

20. See Derrida, *Specters of Marx,* p. 37, p. 100, p. 56.

21. By contrast, two recent Korean films by Kim Ki-duk, *The Isle* (1997) and *Real Fiction* (2000), depict a brutalized everyday world shorn of culturally uncanny forces or redemptive alternatives and thus reduced to the raw master-slave dialectics of exploitation and kill-or-be-killed commodified need, from city to countryside. (I thank Earl Jackson for calling these brilliant and contrarian films to my attention.) On alternative regimes of Korean space-making and subject-position in cinema, see Paul Willemen, "Detouring Through Korean Cinema". *Inter-Asia Cultural Studies* 3 (2002): 167–86.

22. On the spectral commodity-in-reverse, see Derrida, *Specters of Marx,* p. 150.

23. Kim Soyoung and Chris Berry, "Suri Suri masuri: the Magic of Korean Horror Film: A Conversation", *Postcolonial Studies* 3 (2000): 54.

24. I am building upon speculations from Kim Soyoung's "Specters of Modernity", a forthcoming essay, used with permission. On a related set of issues

concerned with genre, national identity, and spectral representation, see also Kim Soyoung, "The Phantom States: Double Exposuring Unfinished Mourning in Korean Melodrama", talk at Inter-Asia Cultural Studies Conference, "Transitional Era, Transformative Work", Kyushu University, Fukuoka Japan Dec. 1–3 2000; and "Modernity In Suspense: The Logic of Fetishism in Korean Cinema", *Traces* 1 (2001): 301–317; and "'Cine-Mania' Or, Cinephilia: Films Festivals and the Identity Question", *UTS Review* 4 (1998): 174–87.

25. Kim Soyoung and Chris Berry, "Suri Suri masuri," p. 54.

26. Esther C. M Yau and Kyung Hyun Kim, "Guest Editor's Introduction" to "Asia/ Pacific Cinemas: A Spectral Surface". *Positions: East Asia Cultures Critique* 9 (fall, 2001): 282–84.

27. Kim Soyoung, "Modernity In Suspense", p. 87.

28. See Lee, *Contemporary Korean Cinema*, p. 72, and chapter two, "Gender and Cinematic Adaptation of the Folk Tale, Ch-unhyangjon".

29. Rob Wilson, "Korean Cinema on the Road to Globalization: Tracking Global/ Local Dynamics, or Why Im Kwon-Taek Is Not Ang Lee", *Inter-Asia Cultural Studies* 2 (2001): 307–18.

30. See Ryan Motteshead, Interview with Im Kwan-Taek in *IndieWire*. http:// indiewire.com/film/interviews/int Kwon-Taek. Accessed on 4 January 2001.

31. Tony Rayns, "Korea's New Wavers". *Sight and Sound* 4:11 (1994): 22–25.

32. Paul Gilroy, *Against Race*, pp. 13–21. Gilroy is specifically addressing the "planetary traffic in the imagery of blackness" (21), which in a Pacific-ethnic context often shifts into a fantasy of evoking indigenous and Asian otherness in American contact-zones of proximity, admiration, trauma, and mixture.

33. On tactics of native ontology and indigenous sovereignty emerging across the contemporary Pacific, see Linda Tuhiwai Smith, *Decolonizing Methodologies: Research and Indigenous Peoples* (London and New York: Zed Books, 1999).

34. See Annie Nakao, "Restless Spirits Lurk Everywhere in Hawaii", *San Francisco Chronicle*, 1 August 2002: D12, who draws this ecological imperative from uncanny Hawaiian beliefs: "But much of the island lore emanates [not just from immigrant Japanese but] from a native Hawaiian culture that respects its spiritual environment — not a bad way to live on the earth".

35. For a "Polyn-Asian" -based updating of "how island paradises are produced for global consumption", see Jonathan Gil Harris and Anna Neill, "Hollywood's Pacific Junk: The Wreckage of Colonial History in *Six Days and Seven Nights* and *Rapa Nui*", *UTS Review* 7 (2001): 68–85: "Consequently, the South Pacific has been colonized by Hollywood as a site of cultural rather than capital production, within which U.S. commercial ambitions can be phantasmatically reimagined and replayed" (76).

36. See Paul Virilio, *War and Cinema: The Logistics of Perception* trans. Patrick Camiller (London: Verso, 1989), fn. p. 95. On the US war movies of John Huston, Anatole Litvak, and Frank Capra made in an era when Nazi-based German cinema (via Joseph Goebbels) sought to overcome "American super-productions" and undermine "the American perceptual arsenal" of world cinema, see Virlio, 9–10.

37. On Hearst's white-nativist Pacific and imperial aspirations for the US, see Gray Brechin, *Imperial San Francisco: Urban Power, Earthly Ruin.* (Berkeley: University of California Press, 1999), p. 230.

38. Hinton Rowan Helper's *The Land of Gold* (1855) is quoted and discussed in Robert G. Lee, *Orientals: Asian Americans in Popular Culture* (Philadelphia: Temple University Press, 1999), p. 49 and p. 26.

39. See Edouard Glissant, *Caribbean Discourse: Selected Essays*, Trans. J. Michael Dash. (Charlottesville: University Press of Virginia, 1989), p. 3.

40. Walt Whitman, "Facing West from California's Shores" in *West of the West: Imagining California*, ed. Leonard Michaels, David Reid and Raquel Scheer (Berkeley: North Point, 1989), p. 328.

41. Iyer, *The Lady and the Monk: Four Seasons In Kyoto* (New York: Vintage, 1992), pp. 332–33 and p. 79.

42. Ping-kwan Leung, *Travelling with a Bitter Melon,* ed. Martha P. Y. Cheung, Foreword by Rey Chow, Hong Kong: Asia 2000 Limited, 2002; and Ping-kwan Leung and Lee Ka-sing [photographer], *Foodscape,* Hong Kong: Original Photograph Club, 1997.

43. Kwai-Cheung Lo, "Transnationalization of the Local in Hong Kong Cinema of the 1990s" in *At Full Speed: Hong Kong Cinema in a Borderless World*, ed. Esther C. M. Yau (Minneapolis: University of Minneapolis Press, 2001), p. 263. On the transnational and localist dynamics of greater Chinese cinema today, see also Sheldon Hsiao-peng Lu, ed. *Transnational Chinese Cinemas: Identity, Nationhood, Gender* (Honolulu: University of Hawaii Press, 1997).

44. See Rey Chow, Foreword to *Bitter Melon*, p. 14.

45. David Bordwell, *Planet Hong Kong: Popular Cinema and the Art of Entertainment.* (Cambridge: Harvard University Press, 2000), p. 82.

46. On the criss-crossing nexus of Hong Kong and Hollywood film production, see Christina Klein, "The Asia Factor in Global Hollywood", *Yale Global Online*, 10 May 2003: http://yaleglobal.yale.edu/article.print?id=1242/; and Christina Klein, "Martial Arts and the Globalization of US and Asian Film Industries", *Comparative American Studies, 2* (2004): 360–84.

47. See Steve Fore, "Life Imitates Entertainment: Home and Dislocation in the Films of Jackie Chan", in Yau, ed., *At Full Speed*, pp. 134–36. For a discussion of global identity-performance, see also Steve Fore, "Jackie Chan and the Cultural Dynamics of Global Entertainment", in Lu, ed., *Transnational Chinese Cinemas*, pp. 239–262.

48. See Gelder and Jacobs, *Uncanny Australia*, p. xiv.

CHAPTER 16

1. Jean-François Lyotard, *The Inhuman: Reflections on Time,* trans. G. Bennington and R. Bowlby (Stanford: Stanford University Press, 1991), p. 37.

2. I choose the term *wuda* in order to lump together *wuxia*, kung fu and martial arts films, since the examples I will be using in the paper can be generically categorized in many ways and my way of discussing them does not require too strict a distinction between them.

3. Mark Hansen, *Embodying Technesis: Technology Beyond Writing* (Ann Arbor: University of Michigan Press, 2000). Further references in parentheses in the text.

4. Timothy V. Kaufman-Osborn, *Creatures of Prometheus: Gender and the Politics of Technology* (New York: Rowman and Littlefield, 1997), Part 1, chapter vi, "The Dialectic of Projection and Reciprocation", pp. 37–56. Further references in parentheses in the text.

    As Kaufman-Osborn explains, he adapts this terminology from Elaine Scarry's *The Body in Pain*: "'Projection' suggests the capacity of human beings to relieve bodies of their more imperious demands by incorporating knowledge of human vulnerabilities into works of artisanal skill. 'Reciprocation' suggests the way artifacts remake agents by releasing potentialities that would remain untapped absent the work done by the fruits of fabrication. Via participation in the dialectic of projection and reciprocation, human beings keep at bay imperatives that would otherwise render them mere bodies in pain" (Kaufman-Osborn, p. 4). [Eds].

5. See Burton Watson's English version of *The Complete Works of Chuang Tzu* (New York: Columbia University Press, 1968), chapter 19, "Mastering Life", pp. 198–200.

6. Gilles Deleuze and Félix Guattari, *A Thousand Plateaus: Capitalism and Schizophrenia* [henceforth *ATP*], trans. Brian Massumi (Minneapolis: University of Minnesota Press, 1987), pp. 410–411. Further references in parentheses in the text.

    On p. 415, Deleuze and Guattari also note: "this hybrid metallurgist, a weapon- and toolmaker, communicates with the sedentaries *and* with the nomads at the same time … In effect, the machinic phylum or the metallic line passes through all of the assemblages: nothing is more deterritorialized than matter-movement". In their *What Is Philosophy?* (New York: Columbia University Press, 1994; trans. Hugh Tomlinson and Graham Burchell), Deleuze and Guattari further suggest that "even when they are nonliving, or rather inorganic, things have a lived experience because they are perceptions and affections" (p. 154).

7. Gilles Deleuze, *Cinema 1: The Movement-Image* [henceforth *C1*], trans. Hugh Tomlinson and Barbara Habberjam (Minneapolis: University of Minnesota Press, 1986), pp. 55 and 51. Further references in parentheses in the text.

8. Manuel Delanda, "Deleuze, Diagram, and the Open-Ended Becoming of the World" in *Becomings: Explorations in Time, Memory, and Futures,* ed. Elizabeth Grosz (Ithaca & London: Cornell University Press, 1999), p. 37.

9. Thomas Lamarre, "Diagram, Inscription, Sensation" in *A Shock to Thought: Expression After Deleuze and Guattari,* ed. Brian Massumi (London and New

York: Routledge, 2002), p. 151. Further references in parentheses in the text.

10. Particularly relevant to the thematic structure (or rather, ideology) of *Hero* is an end-note of Lamarre's on Kenneth Dean and Brian Massumi's *First and Last Emperors* (New York: Autonomedia, 1992), in which Emperor Qin's relation to striated and smooth lines is discussed. Lamarre notes that this book provides "a useful model for thinking about the ways in which the first dynasty of the Qin emperor attempted to reconcile antagonisms between smooth and striated space by evoking modes of warfare, exchange, and social hierarchy which accelerated and blurred the two tendencies (like the spokes of a wheel) within a state that could only implode and explode. This dynamics of imperial formation and dispersion informs subsequent dynasties, courts, commandaries [*sic*], albeit in a muted, tempered form" (Lamarre, p. 168) For Deleuze and Guattari's distinction between smooth and striated space, see *ATP*, pp. 474–550.

11. Brian Massumi, *Parables for the Virtual: Movement, Affect, Sensation* (Durham and London: Duke University Press, 2002), p. 57.

12. Lev Manovich, *The Language of New Media* (Cambridge, MA: MIT Press, 2001), p. 294.

13. Janet Harbord, *Film Cultures* (London: Sage, 2002), p. 142.

14. Andrew Schroeder, "All Roads Lead to Hong Kong: Martial Arts, Digital Effects and the Labour of Empire in Contemporary Action Film", *E-Journal on Hong Kong Cultural and Social Studies* 1 (2002), http://www.hku.hk/hkcsp/ccex/ehkcss/.

15. David Bordwell, *Planet Hong Kong: Popular Cinema and the Art of Entertainment* (Cambridge: Harvard University Press, 2000), pp. 222–24.

16. Manuel DeLanda, *Intensive Science and Virtual Philosophy* (London: Continuum, 2002), p. 62.

17. As DeLanda points out, "An individual organism will typically exhibit a variety of capabilities to form *assemblages* with other individuals, organic or inorganic. A good example is the assemblage which a walking animal forms with a piece of solid ground (which supplies it with a surface to walk) and with a gravitational field (which endows it with a given weight). Although the capacity to form an assemblage depends in part on the emergent properties of the interacting individuals (animal, ground, field) it is nevertheless not reducible to them. We may have exhaustive knowledge about an individual's properties and yet, not having observed it in interaction with other individuals, know nothing about its capacities". *Intensive Science and Virtual Philosophy*, p. 63.

18. Gilles Deleuze, *Cinema 2: The Time-Image* [henceforth *C2*] trans. Hugh Tomlinson and Robert Galeta (Minneapolis: University of Minnesota Press, 1989). Further references in parentheses in the text.

19. Henri Bergson, *Matter and Memory* [henceforth *MM*][1896], trans. N. M. Paul and W. S. Palmer (New York, Zone Books, 1991), p. 17.

20. Keith Ansell Pearson, *Philosophy and the Adventure of the Virtual: Bergson and the Time of Life* (London and New York: Routledge, 2002), p. 145.

21. Dorothea Olkowski, *Gilles Deleuze and the Ruin of Representation* (Berkeley: University of California Press, 1999), p. 93.

22. See Gilles Deleuze, *Bergsonism* trans. Hugh Tomlinson and Barbara Habberjam (New York: Zone Books, 1988), p. 100.

23. Dorothea Olkowski has an interesting description of intensity and body movement and pressure in *Gilles Deleuze and the Ruin of Representation.* Her point is that it is intensity itself that makes the body feel a "sensation of increase" in our using bodily force and that this is a difference in kind (pp. 125–33). I am tempted to make a comparison between the Deleuzian notion of intensity in difference and the Chinese practice of "internal force" (*neigong* 內功) in various kung fu disciplines, but that is beyond the scope of this paper.

24. See Martin Schwab, "Escape from the Image: Deleuze's Image-Ontology" in *The Brain Is the Screen: Deleuze and the Philosophy of Cinema*, ed. Gregory Flaxman (Minneapolis: University of Minnesota Press, 2000), p. 111.

25. The internal citations in Deleuze's text here are from Henri Bergson, *Matter and Memory*, pp. 28 and 29. [Eds].

26. Henri Bergson, *Creative Evolution,* trans. Arthur Mitchell (New York: Henry Holt and Co., 1911), p. 306.

27. Eric Alliez, "Midday, Midnight: The Emergence of Cine-Thinking" in *The Brain Is the Screen: Deleuze and the Philosophy of Cinema*, ed. Gregory Flaxman (Minneapolis: University of Minnesota Press, 2000), p. 296. Emphasis original.

28. D.N. Rodowick, *Gilles Deleuze's Time Machine* (Durham and London: Duke University Press), p. 83.

29. Massumi, *Parables for the Virtual*, p. 8.

30. This term is taken from Deleuze's discussion in *Cinema 2: The Time-Image* of Leibniz's *Theodicy*, sections 414–16: "Leibniz says that [a] naval battle may or may not take place [tomorrow], but that this is not in the same world: it takes place in one world and does not take place in a different world, and these two worlds are possible, but are not 'compossible' with each other" (*C2*, p. 130). [Eds].

31. Rodowick, *Gilles Deleuze's Time Machine*, p. 87.

32. This is the title of chapter 9 in Gregg Lambert, *The Non-Philosophy of Gilles Deleuze* (New York: Continuum, 2002).

33. Jin Yong in *Heaven Sword and Dragon Sabre* (*Yitian tulong ji*) has a famous scene where the Grand Master Taoist Chang first demonstrates in front of everybody, enemies included, a round of his recently created tai-chi *jian* for Chang Wuji's immediate use. Having been attentive and learned by heart the pattern in this tai-chi *jian*, and having digested the moves, the young Chang reports that he has only one move left in his mind. The master, pleased by the young man's quick achievement, then begins another set, this one totally different from the first. The young Chang then walks around the hall, thinking through the whole pattern of moves, and finally announces that not one single

move is left in his mind — henceforth he will be perfectly ready for his eventual triumph over the enemy. I would juxtapose this tai-chi concept with what Deleuze says in *Difference and Repetition* about repetition as "by nature transgression or exception, always revealing a singularity opposed to the particulars subsumed under laws" (p. 5). What the master does the second time is no mere mechanical repetition but a Deleuzian process of "signaling". Such a signaling is a dynamic rhythm process, a repetition of "an internal difference which it incorporates in each of its moments" (p. 20) As for the young Chang, what he will do during actual fights is a difference or a change in itself, armed as he now is with a plurality of positions and modulatory moves that go beyond any representation. Every move he makes in future will be but one among many "free variations" (Massumi, *Parables for the Virtual*, p. 77), and will focus on the "plus" within a structure of "one-plus-one-plus-one", and this "plus" itself constitutes the outside of any relational process of an event.

34. Deleuze cited in Lambert, *The Non-Philosophy of Gilles Deleuze*, p. 90.
35. Gregg Lambert, "Cinema and the Outside" in *The Brain Is the Screen: Deleuze and the Philosophy of Cinema*, ed. Gregory Flaxman (Minneapolis: University of Minnesota Press), p. 287.
36. Andrew Murphie, "Putting the Virtual Back into VR" in *A Shock to Thought: Expression After Deleuze and Guattari,* ed. Brian Massumi (London and New York: Routledge, 2002), p. 188.
37. Stephen Zagala, "Aesthetics: A Place I've Never Seen" in *A Shock to Thought: Expression After Deleuze and Guattari,* ed. Brian Massumi (London and New York: Routledge, 2002), p. 20.
38. Zagala, p. 21. The internal reference here is to the Translators' Introduction to Gilles Deleuze and Claire Parnet, *Dialogues,* trans. Hugh Tomlinson and Barbara Habberjam (New York: Columbia University Press, 1987), p. xii.
39. Murphie, "Putting the Virtual Back into VR", p. 200.
40. Claire Colebrook, *Gilles Deleuze* (London and New York: Routledge, 2002), p. 50.
41. "Chaosmos" ("chaos" plus "cosmos") as a term for the unity of nature of culture is primarily associated with the work of Félix Guattari; see his *Chaosmosis: An Ethico-aesthetic Paradigm,* trans. Paul Bains and Julian Pefanis (Bloomington and Indianapolis: Indiana University Press, 1995). [Eds.]
42. Rodowick, *Reading the Figural,* p. 15.

Index